# Past Trends and Future Prospects of the American City

# Past Trends and Future Prospects of the American City

## The Dynamics of Atlanta

Edited by
David L. Sjoquist

LEXINGTON BOOKS
A division of
ROWMAN & LITTLEFIELD PUBLISHERS, INC.
*Lanham • Boulder • New York • Toronto • Plymouth, UK*

Published by Lexington Books
A division of Rowman & Littlefield Publishers, Inc.
A wholly owned subsidiary of The Rowman & Littlefield Publishing Group, Inc.
4501 Forbes Boulevard, Suite 200, Lanham, Maryland 20706
www.lexingtonbooks.com

Estover Road, Plymouth PL6 7PY, United Kingdom

British Library Cataloguing in Publication Information Available

**Library of Congress Cataloging-in-Publication Data**

Past trends and future prospects of the American city : the dynamics of Atlanta /
edited by David L. Sjoquist.
    p. cm.
  Includes bibliographical references and index.
  Conference proceedings.
    ISBN 978-0-7391-3537-2 (cloth : alk. paper) — ISBN 978-0-7391-3539-6 (elec-
tronic)
   1. Atlanta (Ga.)—Economic conditions. 2. Economic forecasting—Georgia—
Atlanta. I. Sjoquist, David L.
  HC108.A75P37 2009
  330.9758'231—dc22                                      2009025648

Printed in the United States of America

# Contents

# Figures and Tables

*Part I*

# INTRODUCTION AND OVERVIEW OF TRENDS

# Chapter 1

# An Introduction

## David L. Sjoquist

As its title suggests, this book examines the recent changes and the future prospects of the city of Atlanta. The book is comprised of twelve papers presented at a conference on "The City of Atlanta: Recent Trends and Future Prospects," which was held at the Andrew Young School of Policy Studies of Georgia State University and sponsored by the Dan E. Sweat Chair in Educational and Community Policy. The chapters explore the changes that have occurred in the city of Atlanta over the past quarter of a century, and what the future will likely hold, along many dimensions. The book presents multiple perspectives; the authors represent a broad spectrum of academics fields, including economics, geography, history, planning, policy, political science, social work, and sociology. Several of the authors are long-time students of Atlanta and thus bring an insightful perspective.

Atlanta provides a distinctive case study of the changes that cities have experienced over the past twenty years. The chapters tell the story of the city of Atlanta, and to some extent that story is unique. However, the experiences of Atlanta are relevant to other major U.S. cities and are informative as to what changes occurred and what factors drove those changes. The result is a better understanding of how and why cities are changing.

Over the past twenty years or so a number of books have been written that have the city of Atlanta as their focus. Each of these books has a specific focus, but with few exceptions these books deal with race. There has been no book published over the past quarter century that addresses the development of Atlanta from a broad spectrum. This book provides a broader review of how the city of Atlanta has changed over the past twenty-five years and explores what the trends suggest about the future prospects for the city.

In 1994, a headline in the Sunday *Atlanta Journal-Constitution* posed the question: "Is Atlanta the Next Detroit?" Citing the opinion of urban expert David Rusk, who said, "Detroit's on the ropes and Atlanta's in trouble," the paper drew attention to ways Atlanta resembled Detroit. It implied that Atlanta may come to share Detroit's plight: declining employment, high poverty, excessive crime, a vanishing middle class, too many vacant or crumbling buildings, deteriorating infrastructure, high tax rates, and hostile relations with suburban jurisdictions. But today, while Atlanta still faces some of those same problems, virtually no one examining the tea leaves for the city's future is predicting "Detroit, South"; instead a more positive mood has been constructed and has settled around it.

The history of Atlanta's growth and development focuses on transportation, commerce, and race. Atlanta developed because of its location at the terminus of a railroad, not because of any advantageous location to natural resources or water power. That location as a railroad hub led to the city becoming a regional center of commerce; raw materials, such as cotton, destined for the mills in the North were brought to Atlanta for shipping, while goods from the North came to Atlanta for distribution throughout the Southeast region. That function expanded as Atlanta's rail, air, and interstate networks developed.

The city grew until the 1960s, at which point it begin to lose population as a result of white flight, a trend that continued until the later part of the 1990s. Atlanta was not alone since during the 1980s thirty-seven of the largest one hundred U.S. cities experienced a decrease in population. Atlanta's population fell by 7.35 percent, the fourteenth largest decrease. Of those thirty-seven cities, twenty-seven also experienced a decrease in population during the 1990s. However, Atlanta's population increased by 5.8 percent during the 1990s, and by 24.2 percent between 2000 and 2007. Between 1990 and 2007, Atlanta's population growth was the thirteenth largest among the one hundred largest U.S. cities. Of the 63 cities that grew during the 1980s, twelve suffered a decrease in population during the 1990s or 2000s. Twenty-eight cities had negative growth over the entire period 1980 to 2007. Since 2000, the growth rate for the city matched the growth rate for the Atlanta region. Atlanta is the second largest metropolitan area in the Southeast behind Miami. However, while Miami was 32 percent larger in 1990, in 2007 it was only 2.6 percent larger. Today, the city of Atlanta is the thirty-fifth largest city in the U.S. and is located in the ninth largest metropolitan area.

Atlanta's experience is distinctive in some sense, for example, its recent population growth rate. But Atlanta's experience over the past twenty-five years is reflective of many cities, particularly those in the South and West. Thus, the account of how and why Atlanta changed is informative for cities generally. What accounts for the positive turnaround of the city of Atlanta? What can other cities learn from Atlanta's experience? These are the underlying themes of the book.

## SUMMARY OF THE CHAPTERS

The first two chapters provide a review of the population and economic context and set the stage for the remainder of the book. In chapter 2 Charles Jaret, Melissa Hayes and Robert Adelman address the changes in the demographic composition of the city of Atlanta since 1980 and compare Atlanta to other U.S. cities in order to determine whether Atlanta is becoming more or less similar to other major cities. The authors find that the city's population is aging, that there are fewer families and fewer still with children, and that the city is becoming more racially diverse, with a decreasing share of blacks and an increasing share of Hispanics and Asians. Until the mid-1990s the share of residents employed in skilled jobs was increasing, but that trend has reversed. These comparisons with other cities reveal that Atlanta is converging with some other cities in terms of population characteristics, but there is no one city that closely matches the changes experienced by Atlanta. In terms of its future, the authors conclude that Atlanta is evolving from its role as the regional capital to more closely resemble a second-tier global city.

In chapter 3, Glenwood Ross, David Sjoquist, and Matthew Wooten explore the economy of Atlanta. They start with a brief history of the development and growth of Atlanta, noting that Atlanta's development was associated with railroads, which made it a center of commerce for the southeast. While details of the economy have changed, the city of Atlanta and the Atlanta region are still associated with transportation (rail, highways, and air) and make up the distribution center for the growing Southeast. The chapter discusses the decline in employment and population that started in the 1960s and lasted until the late 1990s, and it explores the many potential explanations for the turnaround in the fortunes of the city. The chapter delves into four industries in detail: hospitality (tourism and conventions), logistics, health and hospitals, and professional services. Hospitality is a key industry for the city, and is associated with it long standing position as the center of commerce for the southeast. Professional services have grown as Atlanta has expanded its reach throughout the South and beyond. Logistics has the obvious link to transportation, but is seen as an expanding industry beyond the operations of airlines, railroads, and shipping firms. The health and hospital industry is relatively small given the size of the region and the presence of the Morehouse School of Medicine and Emory's Medical School. Finally, the chapter explores the longer term prospects for the city's economy, noting that the expected growth of the southeast and the Atlanta region provide a potential opportunity for the city if it can capture a share of that growth. While this presents an opportunity for the city, there are potential threats that could prevent the city from participating in the region's growth.

Retailing is the most visible element of commerce and has become a popular node for urban renovation. With the growing importance of sales tax revenue for local governments, retailing has taken on increasing importance. In chapter 4, Katherine Hankins discusses the evolution of retailing in Atlanta in the context of national forces and trends. Retailing has become concentrated among a shrinking number of firms with larger stores, has become more concentrated geographically, and has become increasingly linked to place-identity. After discussing these forces, Hankins describes how the Atlanta retail landscape has changed, driven by outward sprawl. In this sense, Atlanta is an archetypal city—the decline of the CBD as a retail center and the growth in suburban "downtowns," a decrease in the number of retail outlets in the city, an increase in the size of these outlets, and, over the past several years, its evolution as a center for new urbanism developments (or re-developments) in which retailing plays a central role. Hankins points to some dynamics, such as the growth in the city's population and proposed public infrastructure such as the Beltline (a proposed public and private development along a largely abandoned 22-mile rail corridor ringing downtown), which may well change the retail landscape in the city.

Douglas Noonan and Jennifer Chirico (chapter 5) examine the issue of air quality in the Atlanta region. Air quality is a major concern for the city and for the region. There are the obvious health-related factors, but in addition, air quality has implications for transportation planning and for the cost of doing business. In the 1990s the Atlanta region was out of compliance with the standards of the Clean Air Act, resulting in restrictions on transportation spending. After briefly discussing the development of air quality standards, Noonan and Chirico show that, with the notable exception of ozone, air quality in Atlanta has been improving on most counts, and has improved despite the increase in factors that are generally associated with decreased air quality, factors such as population growth, increases in vehicle miles traveled, and growth in certain industries. Given these past trends, Noonan and Chirico then attempt to forecast for various pollutants what air quality in Atlanta might be in the future. While they conclude that air quality may easily worsen, if for no other reason than many types of air pollution have declined so much, they believe there is cause for guarded optimism.

As noted in several chapters, transportation played a major role in the growth of Atlanta, driving both the magnitude and shape of its development. Currently, congestion and the need for additional transportation infrastructure is the issue that commands the most attention in the city and region. Truman Hartshorn (chapter 6) provides a history of post-WW II transportation planning in Atlanta and shows how the implementation of those plans affected the development of the city of Atlanta. While most of the major transportation projects, including freeways and public transit, focused on the CBD as the hub of the system, these projects also promoted sprawl and the decline in the city's population. Hartshorn goes on to discuss the current state of transportation planning, describing the many major projects that have been proposed to deal with mobility. Hartshorn is not particularly optimistic about the ability of the city and region to address its transportation problems. He lists the many barriers to the implementation of these projects, including a complex array of organizations involved in transportation decision making in the region and state and the lack of available funding.

The next two chapters focus on two specific categories of workers; the creative class and the working poor. Hypotheses have been advanced that the creative class, that is, those working in occupations that involve creativity and judgment, is an important source of growth in urban economies. Growth might occur because the creative environment leads to new ways of looking at issues or because it leads to a quality-of-life amenity. In this regard, in chapter 7, Michael Rushton discusses the state of the arts in Atlanta and their role in attracting highly educated workers. Rushton explores the importance of the arts in Atlanta, and finds that in the city the concentration of artists among the population has increased. He then addresses the question of whether the concentration of artists is related to the size of the educated population and to income growth, and finds a positive relationship. Regarding future prospects, Rushton summarizes several studies of the arts in Atlanta and the recommendations made to promote and expand the arts. The future of the arts depends on many factors, not the least of which is increased funding. As to whether the city will be able to expand the arts, Rushton is not particularly sanguine, it is not clear how successful the city will be in addressing the many issues that limit the expansion of the arts.

Fred Brooks (chapter 8) focuses on the other end of the labor market, that is, low-income working families. Brooks puts a face on low-income workers by describing the world faced by three low-income working families and the economic and personal challenges they must cope with as a regular part of their lives. He then goes on to present a more statistical description of the trends in the number and composition of the poor and working poor. He reports that the relative size of the working poor population in the city of Atlanta has increased since 1980, despite the economic growth the city and metropolitan area have experienced. As an example of one effort to raise the wages for the working poor in

Atlanta, Brooks describes the experience of the Living Wage Campaign; it is a story that points to the road blocks that arise and difficulties faced in getting such policies approved. He doesn't see poverty in the City declining in the short run given the current state of the economy and suggests that there is an absence of strong policies and institutions that might be of help to the working poor in the long run. Brooks believes that in the long run the status of the working poor will not improve without serious education reform.

Race and ethnicity is an issue that permeates Atlanta, affecting individual behaviors and shaping public policy. Its importance is demonstrated by the number of books that have addressed the issue of race in Atlanta. Until recently Atlanta was essentially comprised of two races, black and white. However, over the past two decades Atlanta has become much more diverse. In chapter 9, Charles Gallagher explores one dimension of this growing diversity, namely Latino immigration to Atlanta. Gallagher discusses how Latino immigration has challenged the existing black-white political and cultural environment and is reshaping the racial dynamics of Atlanta. Gallagher notes that the rapid growth in the Latino population, largely through immigration of lower-skilled individuals, has strained the economic and political status of blacks. He speculates that the future does not look very positive for Latinos, that the path to upward socioeconomic mobility of previous groups of immigrants may not be available. To the extent that Gallagher is correct, it suggests that Atlanta will continue to have a large underclass.

In chapter 10, Obie Clayton, Cynthia Hewitt, and Gregory Hall consider the changing racial/ethnic composition of Atlanta's population and document the growth in the size of other minority groups. They explore these changes, not just in terms of numbers of various minorities, but also in the context of residential and employment patterns. Despite the increase in diversity, there continues to be geographic separation and inequality with respect to the occupations and earnings. The authors point out in detail the differences in occupations held by blacks and whites and that these distributions are associated with the quality of the occupations, with whites occupying higher quality occupations. Finally, Clayton, Hewitt, and Hall explore how the changing racial/ethnic composition of the city's population will affect the distribution of political power, including control of schools, and suggest that the arrival of another minority group could be an opportunity to change race relations and to develop a more collaborative political structure.

Housing patterns in the city of Atlanta are a reflection of the broad dynamics of race, population change, and government housing policies. Larry Keating (chapter 11) details the change in housing patterns since 1980, focusing on the changes in the nature of the housing stock and on the clash between the low-income indigenous population and new residents to gentrifying neighborhoods. The nature of the city's housing stock changed dramatically over the past twenty-five years with the addition of more dense high-rise apartments and condominiums and the replacement of smaller housing units with larger units or multi-unit complexes. While these changes have added more units and higher quality units, the gentrification has displaced many lower income families, a result that has been aided by government housing policies. Keating argues that the major housing issue that the city faces is increasing the supply of affordable housing; however, given the history of efforts to adopt policies to address this issue, he is not optimistic that there will be significant change in the near future.

In the late 1960s the Civil Rights Act began to break down the barriers that prevented blacks from moving into white neighborhoods. However, Atlanta's experience suggested that racially integrated neighborhoods are very unstable; many communities shifted from near 100 percent white to near 100 percent black in the space of a few years. Douglas Krupka (chapter 12) looks at neighborhood stability in terms of the mix of income levels. Given the differences in income among blacks and whites, the instability of racially mixed neighborhoods might be a reflection of the instability of mixed income neighborhoods. On the other hand, if mixed income neighborhoods are unstable, then racially mixed neighborhoods will also likely be unstable. Krupka explores the dynamics of mixed income community in the city of Atlanta, exploring the determinants of income integration and how those relationships changed over the last two decades of the twentieth century. He finds that mixed income neighborhoods are not stable, but that the relationships changed dramatically over the period considered. Using the results of his analysis to suggest what might happen in the future, he suggests that highly mixed neighborhoods on the city's near southwest side will become more homogenous as gentrification continues, while the more stratified areas on the north and east are likely to become more diverse.

The final chapter, by Glenn Eskew, explores the efforts in the city to develop a venue that would recognize Atlanta's historic role in the civil rights movement. As the home of Martin Luther King, Jr. and many of the civil rights leaders, Atlanta was a natural site to develop a civil rights heritage venue that would be a significant tourist destination. Yet, Eskew argues that other southern cities have been more successful in building on their civil rights heritage. The chapter is a case study of how political, social, and economic dynamics of the city affected the potential development of a public venue. A similar story could be told regarding other efforts. Eskew traces the development of the Martin Luther King, Jr., Center, a place designed to commemorate the life of Martin Luther King, Jr. But the story Eskew tells is one of Atlanta's failure to truly capitalize on its civil rights advantage. Despite substantial public investments in and private contributions to the King Center, its inept management by the family has resulted in the lack of a stable financial base for the nonprofit and little programming for the community. After forty years of supporting the King Center, the city proposes to create its own civil rights venue but Eskew suggests Atlanta will have a difficult time getting out from under the King family in its expensive bid to develop an independent civil rights site that might also attract tourists.

Several chapters refer to many streets, places, and neighborhoods. Figure 1.1 identifies the location of streets and of the Neighborhood Planning Units. The following lists the neighborhoods and their corresponding NPU in parentheses: Adair Park (V); Ansley Park (E); Atlantic Station (E); Atlanta University Center (T); Bedford Pine (M); Ben Hill (P); Blair Villa / Poole Creek (Z); Boulevard Heights (W); Browns Mill (Z); Buckhead (B);

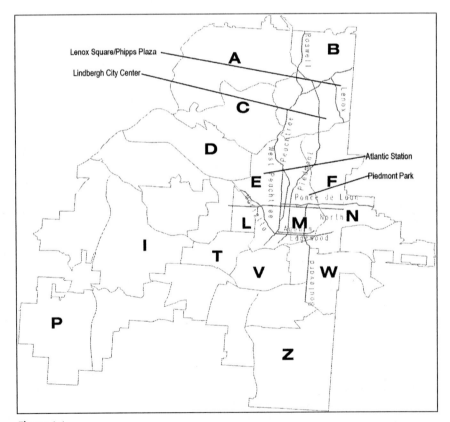

Figure 1.1.

Butler Street (M); Buttermilk Bottom (now part of Old Fourth Ward (M); Cabbagetown (N); Candler Park (N); Castleberry Hill (M); Collier Heights (I); Downtown (M); Druid Hills (N); East Atlanta (W); English Avenue (L); Georgia Tech (E); Grady-Antoine Graves (M); Grant Park (W); Home Park (E); Inman Park (N); Lake Claire (N); Loring Heights (E); Martin Manor (F); McDaniel Glenn (V); Mechanicsville (V); Midtown (E); Morningside-Lenox Park (F); Mt. Paran/Northside (A); Niskey Lake (P); Old Fourth Ward (M); Ormewood Park (W); Peachtree Hills (B); Peoplestown (V); Pittsburgh (V); Polar Rock (Z); Poncey-Highlands (N); Sherwood Forest (E); Summerhill (V); Techwood/Clark Howell (M); Underwood Hills (D); Vine City (L); Virginia Highland (F); West End (T); West Paces Ferry (A); Wildwood-Spring Lake (C).

Maps showing the location of all neighborhoods can be found at www. atlantada.com/atlCompAdvan/neighborhoods.jsp. The interactive map located at www.atlantaga.gov/government/planning/npu_system.aspx shows neighborhoods by NPU, although not all neighborhoods are shown.

## Chapter 2

# Atlanta's Future: Convergence or Divergence with Other Cities?

*Charles Jaret, Melissa M. Hayes, and Robert M. Adelman*

### THE RELEVANCE OF INTER-CITY COMPARISONS

In this chapter we attempt to glimpse the directions in which the city of Atlanta is moving. We do so by examining social, demographic, and economic changes in the city of Atlanta over a twenty-five year period (1980 to 2005) and, more intensively, by comparing social, demographic, and economic trends in the early 2000s in Atlanta with those occurring in other major U.S. cities. We show the cities to which Atlanta is becoming more and less similar, and also indicate what kind of city Atlanta is now and the type of city it may evolve into.

Inter-city comparisons of this sort are relevant because, in trying to shape their cities' futures, community leaders and citizens should be aware of other cities that they either want to emulate or want to avoid resembling. For example, in the 1970s residents of Portland, Oregon, rallied around the call to avoid "becoming another Los Angeles" (Bruegmann 2005:203) and adopted metropolitan-wide planning and an urban growth boundary in hopes of limiting urban sprawl. In 1987 a candidate running for mayor of Nashville used the popular slogan "Let's not become another Atlanta" in his campaign.[1] Locally, urban planners concerned about growth patterns in Atlanta use other places to assess Atlanta's successes and problems (e.g., attracting Fortune 500 corporations, air pollution, population increase, public school standardized test scores). For example, in several reports, the Atlanta Regional Commission (ARC) selected "peer urban regions" for Atlanta and used them as yardsticks in planning and in evaluating Atlanta's strengths and weaknesses.[2]

Readers of the *Atlanta Journal-Constitution* are frequently warned that Atlanta is on its way toward becoming like other places burdened with undesirable social, economic, or political problems. The "Is Atlanta the Next Detroit?"[3] article is the best example of this, but more recently we have been told that "Dallas is Atlanta's big twin"[4]; "Atlanta [is] on [the] road to becoming another L.A. . . ." (i.e., "traffic congestion here in 2030 will be worse than Los Angeles is today")[5]; and a headline from an article taking a regional perspective, proclaims "Metro Atlanta's future—bickering Balkans."[6]

But are these impressionistic observations of resemblance between Atlanta and other places accurate and meaningful guides to Atlanta's development and future? Some of the comparisons alluded to above refer to possible similarities between the Atlanta metropolitan area and other U.S. metropolitan areas. To be clear and explicit, our focus in this chapter is on comparisons between the *city* of Atlanta and *other cities* in the United States.

To provide context for the most recent changes in Atlanta highlighted in this chapter, we point out, in each section below, how the city of Atlanta has changed in terms of trends over a twenty-five year period (from 1980 to 2005). Beyond that, we then examine change between 2000 and 2005, to assess where the city of Atlanta stands and the direction in which it seems to be changing, compared with other major U.S. cities.

In this analysis we focus on four substantive areas of high interest to urban researchers and policy-makers:

a) the age structure and household composition of city-dwellers
b) the occupations and industries in which city residents are employed
c) the residents' income profile
d) the emerging racial/ethnic composition of the city population

We rely on data from the 2000 U.S. Census and the 2005 American Community Survey.[7] From both sources we obtained and compared demographic, social, and economic data about Atlanta and 29 other cities. We use cluster analysis to assist in our comparisons. Cluster analysis is a statistical technique that determines, for every city in the sample, how similar or dissimilar each one is to Atlanta and all other cities on a specified set of variables (i.e., age and type of household variables; occupational and industrial categories; racial/ethnic composition; income levels). Cluster analysis then groups the cities into small sets (clusters) of cities, so that each city in a cluster has strong similarities with the others in its cluster, hence each cluster represents a distinct type of city. In other words, each cluster differs from the other clusters of cities by having a unique profile of traits; cities in the same cluster are similar to other cities in their cluster and different from cities in other clusters.[8] By examining the cluster that Atlanta is in, both in 2000 and in 2005, we can see more clearly what type of city Atlanta is becoming, discern which other cities Atlanta resembles the most (i.e., "peer cities"), and learn whether during the past half decade Atlanta has become more similar to or dissimilar from other cities.

## ATLANTA RESIDENTS' AGE STRUCTURE

Cities vary greatly in their residents' age structure. Some cities have high percentages of older residents, while others are known for concentrations of young residents, primarily single adults. Here we examine how Atlanta's age composition compares with other cities and how it is changing.

Some researchers predict a severe decline in the number of children living in cities. They base this on increasing concerns about poor quality public schools in many cities, the demolition of public housing projects (e.g., due to Hope VI programs), and dispersal of households with children from the city, and the increase in childless couples and empty-nesters due to gentrification. Moreover, birthrates among teenagers and young adults have declined as women delay or defer childbearing.

This section examines Atlanta to determine if it is becoming a "city with few kids." We also focus on young adults (ages 25 to 34) because they are such a potentially important segment of a city's population. As Florida (2003) notes, young adults are highly mobile, innovative, creative, and sensitive to opportunities for advancement and growth. If, as he suggests, the relative prosperity of Austin and Seattle and stagnation of Pittsburgh is due to the former's greater successes in attracting many talented young people, then it is important to see how Atlanta compares with other cities in terms of its percentage of young adults. We also compare the percentage of elderly (age 65 and over) in Atlanta and other places to see how they stand with regard to the broader "graying" of American society.

We first examine changes in the city of Atlanta's age structure between 1980 and 2005, provided in table 2.1, and we see some indications that its population is aging. The average age of the city's residents is about six years older than it was—34.7 years old in 2005 versus 28.9 back in 1980; and the percentage of children under fifteen has declined modestly—21.7 percent in 1980 to 19.5 percent in 2005. On the other hand, the percentage of the city of Atlanta's population that is elderly has actually decreased over the twenty-five year period, from 11.5 percent to 9.3 percent and the number of children under fifteen remains larger than either the number of elderly or the number of young adults (ages 25 to 34). Interestingly, from 1980 to 2005 the percentage of young adults living in the city of Atlanta

**Table 2.1  Profile of the City of Atlanta on Selected Variables: 1980, 1990, 2000, and 2005.**

| Variables | 1980 | 1990 | 2000 | 2005 |
|---|---|---|---|---|
| Total Atlanta City Population | 425,022 | 394,017 | 416,474 | 476,483 |
| % who are Children Under Age 15 | 21.74 | 21.58 | 19.00 | 19.55 |
| % who are Young Adults (25–34) | 18.65 | 19.32 | 19.70 | 18.22 |
| % who are Elderly (65+) | 11.54 | 11.28 | 9.70 | 9.28 |
| Median Age | 28.90 | 31.40 | 31.90 | 34.70 |
| Average Household Size | 2.51 | 2.40 | 2.30 | 2.27 |
| % of Households that are Families | 60.10 | 55.69 | 49.50 | 45.74 |
| % of Households that are Married Couples | 34.70 | 28.28 | 24.50 | 21.76 |
| % of Households that are Married with Children under age 18 | 15.30 | 12.43 | 9.20 | 7.13 |
| % of Households that are Female-Headed with Children under age 18 | 14.00 | 16.62 | 11.75 | 12.39 |
| % Employed in Management, Professional, & Related Occupations | 24.18 | 28.82 | 40.60 | 45.68 |
| % Employed in Sales & Office Occupations | 27.71 | 27.76 | 25.60 | 24.56 |
| % Employed in Construction, Extraction, & Maintenance Occupations | 7.02 | 7.46 | 6.00 | 5.44 |
| % Employed in Production, Transportation, & Material Moving Occupations | 13.12 | 10.64 | 11.20 | 6.87 |
| % Employed in Service Occupations | 19.11 | 17.86 | 16.40 | 16.83 |
| % Employed in Manufacturing Industries | 13.17 | 9.41 | 7.70 | 5.59 |
| % Employed in Transportation, Warehouse, & Utility Industries | 9.30 | 9.66 | 5.90 | 5.50 |
| % Employed in Information Industries | na[a] | na | 5.70 | 3.44 |
| % Employed in Financial, Insurance, & Real Estate Industries | 7.31 | 8.76 | 8.40 | 9.30 |
| % Employed in Professional, Scientific, Management, & Administrative Industries | 8.20 | 12.16 | 17.20 | 17.25 |
| % Employed in Education, Health, & Social Services Industries | 19.72 | 19.07 | 16.80 | 19.19 |
| % Employed in Arts, Entertainment, Recreation, Hotel, & Food Service Industries | 6.54 | 7.90 | 10.40 | 10.15 |
| % Employed in Other Services (except Government) | 8.69 | 7.11 | 4.70 | 4.12 |
| % Employed as "Government Workers" | 20.10 | 16.90 | 13.20 | 13.74 |
| % Households w/ incomes under $10,000 [b] | 45.26 | 26.38 | 17.00 | 14.63 |
| % Households w/ incomes $10,000–14,999 | 16.00 | 9.92 | 7.30 | 9.56 |
| % Households w/ incomes $15,000–24,999 | 20.01 | 17.77 | 13.80 | 12.01 |
| % Households w/ incomes $25,000–34,999 | 8.95 | 13.08 | 12.10 | 9.11 |
| % Households w/ incomes $35,000–49,999 | 5.18 | 12.52 | 12.90 | 13.82 |
| % Households w/ incomes $50,000–74,999 | 4.59 | 10.11 | 14.10 | 13.20 |
| % Households w/ incomes $75,000–99,999 | na | 3.86 | 7.60 | 9.44 |
| % Households w/ incomes $100,000–$149,999 | na | 3.00 | 7.40 | 8.53 |

Table 2.1  Continued on next page

Table 2.1   **Profile of the City of Atlanta on Selected Variables: 1980, 1990, 2000, and 2005.**
(continued)

| Variables | 1980 | 1990 | 2000 | 2005 |
|---|---|---|---|---|
| % Households w/ incomes $150,000–$199,999 | na | 3.35 | 2.70 | 3.43 |
| % Households w/ incomes $200,000+ | na | na | 5.10 | 6.28 |
| Median household income ($) | 11,296 | 22,275 | 34,770 | 39,752 |
| Median household income (equivalent to 2005 $) | 30,387 | 35,083 | 40,760 | 39,752 |
| Per capita income | 6,539 | 15,279 | 25,772 | 33,590 |
| Per capita income (equivalent to 2005 $) | 17,590 | 24,064 | 30,212 | 33,590 |
| % of City Population that is Black | 66.60 | 67.07 | 61.40 | 58.65 |
| % of City Population that is Hispanic | 1.40 | 1.91 | 4.50 | 4.69 |
| % of City Population that is Foreign-Born | 2.30 | 3.39 | 6.60 | 6.69 |
| % of City Population that is Asian | 0.40 | 0.89 | 1.93 | 2.02 |
| % of City Population that is Non-Hispanic White | 31.90 | 30.27 | 31.30 | 33.81 |
| % of City Population with Bachelor's Degree or higher | 20.50 | 26.74 | 34.60 | 42.40 |

Sources: Decennial U.S. Census for 1980, 1990, and 2000; 2005 data are from the American Community Survey (except for the 2005 total Atlanta population, which is from a different U.S. Census survey that provides official estimates of U.S. city population sizes).

[a] na = data not available
[b] Income data for years 1980, 1990, and 2000 are actually the reported incomes from 1979, 1989, and 1999, respectively; income for 2005 is the income reported for 2004 but "inflation adjusted" to 2005 dollars.

has remained almost constant, at just below 20 percent. We conclude that over the last twenty-five years the city of Atlanta's population has aged, but to a lesser degree than has the general American population. It still has substantial numbers of children and young adults. The real test will come during the next twenty years, when, as the baby-boom generation moves into post-sixty-five age brackets, they will make critical residential choices (e.g., moving away from the city of Atlanta; moving from Atlanta's suburbs into the city) that may have a stronger effect on the city's age structure.

## Age Structure in 2000 and in 2005

The cluster analyses we conducted to examine the age structure in 2000 and 2005 are based on three age variables: (1) percentage of children less than fifteen; (2) young adults twenty-five to thirty-four; and (3) adults sixty-five and over. These analyses group together (in clusters) cities that are similar in their percentages of children, young adults, and older

**Table 2.2   Atlanta Compared to 29 U.S. Cities:  Residents' Age.**

**2000**

| | % LT 15 | % 25–34 | % 65+ |
| --- | --- | --- | --- |
| **Cluster #1** | **18.5** | **20.5** | **9.4** |
| *Atlanta* | 19.0 | 19.7 | 9.7 |
| **Other Cities:** | Austin, Boston, Charlotte, Denver, Minneapolis, Raleigh-Durham | | |
| **Description:** | Slightly High Young Adults; Slightly Low Elderly | | |
| **Cluster #2** | **20.5** | **16.4** | **12.3** |
| Washington DC | 17.1 | 17.8 | 12.2 |
| **Other Cities:** | Baltimore, Birmingham, Cincinnati, Indianapolis, Kansas City, Nashville, New York, Philadelphia, St. Louis, San Diego | | |
| **Description:** | Average on all three age categories | | |
| **Cluster #3** | **12.7** | **22.5** | **12.9** |
| San Francisco | 12.2 | 23.2 | 13.7 |
| **Other Cities:** | Seattle | | |
| **Description:** | Very Low Children; High Young Adults | | |
| **Cluster #4** | **17.4** | **14.8** | **16.7** |
| Miami | 18.1 | 15.0 | 17.0 |
| **Other Cities:** | Pittsburgh | | |
| **Description:** | Low Children; Low Young Adults; High Elderly | | |
| **Cluster #5** | **23.5** | **17.4** | **9.9** |
| Chicago | 22.1 | 18.4 | 10.3 |
| **Other Cities:** | Cleveland, Dallas, Detroit, Houston, Memphis, Phoenix, Los Angeles | | |
| **Description:** | High Children | | |
| **Mean (Total Sample)** | **20.2** | **17.8** | **11.3** |

**2005**

| | % LT 15 | % 25-34 | % 65+ |
| --- | --- | --- | --- |
| **Cluster #1** | **22.0** | **15.9** | **10.4** |
| *Atlanta* | 19.6 | 18.2 | 9.3 |
| **Other Cities:** | Baltimore, Birmingham, Charlotte, Chicago, Cincinnati, Cleveland, Dallas, Denver, Detroit, Houston, Indianapolis, Kansas City, Los Angeles, Memphis, Nashville, New York, Philadelphia, Phoenix, St. Louis, San Diego | | |
| **Description:** | Average on all three age categories | | |
| **Cluster #2** | **16.7** | **20.6** | **11.1** |
| Washington DC | 18.6 | 20.5 | 12.1 |
| **Other Cities:** | Boston, Seattle | | |
| **Description:** | Low Children; High Young Adults | | |

Table 2.2   Continued on next page

**Table 2.2  Atlanta Compared to 29 U.S. Cities: Residents' Age.** (continued)

**2005**

|  | % LT 15 | % 25-34 | % 65+ |
|---|---|---|---|
| **Cluster #3** | **12.9** | **18.5** | **14.6** |
| San Francisco | 12.9 | 18.5 | 14.6 |
| **Other Cities:** | None | | |
| **Description:** | Very Low Children; High Elderly | | |
| | | | |
| **Cluster #4** | **17.7** | **13.8** | **16.2** |
| Miami | 19.4 | 14.0 | 17.8 |
| **Other Cities:** | Pittsburgh | | |
| **Description:** | Low Children; Low Young Adults; High Elderly | | |
| **Cluster #5** | **19.8** | **20.5** | **7.4** |
| Austin | 20.7 | 20.3 | 6.6 |
| **Other Cities:** | Minneapolis, Raleigh-Durham | | |
| **Description:** | High Young Adults; Low Elderly | | |
| **Mean (Total Sample)** | **20.6** | **16.8** | **10.7** |

adults. Table 2.2 presents the age structure results for five clusters of cities in 2000 and 2005.

In 2000, Atlanta was a city with an equal balance of children (19.0%) and young adults (19.7%), while it had a much smaller percentage of elderly residents (9.7%). What distinguished Atlanta and the other cities in cluster 1 (Austin, Boston, Charlotte, Denver, Minneapolis, and Raleigh-Durham) is a relatively low percentage of elderly and a fairly equally balanced number of young adults and children. In comparison to Atlanta and its cluster, all the others, except cluster 3 (San Francisco and Seattle), include cities in which children outnumber young adults. Cluster 2 (the largest cluster, with ten cities) was characteristically average across each of the age variables. San Francisco and Seattle (cluster 3) stood out from the others by having, by far, the lowest percentage of children (12.7%), an average percentage of older adults (12.9%), and an especially high number of young adults (22.5%). Thus only San Francisco and Seattle epitomize the alleged trend toward children "disappearing" from cities. In contrast, Miami and Pittsburgh (cluster 4) stood out for their high percentage of older adults (16.7%). At the other end of the spectrum, cluster 5 (which includes Chicago, Dallas, Detroit, and Los Angeles and four other cities) was notable for its high percentage (23.5%) of children. The idea that cities are no longer places with sizable concentrations of children is an exaggeration, since in most cities in 2000 the percentage of young children exceeded the percentage of young adults.

The cluster analysis for 2005 shows variability among the five clusters, though there is little change from 2000. In 2005 Atlanta is slightly less balanced between children (19.6%) and young adults (18.2%), yet it maintains its small percentage of elderly (9.3%). By 2005 Atlanta's age structure converged with many other cities, creating a very large cluster 1 comprised of cities that are close to average in terms of their percentages of children, young adults (though Atlanta is higher on this than most others in cluster 1), and older adults. Surprisingly, Atlanta, from 2000 to 2005, did not exhibit the expected trend toward declining percentages of children and increasing percentages of young adults and older adults. In fact, Atlanta and other cities in cluster 1 have more children (22.0%) than young adults (15.9%). So if having a large pool of young adults is advantageous for cities, then Atlanta will be better off than most cities, but appears to be lagging a little behind some of the pacesetters such as Austin, Minneapolis, Raleigh-Durham, and Washington D.C.

Miami and Pittsburgh (cluster 4) also have more children than young adults, but these cities are distinctive for their high percentages of elderly residents (16.2%) and low percentages of young adults (13.8%). In 2005, the remaining clusters are cities in which young adults are the largest age category. Cluster 2 (Washington D.C., Boston, and Seattle) has the largest percentage of young adults (20.6%) and a below-average percentage of children (16.7%). Similarly, cluster 5 (Austin, Minneapolis, and Raleigh-Durham) contains the second largest percentage of young adults (20.5%) and the lowest percentage of elderly (7.4%). San Francisco (cluster 3) maintains by far the lowest percentage of children (12.9%), and an above-average percentage of elderly (14.6%). However, we note that most of the thirty cities examined in 2005 contain significant percentages of children. In sum, the city of Atlanta did not lose its children between 2000 and 2005; they slightly outnumber young adults and substantially surpass the number of elderly.

## ATLANTA'S HOUSEHOLD TYPES

We now examine shifts in the kinds of households in which Atlantans live.[9] We begin by noting how the percentage of households that are families has changed since 1980. We also investigate whether married couples are vanishing from the city. A recent newspaper article, "Rings Don't Make the World Go Round,"[10] highlights the trend toward remaining single rather than getting married. It notes that in Georgia less than half of all households consist of married couples, and that percentage may be smaller in urban areas. In addition, we look at how the percentage of married couples with young children and the percentage of female-headed households with children have changed in the city of Atlanta.

Changes in the city of Atlanta's types of households between 1980 and 2005 are more dramatic than the age structure changes described above, as shown in table 2.1. Sixty percent of the households in the city of Atlanta were families in 1980, but by 2005 only 46 percent of Atlanta city households were families (i.e., the majority of households now consist of either single individuals or people living together but not related by blood or marriage). Similarly, during this time period, in the city of Atlanta, the percentage of households that contained married couples sharply declined—from 34.7 percent to 21.8 percent, while the percentage of households comprised of married couples with children (under age 18) became remarkably rare (dropping from 15.3% of the city's households in 1980 down to a mere 7.1% in 2005). In contrast, the trend for female-headed households with children has been more stable, with a slight rise from 1980 to 1990 (14% to 17%) followed by a small decline (down to 12% in 2000 and 2005).

## Household Types in 2000 and in 2005

Cluster analyses of the household structure in 2000 and 2005 are based on the percentages of families, married couples, married couples with children under age eighteen, and female-headed families with children under age eighteen in each city. Table 2.3 presents the household structure results for 2000 and 2005, showing percentages of households that are families, married couples with children under age eighteen, and female-headed families with children under age eighteen.

In 2000, Atlanta, like all other cities in our sample, had a much larger number of family households (49.5%) than the other two types of households: female-headed (11.8%) and married couples with children (9.2%). However, Atlanta and other cluster 1 cities (Boston, Charlotte, Cincinnati, Minneapolis, St. Louis, and Washington D.C.) were low in percentage of family households and households containing married couples with children. In fact, Atlanta's cluster had the lowest percentage of married couples with children of all the clusters.

Cluster 1, in 2000, had an average percentage of female-headed households (10.8%), while cluster 2 (Detroit, Baltimore, Birmingham, Cleveland, Memphis, and Philadelphia) had the highest percentage of female-headed households (14.5%). Clusters 2, 4, and 5 are cities with high percentages of family households, but only clusters 4 and 5 contain high percentages of married couples with children. Cluster 4 (Los Angeles, Houston, Phoenix, and San Diego) is the most family-oriented, with the largest percentages of family households (63.1%) and households

**Table 2.3    Atlanta Compared to 29 U.S. Cities:  Household Structure.**

**2000**

| | % Families | % Married with Children | % Female-Headed with children |
|---|---|---|---|
| **Cluster #1** | **48.6** | **10.4** | **10.8** |
| *Atlanta* | 49.5 | 9.2 | 11.8 |
| **Other Cities:** | Boston, Charlotte, Cincinnati, Minneapolis, St. Louis, Washington DC | | |
| **Description:** | Very Low Families; Low Married w/ Children | | |
| | | | |
| **Cluster #2** | **60.6** | **12.6** | **14.5** |
| Detroit | 64.9 | 12.5 | 18.6 |
| **Other Cities:** | Baltimore, Birmingham, Cleveland, Memphis, Philadelphia | | |
| **Description:** | High Families; Low Married w/Children; High Female-headed | | |
| | | | |
| **Cluster #3** | **47.4** | **12.8** | **5.8** |
| San Francisco | 44.0 | 12.2 | 3.4 |
| **Other Cities:** | Denver, Pittsburgh, Seattle | | |
| **Description:** | Very Low Families; Low Female-headed | | |
| | | | |
| **Cluster #4** | **63.1** | **22.7** | **7.9** |
| Los Angeles | 62.6 | 22.6 | 8.2 |
| **Other Cities:** | Houston, Phoenix, San Diego | | |
| **Description:** | Very High Families; Very High Married w/ Children | | |
| | | | |
| **Cluster #5** | **58.6** | **17.2** | **9.0** |
| Chicago | 59.6 | 16.9 | 10.0 |
| **Other Cities:** | Austin, Dallas, Indianapolis, Kansas City, Miami, Nashville, New York, Raleigh-Durham | | |
| **Description:** | High Families; High Married w/ Children | | |
| **Mean (Total Sample)** | **55.8** | **14.9** | **9.9** |

**2005**

| | % Families | % Married with Children | % Female-Headed with Children |
|---|---|---|---|
| **Cluster #1** | **47.8** | **8.4** | **11.8** |
| *Atlanta* | 45.7 | 7.1 | 12.4 |
| **Other Cities:** | Baltimore, Boston, Charlotte, Cincinnati, St. Louis, Washington DC | | |
| **Description:** | Very Low Families; Low Married w/ Children | | |
| | | | |
| **Cluster #2** | **58.5** | **10.8** | **14.5** |
| Detroit | 61.0 | 11.7 | 18.2 |
| **Other Cities:** | Birmingham, Cleveland, Memphis, Miami, Philadelphia | | |
| **Description:** | High Families; Low Married w/ Children; High Female-headed | | |

Table 2.3    Continued on next page

Table 2.3    Atlanta Compared to 29 U.S. Cities:  Household Structure. (continued)

**2005**

|  | % Families | % Married with Children | % Female-Headed with Children |
|---|---|---|---|
| **Cluster #3** | **43.5** | **12.4** | **3.5** |
| San Francisco | 43.8 | 11.7 | 3.0 |
| **Other Cities:** | Seattle | | |
| **Description:** | Very Low Families; Very Low Female-headed | | |
| | | | |
| **Cluster #4** | **59.2** | **17.8** | **9.2** |
| Los Angeles | 61.1 | 20.0 | 8.4 |
| **Other Cities:** | Chicago, Dallas, Houston, Indianapolis, Kansas City, Nashville, New York, Phoenix, Raleigh-Durham, San Diego | | |
| **Description:** | High Families; High Married w/ Children | | |
| | | | |
| **Cluster #5** | **49.6** | **13.6** | **8.3** |
| Austin | 51.7 | 17.3 | 7.0 |
| **Other Cities:** | Denver, Minneapolis, Pittsburgh | | |
| **Description:** | Low Families | | |
| **Mean (Total Sample)** | **54.1** | **13.3** | **10.4** |

containing married couples with children (22.7%). Opposite in nature, cluster 3 (San Francisco, Denver, Pittsburgh, and Seattle) had the lowest percentage of family households (47.4%), and it had the lowest percentage of female-headed households (5.8%). On the whole, the thirty cities had many family households (55.8%), but only a small percentage contained married couples with children (14.9%).

In 2005 the cluster analysis shows consistent patterns with a few changes in cluster composition. Atlanta in 2005 continued to maintain a household structure with more family households (45.7%) than female-headed households (12.4%) or households containing married couples with children (7.1%). However, in the city of Atlanta, from 2000 to 2005, the percentages of family households and households containing married couples with children declined, while female-headed households slightly increased. Clearly, in Atlanta, the trend has been away from households containing traditional families.

Cluster 1 contains Atlanta, Baltimore, Boston, Charlotte, Cincinnati, St. Louis, and Washington D.C. These cities exhibit low percentages of family households (47.8%) and households containing married couples with children (8.4%) compared to the other cities. Low percentages of family households are present in clusters 3 and 5, at 43.5 percent and 49.6 percent respectively. At the other end of the spectrum, clusters 2 and 4 display a relatively high percentage of family households at 58.5 percent and 59.2

percent, respectively. Cluster 4 consistently contains the most family oriented cities; this cluster has the largest percentages of family households
and households containing married couples with children (17.8%). Even
though cluster 2 (Birmingham, Cleveland, Detroit, Memphis, Miami, and
Philadelphia) exhibits an above average percentage of family households,
this cluster has a below average percentage of households containing married couples with children (10.8%). In fact, cluster 2 maintains the largest
percentage of female-headed families with young children. In contrast,
cluster 3 (San Francisco and Seattle) contains the lowest percentage of
female-headed families with children at 3.5 percent, falling far below the
overall mean of 10.4 percent. San Francisco and Seattle, additionally, contain the lowest percentage of family households at 43.5 percent.

The cities in this analysis show a trend toward fewer households containing married couples with children. From 2000 to 2005, the percentage
of married couples with children in Atlanta decreased from 9.2 percent
to 7.1 percent. At the same time, the percentage of family households
decreased from 49.5 percent to 45.7 percent, while the percentage of
female-headed households with children increased slightly. Our analysis
supports the argument that unmarried households are in fact outnumber-
ing married households in Atlanta, and it also appears that households
containing married couples with children are a small and declining percentage of Atlanta's households.

## ATLANTA'S OCCUPATIONAL PATTERNS

Historically Atlanta has been regarded as a city with a mixed and balanced occupational profile. Since the 1980s, however, observers have
noted in Atlanta the impact of two changes that have been altering the
occupational structure of many cities throughout the United States. First,
decline in manufacturing or "factory" jobs ("deindustrialization") as that
economic sector has relocated to other areas of the country or world.
Second, large numbers of people holding middle-class occupations have
moved from the city to the suburbs. Taken together, these changes imply
a severe downgrading of the occupational level of the city of Atlanta's
residents, with growing percentages employed in less skilled (and less
remunerative) service and retail jobs.

However, since the mid-1990s, some observers contend that a counter-
trend is emerging based on the growing impact of gentrification in the
city of Atlanta. Young managers, lawyers, design professionals, entrepreneurs, and other "yuppies" are making the city of Atlanta their home; at
the same time housing costs are rapidly rising in the city and HOPE VI
programs are closing and transforming public housing projects. These

trends, if they are operating on a high magnitude, would imply a different trajectory—occupational upgrading for the city, rather than the decline mentioned above. Is the occupational profile of city residents rising, measured in terms of a higher percentage employed in professional and/or managerial jobs?

The occupational shifts noted in the previous paragraph have important consequences for the income profile of city residents, and we discuss these in a section below. Here we focus on two questions about the occupational distribution:

a) What type of occupational profile does Atlanta actually have, and which other cities are most (or least) like it?

b) Have Atlanta residents experienced much change in occupational composition over the past twenty-five years, particularly between 2000 and 2005; if so, in what direction, and how does it compare with other cities in its cluster?

From 1980 to 2005 one occupational shift among residents of the city of Atlanta overshadows all others—the dramatic increase in people employed in management, professional, and related occupations. In 1980 24.2 percent of workers living in the city were employed in that category, and in ensuing decades it has steadily increased to 45.7 percent in 2005. Closely related to that shift is the upward trend in the educational level of the city's residents. Between 1980 and 2005 the percentage of Atlantans who have graduated college or a post-college program rose from 20.5 percent to 42.4 percent. As the number of employees in management and professional occupations swelled, the percentages working in most other occupational categories declined slightly (see table 2.1). For example, between 1980 and 2005 the percentage of Atlanta residents employed in sales and office occupations dropped from 27.7 percent to 24.6 percent; those employed in the broad blue-collar job category of production, transportation, and material moving declined from 13.1 percent to 6.9 percent; and those employed in service occupations fell from 19.1 percent to 16.8 percent. These numbers clearly support the idea of urban occupational upgrading more than downgrading.

## Occupational Profile of Atlanta and Other Cities in 2000

To compare Atlanta's and other cities' occupational patterns we did cluster analyses (for 2000 and 2005) based on the percentage of employees residing in each city who work in five occupational categories:

1) Management, Professional, and Related Occupations (managerial-professional jobs);

**Table 2.4    Atlanta Compared to 29 U.S. Cities: Occupational Structure.**

**2000**

|  | % Managerial-Professional | % Production-Transport | % Service Occupations |
|---|---|---|---|
| **Cluster #1** | **42.6** | **9.5** | **15.5** |
| *Atlanta* | 40.6 | 11.2 | 16.4 |
| **Other Cities:** | Austin, Boston, Minneapolis, Raleigh-Durham, San Diego | | |
| **Description:** | High Managerial-Professional; Low Production-Transport | | |
| **Cluster #2** | **33.6** | **13.3** | **17.0** |
| Baltimore | 32.4 | 13.4 | 20.0 |
| **Other Cities:** | Birmingham, Charlotte, Chicago, Cincinnati, Dallas, Denver, Houston, Indianapolis, Kansas City, Los Angeles, Memphis, Nashville, Pittsburgh, Philadelphia, Phoenix, New York City, St. Louis | | |
| **Description:** | Average on all three occupational categories | | |
| **Cluster #3** | **22.1** | **22.4** | **21.3** |
| Detroit | 21.6 | 22.5 | 21.6 |
| **Other Cities:** | Cleveland | | |
| **Description:** | Very Low Managerial-Professional; Very High Production-Transport; High Service | | |
| **Cluster #4** | **23.8** | **13.8** | **22.1** |
| Miami | 23.8 | 13.8 | 22.1 |
| **Other Cities:** | None | | |
| **Description:** | Very Low Managerial-Professional; High Service | | |
| **Cluster #5** | **49.3** | **7.0** | **14.8** |
| Seattle | 48.4 | 8.2 | 13.9 |
| **Other Cities:** | San Francisco; Washington DC | | |
| **Description:** | Very High Managerial-Professional; Low Production-Transport | | |
| **Mean (Total Sample)** | **35.9** | **12.5** | **16.9** |

**2005**

|  | % Managerial-Professional | % Production-Transport | % Service Occupations |
|---|---|---|---|
| **Cluster #1** | **42.0** | **7.8** | **17.3** |
| *Atlanta* | 45.7 | 6.9 | 16.8 |
| **Other Cities:** | Austin, Boston, Charlotte, Denver, Minneapolis, Nashville, Pittsburgh, Raleigh-Durham, San Diego | | |
| **Description:** | High Managerial-Professional; Low Production-Transport | | |
| **Cluster #2** | **32.4** | **13.0** | **19.4** |
| Baltimore | 32.9 | 11.3 | 21.8 |
| **Other Cities:** | Birmingham, Chicago, Cincinnati, Dallas, Houston, Indianapolis, Kansas City, Los Angeles, Memphis, New York City, Philadelphia, Phoenix, St. Louis | | |
| **Description:** | Low on Managerial-Professional; Average on others | | |

Table 2.4   Continued on next page

**Table 2.4    Atlanta Compared to 29 U.S. Cities:  Occupational Structure.** (continued)

**2005**

|  | % Managerial-Professional | % Production-Transport | % Service Occupations |
|---|---|---|---|
| **Cluster #3** | **22.2** | **19.8** | **25.4** |
| Detroit | 21.8 | 20.5 | 26.1 |
| **Other Cities:** | Cleveland | | |
| **Description:** | Very Low on Managerial-Professional; High Production-Transport; High Service | | |
| **Cluster #4** | **23.2** | **11.3** | **24.5** |
| Miami | 23.2 | 11.3 | 24.5 |
| **Other Cities:** | None | | |
| **Description:** | Very Low Managerial-Professional; High Service | | |
| **Cluster #5** | **52.2** | **6.1** | **15.5** |
| Seattle | 50.8 | 7.2 | 15.3 |
| **Other Cities:** | San Francisco; Washington DC | | |
| **Description:** | Very High Managerial-Professional; Low Production-Transport; Low on Service | | |
| **Mean (Total Sample)** | **36.6** | **11.0** | **18.9** |

2) Production, Transportation, and Material Moving Occupations (production-transport jobs)
3) Service Occupations
4) Sales and Office Occupations
5) Construction, Extractive, and Maintenance Occupations

Of these occupational categories, managerial-professional was, by far, the most influential in determining which cluster cities fell into. In contrast, the percentages employed in Sales and Office Occupations and in Construction, Extractive, and Maintenance Occupations varied so slightly from city to city that they played little role in placing cities in particular clusters. For that reason, we omit those latter two occupational categories from this discussion and from Table 2.4 and focus instead only on the first three specified above.

Table 2.4 shows that, in 2000, Atlanta and five other cities in cluster 1 (Austin, Boston, Minneapolis, Raleigh-Durham, and San Diego) shared a similar occupational profile marking them as places strongly affected by the growing post-industrial information-based economy. These are all cities with a high percentage of managerial-professional jobs, a slightly lower than average percentage of production-transport occupations, and an average amount of workers in service occupations.

Close in occupational composition to Atlanta and other cluster 1 cities are those in cluster 5: San Francisco, Seattle, and Washington D.C. They represent an even higher degree of emphasis on post-industrial information-based work, with substantially higher percentages of people in managerial-professional jobs (i.e., the mean for cluster 5 is 49.3% compared to 42.6% in cluster 1) and slightly lower percentages in production-transport jobs (i.e., 7.0% in cluster 5 versus 9.5% in cluster 1), but virtually no difference between cluster 1 and 5 in their percentages of residents employed in service occupations (i.e., about 15%).

Atlanta's occupational profile also differs from two small clusters: cluster 3 (only Detroit and Cleveland, but representing the so-called "Rust Belt" cities) and cluster 4 (consisting only of Miami). These cities are much lower than Atlanta in professional-managerial workers (less than 25%), higher (especially Detroit and Cleveland) in production-transport, and higher in percentage of workers in service jobs. Finally, Atlanta can be distinguished from the largest set of cities (cluster 2) mainly by the fact that Atlanta's managerial-professional category is considerably larger (42.6% versus 33.6%) and it has a smaller percentage of residents engaged in production-transport jobs.

## Changes in Atlanta's Occupational Profile from 2000 to 2005

Comparing the 2000 and 2005 results in table 2.4 shows that the overarching pattern in the clusters is one of stability. However, we note three interesting changes pertaining to Atlanta. First, despite Atlanta's substantial increase in its managerial-professional percentage (40.6% to 45.7%) from 2000 to 2005, neither Atlanta nor any of the cities in 2000's cluster 1 increased that percentage enough to move into cluster 5 (comprised of San Francisco, Seattle, and Washington D.C.). However, by 2005 four cities (Charlotte, Denver, Nashville, and Pittsburgh) formerly in the largest cluster (cluster 2) experienced enough growth in managerial-professional workers and/or decline in production-transport to move into the same cluster as Atlanta. In other words, several cities evolved to have a similar type of post-industrial information-based job structure as Atlanta, and evidence suggests that others will do so in the future.

Second, on closer inspection, the data clearly show that Atlanta did not remain in the same position within its cluster during the early 2000s. Instead, Atlanta's growth in percent managerial-professional (from 40.6% to 45.7%) is a larger increase than any other city in its cluster. This increase moved Atlanta from being the city with the lowest percentage of managers and professionals in its cluster to being this cluster's city with the highest percentage of them. Atlanta also had a relatively large decline in its percentage of production-transport workers. These changes in occupational composition mean that Atlanta is on a trajectory of change (assuming it continues unabated) leading to convergence with cluster 5 cities (San Francisco, Seattle, and Washington D.C.) possibly by 2010 and certainly by 2020.[11]

Third, cluster 1 cities (Atlanta to a lesser degree than others) had moderate increases in their percentage of service workers between 2000 and 2005. This, coupled with the rising percentage of managerial-professionals, suggests a change toward the "global city" scenario described by Sassen (2000): a bifurcated or polarized occupational profile comprised of a well-paying upper-middle class in producer services, managerial, and professional jobs, on one hand, and low-paying jobs that provide supportive business, personal, retail, and leisure services, on the other.

## ATLANTA'S INDUSTRIAL STRUCTURE

In this discussion of Atlanta's (and other cities') industrial structure it is important to realize that we are referring to the industries in which the city's residents are employed, which is not equivalent to an industrial profile of the jobs located within the city limits. Many city of Atlanta residents work at jobs that are located outside of the city, and we are counting them in this discussion of the city of Atlanta's industrial structure; conversely, many suburbanites work at jobs located in the city, but those jobs are not included in the data on the city of Atlanta's industrial structure. This also is true with regard to the preceding discussion of occupational structure. This means we are describing the industrial/occupational structure of city residents rather than the industrial/occupational structure of all jobs located in the city (an inevitable result of using Census data tabulated on the basis of where people live rather than where they work).

Several changes in the city of Atlanta's industrial structure from 1980 to 2005 are apparent in table 2.1, and they are consistent with the occupational trends discussed above. The most significant shift was the rise of those working in the industries of the professional–scientific–management–administrative sector of the economy: from 8.2 percent to 17.2 percent. A smaller level of growth occurred between 1980 and 2005 for city of Atlanta residents in arts-entertainment-recreation-hotel-food service industries. On the other hand, the percentage of government workers living in Atlanta declined over time; this was also true for those employed in manufacturing industries as well as for those with jobs in transportation, warehouse, and utilities.

### Industrial Structure in 2000

To compare Atlanta's and other cities' industrial structures we did cluster analyses (for 2000 and 2005) based on the percentage of employees residing in each city who work in seven categories of industries utilized by the Census Bureau:

1) manufacturing
2) finance, insurance, and real estate
3) professional, scientific, management, and administrative
4) information
5) educational, health, and social services
6) arts, entertainment, recreation, hotel, and food services
7) government

However, due to space limitations, table 2.5, which shows the results of these cluster analyses, only contains data on four of these industrial categories: manufacturing; professional-scientific-management-administrative (PSMA); education-health-social services (EHSS); and government.

Two notable traits distinguished Atlanta's industrial structure in 2000 from that of other major U.S. cities. First, the city of Atlanta's economy, long noted for its diversified mix of industries, was still among the most well balanced in terms of the industries in which its residents were employed. Only Dallas, Denver, Nashville, Kansas City, and Los Angeles had residents with a more even spread among industries than Atlanta (with San Francisco about equal). Second, in 2000, although the industrial category that employed the highest percentage of most major cities' residents was (perhaps surprisingly) educational-health-social services (EHSS), Atlanta was one of a few cities where that was not the case. Instead, in Atlanta (and in Dallas and San Francisco) the professional-scientific-management-administrative (PSMA) industrial category employed the highest percentage of residents.

Table 2.5 provides more evidence of Atlanta's distinct industrial structure in 2000. Atlanta, Denver, and San Francisco, form cluster 1. What separates them from most other clusters is their low percentages in manufacturing and EHSS, coupled with high percentages in PSMA and in information industries. Closest to Atlanta's 2000 cluster is cluster 5, comprised of Charlotte, Dallas, Los Angeles and four other cities with balanced economies, but cluster 5 has more manufacturing and lower percentages in information, PSMA, and government work. Most other clusters are easily distinguishable from Atlanta's in that they have strikingly larger percentages in one or two key industries. For example, cluster 4 (Boston, New York, and Pittsburgh) is much higher in EHSS; cluster 6 (Cleveland and Detroit) is much higher in manufacturing; and cluster 7 (Washington D.C.) is much higher in government.

### 2005 Industrial Structure and Changes since 2000

Data from 2005 indicate that the city of Atlanta's industrial structure is changing in the direction of convergence with several other major U.S.

cities. Atlanta is losing the diversified industrial base that characterized it for so long, and the city's residents are becoming more concentrated in fewer industries, especially those that are prominent in other major cities. Specifically, by 2005, no longer is professional-scientific-management-administrative Atlanta's largest industrial sector; instead, in the city of Atlanta (as in most other major cities) the largest percentage of workers is in educational-health-social services.[12] Also, like most other cities in this sample, Atlanta's percentages of residents working in manufacturing and the information industries declined between 2000 and 2005. Perhaps due to its strong housing market (prior to the 2008 downturn), Atlanta's financial, insurance, and real estate sector grew slightly during this period (yet this modest increase outpaced gains in that sector in most other major cities).

The cluster analysis for 2005 indicates the direction in which Atlanta's industrial structure is evolving and shows the other cities with which it is becoming more similar. Atlanta is now in a cluster with seven other cities; besides Denver and San Francisco, Atlanta is also paired with Austin, Minneapolis, Raleigh-Durham, San Diego, and Seattle in 2005's cluster 1. These are all cities that rank high on the size of their "creative class" (Florida 2002) and they are, for their economic base, increasingly reliant on what Metro Atlanta Chamber of Commerce calls "industries of the mind." It appears that, in the future, Atlanta city residents will be increasingly employed in industries in which creative people work with ideas and information to develop new solutions and styles (e.g., science and technology, design professions, the arts, and other problem-solving services).

**Table 2.5   Atlanta Compared to 29 U.S. Cities: Industrial Structure.**

**2000**

|  | % Manufacturing | % PSMA* | % EHSS* | % Government |
|---|---|---|---|---|
| **Cluster #1** | 6.9 | 16.9 | 16.6 | 12.8 |
| *Atlanta* | 7.7 | 17.2 | 16.8 | 13.2 |
| **Other Cities:** | Denver, San Francisco | | | |
| **Description:** | High PSMA, Low EHSS | | | |
| | | | | |
| **Cluster #2** | 10.6 | 12.1 | 21.7 | 15.2 |
| Chicago | 13.1 | 13.6 | 19.0 | 14.3 |
| **Other Cities:** | Austin, Birmingham, Cincinnati, Kansas City, Memphis, Minneapolis, Nashville, Philadelphia, Raleigh-Durham, Seattle, St Louis, San Diego | | | |
| **Description:** | Average on all industries | | | |
| | | | | |
| **Cluster #3** | 7.8 | 10.2 | 26.8 | 22.3 |
| Baltimore | 7.8 | 10.2 | 26.8 | 22.3 |
| **Other Cities:** | None | | | |
| **Description:** | High EHSS, High Government | | | |

Table 2.5   Continued on next page

**Table 2.5   Atlanta Compared to 29 U.S. Cities:  Industrial Structure.** (continued)

**2000**

|  | % Manufacturing | % PSMA* | % EHSS* | % Government |
|---|---|---|---|---|
| **Cluster #4** | **6.3** | **12.6** | **26.7** | **14.0** |
| Boston | 6.1 | 14.9 | 26.8 | 13.3 |
| **Other Cities:** | New York, Pittsburgh | | | |
| **Description:** | Low Manufacturing, High EHSS | | | |
| **Cluster #5** | **10.8** | **12.4** | **16.2** | **10.4** |
| Charlotte | 10.7 | 11.8 | 15.8 | 9.5 |
| **Other Cities:** | Dallas, Houston, Indianapolis, Los Angeles, Miami, Phoenix | | | |
| **Description:** | Low EHSS, Low Government | | | |
| **Cluster #6** | **18.5** | **8.8** | **20.9** | **16.1** |
| Detroit | 18.8 | 9.0 | 20.9 | 17.2 |
| **Other Cities:** | Cleveland | | | |
| **Description:** | High Manufacturing, Low PSMA | | | |
| **Cluster #7** | **1.5** | **18.8** | **18.0** | **25.9** |
| Washington DC | 1.5 | 18.8 | 18.0 | 25.9 |
| **Other Cities:** | None | | | |
| **Description:** | Very Low Manufacturing, High PSMA, Very High Government | | | |
| **Mean (Total Sample)** | **10.0** | **12.6** | **20.4** | **14.3** |

**2005**

|  | % Manufacturing | % PSMA* | % EHSS* | % Government |
|---|---|---|---|---|
| **Cluster #1** | **7.5** | **16.3** | **20.7** | **14.6** |
| *Atlanta* | 5.6 | 17.3 | 19.2 | 13.7 |
| **Other Cities:** | Austin, Denver, Minneapolis, Raleigh-Durham, San Diego, San Francisco, Seattle | | | |
| **Description:** | High PSMA | | | |
| **Cluster #2** | **10.3** | **10.6** | **21.0** | **12.9** |
| Chicago | 11.1 | 13.4 | 20.8 | 13.3 |
| **Other Cities:** | Cincinnati, Indianapolis, Kansas City, Memphis, Nashville | | | |
| **Description:** | Average on all industries | | | |
| **Cluster #3** | **7.1** | **10.4** | **26.3** | **17.5** |
| Baltimore | 6.4 | 10.2 | 27.7 | 20.4 |
| **Other Cities:** | Birmingham, New York, Philadelphia, St. Louis | | | |
| **Description:** | High EHSS, High Government | | | |
| **Cluster #4** | **5.7** | **14.1** | **31.7** | **12.6** |
| Boston | 5.2 | 15.8 | 30.3 | 12.2 |
| **Other Cities:** | Pittsburgh | | | |
| **Description:** | Very High EHSS | | | |

Table 2.5   Continued on next page

**Table 2.5** **Atlanta Compared to 29 U.S. Cities: Industrial Structure.** (continued)

2005

|  | % Manufacturing | % PSMA* | % EHSS* | % Government |
|---|---|---|---|---|
| **Cluster #5** | **8.5** | **13.4** | **16.4** | **9.6** |
| Charlotte | 8.0 | 12.3 | 17.2 | 9.7 |
| **Other Cities:** | Dallas, Houston, Los Angeles, Miami, Phoenix | | | |
| **Description:** | Low EHSS, Low Government | | | |
|  |  |  |  |  |
| **Cluster #6** | **14.9** | **9.2** | **24.4** | **15.9** |
| Detroit | 15.9 | 9.5 | 24.3 | 14.1 |
| **Other Cities:** | Cleveland | | | |
| **Description:** | High Manufacturing, Low PSMA | | | |
|  |  |  |  |  |
| **Cluster #7** | **1.6** | **21.8** | **19.4** | **26.5** |
| Washington DC | 1.6 | 21.8 | 19.4 | 26.5 |
| **Other Cities:** | None | | | |
| **Description:** | Very Low Manufacturing, Very High PSMA, Very High Government | | | |
|  |  |  |  |  |
| **Mean (Total Sample)** | **8.3** | **13.2** | **21.7** | **14.1** |

* PSMA refers to the Professional, Scientific, Management, and Administrative sector; EHSS refers to the Educational, Health, and Social Services sector.

## ATLANTA'S INCOME DISTRIBUTION

A survey of urban experts' assessments about income levels of the inhabitants of America's large cities over the past forty years reveals an amazing turnaround. The 1970s through the early 1990s were dominated by the idea that cities were on a trajectory of increasing impoverishment. Cities were described, metaphorically, as "sandboxes" for the destitute (Sternlieb 1971) or as "reservations for the poor, the deviant, the unwanted, and for those who make a business or career of managing them for the rest of society" (Long 1971:32–33). Research on the growing concentration of poverty in large cities galvanized the attention of urban experts (Wilson 1987; Jencks & Peterson 1991). Locally, it was during this era that fears peaked over Atlanta's loss of affluent residents and possibly ending up like poverty-ridden Detroit.

By the mid-1990s, however, a new perspective appeared, based on observations that in many cities upper-income residents and neighborhoods had real staying power and that gentrification brought significant numbers of high-income residents into formerly low-income parts of cities. Kleniewski (1997:6) disputed the earlier view and offered an "inequality" paradigm: "cities are frequently portrayed as being inhabited overwhelmingly by poor people . . . The reality is . . . that . . . some of the wealthiest neighborhoods in the country are located in large cities. Although there *are* large concentrations of poor residents in urban areas, the chief characteristic of

**Table 2.6   Atlanta Compared to 29 U.S. Cities:  Median Household Income and Per Capita Income.**

**2000**

|  | $ Median Income | $ Per Capita Income |
|---|---|---|
| **Cluster #1** | **55,221** | **34,556** |
| San Francisco | 55,221 | 34,556 |
| **Other Cities:** | None | |
| **Description:** | High Income | |
| **Cluster #2** | **44,282** | **26,273** |
| Austin | 42,689 | 24,163 |
| **Other Cities:** | Charlotte, Raleigh-Durham, San Diego, Seattle, Washington DC | |
| **Description:** | Above-Average Income | |
| **Cluster #3** | **38,262** | **21,976** |
| *Atlanta* | 34,770 | 25,772 |
| **Other Cities:** | Boston, Chicago, Dallas, Denver, Houston, Indianapolis, Kansas City, Los Angeles, Minneapolis, Nashville, New York City, Phoenix | |
| **Description:** | Average Income | |
| **Cluster #4** | **28,402** | **16,601** |
| Baltimore | 30,078 | 16,978 |
| **Other Cities:** | Birmingham, Cincinnati, Cleveland, Detroit, Memphis, Miami, Philadelphia, Pittsburgh, St. Louis | |
| **Description:** | Low Income | |
| **Mean (Total Sample)** 36,745 | | **21,463** |

**2005**

|  | $ Median Income | $ Per Capita Income |
|---|---|---|
| **Cluster #1** | **55,637** | **29,487** |
| San Diego | 55,637 | 29,487 |
| **Other Cities:** | None | |
| **Description:** | High Income | |
| **Cluster #2** | **51,338** | **37,838** |
| San Francisco | 57,496 | 39,554 |
| **Other Cities:** | Seattle and Washington DC | |
| **Description:** | High Income | |
| **Cluster #3** | **41,811** | **26,220** |
| *Atlanta* | 39,752 | 33,590 |
| **Other Cities:** | Austin, Boston, Charlotte, Chicago, Dallas, Denver, Houston, Indianapolis, Kansas City, Los Angeles, Minneapolis, Nashville, New York, Phoenix, Raleigh-Durham | |
| **Description:** | Average Income | |
| **Cluster #4** | **29,438** | **18,546** |
| Baltimore | 32,456 | 20,749 |
| **Other Cities:** | Birmingham, Cincinnati, Cleveland, Detroit, Memphis, Miami, Philadelphia, Pittsburgh, St. Louis | |
| **Description:** | Low Income | |
| **Mean (Total Sample)** 39,067 | | **24,933** |

cities is not so much overwhelming poverty as intense inequality between rich and poor." Other researchers also describe large cities as polarized into income-segregated districts (citadels of the rich, ghettos of the poor [Marcuse 1997]) and some assert that the largest "global" cities are the site of the widest gaps between high-paid and low-paid residents (Sassen 2000).

More recently, some observers offer yet another prediction—the "Parisian" model—in which, due to gentrification, closing of public housing projects, and very high housing costs in the city, most poor residents are displaced outward into a ring of low-rent inner suburbs. Jay Bookman (2006) contends that this, in fact, is the course Atlanta is now on: "if you look at what's happening in Atlanta's urban core and its inner ring of suburbs, you can see that [it is] changing ... toward the European housing pattern, with wealth concentrating in the inner city and the inner-ring suburbs becoming home to large numbers of lower-income residents." We examine the median income levels of residents of Atlanta, and other cities, as well as their distribution across income brackets. This analysis should inform us as to which of the income patterns described above is emerging in Atlanta.

Judging by data on median household income and per capita income, the 1980 to 2005 era saw a marked upward trend, even after taking inflation into account. As table 2.1 shows, in 1980 the median household income in the city of Atlanta was $11,296 (roughly equivalent to $30,387 in 2005 dollars)[13] and by 2005 it had risen to $39,752. The city of Atlanta's per capita income in 1980 was $6,539 (roughly equivalent to $17,590 in 2005) and by 2005 per capita income in the city of Atlanta climbed much higher to $33,590.

## Median Household Income and Per Capita Income in 2000 and 2005

To investigate income inequality in the city of Atlanta in 2000, we began with a cluster analysis of median household income and per capita income; the analysis resulted in four clusters. As seen in table 2.6, Atlanta's 2000 income profile was similar to a dozen other cities in the sample (cluster 3). In 2000, Atlanta's median household income was $34,770 and its per capita income was $25,772. These are similar to cities such as Boston, Los Angeles, and New York City, but Atlanta's median income was a bit lower than the other cities while its per capita income was a bit higher. San Francisco was in a cluster by itself with a median income of just over $55,000 and a per capita income of about $35,000. The next cluster includes a number of cities that had above-average incomes, cities like Austin, Seattle, and Washington D.C. Finally, at the bottom of this economic profile are places like Baltimore, Cleveland, Detroit, and St. Louis, cities that have lower than average median household and per capita incomes.

Much remained the same in 2005: Atlanta's median income went up about $5,000 and its per capita income also went up ($39,752 and $33,590,

**Table 2.7   Atlanta Compared to 29 U.S. Cities:  Household Income Categories.**

**2000**

|  | % LT $15,000 | % $35,000-74,999 | % GT $150,000 |
|---|---|---|---|
| **Cluster #1** | **22.0** | **30.7** | **6.3** |
| *Atlanta* | 24.3 | 27.0 | 7.8 |
| **Other Cities:** | Boston, Chicago, Los Angeles, New York City, Washington DC | | |
| **Description:** | Average Poor; Average Middle; Slightly High Rich | | |
| **Cluster #2** | **15.4** | **35.6** | **4.8** |
| Austin | 14.8 | 35.6 | 5.3 |
| **Other Cities:** | Charlotte, Dallas, Denver, Houston, Indianapolis, Kansas City, Minneapolis, Nashville, Phoenix, Raleigh-Durham, San Diego, Seattle | | |
| **Description:** | Low Poor; Average Middle; Average Rich | | |
| **Cluster #3** | **27.5** | **29.8** | **2.2** |
| Baltimore | 27.1 | 30.5 | 2.4 |
| **Other Cities:** | Birmingham, Cincinnati, Cleveland, Detroit, Memphis, Philadelphia, Pittsburgh, St. Louis | | |
| **Description:** | High Poor; Average Middle; Low Rich | | |
| **Cluster #4** | **34.9** | **23.5** | **3.2** |
| Miami | 34.9 | 23.5 | 3.2 |
| **Other Cities:** | None | | |
| **Description:** | Very High Poor; Low Middle; Average Rich | | |
| **Cluster #5** | **14.8** | **31.0** | **11.4** |
| San Francisco | 14.8 | 31.0 | 11.4 |
| **Other Cities:** | None | | |
| **Description:** | Low Poor; Average Middle; High Rich | | |
| **Mean (Total Sample)** | **21.0** | **32.3** | **4.5** |

**2005**

|  | % LT $15,000 | % $35,000-74,999 | % GT $150,000 |
|---|---|---|---|
| **Cluster #1** | **22.4** | **28.3** | **9.8** |
| *Atlanta* | 24.2 | 27.0 | 9.7 |
| **Other Cities:** | Boston, Washington DC | | |
| **Description:** | Average Poor; Average Middle; High Rich | | |
| **Cluster #2** | **16.7** | **32.3** | **6.4** |
| Austin | 15.6 | 33.1 | 6.9 |
| **Other Cities:** | Charlotte, Chicago, Dallas, Denver, Houston, Indianapolis, Kansas City, Los Angeles, Minneapolis, Nashville, New York City, Phoenix, Raleigh-Durham, Seattle | | |
| **Description:** | Low Poor; Average Middle; Average Rich | | |

Table 2.7   Continued on next page

**Table 2.7    Atlanta Compared to 29 U.S. Cities:  Household Income Categories.** (continued)

**2005**

| | % LT $15,000 | % $35,000-74,999 | % GT $150,000 |
|---|---|---|---|
| **Cluster #3** | **26.5** | **29.7** | **2.6** |
| Baltimore | 25.3 | 30.4 | 3.4 |
| **Other Cities:** | Birmingham, Cincinnati, Detroit, Memphis, Philadelphia, Pittsburgh, St. Louis | | |
| **Description:** | High Poor; Average Middle; Low Rich | | |
| **Cluster #4** | **32.9** | **26.0** | **2.2** |
| Miami | 33.0 | 26.5 | 3.6 |
| **Other Cities:** | Cleveland | | |
| **Description:** | Very High Poor; Low Middle; Low Rich | | |
| **Cluster #5** | **13.7** | **30.2** | **11.6** |
| San Francisco | 16.4 | 27.6 | 13.4 |
| **Other Cities:** | San Diego | | |
| **Description:** | Low Poor; Average Middle; High Rich | | |
| **Mean (Total Sample)** | **20.8** | **30.8** | **5.8** |

respectively), which improved Atlanta's relative position in cluster 3. The cities in Atlanta's cluster stayed similar to 2000 but with the addition of Austin, Charlotte, and Raleigh-Durham, which dropped down from cluster 2 in 2000 to cluster 3 in 2005. San Diego now stands in the highest income cluster by itself, with San Francisco, Seattle, and Washington D.C. in a cluster close behind. Interestingly, San Francisco's median and per capita incomes actually increased but not enough to keep up with San Diego's rising income level. Finally, the lowest cluster in terms of median and per capita income remained composed of exactly the same cities as in 2000, which are a mix of northern and midwestern classic rust-belt cities, plus a few southern cities like Baltimore, Birmingham, Memphis, and Miami.

## Household Income Categories in 2000 and in 2005

We also assessed the economic health of these thirty cities using household income categories. More specifically, we use ten income categories, ranging from less than $10,000, to more than $200,000, to analyze the distribution of household incomes and whether they may or may not be changing between 2000 and 2005. Although we only present three income categories in table 2.7 (corresponding roughly to "poor," "middle-income," and "rich"), all ten income categories were used in the cluster analysis. As we discuss below, Atlanta's profile makes it closer to some of the more economically dominant cities in the United States than what was presented in the table based on median household income and per capita income.

In 2000, Atlanta was in a cluster with Boston, Chicago, Los Angeles, New York City, and Washington D.C. (see table 2.7). About 24 percent of Atlanta's population made less than $15,000, about 27 percent made between $35,000 and $74,999, and around 8 percent made more than $150,000. Overall, Atlanta's 2000 cluster includes cities that had average poor populations, average middle-income populations, and higher than average rich populations. By contrast, cities in cluster 2 (e.g., Austin, Charlotte, Denver) had lower than average poor populations and average sized middle-income and rich populations. The city of San Francisco (cluster 5) had the highest percentage in the rich category and among the lowest percentage of poor residents. Cities like Baltimore and Cleveland (cluster 3) remain places with high proportions of poor people and few rich folks. Miami stood alone in the extent to which it had a large poor population and a lower than average middle-income population.

In 2005, Atlanta's household income profile remained similar to that of 2000. The only major change was an increase in the percentage of rich (up to almost 10%); Atlanta's cluster now only includes Boston and Washington D.C. Some of the other cities that were in the same cluster with Atlanta in 2000 are, in 2005, with Austin (cluster 2) but very little changed between 2000 and 2005 for this cluster. The contrast can best be seen in the lower than average poor populations in cluster 2 and the average middle-income and rich populations. San Francisco, joined by San Diego in cluster 5, is at the top of the household income distribution. At the bottom of the 2005 distribution are Miami and Cleveland (cluster 4), and slightly above them is cluster 3 (which includes relatively poor cities like Baltimore, Detroit, and Pittsburgh).

Clearly, the fears of many social scientists in the 1970s and 1980s that American cities in general were on their way to destitution did not develop across the board, though many cities in the Midwest and Northeast did develop more economic problems over time. Whether because of gentrification, fewer public housing projects, higher housing costs, or the combination of all three dynamics, some cities have shown increases in their affluent populations between 2000 and 2005. Atlanta fits this description: the poor and middle-income populations (as percentages) remained virtually the same but the rich population gained in relative terms. By 2005, almost 10% of the city's household population had incomes greater than $150,000.

Kleniewski's "inequality" paradigm and the Parisian model may be taking place in Atlanta. In other words, while the affluent population grows, the city of Atlanta continues to have a significant above-average sized poor population (and slightly below average sized middle-income population). But it is the difference between the poor and the rich that makes contemporary American cities fit the inequality paradigm. However, supplementary analyses also show that some of the inner-ring suburbs (analyzed by us with county data) have shown increases in their poor populations. Thus, the two income-based models described earlier are not mutually exclusive; the city of Atlanta's poor population remains high and the inner-ring suburbs are also showing an increase in poverty populations. These trends suggest that gentrification and suburban sprawl are taking place at the same time in the Atlanta metropolitan area.

## ATLANTA'S RACIAL AND ETHNIC COMPOSITION

For most of the twentieth century, whites and blacks have dominated Atlanta's racial composition. Indeed, much political energy was spent on maintaining "good" black-white relations in Atlanta during the civil rights movement of the 1960s and 1970s. Not until the last twenty to thirty years has the black-white dichotomy changed with the influx of immigrants from Asia and Latin America. The 1990s saw an increased presence of immigrants as the 1996 Olympics approached, but in the last ten years Atlanta's reputation as an immigrant host has gained even stronger momentum. What does this mean for the city "too busy to hate"? How does Atlanta compare to other U.S. cities in terms of its racial and ethnic composition?

As table 2.1 shows, over the past twenty-five years the percentage of the city of Atlanta's population that is black has declined by over seven percentage points (from two-thirds in 1980 and 1990 to slightly less than 60% in 2005). For most of this period the white population in the city has remained stable (at about 31%), though in the post-2000 years it has increased slightly (to 34% in 2005). These changes have stimulated comments by city leaders and pundits about a possible "whitening" of Atlanta. While those concerns may be relevant in several select neighborhoods or a few voting districts, the citywide numbers show a relatively modest increase in the percentage of white residents in the city of Atlanta as a whole. Perhaps more significant are the increases in the city's other racial-ethnic categories during the years 1980 to 2005. The Hispanic population in the city of Atlanta grew from 1.4 percent in 1980 to 4.7 percent in 2005, with most of that growth occurring between 1990 and 2000. The Asian population in the city of Atlanta also grew, from less that one percent in 1980 to 2 percent in 2005. The increases in both the Hispanic and Asian population in the city of Atlanta is driven to a large extent by the settlement of immigrants, as the percentage of Atlanta's population that is foreign-born rose from 2.3 percent in 1980 to 3.4 percent in 1990, to 6.6 percent in 2000, and to 6.7 percent in 2005. Thus the growth in the level of immigrants in the city of Atlanta was greatest from 1990 to 2000; evidence suggests that in the post-2000 years immigrant settlement in suburban areas of Atlanta has been higher than in the city.

**Table 2.8   Atlanta Compared to 29 U.S. Cities: Percent Black and Percent White.**

**2000**

|  | Percent Black | Percent White |
|---|---|---|
| **Cluster #1** | **58.3** | **33.9** |
| *Atlanta* | 61.4 | 31.3 |
| **Other Cities:** | Baltimore, Birmingham, Cleveland, Memphis, Philadelphia, St. Louis, Washington DC | |
| **Description:** | High % Black; Low % White | |
| | | |
| **Cluster #2** | **8.3** | **53.6** |
| Austin | 10.0 | 52.9 |
| **Other Cities:** | Denver, Phoenix, San Diego, San Francisco, Seattle | |
| **Description:** | Very Low % Black; High % White | |
| | | |
| **Cluster #3** | **29.3** | **58.7** |
| Boston | 25.3 | 49.5 |
| **Other Cities:** | Charlotte, Cincinnati, Indianapolis, Kansas City, Minneapolis, Nashville, Pittsburgh, Raleigh-Durham | |
| **Description:** | Average % Black; High % White | |
| | | |
| **Cluster #4** | **24.7** | **28.9** |
| Chicago | 36.8 | 31.3 |
| **Other Cities:** | Dallas, Houston, Los Angeles, Miami, New York City | |
| **Description:** | Low % Black; Low % White | |
| | | |
| **Cluster #5** | **81.6** | **10.5** |
| Detroit | 81.6 | 10.5 |
| **Other Cities:** | None | |
| **Description:** | Very High % Black; Very Low % White | |
| | | |
| **Mean (Total Sample)** | **33.7** | **43.5** |

**2005**

|  | Percent Black | Percent White |
|---|---|---|
| **Cluster #1** | **54.9** | **36.1** |
| *Atlanta* | 58.6 | 33.8 |
| **Other Cities:** | Baltimore, Cincinnati, Cleveland, Memphis, Philadelphia, St. Louis, Washington DC | |
| **Description:** | High % Black; Low % White | |
| | | |
| **Cluster #2** | **8.9** | **52.9** |
| Austin | 8.9 | 51.2 |
| **Other Cities:** | Denver, Minneapolis, Phoenix, San Diego, San Francisco, Seattle | |
| **Description:** | Very Low % Black; High % White | |
| | | |
| **Cluster #3** | **29.1** | **56.4** |
| Boston | 24.6 | 48.6 |
| **Other Cities:** | Charlotte, Indianapolis, Kansas City, Nashville, Pittsburgh, Raleigh-Durham | |
| **Description:** | Average % Black; High % White | |

Table 2.8   Continued on next page

**Table 2.8   Atlanta Compared to 29 U.S. Cities:  Percent Black and Percent White.** (continued)

| 2005 | Percent Black | Percent White |
|---|---|---|
| **Cluster #4** | **23.2** | **27.1** |
| Chicago | 34.9 | 30.3 |
| **Other Cities:** | Dallas, Houston, Los Angeles, Miami, New York City | |
| **Description:** | Low % Black; Low % White | |
| **Cluster #5** | **78.9** | **14.5** |
| Detroit | 82.1 | 9.2 |
| **Other Cities:** | Birmingham | |
| **Description:** | Very High % Black; Very Low % White | |
| **Mean (Total Sample)** | **33.4** | **41.5** |

### Black-White Composition of Atlanta and Other Cities in 2000 and in 2005

The city of Atlanta remains a place that is predominantly African American (see table 2.8). In 2000, about 61 percent of the city's population identified as black whereas about 31% identified as white. This put Atlanta in a cluster with similar cities, mostly in the South, like Baltimore, Birmingham, Memphis, and Washington D.C., as cities with high proportions of blacks and relatively low proportions of whites. Cleveland, Philadelphia, and St. Louis are northern cities that also fit into this cluster. Except for Detroit, which had a black population at almost 82 percent (and is in a cluster by itself), the cities in the three other clusters do not come close to Atlanta's cluster. First, Austin is in a cluster with other western cities that have low black populations and higher than average percentages of whites. A second pattern is represented by Boston in a cluster with cities across different regions (e.g., Charlotte, Kansas City, Minneapolis) having average black populations but higher than average white populations. Finally, a number of cities have low black and white populations, such as Dallas, Houston, Los Angeles, Miami, and New York City, which, as will be seen below, have higher than average immigrant populations.

In 2005, Atlanta's black population decreased to about 59 percent and the white population went up to about 34 percent. Consequently, there were small changes but the overall characterization of Atlanta and the other cities in the cluster remains the same: high percent black and lower than average percent white. Birmingham joined Detroit as a city with a very large black population and a very small white population (2005 cluster 5). The other cities remained quite similar to the 2000 characterizations. There are the mostly western cities with low proportions of blacks and higher than average proportions of whites (e.g., Austin and Denver). There are the mix of cities, including Boston and Charlotte, with average

**Table 2.9   Atlanta Compared to 29 U.S. Cities:   Racial and Ethnic Composition.**

**2000**

|  | % Black | % White | % Hispanic | % FB |
|---|---|---|---|---|
| **Cluster #1** | **58.3** | **33.9** | **4.6** | **6.2** |
| *Atlanta* | 61.4 | 31.3 | 4.5 | 6.6 |
| **Other Cities:** | Baltimore, Birmingham, Cleveland, Memphis, Philadelphia, St. Louis, Washington DC | | | |
| **Description:** | Low % Immigrant; High % Black; Low % White | | | |
| **Cluster #2** | **17.5** | **42.2** | **29.3** | **26.5** |
| Austin | 10.0 | 52.9 | 30.5 | 16.6 |
| **Other Cities:** | Boston, Chicago, Dallas, Denver, Houston, Los Angeles, New York City, Phoenix, San Diego, San Francisco | | | |
| **Description:** | High % Immigrant; Low % Black; Average % White | | | |
| **Cluster #3** | **27.4** | **60.8** | **5.1** | **9.0** |
| Charlotte | 32.7 | 55.1 | 7.4 | 11 |
| **Other Cities:** | Cincinnati, Indianapolis, Kansas City, Minneapolis, Nashville, Pittsburgh, Raleigh-Durham, Seattle | | | |
| **Description:** | Low % Immigrant; Slightly Low % Black; High % White | | | |
| **Cluster #4** | **22.3** | **11.8** | **65.8** | **59.5** |
| Miami | 22.3 | 11.8 | 65.8 | 59.5 |
| **Other Cities:** | None | | | |
| **Description:** | Very High % Immigrant; Low % Black; Very Low % White | | | |
| **Cluster #5** | **81.6** | **10.5** | **5.0** | **4.8** |
| Detroit | 81.6 | 10.5 | 5.0 | 4.8 |
| **Other Cities:** | None | | | |
| **Description:** | Very Low % Immigrant; Very High % Black; Very Low % White | | | |
| **Mean (Total Sample)** | **33.7** | **43.5** | **15.9** | **16.2** |

**2005**

|  | % Black | % White | % Hispanic | % FB |
|---|---|---|---|---|
| **Cluster #1** | **54.9** | **36.1** | **5.2** | **7.3** |
| *Atlanta* | 58.6 | 33.8 | 4.7 | 6.7 |
| **Other Cities:** | Baltimore, Cincinnati, Cleveland, Memphis, Philadelphia, St. Louis, Washington DC | | | |
| **Description:** | Low % Immigrant; High % Black; Low % White | | | |
| **Cluster #2** | **16.3** | **40.1** | **32.2** | **27.7** |
| Austin | 8.9 | 51.2 | 32.9 | 18.2 |
| **Other Cities:** | Boston, Chicago, Dallas, Denver, Houston, Los Angeles, New York City, Phoenix, San Diego, San Francisco | | | |
| **Description:** | High % Immigrant; Low % Black; Average % White | | | |

Table 2.9   Continued on next page

**Table 2.9   Atlanta Compared to 29 U.S. Cities:  Racial and Ethnic Composition.** (continued)

**2005**

|  | % Black | % White | % Hispanic | % FB |
|---|---|---|---|---|
| **Cluster #3** | **25.5** | **59.0** | **7.6** | **11.9** |
| Charlotte | 34.3 | 50.3 | 9.7 | 13.2 |
| **Other Cities:** | Indianapolis, Kansas City, Minneapolis, Nashville, Pittsburgh, Raleigh-Durham, Seattle | | | |
| **Description:** | Low % Immigrant; Low % Black; High % White | | | |
| **Cluster #4** | **21.9** | **11.0** | **67.4** | **58.2** |
| Miami | 21.9 | 11.0 | 67.4 | 58.2 |
| **Other Cities:** | None | | | |
| **Description:** | Very High % Immigrant; Low % Black; Very Low % White | | | |
| **Cluster #5** | **78.9** | **14.5** | **4.3** | **5.4** |
| Detroit | 82.1 | 9.2 | 5.6 | 6.3 |
| **Other Cities:** | Birmingham | | | |
| **Description:** | Very Low % Immigrant; Very High % Black; Very Low % White | | | |
| **Mean (Total Sample)** | **33.4** | **41.5** | **17.8** | **17.6** |

black populations and higher than average white populations. And, finally, there are the cities with both low black and white populations such as Dallas and Miami.

## Racial-Ethnic Composition of Atlanta and Other Cities in 2000 and in 2005

In table 2.9 we add percent Hispanic and percent foreign-born to our cluster analysis. While much of the story is similar to that from the results in table 2.8, there are some key differences in both years. In both years, Atlanta had a Hispanic population that comprised about 5 percent of the population. In terms of the city of Atlanta's foreign-born residents, the foreign-born population remained at about 7 percent of the city's population in 2000 and 2005. Atlanta's cluster stayed the same across the two tables; that is, Atlanta, along with places like Baltimore, Cleveland, and Philadelphia had higher than average black populations, lower than average white populations, and lower than average immigrant populations across the timeframe. Similarly, but to a more extreme degree, Detroit in 2000, and Detroit and Birmingham in 2005 (see cluster 5) had large black populations, and below average white, Hispanic, and foreign-born populations. Cluster 3, comprised of cities such as Charlotte, Indianapolis, and Seattle, also had below average immigrant populations, but these cities have lower than average black populations with higher than average white populations.

Separate from the three clusters described above, are two remaining ones. First, there are the cities in cluster 2 (e.g., Austin, Boston, Dallas, Denver, Los Angeles, and New York City), with above-average immigrant populations, relatively small black populations, and average white populations. Standing alone, though, is Miami: in both 2000 and 2005, nearly 60 percent of the city's population is foreign born and about 65 percent of the population identifies as Hispanic (native- or foreign-born). Miami shows consistency across the timeframe and has a much different racial and ethnic composition than Atlanta. If anything, although Atlanta's non-black and non-white populations have grown, its immigrant population is far below that of Miami and the cities in cluster 2, such as Boston, Chicago, Dallas, Houston, Los Angeles, New York, and San Diego.

## SUMMARY

What does the city of Atlanta's future hold for her residents? Is Atlanta converging with other cities or is it an entirely different context from other U.S. cities? We do not pretend to hold a crystal ball in front of us, and we realize that it is dangerous to project trends based on the developments we have found in the short five year period between 2000 and 2005. However, we think our analyses and results do offer a few good suggestions about what lies ahead for the city of Atlanta in the early twenty-first century.

At the outset, it is important to note that Atlanta is converging with (i.e., becoming more similar to) certain other U.S. cities, but there is not one particular city that Atlanta increasingly resembles on the variables studied here. This is evident because no single other city is in the same cluster as Atlanta in all eight cluster tables we have presented. However, several other cities are often in the same cluster as Atlanta, particularly Austin, Boston, Charlotte, Denver, San Diego, and Washington D.C. For example, in 2005, Boston has similar household, occupational, and income profiles as Atlanta, while San Diego and Atlanta were similar in their age, occupational, and industrial profiles. Interestingly, Atlanta has a similar racial and ethnic profile as Washington D.C., but it is different from that of Austin, Boston, Charlotte, Denver, and San Diego. At the same time, Atlanta definitely is not becoming the next Detroit. In fact, Detroit is among a series of cities such as Miami, Pittsburgh, and St. Louis that fall at the bottom of the city hierarchy in terms of the socioeconomic variables in our research. These are places with very high levels of poverty and rising income inequality, and while Atlanta also has rising poverty, it also has rising incomes which may increase income inequality on the one hand but offset some of the negative consequences on the other.

Several key findings have implications for Atlanta's future. First, Atlanta is not following places like San Francisco and Seattle with decreasing numbers of children. Atlanta is holding steady in this regard. Second, Atlanta is following a national trend with ever-lower percentages of married persons with children. Third, Atlanta now has a bifurcated occupational structure. Specifically, Atlanta has a growing managerial-professional class as well as an increasing proportion of persons working service jobs. At the same time, the percentage of production-transportation occupations has gone down. We believe that this means Atlanta is becoming more like a global city with sharp inequality, though not at the level of New York City, for example. The industrial distribution results support this conclusion that Atlanta is now a second-tier global city (see Markusen, Lee, and DiGiovanna 1999; Hodos 2007 for discussion of this concept). Fourth, income differences also support these contentions with an increasing percentage of rich residents and a consistent percentage of middle-class and poor households. Finally, Atlanta is increasingly known as a new immigrant gateway, but the data (not shown here) indicate that this is a more fitting description of its suburbs—particularly Gwinnett, DeKalb, and Cobb counties —than the city itself where the black-white dichotomy remains dominant.

Taken together, our analyses suggest that Atlanta is neither at the top of the city hierarchy nor is it at the bottom. Although Atlanta city leaders and boosters often compare Atlanta to New York or Chicago and aspire for Atlanta to be like those cities, our analyses show that Atlanta is really a different kind of city than those places, and that Atlanta is on a developmental path more similar to Boston, Denver, or San Diego. In some respects Atlanta is becoming more like a second-tier global city than the old regional capital it used to be, especially with regard to economic factors, but in other respects Atlanta remains clearly a part of the South. Race, especially the disadvantaged position of African Americans even in a city with a relatively large middle- and upper-class black population, continues to be a salient feature of the Atlanta experience and this continues into the twenty-first century. Our analyses do suggest that inequality and conflict between the haves and have-nots of Atlanta will continue, and that this is indeed like the rest of urban America.

## NOTES

1. "Booming Nashville struggles not to become 'another Atlanta'" by Tom Eblen, *Atlanta Journal-Constitution*, March 29, 1987: 10B.

2. The ARC Peer Region Report (2002) chose Baltimore, Charlotte, Chicago, Cleveland, Dallas, Denver, Minneapolis, San Diego, and Seattle as Atlanta's peer urban regions. Its "Envision 6+" tables list Boston, Chicago, Dallas-Fort Worth,

Detroit, Houston, Los Angeles-Long Beach-Santa Ana, Miami, New York-Newark, Philadelphia, Phoenix, San Francisco-Oakland, and Washington D.C. as peer regions to compare with Atlanta.

3. *Atlanta Journal-Constitution*, December 18, 1994: Section D.

4. Maria Saporta, *Atlanta Journal-Constitution*, May 24, 1999: E1.

5. *Atlanta Journal-Constitution*, "Atlanta on road to becoming another L.A., report says" September 4, 2006: B4.

6. E. Wycliffe Orr, *Atlanta Journal-Constitution*, December 19, 2006: A19.

7. Unlike the decennial Census, the American Community Survey in 2005 and in prior years only included people residing in "housing units" and excluded people living in "group quarters" (e.g., military barracks, college dorms, nursing homes, correctional facilities). This creates some comparability problems for the 2000 and 2005 data, but in most cases we think they are relatively small. The only adjustment we have made is that for the city of Atlanta's 2005 total population (given in table 2.1) we use the Census Bureau's official estimate rather than the number given in the American Community Survey.

8. More technically, our research used agglomerative hierarchical cluster analysis, in which distance was measured as squared Euclidian distance and the clustering method is average linkage between groups.

9. We use the U.S. Census Bureau's typology of households. A household consists of one of the following living in a "housing unit": a person living alone, two or more unrelated people living together, or a family ("housing units" are houses, apartments, mobile homes, or rooms that are intended as separate living quarters; "group quarters," such as dormitories, nursing homes, prisons, shelters, or barracks are not considered "housing units"). Households that are "families" are those in which two or more people related by birth, marriage, or adoption live in the same housing unit. In our analysis, we also focus on two subcategories of family households: (a) those in which a married couple and their child less than eighteen live together, and (b) those in which a woman is living with her child less than eighteen and no husband is present.

10. Helena Oliviero, *Atlanta Journal-Constitution*, November 28, 2006.

11. Whether it will continue unabated is the key question for Atlanta's future. Several recent changes have implications for this:

1) Business mergers that reduce the number of corporate headquarters in Atlanta may slow growth of managerial-professional jobs.
2) Closure of Atlanta's automobile factories and uncertainties in Delta Airlines' future will affect production-transport jobs.
3) Rising housing costs reduce the number of workers with service jobs who can afford to live in the city of Atlanta.
4) The economic crisis starting in 2008 has pushed unemployment rates up to levels not seen in over a decade.

12. Dallas and San Francisco remain, in 2005, cities in which PSMA is the industrial category that employs the highest percentage of city residents.

13. Conversion from dollars in earlier years to equivalent dollars (i.e., similar purchasing power) in 2005 was done using the inflation calculator on the Bureau of Labor Statistics' website.

# REFERENCES

Bookman, Jay. 2006. "As inner cities transform, so do suburbs." *Atlanta Journal-Constitution,* October 30: A17.

Bruegmann, Robert. 2005. *Sprawl: A Compact History.* Chicago: University of Chicago Press.

Florida, Richard. 2002. *The Rise of the Creative Class.* New York: Basic Books.

Hodos, Jerome. 2007. "Globalization and the Concept of the Second City." *City & Community* 6: 315–333.

Jencks, Christopher and Paul E. Peterson (eds.). 1991. *The Urban Underclass.* Washington DC: Brookings Institute.

Kleniewski, Nancy. 1997. *Cities, Change, and Conflict.* Belmont, CA: Wadsworth Publishing.

Long, Norton E. 1971. "The City as Reservation." *The Public Interest* 25 (Fall): 22–28.

Marcuse, Peter. 1997. "The Enclave, the Citadel, and the Ghetto: What Has Changed in the Post-Fordist U.S. City." *Urban Affairs Review* 33: 228–264.

Markusen, Anne R., Yong-Sook Lee, and Sean DiGiovanna (eds.). 1999. *Second Tier Cities.* Minneapolis: University of Minnesota Press.

Sassen, Saskia. 2000. *Cities in a World Economy,* 2nd edition. Thousand Oaks, CA: Pine Forge Press.

Sternlieb, George. 1971. "The City as Sandbox." *The Public Interest* 25 (Fall): 14–21.

Wilson, William J. 1987. *The Truly Disadvantaged.* Chicago: University of Chicago Press.

*Part II*

# THE ECONOMY

*Chapter 3*

# Tracking the Economy of the City of Atlanta: Past Trends and Future Prospects

*Glenwood Ross, David L. Sjoquist, and Matthew Wooten*

Metropolitan growth in the United States during the second half of the twentieth century redefined American cities. Once primarily urban manufacturing centers, they were transformed into suburban and urban areas whose industrial composition went through a major metamorphosis. As a logistics-based city with expanding service industries, significant labor pooling, and low costs, the city of Atlanta provides a useful example for examining modern urban economic growth.

This chapter explores the changes over the last twenty-five years in the level and composition of employment in the city of Atlanta. Further, this report seeks to understand how and why the employment level and industrial composition of the city changed, and to understand the future prospects of the city's economy. We start with a brief history of the growth and development of the city and region, and then turn to a discussion of the current economic structure and how it evolved over the past twenty-five years. We also provide a detailed discussion of four important specific sectors: the hospitality industry, logistics, professional services, and the health sector. After exploring why these changes occurred, we turn to a discussion of what might be in store for the city's economy.

## THE CONTEXT OF ATLANTA

Atlanta is unique in terms of what caused its creation. Most cities that existed in the nineteenth century were established as seaports or as manufacturing centers close to water power needed to run manufacturing equipment or to raw materials such as coal. Atlanta, however, developed because of its transportation access to the Southeast.

Compared to most other major U.S. cities, Atlanta developed late. Atlanta's origin dates to 1837 when the Western and Atlantic Railroad marked the end of the rail line coming from Tennessee. The railroad established Atlanta as a collection and distribution center for the state, with food and cotton brought to Atlanta for shipment north and finished goods from the north shipped to Atlanta for distribution to other parts of the state. The Atlanta economy thus focused on retailing, wholesaling, and distribution based on the advantage it had as the terminus of the railroad.

By 1890, eleven rail lines converged on Atlanta, and as a result Atlanta became the center of the distribution network of the Southeast. As the population of the geographic area served by the railroads coming from Atlanta grew, Atlanta also became an increasingly important commercial center.

To further expand the economy, efforts such as the 1881 International Cotton Exposition were made to increase northern investment in the area, particularly in establishing textile mills. The result of these efforts was that by the end of the nineteenth century, Atlanta had become a center of manufacturing as well as commerce.

Its role as a transportation hub further expanded in the twentieth century. In 1925, William Hartsfield, then a member of the board of aldermen and later mayor, encouraged the city to buy the land that is now the site of Hartsfield-Jackson International Airport. The airport is now the world's busiest airport. And when the interstate system was built, three major interstates intersected in Atlanta. Thus, originally built as a rail center, Atlanta evolved into a major regional transportation center for rail, air, and trucking.

Atlanta grew in the first half of the century for two reasons. First, Atlanta's commercial economy was based on the needs of the Southeast region, and that region grew. Between 1900 and 1950, the population of Georgia and its border states increased at an annual average rate of 1.26 percent.[1] Second, Atlanta grew because it extended its economic reach beyond the Southeast and because the changing nature of the U.S. economy made urban locations economically more sensible.

As a result of these forces, Atlanta grew faster than the Southeast region as a whole. In 1900, the city's population was 89,872. By 1950, the city's population had increased to 331,314, an annual increase of 2.6 percent, and the Atlanta metropolitan area population had increased to 671,797, an annual increase of 4.1 percent.[2]

Despite its growth during the first half of the twentieth century, the end of World War II is often cited as the point at which Atlanta takes on national importance. The economy had diversified by 1950 and Atlanta had become a regional center for finance and insurance, as well as commerce.

Manufacturing employed nearly 17 percent of city residents, although in the United States, 29.5 percent of urban residents were employed in manufacturing. Generally, city and suburban residents were employed in the same industries. A major exception was personal services, a sector in which 93.7 percent of the workers were black; these workers were largely employed as domestics and generally lived in the city.

During the latter half of the twentieth century, suburban expansion in the United States became a national phenomenon, and Atlanta was no exception. In 1950, the Atlanta region was the economic center serving the Southeast, and as the economy of the Southeast grew, the Atlanta region grew. Initially, the city of Atlanta captured a large share of that growth. The period from the 1950s to the mid-1960s was one of substantial growth and development for the city, with its population increasing by over 150,000 people, including 100,000 added through the 1953 annexation called for in the Plan of Improvement.[3] By 1970, the city's population had reached 496,973. But the region's growth increasingly spilled out from the boundaries of the city, in part because the city could not expand its borders. As a result, the city's population growth at first stagnated and then declined from the late 1960s into the 1990s.

However, the Atlanta region grew, adding over 3 million people between 1950 and 2000, and another million by 2005, to bring the population to 4.9 million. While the metropolitan statistical area (MSA) consisted of three counties in 1950, it grew to five counties in 1960, fifteen counties in 1973, eighteen counties in 1983, twenty counties in 1993, and twenty-eight counties in 2005.

Following World War II, the suburbanization of urban economies accelerated. Manufacturing and commercial activities, which had traditionally resided in the central cities, began to spread out beyond the urban centers. Thus, urban economies grew into larger commuter areas. Mills and Lubuele (1997) note that suburbanization "has pervaded United States MSAs for at least fifty years and has characterized every metropolitan area in the world" (p. 750). The interstate system reduced commuting costs, which allowed households to move even further from the central city. Higher-wage workers moved further from urban centers, resulting in increasing income segregation between high-wage residents of suburban areas and lower-wage earners in inner cities. Suburbanization of workers has also meant a relocation of employers and industries. "Not only manufacturing but also offices and retail shops have suburbanized during the last half-century. In 1950 about 70 percent of MSA employment was in inner cities, and in 1980 it was somewhat more than 50 percent. By 1990, it was certainly somewhat less than half" (Mills and Lubuele 1997, 750–51).

Beginning in the mid- to late-1960s, the City of Atlanta succumbed to the economic and social pressures facing central cities nationwide. The development of the interstate system in the region allowed households to live further from their jobs in the central city. The growth of the middle class in the suburbs provided the economic basis for retailing to move to the suburbs, particularly in the form of regional shopping centers made possible by the increase in automobile ownership after World War II. Likewise, shipping became less tied to railroads and so wholesaling and warehousing operations were no longer tied to rail lines and the central city. Manufacturing technology changed from vertical to horizontal production processes; the resulting need for one-story buildings with large land requirements drove manufacturing firms to seek lower cost land in the suburbs and exurbs.

Social issues were also a force driving the middle class to the suburbs. Increasing social problems associated with the growing concentration of poverty in the central city along with school integration led many to flee the city. The suburbanization of the skilled work force, along with the increase in mobility and communications technology, led to office jobs moving to the suburbs. The interstate's exits and interchanges provided an attractive location for the development of office parks such as Executive Park at Druid Hills and I-85 in DeKalb County.

As mentioned previously, the population of the city began to decline sometime in the mid-1960s and employment likely declined as well.[4] By 1990, population had fallen to 394,017 according to the Bureau of the Census and to 415,200 according to the Atlanta Regional Commission (ARC).[5] But the city's population began increasing again at least by the late 1990s. Current (2006) population of the city is estimated by ARC to be 451,600, while the city's own estimate is 499,000.[6] ARC forecasts population to increase, reaching 602,783 by 2030, while the city's forecast is 783,000.

## TRENDS IN EMPLOYMENT PATTERNS

Like most U.S. cities and metropolitan areas, over the past twenty-five years Atlanta has redefined itself in economic terms. We start by considering the growth in employment for the city and the ten-county ARC region.[7] We then turn to a look at the changing industrial composition, considering first the Atlanta MSA because the employment patterns in the city of Atlanta are driven in large part by regional changes. We then turn to a discussion of employment in the city.

### Employment Growth

Table 3.1 shows total employment as estimated by ARC for the city and the ten-county ARC region for the period 1980 to 2005 and forecasts to

2030.[8] During the 1970s the city added about 1,700 jobs per year. The growth increased to 3,700 per year during the 1980s, and 4,500 per year during the 1990s. Employment dropped in the early 1990s, which coincides with the 1991 recession, but rose from 1993 through 2000 before dipping again with the onset of the 2001 recession. But unlike the 1990s, city employment has yet to recover from the 2001 recession.

Employment growth in the ARC region grew faster over the period 1980 to 2005 than did employment growth in the city. For the entire period, regional employment increased at an annual rate of 3.2 percent while employment in the city increased at an annual rate of 0.5 percent.

The Atlanta Regional Commission does expect employment in the city and the ARC region to grow over the next twenty-five years. However, they forecast that it will be almost 2015 before the city reaches the employment level it had in 2000. In 2005, the city had 20.3 percent of the ARC region's employment. The city's share is expected to fall to 17.3 percent by 2030.

## Industrial Composition of the Atlanta MSA

Making comparisons of employment over time is difficult because of changes in how the Federal government defines industry sectors. In

**Table 3.1   Employment in the City of Atlanta and Atlanta Region for Selected Years**

| Year | Employment | | City Share |
|------|------|------------|------------|
|      | City | ARC Region | |
| 1980 | 355,526 | 901,157 | 39.4% |
| 1990 | 392,147 | 1,426,000 | 27.5% |
| 1991 | 384,959 | NA | |
| 1992 | 382,866 | 1,414,000 | 21.1% |
| 1993 | 387,954 | 1,478,000 | 26.2% |
| 1994 | 398,108 | 1,567,000 | 25.4% |
| 1995 | 402,911 | 1,640,000 | 24.6% |
| 1996 | 417,683 | 1,706,000 | 23.5% |
| 1997 | 418,321 | 1,774,000 | 23.6% |
| 1998 | 425,594 | 1,840,000 | 23.1% |
| 1999 | 431,133 | 1,918,000 | 22.5% |
| 2000 | 437,195 | 1,991,450 | 22.0% |
| 2001 | 435,492 | NA | |
| 2002 | NA | NA | |
| 2003 | 411,117 | 1,934,000 | 21.3% |
| 2004 | NA | NA | |
| 2005 | 403,110 | 1,980,500 | 20.3% |
| 2010 (forecast) | 419,596 | 2,168,669 | 19.3% |
| 2030 (forecast) | 534,073 | 3,086,304 | 17.3% |

Source: Atlanta Regional Commission.
NA: Not Available.

1997, in order to better represent the industrial composition of the U.S. economy, the federal government switched from the Standard Industrial Classification (SIC) industry codes to the North American Industrial Classification System (NAICS) for reporting employment by industry sector. In changing the system, all industry classifications were at least partially altered, and a number of them were significantly restructured. The NAICS system defined new industries, for example, Information, and switched sub-sectors between sectors, for example, durable goods went from wholesale trade to retail trade. These changes make comparisons of employment between SIC and NAICS impossible. However, the NAICS better reflects the nature of today's economy.[9]

Thus, to show the changes in employment by sector between 1980 and 2006, it is necessary to use data reported by SIC code and by NAICS codes. Table 3.2 shows the changes for 1990 to 2006 by NAICS code.[10]

Table 3.2 shows the change in the composition of employment for the Atlanta MSA by major industry categories (and for some subcategories) over the 1990–2006 timeframe. The table illustrates the continued decline of the manufacturing sector and the increased importance of the service sector in the Atlanta MSA. Not only did the manufacturing sector lose employment share, it actually lost ground in absolute terms as well. Since 2000, manufacturing has lost twenty-nine thousand jobs and now employs nearly nine thousand fewer people than it did a quarter of a century ago. Service employment, on the other hand, increased by over 80 percent from 1990 to 2006 and its corresponding share of total employment grew from 33.1 percent to 40.2 percent. More than four hundred thousand new jobs were created in the service sectors during this period. Forty-five percent of this increase was accounted for by professional and business services. The food and drink service sector made up about a fifth of the increase while health care services accounted for 16.9 percent of the employment increases. Other significant employment gainers include construction, financial activities, transportation and warehousing, wholesale and retail trade, and government—particularly at the local level.

Employment in construction increased by 77.7 percent between 1990 and 2006. Construction employment reflects the employment and population growth, including a booming housing sector in an expanding suburban area. Employment in wholesale trade increased by 43,200 jobs between 1990 and 2006, although employment in the sector declined by around 4,000 jobs after 2000. Transportation and warehousing also saw strong growth in the 1990s, but has been stagnant since.

Compared to the Atlanta regional economy of 1950, today's economy retains some of the same characteristics. Atlanta is still a major distribution center, as evidenced by its strong logistic sector (transportation, warehousing, and wholesale trade), which remains a dominant sector

**Table 3.2  Atlanta MSA Employment and Share by Sector: 1990, 2000, and 2006 (in 1000s)**

| Industry (NACIS) | 1990 Emp | Share | 2000 Emp | Share | 2006 Emp | Share | %Change 1990–2006 |
|---|---|---|---|---|---|---|---|
| Natural Resources and Mining | 2.2 | 0.1% | 2.2 | 0.1% | 2.1 | 0.1% | -4.5% |
| Construction | 77.5 | 4.8% | 128.5 | 5.6% | 137.7 | 5.7% | 77.7% |
| Manufacturing | 186.9 | 11.6% | 207.2 | 9.0% | 178.1 | 7.4% | -4.7% |
| Food | 20.4 | 1.3% | 22.8 | 1.0% | 24.8 | 1.0% | 21.6% |
| Transportation | 18.4 | 1.1% | 21.7 | 0.9% | 19.3 | 0.8% | 4.9% |
| Wholesale Trade | 114.1 | 7.1% | 160.9 | 7.0% | 157.3 | 6.6% | 37.9% |
| Retail Trade | 196.4 | 12.2% | 263.4 | 11.5% | 265.3 | 11.1% | 35.1% |
| Utilities | 12.9 | 0.8% | 10.8 | 0.5% | 10.9 | 0.5% | -15.5% |
| Transportation & Warehousing | 83.1 | 5.2% | 116.5 | 5.1% | 114.7 | 4.8% | 38.0% |
| Information | 74.4 | 4.6% | 111.1 | 4.9% | 89.8 | 3.7% | 20.7% |
| Telecommunications | 29.2 | 1.8% | 53.8 | 2.3% | 35.5 | 1.5% | 21.6% |
| Wired Telecommunications Carriers | 21.8 | 1.4% | 35.4 | 1.5% | 19.1 | 0.8% | -12.4% |
| Financial Activities | 106.8 | 6.6% | 148.4 | 6.5% | 161.9 | 6.8% | 51.6% |
| Finance & Insurance | 81.0 | 5.0% | 108.7 | 4.7% | 115.4 | 4.8% | 42.5% |
| Real Estate & Rental & Leasing | 25.9 | 1.6% | 39.7 | 1.7% | 46.6 | 1.9% | 79.9% |
| Services | 532.4 | 33.1% | 868.0 | 37.9% | 963.3 | 40.2% | 80.9% |
| Professional & Business Services | 203.1 | 12.6% | 392.0 | 17.1% | 398.6 | 16.6% | 96.3% |
| Education | 23.1 | 1.4% | 39.5 | 1.7% | 51.5 | 2.1% | 122.9% |
| Health Care | 86.7 | 5.4% | 129.3 | 5.6% | 159.4 | 6.6% | 83.9% |
| Social Assistance | 11.3 | 0.7% | 22.4 | 1.0% | 31.3 | 1.3% | 177.0% |
| Arts & Entertainment | 21.3 | 1.3% | 23.8 | 1.0% | 26.8 | 1.1% | 25.8% |
| Accommodations | 26.6 | 1.7% | 26.9 | 1.2% | 24.3 | 1.0% | -8.6% |
| Food & Drink | 94.6 | 5.9% | 145.7 | 6.4% | 174.6 | 7.3% | 84.6% |
| Other Services | 65.7 | 4.1% | 88.4 | 3.9% | 96.8 | 4.0% | 47.3% |
| Government | 219.6 | 13.7% | 272.8 | 11.9% | 317.2 | 13.2% | 44.4% |
| Federal | 47.1 | 2.9% | 46.6 | 2.0% | 46.0 | 1.9% | -2.3% |
| State | 47.4 | 3.0% | 56.1 | 2.5% | 62.9 | 2.6% | 32.7% |
| Local | 125.2 | 7.8% | 170.1 | 7.4% | 208.3 | 8.7% | 66.4% |
| Total | 1,606.2 | 100.0% | 2,289.7 | 100.0% | 2,398.3 | 100.0% | 49.3% |

Source: Bureau of Labor Statistics.

in Atlanta. The area's transportation sector accounts for a larger proportion of jobs than in any other domestic MSA (Keating, 2001, 11). Atlanta is also a major commerce center, as reflected in its large retail trade, food services, and accommodation sectors. What have changed are the large decline in manufacturing and the substantial increase in services such as health and professional services.[11]

Finally, as an indication of its economic role, the Atlanta region has the third largest concentration of Fortune 500 firms of any MSA in the country (12), behind New York with forty-four and Houston with twenty-two (*Fortune*, 2007). The twelve Fortune 500 firms in the Atlanta region and their ranking are The Home Depot (17th), United Parcel Service (43rd),

The Coca-Cola Company (94th), Coca-Cola Enterprises (118th), Delta Air Lines (136th), Southern Company (168th), SunTrust Banks (183rd), Genuine Parts (244th), Newell Rubbermaid (343rd), Beazer Homes (420th), Bluelinx Holdings (456th), and Mirant (474th).

### Industrial Composition of the City of Atlanta

Like the MSA, the employment pattern for the city of Atlanta has also undergone significant restructuring (table 3.3). Since 1980, the number of manufacturing jobs in the city declined by 41.8 percent (over 20,000 jobs). In 1980, this sector accounted for about one out of every seven jobs in Atlanta and was second only in importance to the service sector. However, by 2005, less than one out of every fourteen jobs in Atlanta were manufacturing jobs and this sector had been surpassed in importance by the retail trade sector, by the finance, insurance, and real estate (FIRE) sector, and by the local government sector. In contrast, the service sector had employment gains of more than fifty-six thousand and it remained the leading employer in the city throughout the 1980–2005 period. Today, the service sector accounts for over one-third of all jobs in the city, up from a quarter of all jobs in 1980.

Manufacturing was not the only sector with a declining presence in the city of Atlanta. Employment in wholesale trade, transportation, and construction lost ground during the past quarter century as well. These three sectors together accounted for a loss of more than seventeen thousand jobs. While these sectors were becoming less important to Atlanta in terms of employment opportunities, the retail trade, FIRE, and government sectors—in addition to the aforementioned service sector—were playing an ever-increasing role. Today, these four sectors account for more than three-quarters of all of Atlanta's employment and for three hundred ten thousand jobs.

From a regional perspective, jobs in FIRE, services, and government sectors were each highly concentrated in the city. For instance, Atlanta accounts for 23.3 percent, 25.3 percent, and 31.0 percent of all service, FIRE, and government jobs, respectively, in the ARC Region. Agglomerative economies, no doubt, play an important role in the clustering of many types of FIRE and service sector firms in the city while the presence of a large local government combined with an expanding Georgia State Capitol complex and a high concentration of federal government regional offices helps to explain the city's dominance in this sector.

One way to gauge the relative importance of various industry sectors is to calculate a location quotient, which is the share of employment in a sector within a particular geographic area, in this case Atlanta, divided by the equivalent share for the United States. A location quotient that is greater than one suggests that that industrial sector in Atlanta is relatively

Table 3.3   City of Atlanta Employment by Industry: 1980–2005

|  | 1980 | | 1990 | | 2000 | | 2005 | | %Change |
|---|---|---|---|---|---|---|---|---|---|
| Industry | Emp | Share | Emp | Share | Emp | Share | Emp | Share | 1990-2005 |
| Construction | 12,831 | 3.6% | 12,122 | 3.1% | 10,209 | 2.3% | 8,495 | 2.1% | -33.8% |
| Manufacturing | 48,986 | 13.8% | 36,882 | 9.3% | 33,211 | 7.6% | 28,487 | 7.1% | -41.8% |
| Transportation, Communications, Utilities | 32,430 | 9.1% | 30,014 | 7.6% | 32,404 | 7.4% | 28,323 | 7.1% | -12.7% |
| Wholesale Trade | 30,155 | 8.5% | 32,683 | 8.2% | 25,913 | 5.9% | 21,106 | 5.3% | -30.0% |
| Retail Trade | 46,020 | 12.9% | 48,994 | 12.3% | 53,861 | 12.3% | 49,550 | 12.4% | 7.7% |
| Finance, Insurance, Real Estate | 31,181 | 8.8% | 34,990 | 8.8% | 35,295 | 8.1% | 36,400 | 9.1% | 16.7% |
| Services | 84,694 | 23.8% | 121,202 | 30.5% | 157,917 | 36.1% | 141,581 | 35.3% | 67.2% |
| Private Total | 286,899 | 80.7% | 317,709 | 80.0% | 351,483 | 80.3% | 317,381 | 79.2% | 10.6% |
| Federal Government | 20,417 | 5.7% | 24,342 | 6.1% | 24,703 | 5.6% | 21,987 | 5.5% | 7.7% |
| State Government | 19,091 | 5.4% | 25,577 | 6.4% | 29,957 | 6.8% | 29,910 | 7.5% | 56.7% |
| Local Government | 29,119 | 8.2% | 29,519 | 7.4% | 31,429 | 7.2% | 31,328 | 7.8% | 7.6% |
| Government Total | 68,627 | 19.3% | 79,438 | 20.0% | 86,089 | 19.7% | 83,225 | 20.8% | 21.3% |
| Miscellaneous | 602 | 0.2% | 822 | 0.2% | 2,673 | 0.6% | 3,439 | 0.9% | 471.3% |
| Total | 355,526 | 100% | 397,147 | 100% | 437,572 | 100% | 400,606 | 100% | 12.7% |

Source: Atlanta Regional Commission.

more important than for the United States as a whole. It is not possible to calculate the location quotients for the city of Atlanta because of the lack of available data, although we can do so for Fulton County for 2004. Table 3.4 contains the location quotients for the three-digit NAICS sectors for which the location quotient for Fulton County is above 1.20, along with the city's share of Fulton County's 2002 employment for each of these sectors for which data are available.

There are some very large location quotients, particularly in NAICS sector 51, information, and sector 52, finance and insurance. Broadcasting (NAICS sector 515) has a location quotient of over 4 and over 70 percent of Fulton County's employment in that sector is located in the city. On the other hand, Internet publishing has a location quotient of over 6, but less than 10 percent of the jobs are in the city.

These data suggest that the economy of the city of Atlanta is dominated by real estate, communications/information, services, especially professional services, and government. Generally, these are industries with higher wage rates. For example, the Georgia Department of Labor reports that the average weekly earnings in the ARC region in 2006 was $1,245 in the wholesale trade sector, $1,438 in the information sector, $1,327 in the professional, scientific, and technical services sector, and $1,416 in the finance and insurance sector. This compares with average weekly earnings of $902 for private sector workers and $892 for government workers.

**Table 3.4   Location Quotients, 2004**

| NAICS | NAICS Description | Location Quotient | City of Atlanta's Share, 2002 |
|-------|-------------------|-------------------|-------------------------------|
| 312 | Beverage and Tobacco Product manufacturing | 1.36 | 55.6%[a] |
| 424 | Merchant Wholesalers, Nondurable Goods | 1.49 | 42.9% |
| 488 | Support Activities for Transportation | 1.54 | NA |
| 492 | Couriers and Messengers | 2.66 | NA |
| 511 | Publishing Industries | 1.90 | 67.3% |
| 512 | Motion Picture and Sound Recording Industries | 1.60 | 83.4%[a] |
| 515 | Broadcasting (except Internet) | 4.03 | 71.9% |
| 516 | Internet Publishing and Broadcasting | 6.29 | 9.4% |
| 517 | Telecommunications | 3.46 | 56.5% |
| 518 | Internet Service Providers, Web Search Portals, and Data Processing Services | 3.40 | 39.4% |
| 522 | Credit Intermediation and Related Activities | 1.32 | NA |
| 523 | Securities, Commodity Contracts, and Other Financial Investments and Related Activities | 1.36 | NA |
| 524 | Insurance Carriers and Related Activities | 1.51 | NA |
| 531 | Real Estate | 1.65 | 63.3% |
| 533 | Lessors of Nonfinancial Intangible Assets | 3.91 | 22.4% |
| 541 | Professional, Scientific, and Technical Services | 1.53 | 61.9% |
| 551 | Management of Companies and Enterprises | 2.45 | NA |
| 561 | Administrative and Support Services | 1.48 | 41.3% |

Source: Location Quotients are author's calculation based on 2004 County Business Pattern data; City shares are based on 2002 Census of Business data.  NA: not available.
[a]City share for this sector is based on number of establishments since employment information is not available.

## ANALYSIS OF FOUR INDUSTRY SECTORS

In this section we discuss in detail four specific industrial sectors: the hospitality, convention, and tourism sector, the logistics sector, the health and hospital sector, and the professional services sector.

### The Hospitality, Convention, and Tourism Sector

From its inception, Atlanta attracted individuals engaged in commerce. Atlanta was a collection point for raw materials being sent north and a distribution center for finished products coming from the north.[12] As evidence, in 1880 the city's population was 37,400, but it had eight hotels and sixty-two boarding houses (Newman 1999, 25). Efforts to expand the number of visitors also have a long history. The city organized the International Cotton Exposition in 1881 and held a commercial convention in 1885, which was attended by more than 300 representatives from thirty states (Newman 1999, 40). By 1900, nearly 16 percent of the city workforce was engaged in tourism (Newman 1999, 62). The Atlanta Convention and

Visitors Bureau was formed in 1912 and in 1939 Atlanta was host to 495 conventions. By 1980, Atlanta was the third most popular convention site in the U.S. (Newman 1999, 202).

One reflection of the growing importance of the hospitality industry is the number of hotel rooms. The number of rooms in the metro area increased from 30,422 in 1982 to 51,097 in 1989, and by another 6,000 in the mid-1990s (Newman 1999, 221, 271).

There are several factors that have led to the continued increase in the size of the hospitality industry. First, Hartsfield-Jackson International Airport provides ease of access from anywhere in the United States, and increasingly from anywhere in the world. The current passenger terminal opened in 1980, a fourth runway was added in 1984 and a fifth in 2006. Today there are thirty-two passenger airlines and nineteen all-cargo airlines that operate out of Hartsfield-Jackson.[13] In 2006, there were nearly 85 million passengers that came through the airport.

Second, the construction of the Merchandise Mart in 1961, the Apparel Mart in 1979, and the Gift Mart in 1992, and the subsequent expansion of those buildings made Atlanta a draw for representatives of the manufacturers of the products associated with the Mart and the retailers of those products. Annually, the Marts draw nearly 300,000 individuals from around the world to Atlanta.

Third, the World Congress Center opened in 1976 with 350,000 square feet of exhibit space. It has been expanded several times, and today has 1.4 million square feet of exhibit space. In fiscal year 1981–82, attendance was 794,814, while in fiscal year 2005–06, attendance was 1,380,617, of which 807,549 were from out of state. The Georgia Dome, which opened in 1992, is the home venue for the Atlanta Falcons. But its existence was important to securing the Super Bowl in 1994 and 2000, and the 1996 Olympic Games. The Dome hosts the Atlanta Football classic, the SEC Football Championship, and the Chick-fil-A Bowl, as well as major trade shows, concerts, and religious events. In fiscal year 2005–06, attendance at the Dome was 1.5 million.[14]

The economic impact of these facilities on the city is substantial, resulting in jobs associated with hotels, restaurants and catering, and the firms that provide services in support of the conventions and other events that bring individuals to the city. There is no way of determining how many jobs are created in the city of Atlanta by the events hosted in these facilities. But one indication of the size of the hospitality industry is that in 2002 over 37,000 individuals were employed in the city of Atlanta in establishments associated with the accommodations and food and drink sectors. Certainly, not all of these jobs are associated with the convention and tourism business, but these industries are only the most obvious of the industrial sectors that support the hospitality industry.

The convention business is very competitive. Conventions are seen as attractive and a valuable economic contributor to host cities. As a result, cities have increased their efforts to attract meetings and conventions, resulting in increased competition. As with any business, to compete for meetings and conventions, cities have to do well on the factors that determine site selection. Several studies have been conducted to determine the relative importance of various factors in determining the site selection of meetings and conventions. Crouch and Ritchie (1998) identify eight primary factors: accessibility, local support, extra-conference opportunity, accommodation facilities, meeting facilities, information (including reputation and marketing attributes), site environment, and other criteria such as novelty attributes.

Atlanta does well on access, local support, accommodations, and meeting facilities. But as Crouch and Louviere (2004) find, while convention facilities and costs are critical, a destination must offer other attributes to compete in the convention business. In the early 1980s Research Atlanta (1982 and 1983) noted that the most pressing need for the city's convention business was entertainment. In response, efforts began to renovate Underground Atlanta, which reopened in 1989. While Underground Atlanta is not the attraction it was when it opened, it still attracted 6 million individuals in 2005 (compared to 13 million the year it opened). In the past twenty-five years, a number of attractions have opened in the region. These include the World of Coca-Cola in 1990 (which moved to a new, expanded site in 2007), Fernbank Museum in 1992, Centennial Olympic Park in 1998, and the Georgia Aquarium in 2005. The increase in the number of individuals living in the central city has resulted in some additional amenities downtown, but downtown is not yet the twenty-four-hour venue that is thought to be important to making the city more attractive to conventioneers and tourists. Other facilities are in the planning stage, including a human rights museum.

In addition to competition for convention business from other metropolitan areas, the city of Atlanta is also facing increasing competition from suburban sites. There are 5,000 first-class hotel rooms near the airport where College Park opened a new 150,000 square foot Georgia International Convention Center in 2004, with plans to link it to the terminal at Hartsfield-Jackson with a light rail system. Surrounding counties have also built convention and meeting facilities. Cobb County and Gwinnett County have both built convention facilities; the Cobb Galleria Centre has 280,000 square feet of meeting space and the Civic and Cultural Center in Gwinnett has 50,000 square feet of space (Newman, 2002). In 2000, there are almost as many hotel rooms in the Cumberland/Galleria area as in downtown (Newman, 2002). In addition, Marietta and Decatur have built small meeting facilities.

The convention business can undergo a substantial change as the result of one event. As a result of the events of 11 September, 2001, attendance at conventions dropped significantly. As a result of Katrina, New Orleans lost most of its conventions to other cities, including Atlanta. It is reported that Atlanta was not chosen as a future Super Bowl site because of the ice storm the city experienced last time the Super Bowl was in Atlanta. High crime rates or negative publicity associated with crime, panhandling, and police enforcement of jaywalking laws can turn conventions to other cities.

The city has become one of the leading convention sites in the country and, along with other sources of visitors to the city, is an important driver of the city's economy. The city, along with the state, has worked to provide the meeting facilities. The increase in visitors has resulted in an expansion of the number of hotels, furthering the attractiveness of the city to the convention industry. But if this industry is to continue to grow in the face of increasing competition, the city will have to continue to focus on the other factors that go into the decision of where to hold conventions and major sporting events. There are major new entertainment venues and more planned for Atlanta. Crime downtown is down from a decade ago. The city has tried to address the homeless issue, panhandling, and taxis, but without much visible success. While the focus has been on competing with other major cities, the growth in the suburban markets for smaller conventions and meetings could have an effect on the growth of the convention business in the city.

## The Logistics Sector

### Logistics in the Atlanta Region

As mentioned earlier, almost from its beginning Atlanta's strategic location has caused it to be a major transportation hub for people and for goods. Today, more than 80 percent of the U.S. population market is within a two-hour flight or a one-day interstate truck trip from Atlanta. According to the Metro Atlanta Chamber of Commerce, metropolitan Atlanta's extensive intermodal network of air, road, and rail services, together with its connection to port facilities and world-reaching telecommunications network provides businesses with several competitive options for transporting people, goods, and information. Logistics, which is concerned with the various facets of the movement and storage of goods, is playing an ever-increasing role in the region's economy in general and that of the city of Atlanta in particular.[15]

Recent U.S. Bureau of the Census data on employment levels in various segments of the logistics sector in metropolitan Atlanta appears to substantiate an overall growing trend. Table 3.5 examines recent employment levels for the ten-county Atlanta Regional Commission (ARC) area and the city of Atlanta in four major logistics categories: air freight, truck freight, warehousing and storage, and process, physical distribution, and logistics consulting services (PPD&L).

In the seven year period 1998–2005, overall logistics employment in the ARC Region grew by nearly 16,000 jobs, an increase of more than 50 percent. With the lone exception of Clayton County, each of the ARC counties experienced growth in logistics employment over this period. Fulton (including the city of Atlanta) and DeKalb counties accounted for more than two-thirds of regional growth.[16]

By 2005, nearly forty-seven thousand people were employed in these four logistics sectors. Employment growth was dominated by the warehousing and storage sector, which experienced a robust three and a half fold increase in employment, representing a gain of 13,500 new jobs. More than four out of every five logistics jobs created during the 1998–2005 period in the ARC region were in warehousing and storage. Even though each of the warehousing and storage sub-sectors experienced growth, the increase in employment was most pronounced in the general warehousing and storage category (NAICS 493110), which saw employment grow from 1.8 thousand in 1998 to 11,100 in 2005. The only other logistical sector besides warehousing and storage that experienced significant growth was the PPD&L Sector (NAICS 541614) which added 2,200 new jobs.

In regards to the truck freight sector, 2005 employment remained virtually unchanged from 1998 totals. However, this stagnant overall growth trend for truck freight masks considerable employment changes among its sub-sectors. For example, nearly all of the roughly 3,000 new jobs created in the long distance general freight trucking by the truckload sub-sector were offset by job losses in the long distance general freight trucking by less than the truckload sub-sector and in the long distance specialized freight trucking sub-sector. Furthermore, there were substantial geographic shifts. Three counties—Fulton, Clayton, and Cobb—experienced significant job losses in this sector while three others—DeKalb, Gwinnett, and Henry—experienced significant job gains. DeKalb County is now the largest truck freight employer, up from third in 1998, while Clayton County is now the third largest, down from first in 1998.

## Logistics in the City of Atlanta

The city of Atlanta accounted for roughly one out of every four new logistics jobs created in the ten-county ARC area during the period 1998–2005. The city added an estimated 4,200 new logistics jobs, an increase of 61 percent over 1998 levels (table 3.5). More than 80 percent of the increase

**Table 3.5 Employment in Selected Logistics Sectors for the Ten-County ARC Area[a]**

| NAICS | Description | 1998 Employment | 2005 Employment | %Change |
|-------|-------------|-----------------|-----------------|---------|
| 481112 | Total Air Freight | 180 | 175 | -3.1 |
| 484110 | General Freight Trucking, Local | 1,625 | 1,949 | |
| 484121 | General Freight Trucking, Long-Distance, Truckload | 6,389 | 9,372 | |
| 484122 | General Freight Trucking, Long-Distance, < Truckload | 9,912 | 8,523 | |
| 484210 | Used Household and Office Goods Moving | 2,345 | 1,933 | |
| 484220 | Specialized Freight Trucking, Local | 1,812 | 1,892 | |
| 484230 | Specialized Freight Trucking, Long Distance | 3,468 | 2,036 | |
| | Total Truck Freight | 25,550 | 25,704 | 0.6 |
| 493110 | General Warehousing and Storage | 1,804 | 11,147 | |
| 493120 | Refrigerated Warehousing and Storage | 688 | 1,986 | |
| 493130 | Farm Product Warehousing and Storage | 3 | 15 | |
| 493190 | Other Warehousing and Storage | 918 | 3,631 | |
| 531130 | Lessors of Mini-Warehouses and Self-Storage Units | 346 | 478 | |
| | Total Warehousing and Storage | 3,758 | 17,256 | 359.2 |
| 541614 | Total Process, Physical Distribution, and Logistics Consulting Services | 1,470 | 3,691 | 151.1 |
| | Total | 30,957 | 46,824 | 51.3 |

Source; U.S. Bureau of the Census, *County Business Patterns.*
[a] Data for this table was obtained from the U.S. Bureau of the Census' County Business Patterns database. Employment figures for North American Industry Classification system (NAICS) codes for the selected logistical sectors were tallied for every county in the 10-county Atlanta Regional Commission (ARC) area and summarized.

in logistics jobs in Atlanta and about 85 percent of the growth in the suburbs were in the warehousing and storage sector.[17] Despite this similarity, almost three times as many jobs were created in the suburbs than in the city of Atlanta, as warehouse distribution centers and trucking companies increasingly sought less expensive locations along the interstate highways outside of the city. Indeed, as Atlanta was losing 800 jobs in the truck freight sector during the 1998–2005 period, the suburbs was gaining 950 of these positions and while Atlanta added 3,400 new warehousing and storage sector jobs the suburbs were adding more than ten thousand of these. The estimated 3,400 gain in warehousing and storage employment by the city of Atlanta was greater than that for any of the counties in the ARC region with the exception of DeKalb County.

In regards to process, physical distribution, and logistics consulting services, Atlanta was truly the focus of activity. Roughly two out of every three new PPD&L sector jobs in the ARC region were accounted for by the city of Atlanta. Employment growth in this sector was quite robust. In 1998, a little more than four hundred people were employed in the PPD&L sector; however by 2005 the city had acquired nearly 1,900 jobs in this sector. Clearly, PPD&L is a growth sector for both Atlanta and its nearby suburbs. Because of the presence of Hartsfield-Jackson International Airport the city of Atlanta dominates the air freight sector.

*Why has the Logistics Sector Grown?*

According to the Metro Atlanta Chamber of Commerce, metropolitan Atlanta has become a leading global logistics center, with more than half of the top one hundred third-party logistics providers housing operations in the area.[18] In addition, metropolitan Atlanta is home to nearly 90 percent of the top twenty-five third-party logistics providers in the country based on revenues. A number of these third-party logistics providers have located to the Atlanta area in recent years and have expanded operations. For instance, Manhattan Associates relocated from California to Atlanta in 1995 with just twenty-five employees. It now has more than 1,200 employees, more than half of whom are based in metropolitan Atlanta. Initially a manager of warehouses for retailers, Manhattan Associates has expanded operations to include logistics software—*Integrated Logistics Solutions*™—that manage the entire source to consumption supply chain. These companies and others like them have contributed to Atlanta's recent and rapid growth in the PPD&L Sector.

A number of factors have contributed to the significant expansion in logistics employment in metropolitan Atlanta in recent years. One factor has been Atlanta's designation as the first U.S. Customs Inland Port, a general purpose foreign trade zone. In preparation for the 1996 Olympic Games, Atlanta was given this designation, which allows containers from abroad to travel inbound duty free from coastal ports. This development, together with the growing operations at Georgia's two deepwater ports in Savannah and Brunswick, has helped Atlanta's cargo business to boom.[19] According to the Metro Atlanta Chamber of Commerce, the Atlanta region's cargo output ranks tenth in the United States.

Developments at Hartsfield-Jackson International Airport have also led to increased logistics employment opportunities in Atlanta. With more than thirty cargo carriers serving the airport, Atlanta's Hartsfield-Jackson is increasingly becoming a major world port for air cargo.[20] Currently ranked as the eleventh-busiest airport in the United States for total air freight tonnage, Hartsfield-Jackson's major growth area is in international cargo. For example, through the first six years of this decade Hartsfield-Jackson has increased its international cargo tonnage by almost two-thirds. International freight represents a growing share of

Hartsfield-Jackson air freight business. International cargo now accounts for 52 percent of the airport's throughput, more than double its share in 1999. The addition of a fifth runway in June of 2006 and expanded and improved cargo operations at the airport should contribute to the sector's continued growth.

Local expertise has likely spurred logistics employment growth in Atlanta. For instance, as noted by the Metro Atlanta Chamber of Commerce, Georgia Institute of Technology boasts the nation's best industrial engineering program and its Logistics Institute is the world's largest research and education center focused on global logistics and supply chains. In addition, four of Georgia's six research universities—Georgia Institute of Technology, Georgia State University, Clark Atlanta University, and Emory University—are clustered in metro Atlanta with the others, the University of Georgia and the Medical College of Georgia, less than a two-hour drive away. Two of these research universities offer logistics-related degrees. According to the Atlanta Regional Consortium on Higher Education, in 2000 Atlanta ranked as the fourth major research center in the nation behind only Los Angeles, New York, and Boston and ahead of Raleigh-Durham, North Carolina. The contribution of logistics personnel provided by Atlanta's research institutions is augmented by the logistics talent pool generated by companies like UPS and Delta Air Lines, which are both headquartered in Atlanta. The clustering of those companies and others like them allows for knowledge spillovers and has increased the pool of logistics and supply chain professionals.

## Prospects for Atlanta

The city of Atlanta appears to be well-poised to continue as a focus of logistics activity in the years ahead, particularly in the air freight, warehousing and storage, and the PPD&L sectors. The presence of Hartsfield-Jackson International Airport ensures that the city of Atlanta will continue to dominate the air freight sector and, with the recent emphasis on international cargo the prospects for future growth in this sector are good. Location advantages that made Atlanta a transportation hub will continue to attract many kinds of warehousing and storage facilities to the city, while the intellectual capital and logistical expertise as provided by Atlanta's research universities and many logistics enterprises combine to form a synergy that encourages PPD&L firm development and growth.

## The Health and Hospitals Sector

Health care is a rapidly growing sector of the U.S. economy. In 1980, medical care as a share of gross domestic product was 10.5 percent. By 1990, its share had increased to 14.5 percent, and in 2005 it was 17.1 percent.[21] Given its growing importance, we explore its role in the Atlanta economy. However, data at the city level is limited.

In 1980, the metropolitan area had 3,825 physicians, while in 1995 there were 7,937 physicians, an increase of 212.4 percent.[22] In 2003, in the Atlanta MSA there were 11,948 physicians, which ranked Atlanta thirteenth in the country.[23] Physicians per 100,000 persons increased from 164.4 in 1980 to 259.0 in 2003, an increase of 57.5 percent. However, the metropolitan area does not rank very high in terms of physicians per capita; it ranked ninety-fifth in 1995 and 175th in 2003. Areas with medical schools, which tend to be located in areas with smaller populations, rank high on a per capita basis. But, even among the twenty-five metropolitan areas with a population of more than 2 million, the Atlanta metropolitan area ranks twenty-second in terms of physicians per 100,000. This is somewhat surprising given that the Emory Medical School and the Morehouse School of Medicine are located here, as is the Centers for Disease Control and Prevention.

While the number of physicians per capita has increased, the number of hospitals and hospital beds has decreased. In 1980, there were seventy community hospitals in the Atlanta metropolitan area, but only forty-one in 2003. The number of community hospital beds declined from 11,916 to 9,061 over that period. This reflects a national trend, but the relative decline was greater for the Atlanta area. The number of community hospitals in the United States fell from 5,830 in 1980 to 4,919 in 2004, while the number of beds fell from 988,000 to 808,000 over that period.[24] Using the business telephone directory, we identified twenty-three hospitals that were located within the city of Atlanta in 1980. By 2006, thirteen of those hospitals had closed, while two specialty hospitals opened.

Employment in health care in the city of Atlanta in 2002 was between twenty-five and thirty thousand.[25] This represents between 5.9 and 7.1 percent of employment in the city of Atlanta, while for the U.S. the health care sector accounts for 11.4 percent of employment. Health care employment in Fulton County in 1993 was 47,532, which increased to 53,399 in 2004.[26] For DeKalb County, health care employment increased from 25,059 in 1993 to 32,810 in 2004.

Health care is an important sector in the city of Atlanta and the region, but it is not a dominant industry, despite Grady Memorial Hospital, the Emory Medical School, and Morehouse School of Medicine. It is not clear why employment in health care is low as compared to other communities. There do not appear to be any barriers that would prevent the Atlanta area from having a larger health care sector and thus it appears to be a sector that could grow. It would seem that identifying the reason why the sector is relatively small would be potentially advantageous to the city and the region.

## The Professional Services Sector[27]

The distribution of professional services in the ARC region is becoming more decentralized as service providers migrate towards population centers in the close-in suburbs. During the 1998–2005 time period, Atlanta's share of the region's professional services employment fell by more than 4 percent, while its share of the number of establishments in this sector dropped by three percent. Nevertheless, Atlanta remains an important player in the professional services sector since two out of every five jobs in the ARC region and more than one out of every four establishments are located in the city.

Between 1998 and 2005, the ARC region gained an estimated 25,000 jobs and 4,000 establishments in professional services (table 3.6). Most of the growth occurred in the Atlanta suburbs located in Cobb County, Gwinnett County, and Fulton County outside the city of Atlanta. These three areas accounted for nearly 80 percent of the job growth and almost 60 percent of the growth in the number of establishments in the ARC region.

To a large extent, the pattern of job growth in professional services mirrors changes in the regional population. For example, during the period 1990–2005 the top three gainers in population were Gwinnett County, Cobb County, and Fulton County outside the city of Atlanta. Together, they accounted for 56 percent of the total population growth in the ARC region. It makes sense that many professional service firms would tend to follow the movement of people to these areas. DeKalb County (which achieved significant population gains amounting to more than one

**Table 3.6   Professional Services Employment Growth**

|  | 1998 Employment | 2005 Employment | 1998–2005 Employment Growth | Percent Share of Growth |
|---|---|---|---|---|
| Fulton | 66,578 | 79,424 | 12,846 | 51.2% |
| Atlanta-Fulton est. | 58,000 | 62,240 | 4,240 | 16.9% |
| Cherokee | 1,194 | 2,219 | 1,025 | 4.1% |
| Clayton | 1,700 | 1,505 | -195 | -0.8% |
| Cobb | 20,583 | 27,295 | 6,712 | 26.7% |
| DeKalb | 21,602 | 18,261 | -3,341 | -13.3% |
| Douglas | 737 | 1,029 | 292 | 1.2% |
| Fayette | 962 | 1,844 | 882 | 3.5% |
| Gwinnett | 15,624 | 21,205 | 5,581 | 22.2% |
| Henry | 748 | 1,774 | 1,026 | 4.1% |
| Rockdale | 875 | 1,149 | 274 | 1.1% |
| Totals | 130,603 | 155,705 | 25,102 | 100.0% |

Source: U.S. Bureau of the Census, *County Business Patterns.*

hundred fifty thousand during the 1990-2005 period) and Clayton County were the only counties to experience a loss of professional service jobs. For DeKalb County, this was largely due to the substantial loss of jobs in two major sectors; computer system design and related services (NAIC 5415) and architectural, engineering, and related services (NAIC 5413).

It is interesting to note that one of the major professional services sub-sectors—offices of lawyers—exhibited patterns of growth that diverged significantly from the overall trend of decentralization. For this subsector, the city of Atlanta remains the primary focus, probably because the benefits of agglomeration economies derived from the need for face-to-face contact with business clients far outweigh the gains from cheaper land in more distant locations. During the 1998–2005 period, Atlanta retained its regional share of lawyers both in terms of employment and number of establishments, accounting for almost two-thirds of the former and more than two-fifths of the latter. Atlanta is more dominant in regards to the employment of lawyers because on average law firms in Atlanta are larger than the law firms elsewhere in the ARC region. In terms of growth, the city of Atlanta accounted for an estimated 64 percent of the lawyer jobs and 30 percent of lawyer establishments created during the 1998–2005 period (table 3.7).

Despite Atlanta's stable and dominant position in regards to this sub-sector during the 1998–2005 period, there has been considerable intra-city movement of law firms and employment. Law firms continue to exit the central business district (CBD) for other parts of the city, most notably the Midtown area.[28] For example, during the seven year period 1998–2005

**Table 3.7   Offices of Lawyers Employment Growth**

|  | 1998 Employment | 2005 Employment | 1998–2005 Employment Growth | Percent Share of Growth |
|---|---|---|---|---|
| Fulton | 10,922 | 14,783 | 3,861 | 70.0% |
| Atlanta-Fulton est. | 10,680 | 14,220 | 3,540 | 64.1% |
| Cherokee | 175 | 256 | 81 | 1.5% |
| Clayton | 175 | 375 | 200 | 3.6% |
| Cobb | 1,446 | 2,176 | 730 | 13.2% |
| DeKalb | 1,838 | 2,159 | 321 | 5.8% |
| Douglas | 175 | 111 | -64 | -1.2% |
| Fayette | 175 | 176 | 1 | 0.0% |
| Gwinnett | 1,055 | 1,343 | 288 | 5.2% |
| Henry | 175 | 240 | 65 | 1.2% |
| Rockdale | 98 | 134 | 36 | 0.7% |
| Totals | 16,234 | 21,753 | 5,519 | 100.0% |

Source: U.S. Bureau of the Census, *County Business Patterns*.

the CBD lost eleven law offices while at the same time Midtown gained fifteen. This represents a continuation of a two-decade trend that saw businesses leave the downtown area only to relocate a few miles north to Midtown and well within the city limits.

## EXPLAINING THE CHANGE IN EMPLOYMENT

### The Atlanta Region

The city of Atlanta is not an economy separate from the regional economy, and thus, a large factor driving the city's employment is what is happening in the region. As Jordan Rappaport (2003) notes, urban growth experiences of American cities over the latter half of the twentieth century were the result of a mixture of national, regional, metropolitan, and local factors. Thus, to explain the change in the level and composition of employment in the city of Atlanta, we should start by discussing the causes of employment changes at the Atlanta metropolitan statistical area (MSA) level.

Given the significance of metropolitan MSAs in the United States, a large volume of literature has contributed to our understanding of what makes metropolitan areas more or less attractive places for firms and individuals. Many researchers have sought explanations through traditional urban economic theory of agglomeration economies, labor pooling, and capital spillover. Mills and Lubuele (1997), for example, point to agglomeration economies to explain why MSAs exist in the first place: "proximity of workers to jobs, of firms to customers, of firms to other firms with whom they do business, and of workers and firms to information generating and dispersing institutions. Not only are traditional economies of scale and scope important in producing large concentrations of workers and producers, but also the lower costs of moving people, goods, and information because of proximity within large MSA's" (p. 729). Glaeser and Shapiro (2003; 154–58) suggest a mixture of geographic determinism and human capital presence as the driving forces in explaining the level and composition of economic growth. Metropolitan growth has also required an explanation for the resulting disparities of income between inner cities and surrounding suburbs.

In *The Rise of the Creative Class*, Florida (2002) attempts to explain successful city growth through the ability to attract and retain members of what he calls the "creative class," the expanding, highly educated, workforce involved in idea-based professional services. However, he also notes that "the key to economic growth lies not just in the ability to attract the creative class, but to translate that underlying advantage into creative economic outcomes in the form of new ideas, new high-tech businesses and regional growth" (p. 49).

Trends in industrial composition and employment in the Atlanta MSA and city of Atlanta reflect many of the changes experienced over the past twenty-five years by metropolitan areas in general, namely continued suburban expansion, service-related industry growth, and income and employment discrepancies between suburbs and inner cities. These changes have been attributed to the rise in the ownership of automobiles, the interstate system, changes in production and information technology, and more general economic forces associated with increased globalization. Yet, the Atlanta MSA experienced growth that was not shared by all large metropolitan areas. Thus, we focus on those factors more closely associated with explaining why the Atlanta metropolitan area experienced growth and change in employment that differed from other metropolitan areas.

Part of Atlanta's growth had to do with Atlanta's low share of declining industries, resulting in less severe losses in employment. The fact that the Atlanta MSA recently lost a significant number of manufacturing jobs was not so remarkable since in comparison to other large MSAs, Atlanta historically had a much smaller manufacturing base, and thus had less to lose. Historic manufacturing cities like Pittsburgh, Detroit, and Cleveland have all lost more than a third of their population since 1970, and their MSAs lost hundreds of thousands of workers from 1970 to 1990 (Rappaport, 2003, 37). The Atlanta MSA has not stopped expanding in more than fifty years, and the expanding non-manufacturing industries have more than offset the losses from declining industries.

As noted above, there has been a large migration from northeastern and midwestern areas to the South and West. Thus, in part, Atlanta's growth reflects the increased regional importance of the South, where Atlanta is the dominant wholesale and retail trade center, as well as the transportation hub. As Glaeser and Shapiro (2003) note, the rise of the Sunbelt simply marks the declining importance of production advantages relative to consumption advantages. Growth in the South is also part of a strong migratory trend towards better weather. The warm and generally humid climate in the South once stifled growth, but the invention of air conditioning overcame that deterrent.

The South, and the Atlanta area in particular, now maintain a different political climate than was present fifty years ago. Once a bastion of racial tensions and civil rights abuses, the South now has a solid legal infrastructure and a political climate which is much more accommodating to businesses than the more regulatory North. Thus, new political leadership has made businesses and individuals more comfortable locating in the Atlanta area (Glaeser and Shapiro, 2003, 154–8). The 2003 ING Gazelle Index, which measures confidence and expectations of African American

CEOs, overwhelmingly identified Atlanta as the best metropolitan area and Georgia as the best state for fast growing black businesses to relocate. Thus, Atlanta no longer represents a place where minorities are unable to succeed.

The southeastern United States in general has become an even greater regional economic center, and is currently growing at a faster rate than any other region. Atlanta has been successful in capturing a large amount of growth and employment associated with that. The Atlanta economy also benefits from the largest concentration of federal agencies outside of Washington D.C. (Garoogian, 2006, 30).

However, geographic determinism does not provide a complete explanation. Atlanta's MSA growth is also influenced by local factors, including investments in transportation and higher education, its low cost of doing business, efforts at marketing the area, and improvements in the quality of life.

Atlanta grew in its early history as a city because its location made it a natural transportation hub for railroads, and those transportation benefits have continued until today. As mentioned earlier, more people are employed in the transportation industry in Atlanta than in any other domestic MSA. The nearby Hartsfield-Jackson Airport has capitalized on the increased importance of air transportation, as it has become the busiest airport in the world, carrying around 85 million passengers each year (Quinn, 2006). The cargo port of Savannah, Georgia, currently the fifth largest port in the United States, has tapped into primarily Asian imports and is assuring Atlanta's status as a distribution hub for imported goods (Barry, 2005).

Importance as a logistics and professional services city would not be nearly as defined if Georgia did not provide sufficiently educated human capital. Although there is debate as to whether local skills matter because of education spillovers in production, it is obvious that there is a strong connection between workforce skills and city growth. Local human capital is important because places with more skilled workers grow faster than cities with weaker human capital bases. The percentage of college educated workers is a strong predictor for urban growth (Glaeser and Shapiro, 2003, 154–58) and, according to the Brooking Institution's Center on Urban and Metropolitan Policy, Atlanta has the second largest concentration of college graduates (68 percent) in the fifty largest American cities (Harden, 2005, 64).

The increased importance of highly skilled service-oriented professionals has been supported by leading research universities, which have spurred development around them. The University System of Georgia consists of thirty-five public colleges and universities and almost forty private colleges and universities. Georgia also has the most extensive technical education program in the nation, with forty technical colleges and, in 2002, over 700,000 enrolled students. Thus, Georgia technical and higher education has created a highly skilled and varied worker population capable of accommodating and bolstering new industry growth.

Evidence for high quality of human capital can be seen in the location economies which have taken place in a number of industries, particularly in logistics and bioscience. Logistics (wholesale trade and transportation and warehousing) industry in the state of Georgia employs over 263,000 workers and is projected to grow by 17 percent by 2012 (Youtie, 2005, 7). Georgia has also seen localization in the biosciences, which employed more than 14,000 people in Georgia in 2003. From 2000 to 2010, demand for biochemists and biophysicists was expected to increase by 50 percent (Drummond and Youtie, 2003, 2–4).

The costs of doing business in Atlanta are low as compared to other metropolitan areas, which have given large firms and professional services a reason to either expand inside or relocate to the Atlanta MSA. The Atlanta MSA also presents relatively lower housing costs, costs of living, and tax rates than other large MSAs. In fact, based on after-tax cost of business startup and operations of ten years, KPMG's guide to international business costs showed Atlanta as the least costly large U.S. city in which to do business (Metro Atlanta Chamber of Commerce, 2006). MSA median home price and average new home prices are significantly lower than national averages, as are construction, rental, and utility costs. Tax incentive packages offered to firms are extremely competitive on a national level.

The area has also benefited from efforts to market the region. The 1996 Olympic Games contributed to Atlanta's growth as a consequence of its greater recognition as an international city. The area has also been successful in attracting large national sporting events such as the Super Bowl, which also provides exposure. In addition, public efforts to increase the arts and green space, combined with the private sector-provided amenities such as restaurants and entertainment venues, have increased the quality of life in the area.

There are also factors that have hindered economic growth of the Atlanta metropolitan area. Georgia has a very weak public K–12 education system and scores on standardized tests consistently rank below U.S. averages. While public schools in the Atlanta metropolitan area are somewhat better, there is concern that the absence of a high performance education system deters firms that might otherwise locate in the Atlanta MSA.

Substantial population growth, suburban sprawl, and a lack of investment in transportation infrastructure have led to very serious traffic congestion throughout the entire twenty-eight-county metropolitan region. As an indicator of that problem, the average commute time in the Atlanta

MSA is one of the longest in the nation. It is believed that relocating firms are less inclined to consider Atlanta because of the traffic congestion.

The reliance on automobiles combined with the hot summer weather has contributed to air quality problems. In 2005, the Atlanta MSA was the ninth worst polluted area in the United States, worse than New York, Washington D.C., and Chicago (American Lung Association, 2005). This has contributed to other less glorious rankings, such as one of *America's Worst Cities for Respiratory Infections* and as one of the *U.S. Asthma Capitals* by the Asthma and Allergy Foundation of America (Garoogian, 2006, 26–29).

## The City of Atlanta

Rappaport (2003) shows that city population growth is significantly correlated with strong MSA growth—providing evidence that MSA population growth is a primary contributor to the city's population growth. And, as has been suggested, a city's economy is dependent on its region's economy. However, the city of Atlanta certainly has not captured the same share of the Atlanta MSA's industry growth. Employment in the city of Atlanta grew by 13.4 percent from 1980 to 2005, while employment in the ARC region grew by 120 percent (table 3.2).

While the region's growth may have had a strong influence on the city's growth, the question of why the city's growth rate was so much lower needs to be addressed. There are several possible explanations, including land-area limitations, differential growth rates of industries located in the city versus the suburbs, population decentralization and demographic shifts, changes in the significance of agglomerations for particular industries, and differences in costs and amenities.

Land area might have been one of the most basic factors in limiting city growth. City size and industry density limit the amount of new growth which can take place within the city's boundaries. The geographic size of the city of Atlanta has been essentially unchanged since 1953. The MSA, on the other hand, saw a huge increase in total area as it grew from fifteen to twenty-eight counties. In 2005, the area of the MSA was 8,376 square miles compared to 132.4 square miles for the city. Building upwards is generally more costly than building out into surrounding areas, increasing prices in more densely populated areas. Industries like manufacturing, wholesale trade, and transportation (which saw employment losses) generally require greater land area and had an incentive to move towards cheaper land. Employment density also affects the demand and cost of leased space, as well as basic amenities such as parking.

In a number of instances, jobs followed people to the suburbs. As previously noted, many industries such as retail trade, wholesale trade,

FIRE, and construction grew most in the counties where population was expanding most rapidly. In general, northern metropolitan counties were home to the most educated portion of MSA residents, providing an incentive for idea-based and professional service firms to grow nearer to their employees.

Innovations such as the Internet, e-mail, and videoconferencing might have decreased the importance of agglomerations for industries like financial and professional services, allowing for greater distancing from the historical CBD. Back office functions could be separated from central administration and relocated to cheaper space in the suburbs. Evidence for this can be seen in the clusters of professional services and warehousing in suburban areas just north of the city, such as the Cumberland district and Alpharetta. Thus, a location in the center of the city has become relatively less important.

The city's share of the region's employment is dependent on which employers experience an increase in employment because of an increase in their economic activity and on the location decisions of employers. The former is more of a short-run dynamic effect dependent on the nature of the growth in the U.S. and regional economy, while the latter is the result of more long-run decisions about location. Thus, if there is a significant increase in conventions or state and federal employment, then employment in the city is likely to increase as a result.

Over the longer term, employment patterns within the metropolitan area depend on the location decisions of employers. There are several factors that are thought to affect the location of employers. The factors that are thought to be most important are the cost of land, availability of workers with the appropriate skills, market, agglomerations, and transportation costs. But there are other factors that affect the cost or desirability of a particular site, including tax rates, crime rate, and the availability of supportive services. The relative importance of these factors will differ by industrial sector. A location near the market is very important for retail. A location near rail and interstates is important for shipping.

As discussed elsewhere in this report, long-run changes in technology have had significant effects on where businesses locate. But we can consider more marginal factors. Taxes and crime are two such factors. Over the past decade, the property tax rate in the city has declined, but the rate is still higher than most suburban jurisdictions. The crime rate in the city has fallen substantially since 1990. For example, the violent crime rate was 4085 per 100,000 in 1990 but fell to 1675 per 100,000 in 2005, although the crime rate is reported to by increasing in 2007.

Commuting times more directly affect workers, but they indirectly affect employers who seek locations that are more accessible to employees. Commuting times have increased in the Atlanta metropolitan area, but have increased more outside the city. In 1990, for example, 43 percent of metro workers took more than thirty minutes to get to work, while in 2000, 50 percent took at least that long. For city workers, 35 percent took more than thirty minutes in 1990, but by 2000 that had increased to just 38 percent.

As mentioned earlier, the city's population has started to grow in the past decade after more than twenty years of decline. The increasing congestion in the suburbs is thought to be a factor driving the increase in population in the city, although we know of no direct evidence of this. It is thought that these new residents are more skilled and are more likely to be employed in professional positions. This growth in the city's population is increasing the work force in the city, which should have a positive effect on location of firms within the city. However, while the education level increased in the city, the percent of the adult population with more than a high school degree is still higher in the suburbs.

## PROSPECTS FOR THE FUTURE

It appears that on balance the prospects for future job growth in the city of Atlanta are quite good. The Atlanta Regional Commission forecasts that employment in the city of Atlanta will grow by twenty to thirty-five thousand every five years and will reach a total of 534,000 by 2030. In other words, between the years 2005 and 2030 the ARC expects employment opportunities in Atlanta to grow by nearly a third. Atlanta job growth during the previous twenty-five-year period (1980–2005), by comparison, amounted to just 12.1 percent. There are a number of reasons for such optimism.

First of all, the city's population is likely to grow appreciably and as it does it will likely attract additional retail and personal service firms. After losing about a sixth of its population (nearly 80,000 people) during the 1970–2000 period, it appears that the city of Atlanta is in the throes of a significant rebound. According to the ARC, the city of Atlanta gained almost forty-eight thousand residents during the 2000–2007 period. Forty-four percent of this increase came within the last two years. The city is becoming increasingly attractive as commuting costs increase and as the quality of life improves. Longer suburban commute times together with higher gasoline prices create a substantial incentive for in-town living.[29]

Second, changing demographics and a renewed emphasis on high density middle-class housing developments suggest that incomes in Atlanta may be growing, which provides an additional incentive for retailers and personal service firms to locate in the city. The Atlanta Housing Authority is continually replacing its low-income public housing units with mixed income developments. Many of the former low-income residents have relocated outside of the city, and this trend is likely to continue as more public housing units are converted. In addition, a number of developers have embraced "New Urbanism" projects, which place an emphasis on high density developments where one can live, work, and play. These developments appeal to the highly educated, young upwardly mobile resident.

Third, industries that rely on localization economies and knowledge spillovers will continue to find the city of Atlanta attractive. This will be particularly true for the fast-growing logistics sector and also for some of the professional service firms. The large percentage of Atlanta's workforce that holds college degrees, together with the several research institutions and numerous high-tech firms located in the city, provides an incentive for more of these types of firms to locate to the city.

Fourth, new entertainment venues—such as the Georgia Aquarium, the New World of Coke, the expanded Zoo Atlanta, and the proposed human rights museum—combine to improve the attractiveness of the city for conventions and visitors. If the proposed reconstruction of Peachtree Street, the Beltline Project, and the decommissioning of Fort McPherson come to fruition, it is expected that they will generate a substantial number of new jobs in the city.

Despite these advantages, Atlanta's expected job growth could be derailed by any number of events. For instance, an increase in crime, either real or perceived, would have a serious negative effect on the attractiveness of the city to businesses and conventions. In addition, moves by any of the city's major employers could adversely impact employment growth. For example, if CNN were to move to New York, or if Delta were to go bankrupt or get bought out, or if the new owners of Georgia Pacific and BellSouth were to downsize these divisions, it would have a major negative effect on the city as well as the region. In addition, Charlotte, North Carolina could emerge as a major competitor, not just for banking but for logistics and distribution, which could dampen employment growth in Atlanta in those sectors. And finally, another terrorist attack or a big increase in jet fuel prices would, no doubt, reduce Atlanta's convention, travel, and tourism business and pose serious consequences for employment in those areas.

## SUMMARY AND SUGGESTIONS

The urban economy is in a constant state of flux in which businesses are continuously being added while others are being cast aside. At the same time, people are regularly moving into and out of the urban area.

To complicate matters further, there is a constant relocation of businesses and people within the urban area. In the Atlanta region, this relentless churning of economic activity over the past twenty-five years has led to substantial growth as the added jobs and populations during this period far exceeded those that had been taken away. It has also resulted in Atlanta being a more service-oriented and suburbanized region. The growth of the Atlanta region over the past quarter century reinforces many classic urban theoretical explanations for economic growth. Atlanta MSA's growth shows that low costs, access to qualified human capital, localization economies, and knowledge spillovers are still important. Atlanta has also been the beneficiary of inherent advantages of its location, including its weather, centrality within the Southeast region, and lack of barriers to geographic expansion.

In an economy which is increasingly oriented around the services and the production of ideas, investment in human capital that is able to perform those jobs is also important. The Atlanta MSA provides strong evidence for how a skilled and varied workforce allows for growth, but also where it can be improved by providing better K–12 schools. As noted by Glaeser and Shapiro, "the primary fact about urban growth is that skills predict growth," and that it is "better to concentrate on human capital than building denser downtowns" (Glaeser and Shapiro, 2003, 154–58). As shown by differences between the city and the MSA, density related to agglomerations in some financial and professional services may not be as important as they once were due to technology advances, signaling that more energy should be spent on creating less congestion in existing infrastructure than on constructing new high-rise buildings.

Maintaining a pro-business, pro-"creative class" climate also gives firms from base-industries a reason to locate in a city. It seems unreasonable that attracting members of the "creative class" is the only key to economic growth; as noted by Joel Kotkin and Fred Siegel (2005, 57), "it requires a mix of 'common-sense' policies that stress basic services like police and firefighters, innovative public schools that are not beholden to teachers unions, breaking down the barriers to new housing construction, and policies that lead local businesses to expand within the urban area." To its credit, Atlanta has fulfilled many of the basics needed to allow individuals and families to live well and for businesses to expand their ideas. However, continuous attention needs to be paid to issues dealing with crime, water shortages, and air pollution. If left unchecked these problems could become impediments to growth. At the same time, it is imperative that the Atlanta region continues to recognize the importance of maintaining high caliber research-oriented educational programs and projects that promote healthy public infrastructure. Policies that foster such programs and projects enable job growth.

One basic rule that cities often forget is the importance of comparative advantage. Cities ought to spend their time maintaining their current advantages, while at the same time dismantling obstacles to progress. Atlanta's inherent advantages were location (convenient for transportation services), being culturally diverse (making minority business-owners feel comfortable in the city), and a large pool of college-educated workers. Atlanta could also a do better job in maintaining those things which make it an attractive place to be. Maintaining transportation advantages means providing efficient connections to high-demand areas such as China, and more proximate ones like Savannah. At some point, suburban sprawl begins to diminish the natural resources and environment which make the state of Georgia attractive to people. Although tax abatement policies are important for industry growth, so too are policies which reduce congestion and improve environmental standards.

While examining Atlanta does not provide solutions for every obstacle to urban growth, it certainly provides a number of examples which both reinforce older theories on, and make suggestions about, how MSAs change and why they grow. It also provides evidence for explaining why residents of inner cities are often left with higher unemployment rates and lesser shares of jobs.

## NOTES

1. Unless otherwise noted, population data in this section are from the Bureau of the Census.

2. The concept of a metropolitan area did not exist in 1900. However, we assume that in 1900, the population of the city was essentially equal to the population of the region.

3. See Martin (1987) for a discussion of the Plan of Improvement.

4. There are no population estimates for years between the decennial censuses until 1990, nor are there employment estimates for the city during this time.

5. There was a widely held belief that there was a substantial population undercount of the city's population in the 1990 Census.

6. The Bureau of the Census estimates that the 2005 population of the city was 394,929.

7. The ten ARC counties are Cherokee, Clayton, Cobb, DeKalb, Douglas, Fayette, Fulton, Gwinnett, Henry, and Rockdale.

8. Employment for the city of Atlanta is based on estimates by census tracts. Since census tract boundaries do not align with city boundaries, employment figures may slightly overstate employment for the city.

9. The Bureau of Labor Statistics, the source of regional employment data, converted employment back in 1990 to NACIS. Thus, employment patterns according to SIC and NAICS can be compared over the 1990s.

10. The Bureau of Labor Statistics converted 1990–96 employment data to the NAICS and, as a result, we have consistent statistics over the entire 1990–2006 period.

11. Professional Services represents the sum of business services, legal services, and engineering and management services under SIC classification; and under NAICS classification consists of professional, scientific, technology; management of companies and enterprises; and administration, support, waste management.

12. For an excellent history of the hospitality industry in Atlanta, see Newman (1999).

13. www.atlanta-airport.com/Default.asp?url=sublevels/airport_info/ gm-page.htm (accessed 24 October, 2007).

14. Annual Reports of the Georgia World Congress Center Authority and the Center's website at www.gwcc.com.

15. Logistics is defined as part of the supply chain that plans, implements, and controls the efficient, effective forward and reverse flow and storage of goods, services, and related information between the point of origin and the point of consumption in order to meet customer's requirements. (Source: *Council Supply Chain Management Professionals.*)

16. A portion of the city of Atlanta is actually in DeKalb County; however, the bulk of the city is located in Fulton County. We include all of Atlanta's employment in the Fulton County totals.

17. The Atlanta suburbs are defined here as the ten-county region outside of the city of Atlanta.

18. A third-party logistics provider is a firm that provides outsource of "third-party" logistics services to companies for part or sometimes all of their supply chain management function. Third-party logistics providers typically specialize in integrated warehousing and transportation services that can be scaled and customized to customer's needs based on market conditions and the demands and delivery service requirements for their products and materials.

19. According to the *Georgia Port Authority's Annual Report for Fiscal Year 2006*, the port of Savannah is the largest single container facility on the entire east coast and is also the fastest growing container port. Between fiscal year 2002 and fiscal year 2006 Savannah's throughput has grown by 78 percent from 1.1 million containers to 2.0 million containers. In April 2006, a new container berth increased Savannah's port capacity by 20 percent and by 2015 planned capital improvements will increase annual capacity to 6 million containers. The Port of Brunswick is a major automobile entry point and is ranked among the most efficient ports in the United States.

20. Metro Atlanta Chamber of Commerce (2005). This includes both all cargo airlines as well as other airlines that carry cargo.

21. Table 2.4.5 of the National Income and Product Accounts produced by the Bureau of Economic Analysis.

22. These numbers are for the metropolitan area as defined in 2003.

23. *State and Metropolitan Area Data Book 2006*, table B-6.

24. *2007 Statistical Abstract*, table 162.

25. The 2002 Census of Business provides only a range for employment in health care for the City of Atlanta.

26. U.S. Bureau of the Census, *County Business Patterns.*

27. Professional services is the shortened title for the professional, scientific, and technical services sector (NAIC 54). It is comprised of businesses whose major input is human capital, and that are defined by the expertise and training of the service provider. The sector includes such industries as law offices, accounting firms, engineering services, architectural services, advertising agencies, veterinary services, and interior design services.

28. The CBD is defined as zip code 30303 while Midtown is defined as zip code 30309.

29. According to the Transportation Research Board, from 1990 to 2000 metro Atlanta's average commute rose from 26 minutes to 31.2 minutes, the highest jump in the nation.

## REFERENCES

American Lung Association. *State of the Air 2005: Best and Worst Cities.* www.lungusa.org (2005).

Atlanta Regional Commission. www.atlantaregional.com.

Barry, Tom. "Partners in Trade: As the Port of Savannah Grows, It Assures Atlanta's Status as a Distribution Hub." *Atlanta Business Chronicle* 7 (November 2005). Atlanta.Bizjournals.com/atlanta/stories/2005/11/07/focus1.html.

Crouch, Geoffrey J. and Jordan J. Louviere. "The Determinants of Convention Site Selection: A Logistic Choice Model from Experimental Data." *Journal of Travel Research* 43 (2004): 118–30.

Crouch, Geoffrey J. and J.R. Brent Ritchie. "Convention Site Selection Research: A Review, Conceptual Model and Propositional Framework." *Journal of Convention and Exhibition Management* 1, no. 1 (1998): 49–69.

Drummond, William J. and Jan L. Youtie. "Supply and Demand of Human Capital for the Biosciences Industry." Atlanta: Georgia Institute of Technology, 2003.

Florida, Richard. "The Rise of the Creative Class." *Washington Monthly* (May 2002). www.washingtonmonthly.com/features/2001/0205.florida.html.

*Fortune.* "Fortune 500." 155, no. 8 (2007): F1–F26.

Garoogian, David. "Atlanta." Pp. 25–56, in *America's Top Rated Cities: A Statistical Handbook.* Millerton, NY: Grey House Publishing, 2006.

Glaeser, Edward and Jesse Shapiro. "Urban Growth in the 1990's: Is City Living Back?" *Journal of Regional Science* 43, no. 1 (2003): 139–65.

Harden, Blaine. "Urban Warfare: American Cities Compete for Talent, and the Winner Takes All." Pp. 63–67, in *Urban Society,* edited by Fred Siegel and Harry Siegel. New York: McGraw-Hill, 2005.

Keating, Larry. *Atlanta: Race, Class and Urban Expansion.* Philadelphia: Temple University Press, 2001.

Kotkin, Joel and Fred Siegel. "Too Much Froth: The Latte Quotient is a Bad Strategy for Building Middle Class Cities." Pp. 56–57, in *Urban Society,* edited by Fred Siegel and Harry Siegel. New York: McGraw-Hill, 2005.

Martin, Harold H. *Atlanta and Environs: A Chronicle of Its People and Events: Years of Change and Challenge* (Volume III). Athens: University of Georgia Press, 1987.

Metro Atlanta Chamber of Commerce. *Metro Atlanta Logistics Directory*. Atlanta: Metro Atlanta Chamber of Commerce, 2005.

———. *Study: Atlanta Least Expensive to Do Business*. News Release. Atlanta: Metro Atlanta Chamber of Commerce, 22 March 2006.

Mills, Edwin and Luan Sende Lubuele. "Inner Cities." *Journal of Economic Literature* (June 1997): 727–56.

Newman, Harvey K. *Southern Hospitality: Tourism and the Growth of Atlanta*. Tuscaloosa: University of Alabama Press, 1999.

———. "Decentralization of Atlanta's Convention Business." *Urban Affairs Review* 38, no. 2 (2002): 232–52.

Quinn, Christopher. "Atlanta Still Ahead of O'Hare in Passengers." *Atlanta Journal-Constitution* 6 July 2006.

Rappaport, Jordan. "U.S. Urban Decline and Growth, 1950–2000." *Economic Review*. Federal Reserve Bank of Kansas City, 2003.

Research Atlanta. *The Convention Industry in Atlanta*. Atlanta: Research Atlanta, 1982.

———. *Atlanta Tourism and Convention Market: A Synopsis of Several Studies*. Atlanta: Research Atlanta, 1983.

Youtie, Jan. *Logistics Centered Talent: A Perspective on Supply and Demand* (Final Report). Atlanta: Georgia Institute of Technology, 2005.

## Chapter 4

# Retail Concentration and Place Identity: Understanding Atlanta's Changing Retail Landscape

### Katherine B. Hankins

Target, Gap, Victoria's Secret, California Pizza Kitchen, and Bath and Body Works all recently opened in Atlantic Station, a 138-acre new urbanist development that is located northwest of Atlanta's central business district. Atlantic Station has been celebrated by planners, architects, and city builders as a stunning success of a viable "intown" development strategy, combining the amenities of suburban spaces (townhomes and single-family detached homes, manicured lawns, and private security) with the conveniences of a walkable retail environment, complete with a movie theater and grocery store. The development is seen as bringing a sense of place to midtown Atlanta and to the west side of the city in general (Pendered 2005). Walking around Atlantic Station, however, one is struck by the sameness of the retailing environment. It contains the same stores that most suburban malls offer, yet it is branded and marketed as a destination with a unique identity in Atlanta's cityscape. The tension around this dynamic—the increasing ubiquity of retailing that reflects the concentration of retail capital and the explicit desire among residents (and consumers) to experience unique, identifiable places—is one which warrants investigation. Shaping this dynamism are complex economic and social processes that influence the expression that retail capital takes—from large big box, multinational establishments (e.g., Wal-Mart or Target) to smaller, boutiques and locally-owned establishments—and *where* retail investment is desirable. In this chapter, I explore both the theoretical complexity of the tension between retail sameness and place-uniqueness and some of the ways in which Atlanta's retail landscape has been shaped by this tension. I take a historical-geographical approach to understand the changing form of retail capital, its expression on the landscape, and the complexities inherent to understanding how 'place-identity' itself is negotiated and contested. I do so by examining Atlanta's overall retail geography as well as specific retail nodes within the city.

## RETAIL CAPITAL

Retail capital refers to profit-seeking investments in the infrastructure and technologies that enable the moment of retail exchange to take place. The retail moment is one in which buyers seek goods and services from retailers hoping to make a profit from the exchange. The conditions under which retail exchange takes place vary, based on the nature of the goods or services that are bought and sold and the logic guiding the ability of retailers to make a profit and consumers to purchase goods. Of course, retail exchange happens in a range of different kinds of stores and different kinds of places, and this totality is the expression of the logic and contradictions of retail capital (Ducatel and Blomley 1990; Wrigley and Lowe 1996; 2002). Importantly, as I show below, the form that retail capital takes in the 2000s is much different than the retailing dynamics of the early twentieth century.

Urban form both shapes and is shaped by the changing dynamics of retail exchange. For example, in the early twentieth century when American cities were dense and walkable, retail nodes and retail establishments looked quite different from today (see Jackson 1985). More recently, the creation of automobile-centered metropolitan regions required a rethinking of the logic of retail exchange. No longer could stores rely on small, less contested market areas but instead were compelled to compete for retail consumers across larger regions of the cities and suburbs. Additionally, retailers had to accommodate the parking requirements of the automobile-culture (Jackson 1985). As a result of these changes, small, neighborhood-based grocery stores and specialized dry goods shops gave way to large drive-in shopping centers, malls, and eventually supercenters (Longstreth 1997).

Throughout the transformation of urban (and suburban) America, the physical space in which retail exchange takes place also changed. This space includes the physical establishment and both its internal configuration (how aisles are configured to enable the desired flow of customer travel, for example) and where the establishment itself is located (a city block, a mall, a stand-alone space). The spatial expression that retail capital takes, of course, is the result of the logic of capital accumulation, where profit is the ultimate goal of the retailer. As such, the spaces of retailing change over time as new technologies (bar code scanning, automobile travel, reconfigured distribution systems, etc.) enable different strategies of profit maximization. Retail spaces are, then, a material expression of the restructuring of retail capital.

Ducatel and Blomley (1990) identify several trends that capture the contemporary logic of capital accumulation in the retail sector of the economy, including the increasing concentration of retail capital and the attempt by retailers to reduce circulation costs. The increasing concentration of retail capital refers to "the growth in market share attributable to the largest retailers and the local market concentration of retail outlets" (219). That is, fewer and fewer firms control a larger and larger share of the retail market. As Wrigley and Lowe (2002, 22) point out, in the mid-twentieth century small independent firms dominated the retail landscape in the United States, where 70 percent of total of retail sales were from independent stores. Within just three decades, that share had fallen to less than half of all retail sales. More significant, however, is the rise of the retail corporation, or the mega-chain (Wrigley and Lowe 2002), which gained unprecedented power beginning in the 1980s.

The mega-chain, illustrated by Wal-Mart and its rise to prominence as a corporate giant, has significantly shifted the power relationship between producers and retailers (Bianco and Zellner 2003; Petrovic and Hamilton 2006). For example, because of its command of a large market share in the United States (and its virtual monopoly in many suburban and rural areas), Wal-Mart can dictate its terms of sale to producers, often forcing producers to find cheaper sources of labor and materials (Young 2004; Petrovic and Hamilton 2006). Furthermore, with a workforce of approximately 1.3 million, Wal-Mart is the largest private employer in the United States (Wal-Mart Fact Sheet 2007). Part of Wal-Mart's success is built upon an explicitly spatial strategy, requiring consumers to drive outside of traditional downtowns to shop at large, warehouse-like establishments. This enables the retailer to reduce its circulation costs, or the cost/time of moving items from inventory to the checkout counter, which includes costs associated with warehousing and transportation. By driving longer distances, consumers participate in the work of retail exchange and absorb a larger portion of the circulation costs (Precteceille and Terrail 1985 in Ducatel and Blomley 1990). Another circulation cost-cutting strategy mega-chains employ is to reduce the number of retail establishments by increasing the average selling space of each one (therefore covering a larger market share with fewer establishments). The larger spaces enable firms to realize economies of scale in expanded on-site inventory and to reduce the redundancies associated with operating too many retail establishments. As Ducatel and Blomley (1990, 222) succinctly put it, "Size garners a number of efficiencies."

These processes—the concentration of retail capital and the drive to reduce circulation costs for retailers—have qualitatively changed the retailing experience for consumers. Theoretically, consumers have fewer choices in terms of retail outlets but more choices in terms of the kinds of goods and services offered in retail establishments that are designed to garner maximum efficiency and profit for retail firms. The danger is that retailers overly standardize the retail experience in terms of the efficient delivery of goods and services by standardizing the spaces, as well. While this dynamic is apparent in the U.S. retail landscape (and also in Britain, see Wrigley and Lowe 1996; 2002), increasingly retailers are attuned to a potentially contradictory force: consumers' desire to reside in and shop in unique *places*.

## PLACE-IDENTITY

In basic terms, the concept of place refers to a particular location that has meaning. Agnew (1987 in Miller 2001: 16) argues that place is a product of three elements: *locale*, or the "settings in which social relations are constituted"; *location*, which is the geographical area where social interaction takes place, and *sense of place*, or the local "structure of feeling." According to Martin (2003: 732), place is "both a setting for and situated in the operation of social and economic processes, and it also provides a 'grounding' for every day life and experience." In both of these definitions of place, there is a suggestion of emotional attachment to a discrete location. How this location comes to gain meaning is based on the interactions between how spaces are created (or produced) and how they are understood (or consumed).

Linking place-identity to the changing dynamics of retail capital suggests that we pay attention to how retail places are deliberately created. Cues, such as the naming of a development like Atlantic Station and the subsequent symbolism attached to the development in the form of steel sculptures from the area's history as Atlantic Steel, a steel mill, results in the creation of an identifiable place that is unique from others (see figures 4.1, 4.2). This strategy of producing spaces with particular meaning, then, requires a rethinking of the circulation costs of retail capital—and indeed requires that place itself become part of the understanding of the contemporary logic of capital accumulation.

As geographers are well aware, the process of capitalism is inherently spatial (Harvey 1989). Indeed, it is *place*—space that is imbued with particular culturally-significant meaning—that enables retail capital to exist. Retail capital as the infrastructure of exchange always happens *somewhere*, and this somewhere holds meaning for retailers and consumers (and residents, tourists, etc.). By extension, there is a relationship between the meanings associated with particular locations of retail exchange and the

IMG_3499

**Figure 4.1.   Atlantic Station steel sculpture**

nature of the exchange itself. For example, high-end luxury goods are often sold in retail districts that self-consciously exhibit cues of exclusivity, such as beautified streetscapes, doormen, or, in the case of malls, chandeliers, live piano, and fountains. Likewise, low-end retailing nodes rarely contain the same kinds of aesthetic cues as their high-end counterparts. Focusing on the creation of place identity—to construct a location's meaning in a particular way—to facilitate retail exchange is increasingly a strategy of developers and retailers.

The deliberate creation of place-identity as a way to enhance the appeal (and marketability) of a place is not a new strategy, of course. As scholars have pointed out, place-marketing (for neighborhoods, whole cities, states, or even countries) is an increasingly popular approach to attract consumers, be they residents or tourists (Harvey 1989; Hall and Hubbard 1996). Place promotion has become professionalized (Warnaby and Medway 2004), and some argue that places themselves have become commodities whose elements are overtly produced (Hughes 1992 in Warnaby and Medway 2004). This relationship between retailing and the production of place has been largely ignored by academics (for an exception, see Warnaby and Medway 2004). Nevertheless, the marketing of developments such as Atlantic Station (and other retail developments discussed

**Figure 4.2.   Atlantic Station retail district**

below) and the construction of place identity suggest that profit-making
in retailing now requires an identifiable place experience. Retailers need
to pay attention not just to the physical spaces of store layout and design
but to the meanings associated with the retail districts in which consumers participate in the moment of exchange.

## ATLANTA'S RETAIL LANDSCAPE

A review of Atlanta's retail landscape provides an empirical example of
how retailing has changed—both through the increasing concentration of
retail capital and the various ways in which retail capital has structured,
and been structured by, time and space. Atlanta's recent retailing history
reveals both the trend of retail concentration and the turn to place identity—both Atlanta's identity as a city and the identity of retail nodes within
the city. A critical point is that place identity is not always at the whim of
the retailers—rather, it is "constructed," through a complex social and economic negotiation among residents, retail corporations, investors, and city
leaders. Finally, I conclude the chapter by contemplating the future direction of Atlanta's retail landscape in light of these paradoxical retail trends.

**Atlanta's Recent Retail Past**

The landscape of retail activity in the city of Atlanta has changed dramatically over the past several decades. Following a population exodus out of the city into suburban areas in the latter part of the twentieth century (Hartshorn and Ihlanfeldt 2000), the location and mix of retailing activity in the city has moved within and beyond the historic central business district. From centralized retail activity on Peachtree Street at the turn of the twentieth century, to an elongated strip of retail and business functions extending northward towards Buckhead, to countless pockets of neighborhood centers as well as renewed interest in integrating retail with residential and office functions, by the twenty-first century the city of Atlanta exhibited a dynamic retail landscape.

Atlanta's retail landscape has followed the urban morphology patterns exhibited by many Sunbelt cities that sprawled outward from their centers in the latter part of the twentieth century (see Bullard et al. 2000). Population growth and residential development occurred well beyond the city limits, primarily in suburban regions where land was cheaper and access was facilitated by the new interstate highway system (Jackson 1985; see Hartshorn, this volume). Atlanta also experienced a reconfiguration of urban space around the desegregation of the Atlanta public schools, which occurred in the 1960s and facilitated the departure of many of Atlanta's white residents from the city to outlying suburbs (Pomerantz 1996). Retail investment patterns reflected a bifurcated landscape, with major retail nodes following the suburban market in the form of large regional shopping malls, and the continued but steadily declining existence of downtown retailing, anchored by department and specialty stores. In what follows, I examine what might be termed "non-everyday" retailing (or high-end goods), or the kinds of retail goods and services that consumers need on an occasional basis.

Atlanta is an archetypal city in which to examine the dynamics of rapid suburbanization that has occurred since the 1950s to the present. Hartshorn and Muller (1989) articulate the presence of city-like clusters of offices, retail, and residential in suburban areas as "suburban downtowns." Their definition of a suburban downtown is predicated on the presence of a regional shopping center of more than one-million square feet of retail space in addition to the presence of high-rise office buildings, hotels, and an employment level of no less than 50,000 (Hartshorn and Muller 1989). Shopping centers of this size revealed a new moment in the logic of retail capital and the search for profit. By enclosing and grouping retail establishments together under a single roof (and by private management), retailers (and developers) essentially changed the retail experience for many consumers. No longer did consumers have to fight congested central cities to experience shopping; instead, they could utilize the world of the automobile and large parking lots. Malls, as a spatial expression of late twentieth century retail capital, have been a mainstay in the retail landscape since the 1960s (Marston and Modarres 2002).

Examining the geography of mall development from the 1960s to the present reveals the stages of suburbanization experienced by metropolitan Atlanta. It also illustrates the changing spatiality of malls themselves (which have almost doubled in square footage over the past fifty years). That is, as suburban areas grew farther from the city, and as retail firms realized advantages from larger and larger spaces, malls themselves grew dramatically in size.

In Atlanta, the earliest malls include Lenox Square Mall, opened in Buckhead in 1959, the Avondale Mall (previously Columbia Mall) in 1964, and Greenbriar Mall and the North Dekalb Mall in 1965, all of which are located between five and fifteen miles from Atlanta's CBD. These early malls reflected the movement of population centers northward and eastward. The next wave of development included malls developed within twelve miles of downtown Atlanta, including the South Dekalb Mall (1968), Phipps Plaza (1969), Perimeter Mall (1971), and Cumberland Mall (1973). These malls reflected the rise of suburban areas which grew substantially in the northern and northwestern regions of the metropolitan area.

The square footage of these early malls represented an unprecedented amount of concentrated retail space under the same roof, around 650,000 square feet. However, as table 4.1 reveals, the size of malls built after the 1970s averaged over a million square feet of retail space. Again, this increase in the size of malls reflects the changing spatiality of retailing whereby larger spaces for individual stores as well as larger spaces for mall complexes became desirable and profitable.

Atlanta's most recently constructed malls reflect the contemporary logic of capital accumulation, which is to locate in suburban (some would argue exurban) locations in immense developments. For example, two of the newest malls serving the metro Atlanta area were completed in such locations in 2001. Discover Mills, with 1.2 million square feet of retail and more than 200 stores opened 23 miles northeast of the city along Interstate 85 in Gwinnett County. The Mall at Stonecrest contains about 1.3 million square feet of retail and is located approximately 17 miles east of downtown along Interstate 20 in DeKalb County.

Clearly, these malls extend the logic of economies of scale by providing large physical establishments on relatively inexpensive land, where greater stock can be maintained at reduced cost, and where consumers travel long distances but spend potentially more time and money shopping. Furthermore, these large super-regional centers (as they are termed in retail literature) host multinational and national chain stores, which cluster to take

**Table 4.1:   Malls in the Atlanta area, 1959 to 2007**

| Name | Date opened (renovated and closed*) | Size (renovated) in square feet | Distance from CBD |
|---|---|---|---|
| Lenox Square Mall | 1959 (1972, 1987, 1993, 1995) | 665,000 (1.5 million) | 6.5 miles |
| Cobb Center Mall (previously Cobb County Shopping Center) | 1963 (1986, 1998*) | No data | 13 miles |
| Avondale Mall (previously Columbia Mall) | 1964 (1980s, 2001*) | 350,000 | 7 miles |
| Greenbriar Mall | 1965 | 678,000 | 7.5 miles |
| North Dekalb Mall (previously Market Square | 1965 (1986) | 650,657 | 7.5 miles |
| The Gallery at South Dekalb (previously South Dekalb Mall) | 1968 | 800,000 | 7.3 miles |
| Phipps Plaza | 1969 (1992) | 821,000 | 7 miles |
| Perimeter Mall | 1971 (1982, 1993) | 1.2 million | 12 miles |
| Cumberland Mall | 1973 (1989) | 1.2 million | 9.8 miles |
| Southlake Mall | 1976 | 1 million | 12.5 miles |
| Shannon Southpark Mall | 1980 (1986) | 770,651 | 15 miles |
| Gwinnett Place | 1984 (1993) | 1.2 million | 21 miles |
| Town Center Mall | 1986 | 1.2 million | 20.7 miles |
| North Point Mall | 1993 (2003) | 1.4 million | 21 miles |
| Arbor Place Mall | 1999 | 860,000 | 20.3 miles |
| Discover Mills | 2001 | 1.2 million | 23.6 miles |
| The Mall at Stonecrest | 2001 | 1.3 million | 17.3 miles |

advantage of cost savings associated with the mall format. The presence of these super-regional centers can be understood as an expression of the ways in which retail capital has shifted over time to reduce circulation costs by taking advantage of economies of scale and new retail geographies.

While malls are a mainstay of today's retail landscape, the same might have been said for the central business district of most major cities at the turn of the twentieth century. In the case of Atlanta, at the same time that the city experienced tremendous growth outward, the central business district declined in its importance as a major retail hub. This decline reflects a fairly typical pattern observable in most U.S. cities in the second half of the twentieth century (Robertson 1983; Teaford 2006). In some respects, Atlanta's central business district remained a symbolic hub of retail activity for decades longer than it deserved because of the presence of the flagship stores of major retailers. For example, the downtown department stores Rich's and Macy's only closed their doors in 1991 and 2003, respectively.

Figure 4.3 reveals the geographic distribution of shopping centers across the metropolitan Atlanta region as of 2005. Shopping centers are clustered near the interstate system, and within the city limits of Atlanta the number of shopping centers north of Interstate 20 is more than twice that of shopping centers south of the interstate. This northward trend reflects a spatial concentration of retail capital in wealthier residents in the northern portion of the city (see Jaret et al. 2000 and Keating 2001).

Within the city, the primary retail node that was centered in the CBD for much of the twentieth century moved northward towards the Buckhead region. A brief examination of economic census data for 1982, 1992, 1998, 2002, and 2005 by zip code reveals the mobility of retail investment over a twenty-year period in Atlanta. The general trend of retail establishments with the greatest sales volume moved from the

Figure 4.3.  Map of Atlanta's shopping centers

central areas of the city northward. For 1982, retail investment is relatively centralized, including intense retail activity in the CBD (zip code
30303). At this time, the major department stores anchored the central
business district. The data also show areas of investment to the south,
west, and north of the CBD. As with many cities in the late twentieth
century, Atlanta experienced a "doughnut" effect around the CBD,
with immediately adjacent areas in the last tier of investment (relative
to other zip codes).

By 1992, there was still significant investment in the downtown area,
with the CBD (zip code 30303) maintaining its position as one of the top
sites of investment in the metropolitan area. Indeed, city leaders made
concerted attempts to attract consumers downtown by reopening Underground Atlanta in 1989 with retail and entertainment venues drawing
upon Atlanta's past for the explicit purpose of generating tourist dollars
(Monroe 2007). The general trend, however, was that by 1992 retail inten-
sity was moving discernibly northward.

Finally, as depicted in Figure 4.4, by 2005, retail investment was centered considerably north of the CBD, and much of it around or near the
Buckhead region. Indeed, the 1990s saw the closing of several of Atlanta's
long-established downtown department stores and the simultaneous
investment in luxury retailers in Lenox Mall and Phipps Plaza in the
Buckhead region of Atlanta. Although these malls were opened in 1959
and 1969, respectively, the transformation of the region to high-end retail
establishments (including Saks Fifth Avenue, Nordstrom, and Bloom-
ingdales by 2005), reinforced its reputation as one of Atlanta's premier,
high-end retailing destinations. Likewise, examining the number of retail
outlets per area in 2005 reveals a continuation of this geographic pattern,
with retail activity continuing to cluster in the northern portions of the
city limits. Not only has the city experienced waves of investment in different regions of the city, whereby retailers sought to capitalize on the
movement of population centers and changing social conditions, but the
ownership structure in Atlanta's retail industry has also changed over the
past several decades.

## Concentration of Retail Capital in Atlanta

Figure 4.5 illustrates the number of retail establishments in the city of Atlanta between 1982 and 2002. The number of retail establishments in all of
Atlanta city zip codes declined over the years, from almost 3000 in 1982 to
just under 2000 by 2002. This decline occurred while the value of the sales
from these outlets significantly increased, a divergence explained partly
by the concentration of retail capital which resulted in an increasing number of very large firms but fewer retail firms overall. These larger firms

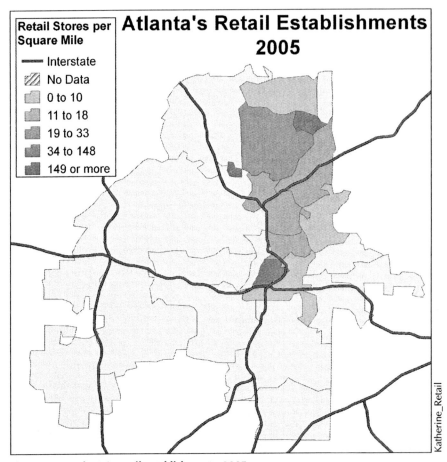

Figure 4.4.   Atlanta's retail establishments, 2005

control much of the retail sector, and often force out smaller competitors, as discussed above.

In effect, the concentration of retail capital in the form of fewer retail establishments has meant that consumers have fewer choices in terms of where they can purchase different goods (although many would argue that the selection within these large stores is so much larger given that the scale of many retail establishments outstrips what many smaller firms could offer). Thus, Atlanta exhibits precisely the conditions that Ducatel and Blomely (1990) and others (Wrigley and Lowe 2002) observe generally regarding the growing market share of retailers among fewer and fewer firms. The transformation of the number of retail outlets into fewer and fewer establishments alongside other changes occurring in the retail

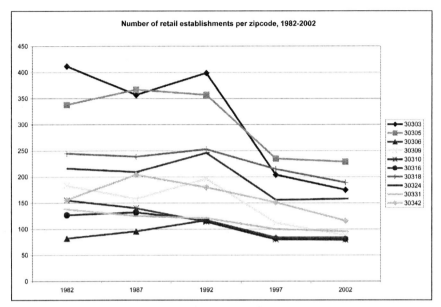

Figure 4.5.   Number of retail establishments per zipcode

sectors reveals a dynamic retail environment in Atlanta. In addition to, and in part because of, these changes, retail establishments are increasingly seen as integral elements in place-making processes—and vice versa, "made" places effectively reveal the retail offerings of the city and shopping nodes within it.

### Retail Place-making in Atlanta

Atlanta has been the site of several high-profile urban developments that draw from new urbanist and neotraditional planning principles (see Duany and   Plater-Zyberk 1994). These developments, profiled below, emphasize retail establishments that are integrated into residential and office space. And, importantly, they all rely on place-based identities in an attempt to attract consumers by fostering a sense-of-place for them.

As figure 4.6 illustrates, Lindbergh City Center seeks to integrate pedestrian-friendly retail and office with residential spaces. Touted as "the country's first true Transit-Oriented Development" according to the developer's brochure,  when complete, the complex will include almost 230,000 square feet of office space, 208,000 square feet of retail, a hotel, and apartments and condos (Lindbergh City Center 2007). The attempt by developers is to make Lindbergh into a place that has a distinct identity. Given the name and the landscape the developers have created, the development is intended to invoke reference to the convenience of the city center, while occupying a transit node five miles north of the central city of Atlanta.

Of course, Lindbergh City Center pales in comparison to the country's largest new urbanist development, Atlantic Station, which, when complete will have two million square feet of open air retail and entertainment space and eleven acres of green space on the 138 acre site. With its own zip code, Atlantic Station has been lauded as a model of retail development with up-scale restaurants, a grocery store, and a host of more common "mall stores." As mentioned in the introduction, tenants at Atlantic Station include many multinational chain stores within a walkable retail node, known as "The District." Parking for more than seven thousand cars is underground, en-abling daily visitors to drive into the development, park, and then walk among the shops. Atlantic Station is clearly a created place that includes the historic referent of a steel mill and a romantic notion of what a walkable city space ought to be. What this development suggests is that retail capital is seeking more than a reduction in circulation costs vis-à-vis the increase in retail space (although this is illustrated by the immense scale of the Atlantic Station development) by addressing the perceived notion that people want identifiable places to consume.

Other development plans in the city include the vision articulated by the Midtown Alliance, a nonprofit organization of business leaders and Midtown citizens, to create Atlanta's own version of Chicago's Magnifi-cent Mile—dubbed Midtown Mile (Midtown Mile 2007). The Midtown Alliance is seeking to turn fourteen blocks of Peachtree Street in Midtown into a main retail thoroughfare with one-million square feet of retailing. Existing retail spaces will be oriented towards the sidewalk, and hundreds of thousands of square feet of ground-floor retail space is proposed in new construction along the thoroughfare. The proposal for Midtown Mile is complete with a branded logo, uniform signage for the retail district, and a beautified streetscape with wide, tree-lined sidewalks to encourage pedestrian shoppers. As the Midtown Alliance website articulates, the plan for Midtown, called "Blueprint Midtown" envisions a vital, vibrant city center inspired by what people want in an urban community:

- Balanced blend of residential, retail, office & mixed-use properties
- Plenty of greenspace
- Multiple transit options
- Unique, welcoming & thoroughly pedestrian streetscape environ-ment

By following the requirements of the Blueprint, Midtown stakeholders will create the community imagined from the outset: a vibrant, successful city cen-ter that is uniquely Midtown Atlanta (Blueprint Midtown: The Vision 2008).

**Figure 4.6.** **Photo of Lindbergh City Center**

Through the civic organization, the Midtown Alliance is trying to lead a concerted effort to shape the kind of retail and residential development to be "uniquely" Midtown. Developers are invited to share in the group's vision of making that particular part of the city "vibrant" and "successful."

What these three places have in common—Lindbergh City Center, Atlantic Station, and Midtown Mile—is a deliberate attempt among developers, business leaders, and civic groups to create a sense of place around retail investment. Indeed, developers and place-based organizations, such as the Midtown Alliance, spent a tremendous amount of capital to market—and indeed create—place-identity through retail spaces and experiences. Lindbergh Center, Atlantic Station, and Midtown Mile are all identifiable *places* that are intended to be unique destinations for consumers.

This dynamic of place-identity is evident in much of the retail landscape (dating back to the naming of malls and subdivisions). And it is important to recognize that place-identity is not static or monolithic, and as such, we need to examine how place-identity is negotiated and contested. In fact, the vision of what a neighborhood or thoroughfare ought to look like—indeed, the retail establishments and consumers it ought to have—can be, and usually is, contested.

Place-identity complicates the realization of profit in retail capital accumulation. The meaning of a particular place is bound up with the "sunk costs" associated with property and infrastructure (in that older buildings may garner a reputation as "run down" or "out of style") and yet it is distinct from such material processes (just as older buildings may become "historical gems" with the passage of time). Therefore, place-identity, which encapsulates the geographical imaginaries of both retailers and consumers, is critical to understanding retail capital.

## Atlanta's Retailing Future

Suggesting what the future might hold is clearly complex, given that one cannot separate out phenomena such as retailing from broader social, political, cultural events. At the same time, I think we are likely to see the continuation of several trends, which have contradictory tendencies. The first is the increasing concentration of the retail industry as retail multinational corporations continue to grow. More and more of the same retail brands are offered in malls and inner city or urban developments across the country. This, of course, poses challenges for smaller business owners who must compete with the economies of scale that large corporations can attain. At the same time, I think we will see the continued importance of place-based retailing. This may require that those large corporations carefully respond to local, place-based needs—beyond simply creating logos and place-names for shopping centers. Furthermore, an important piece of the place-identity equation is the kind of activities that local organizations—including business associations, neighborhood groups, and municipalities—engage in to create and maintain a vision of what their place ought to be. Indeed, place-based organizations working in concert with the city and with developers seems to be the most promising strategy for sustained retail investment, which, as the broader economic, social, and cultural context suggests, can be quite fleeting.

The future retail picture in Atlanta is one of continued change. The Atlanta Regional Commission predicts the population of the city of Atlanta to increase by 43 percent between 2000 and 2030 (City of Atlanta Tomorrow 2008), and an increasing share of this population is expected to be older and childless. Much of this increasing, older population will require a reshuffling of retail establishments. Mixed-use centers with a collection of big box stores, such as the Edgewood Retail Center, which opened in 2005 in an in-town neighborhood, may find that building dense housing and senior residences around shopping nodes can accommodate the growing population. While the corner store may be harder to find in Atlanta's neighborhoods, as more residents move into the city, everyday retailers, such as grocery stores and pharmacies, will likely follow, as is evidenced by the increasing number of such stores that have been built in the urban core since 2000.

Another project that is likely to shape urban development patterns—and by extension retail—is the proposed Beltline project, which anticipates creating and connecting twenty-two miles of rail segments that circle the central part of the city (see Beltline Atlanta Connected 2008). This project will likely inspire a renewed interest in providing more everyday retailing goods and services within Atlanta's urban neighborhoods.

Given that place-making has been critical to the success of some retail centers, I think the city is likely to experience more retail development that emphasizes a sense of place. Developments will likely provide pockets of walkable space that, like Atlantic Station, are most easily accessible by car. This can lead to a heightened sense of difference among regions of the city, as retail becomes (more deliberately) imbued with particular experiences of place.

The paradox of the increasing concentration of retail capital and the heightened demand for unique places will likely shape Atlanta into centers of "placeful" big box retail establishments. At the same time, the increasing interest in intown living and the projected population increases for the city suggest that there may yet be room for smaller specialty retailers to dot neighborhoods, strengthening neighborhood identities through retail.

This placeful retailing narrative largely leaves out areas that are underserved or marginalized in terms of their retail offerings. As Keating (2001) and the authors in Sjoquist's (2000) edited volume point out, Atlanta has long suffered from racial and income inequalities within the city and the larger metropolitan region. While these inequalities may be heightened by future population shifts (many of Atlanta's urban neighborhoods are undergoing rapid gentrification), retailers will continue to follow their markets, clustering in areas that draw in consumers and deliberately creating unique places in the process.

## NOTE

A special thank you to David Sjoquist for organizing this volume, to Dan Miller Runfola for tireless assistance, and to Andy Walter for encouragement and support.

## REFERENCES

Agnew, J. *Place and Politics*. Boston, MA: Allen and Unwin, 1987.
"Beltline: Atlanta Connected" Atlanta Beltline, Inc. 2008. www.beltline.org (8 April 2008).
Bianco, A. and W. Zellner. "Is Wal-Mart too powerful?" *BusinessWeek*. October 6, 2003.
"Blueprint Midtown: The Vision." Midtown Alliance, 2008. www.midtownalliance. org/BM_vision.html (8 April 2008).
Bullard, R., G. Johnson, and A. Torres (eds). *Sprawl City: Race, Politics, and Planning in Atlanta*. Washington, D.C.: Island Press, 2000.
"City of Atlanta Tomorrow." Atlanta Regional Commission. 2008. www. atlantaregional.com/html/207.aspx (8 April 2008).
Duany, A. and E. Plater-Zyberk. "The Neighborhood, the District, and the Corridor." Pp. 17–20 in *The New Urbanism: Toward an Architecture of Community*, edited by P. Katz. New York: McGraw-Hill, 1994.
Ducatel, K.J. and N.K. Blomley. "Rethinking Retail Capital." *International Journal of Urban and Regional Research* 14, no. 2 (1990): 207–27
Hall T. and P. Hubbard. "The Entrepreneurial City: New Urban Politics, New Urban Geographies?" *Progress in Human Geography* 20, no. 2 (1996): 153–74.
Hartshorn, T. and K. Ihlanfeldt. "Growth and Change in Metropolitan Atlanta." Pp. 15–41 in *The Atlanta Paradox*, edited by D. Sjoquist. New York: Russell Sage, 2000.
Hartshorn, T. and P. Muller. "Suburban downtowns and the transformation of Atlanta's business landscape." *Urban Geography* 10 (1989): 375–95.
Harvey, D. "From Managerialism to Entrepreneurialism: The Transformation of Urban Governance in Late Capitalism." *Geografiska Annaler* 71B (1989): 3–17.
———. *The Limits to Capital*. London and New York: Verso, 1989.
Hughes, G. "Tourism and the Geographical Imagination." *Leisure Studies* 11 (1992): 31–42.
Ihlanfeldt, K. and D. Sjoquist. "Earnings Inequality." Pp. 128–57 in *The Atlanta Paradox*, edited by D. Sjoquist. New York: Russell Sage, 2000.
Jackson, K. *Crabgrass Frontier*. New York and Oxford: Oxford University Press, 1985.

Jaret, C., E. Ruddiman, and K. Phillips. "The Legacy of Residential Segregation." Pp. 111–38 in *Sprawl City: Race, Politics, and Planning in Atlanta*, edited by R. Bullard, G. Johnston, and A. Torres. Washington, D.C.: Island Press, 2000.

Keating, L. *Atlanta: Race, Class and Urban Expansion*. Philadelphia: Temple University Press, 2001.

"Lindbergh City Center." 2007. www.carterusa.com/flyersHTML/Lindbergh. html (20 February 2007).

Longstreth, R. *City Center to Regional Mall: Architecture, the Automobile, and Retailing in Los Angeles, 1920-1950*. Cambridge, MA: MIT Press, 1997.

Lowe, M. and N. Wrigley. "Towards the New Retail Geography." Pp. 3–30 in *Retailing, Consumption, and Capital: Towards the New Retail Geography*, edited by N. Wrigley and M. Lowe. London: Longman,1996.

Marston, S. and A. Modarres. "Flexible Retailing: Gap, Inc. and the Multiple Spaces of Shopping in the United States." *Tijdschrift: the Journal of Economic and Social Geography* 93, no. 1 (2002): 83–99.

Martin, D. "'Place-framing' as Place-making: Constituting a Neighborhood for Organizing and Activism" *Annals of the Association of American Geographers* 93, no. 3 (2003): 730–50.

Midtown Mile. 2007. www.midtownmile.com (20 February 2007).

Miller, B. *Geography and Social Movements*. Minneapolis and London: University of Minnesota Press, 2001.

Monroe, D. "Burning Question: What's Up with Underground?" *Atlanta Magazine Online*. 2007. www.atlantamagazine.com/article.php?id=310 (6 March 2007).

Pendered, D. "Atlantic Station Opens: A City within the City." *The Atlanta Journal-Constitution*, 16 October 2005, 1E.

Petrovic, M. and G. Hamilton. "Making Global Markets: Wal-Mart and Its Suppliers." Pp. 107–41 in *Wal-Mart: The Face of Twenty-First-Century Capitalism* edited by N. Lichtenstein. New York and London: The New Press, 2006.

Pomerantz, G. *Where Peachtree Meets Sweet Auburn*. New York: Penguin Books, 1996.

Precteceille, E. and J.P. Terrail. *Capitalism, Consumption and Needs*. Oxford: Basil Blackwell, 1985.

Robertson, K. "Downtown Retail Activity in Large American Cities 1954–1977." *Geographical Review* 73, no. 3 (1983): 314–23.

Sjoquist, D. *The Atlanta Paradox*. New York: Russell Sage, 2000.

Teaford, J. *The Metropolitan Revolution: The Rise of Post-Urban America*. New York: Columbia University Press, 2006.

Wal-Mart Fact Sheet. 2007. walmartfacts.com/FactSheets/1242007_Employment_ and_Diversity.pdf (20 June 2007).

Warnaby, G. and D. Medway. "The Role of Place Marketing as a Competitive Response by Town Centres to Out-of-Town Retail Developments." *International Review of Retail, Distribution and Consumer Research* 14, no. 4 (2004): 457–77.

Wrigley, N. and M. Lowe. *Reading Retail*. London: Arnold, 2002.

———. *Retailing, Consumption and Capital*. Harlow, UK: Longman, 1996.

Young, R. "Is Wal-Mart Good for America?" *Frontline*, 16 November 2004.

*Part III*

# AIR AND TRANSPORTATION

## Chapter 5

# Air Today, Gone Tomorrow: Atlanta's Air Quality Past and Future*

## *Douglas S. Noonan and Jennifer Chirico*

Atlanta residents tend to worry a lot about the local air quality. Atlantans commonly link air pollution, sprawl, and traffic congestion as a major regional problem (CVIOG 2002). The signs of Atlanta's air pollution are everywhere. Along Atlanta's main interstates are overhead signs that warn citizens about high smog days during the summer months, news reports advise people to carpool or take public transportation on "red alert" days (days when the ozone level reaches "unhealthy" levels), and parents are warned to keep children with asthma indoors. "Better Air Campaigns" are in action around the city, encouraging citizens to find alternative means of transportation and to adopt more energy efficient behaviors. While pursuing the worthy goal of better air quality, the average Atlanta citizen might find it surprising to discover that the overall air quality in Atlanta actually steadily improved over the last three to four decades. Sometimes a little history can help put matters into perspective.

The purpose of this chapter is to provide an overview of the history of air quality in Atlanta, the present state of Atlanta's air quality, and what we might expect air quality to be in the future. Section II provides a brief history of air quality prior to the Clean Air Act. Section III reviews the Clean Air Act and provides an overview of each of the criteria air pollutants. Section IV provides an overview of typical air pollution indicator trends, and discusses possible reasons why these trends do not appear to follow the air quality trends in Atlanta. Section V provides our projections of Atlanta's

* This research is based in part on research funded by EPA STAR grant, "Air Quality, Emissions, Growth, and Change."

air quality in the future. Throughout this chapter we refer to the "City of Atlanta" as "Atlanta," and to "Metropolitan Atlanta" as "Metro Atlanta."

## AIR QUALITY BEFORE ATLANTA

Up until the twentieth century, the term "air pollution" did not exist. Air pollution was referred to as 'smoke,' 'kiln,' 'nuisance,' and 'coal' (Bowler and Brimblecombe 1992). Without a common term for air pollution, measuring historical air pollution trends is somewhat difficult. One might suspect that air pollution has been around since the beginning of time—or at least since the first fire.[1] During medieval times, air pollution became a concern to society when coal replaced wood as the primary source of fuel (Goklany 1999). Urban air pollution regulation can be traced very far back indeed. Air pollution regulation existed in 1257, following Queen Eleanor of England complaining about smoke while visiting Nottingham (Brimblecombe 1976). Much like we see in Atlanta some 750 years later, the national governing authorities in England regulated the use of emitting technologies (e.g., kilns) and fuels (e.g., coal) to control air pollution.

During the first hundred years of the United State's existence, "smoke" complaints were considered a common law nuisance and were resolved by litigation among involved parties instead of through legislation. Around 1881, the first legislation was enacted that declared smoke emissions a public nuisance, and by the early 1900s, smoke was prohibited if it was considered "dense," "black," or "grey." This led to the establishment of the first formal measure of air pollution, defined by the Ringelmann Chart. By 1950, over 1,030 American communities had enacted a variety of emission standards (Stern 1981), and by the mid-1950s, a few air control programs were implemented in several large cities, including New York, Pittsburgh, and Los Angeles (Sabatier 1988). It is interesting to note, however, that even as late as the 1950s when air control programs were becoming more common at the city level, "air pollution" was not yet an official term and was still referred to as "dirty air arising from coal combustion" (Sabatier 1988).

## AIR QUALITY AFTER 1970

While it is clear that air pollution was an issue to societies for many centuries, federal legislation on air pollution in the United States was not enacted until 1970. After passage of the Clean Air Act (CAA) in 1970, air pollution control became the responsibility of the U.S. Environmental Protection Agency (EPA). The new, strict regulations imposed by the CAA coincided with a change in the public perception of air quality. The public began to perceive air pollution as not only dirty, but also unhealthy. In addition, the perception of the sources of air pollution shifted from coal-burning and factory emissions to automobiles (Sabatier 1988). The passage of the CAA also accompanied the first Earth Day celebration, a rise in environmental concerns that coincided with rising affluence and scientific understanding of air pollution problems. Under the CAA, the EPA established National Ambient Air Quality Standards (NAAQS) that included six criteria air pollutants: lead, particulate matter, ozone, sulfur dioxide, carbon monoxide, and nitrogen dioxide (EPA 2006a). The NAAQS provides national air quality standards for each pollutant.

## Measuring Air Quality

Prior to 1970, very little was known about the distribution of the criteria pollutants in many areas. With the passage of the Clean Air Act, the United States Environmental Protection Agency (EPA) began tracking air quality from over 3,000 locations around the country. Under the CAA, the EPA sets standards for air quality to protect human, plant, and animal health. The EPA identified six principle criteria pollutants and measured the pollutants in the air and from emissions to evaluate how air quality changes over time. Since the CAA established the first national air quality standards, setting these standards and providing clear guidance was a challenge for the EPA. In an EPA press release in 1971, then-current EPA administrator William Ruckelshaus stated, "[These standards] are based on investigations conducted at the outer limits of our capability" (EPA 1971). The NAAQS shifted the focus of air quality improvement from the state and local level to cross-sectional conformity at the national level. Below are descriptions and trends for these primary pollutants in Atlanta.

### Lead

Lead (Pb) is an air pollutant that is found in manufactured products and in the natural environment. Exposure to lead has serious health effects, such as organ, brain, and nerve damage, and it can increase the risk of high blood pressure and heart disease. Historically, the major source of lead emissions was from leaded gasoline from cars and trucks. Lead exposure has decreased significantly over the last thirty years with the reduction in car and truck emissions. Lead emissions sharply declined when leaded gasoline was phased out, and today, most lead emissions come from industrial operations (EPA 2006b). As illustrated in figure 5.1,[2] annual lead concentrations in Atlanta substantially decreased in the late 1970s and continued to steadily decline through 2005 (EPA 2003; 2007). (The straight line denoted by squares indicates the NAAQS level for lead.)

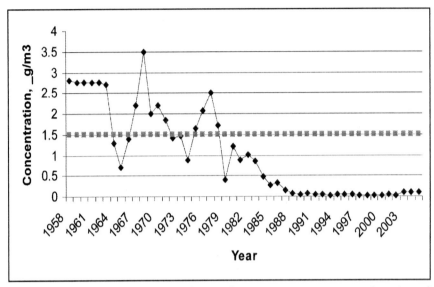

**Figure 5.1. Annual Lead Concentrations, Atlanta, GA, 1958–2005 Based on Annual Maximum Average**

*Particulate Matter*

Particulate matter (PM) is made up of small particles derived from a mixture of different components, such as acids, metals, organic chemicals, and dust particles. PM is generally measured in terms of the size of the particles, specifically by the diameter of the particles measured in micrometers. PM measurements are usually split into two categories: $PM_{10}$ and $PM_{2.5}$. $PM_{10}$ is made up of inhalable coarse particles that are smaller than 10 and larger than 2.5 micrometers. $PM_{10}$ particles include mold, spores, and pollen, and dirt and dust from factories, farming, and roads. In contrast, $PM_{2.5}$ particles are made up of fine particles that are 2.5 micrometers in diameter or smaller. $PM_{2.5}$ particles include toxic organic compounds and heavy metals that are created from driving automobiles, burning plants (e.g., forest fires), and smelting and processing metals (EPA 2008). Prior to formal measurements of $PM_{10}$ and $PM_{2.5}$, the EPA measured particulate matter in the form of total suspended particles (TSP). TSP, while not a criteria pollutant as such, is a common measure of air pollution in international studies. TSP is made up of particles that are suspended in the air and are larger than 10 micrometers in diameter. TSP is not considered as dangerous as $PM_{10}$ and $PM_{2.5}$ since the particles are not small enough to get into the lungs. Nevertheless, public measurement records of TSP date back into the 1950s, which provides a good indicator for examining older trends

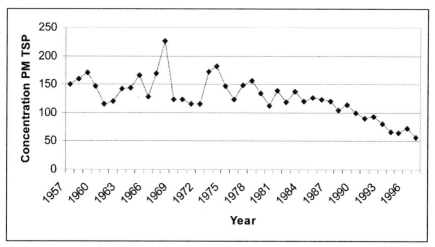

**Figure 5.2.** Annual TSP Concentrations, Atlanta, GA, 1957–1997 Based on Annual 24 Hour 4th Maximum Average

in $PM_{10}$ and $PM_{2.5}$. As illustrated in figure 5.2, TSP varied dramatically between 1957 and 1975 and then steadily declined from 1975 into the 1990s.

Unlike TSP, $PM_{10}$ was not systematically measured by the U.S. EPA until the late 1980s, and $PM_{2.5}$ was not measured until the late 1990s. $PM_{2.5}$ is more harmful to the environment and human and animal health than $PM_{10}$ because the particles can easily be inhaled into the lungs due to the small size. Emissions of $PM_{2.5}$ are usually in the form of smoke coming from power plants, industries, and automobiles reacting with the air (EPA 2006b). Figures 5.3 and 5.4 depict the particulate matter concentrations for Atlanta for $PM_{10}$ and $PM_{2.5}$, respectively. Overall, $PM_{10}$ decreased by about 55 percent from 1986 to 2005 and remained well below NAAQS (the EPA standard). $PM_{2.5}$ only slightly decreased (11.6%) from 1999 to 2005 and remained consistently above NAAQS (EPA 2007).

In comparing the trends for PM to the trends for lead, a few observations merit emphasis. First, the time span for EPA tracking and reporting ambient air concentrations for particulate matter is greatly truncated relative to lead. For example, lead has measures back to the 1950s for Atlanta, whereas the PM measures begin in 1986 for the larger particles and not until 1999 for the smaller particles. Second, while compliance (pollutant measures below the NAAQS levels) has been achieved for lead and $PM_{10}$ but not for $PM_{2.5}$, these trends and comparisons are very difficult to make for PM generally and $PM_{2.5}$, in particular because of the lack of data.

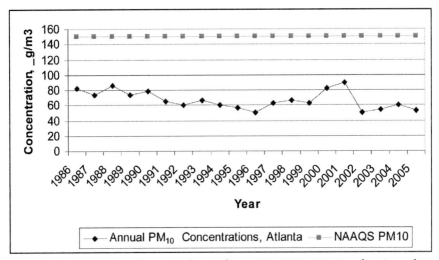

**Figure 5.3.   Annual PM$_{10}$ Concentrations, Atlanta, GA, 1986–2005 Based on Annual 24 Hour 4th Maximum Average**

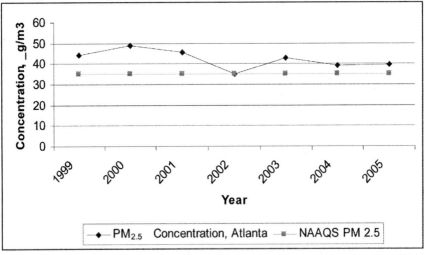

**Figure 5.4.   Annual PM$_{2.5}$ Concentrations, Atlanta, GA, 1999–2005 Based on Annual 24 Hour 4th Maximum Average**

*Ozone*

Ozone (O$_3$) is a gas made up of three oxygen atoms. It is created when volatile organic compounds and nitrogen oxide react with sunlight. The focus here is on ground-level ozone rather than stratospheric ozone.[3] Ground-level ozone can cause health problems, particularly respiratory related, such as asthma, wheezing, and reduced lung capacity. Ongoing exposure can be a serious health concern for some people, causing permanent lung damage. Ground-level ozone is typically a seasonal pollutant (EPA 2006b). Atlanta's ozone levels are highest during the hot summer months (May through September) and when exposed to sunlight. From 1987 to 2005, the ozone concentration fluctuated up and down and had an overall decrease of about 17 percent (figure 5.5). For most of these years, Atlanta's peak ozone concentrations were above the NAAQS (EPA 2007). EPA (2007) records show the fourth-highest ozone levels in years immediately prior to 1987 were generally considerably higher. While the average ozone levels vary somewhat from year-to-year, they fell markedly following the 1986 ozone season.

## Sulfur Dioxide

Sulfur dioxide ($SO_2$) is in all raw materials that contain common metals. It is an air pollutant that is formed when fuel is burned. Most $SO_2$ emissions are derived from electric utilities. $SO_2$ is harmful to humans and the environment when it dissolves in water and interacts with other particles and gases in the air. It can cause serious respiratory problems to humans, and it facilitates the production of acid rain, which can cause considerable damage to plants and water animals (EPA 2006b). In Atlanta, the average annual $SO_2$ concentration dropped dramatically in 1973 and then steadily decreased through 2005 (figure 5.6). After the significant decrease

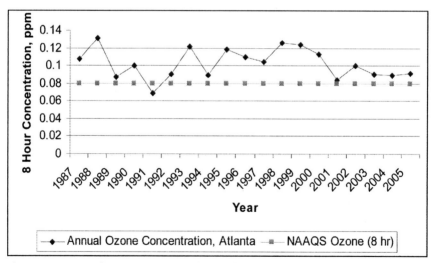

**Figure 5.5. Annual Ozone Concentrations, Atlanta, GA, 1987–2005 Based on Annual 8 Hour 4th Maximum Average**

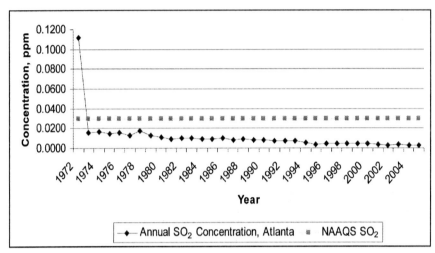

Figure 5.6. Annual $SO_2$ Concentrations, Atlanta, GA, 1972–2005 Based on Annual Averages

in 1973, Atlanta's $SO_2$ concentrations remained below the NAAQS level (EPA 2007).

### Nitrogen Dioxide

Nitrogen dioxide ($NO_2$) is a part of the nitrogen oxide ($NOx$) family of reactive gases that contain various amounts of nitrogen and oxygen. $NO_2$ often creates a reddish-brown layer of air over urban areas and is a component of automobile exhaust fumes. Some of the concerns with $NO_2$ are that it is the primary ingredient in the creation of ground-level ozone, which can lead to respiratory problems in humans; it contributes to the formation of acid rain, water quality deterioration, global warming, and visibility impairment in urban areas. The EPA has developed emission standards to reduce $NO_2$ emitted from motor vehicles and coal-fired electric utilities (EPA 2006b). Figure 5.7 depicts the trends in Atlanta's $NO_2$ levels over the past thirty years (EPA 2007).

### Carbon Monoxide

Carbon monoxide (CO) is the final of the six criteria pollutants regulated by the U.S. EPA. CO is a poisonous gas that is created when carbon is not completely burned in fuel. Nationwide, the EPA estimates that 56 percent of CO emissions come from on-road vehicles, while 22 percent derive from non-road vehicles (e.g., construction equipment, boats). In urban areas, motor vehicles typically account for an even greater share of CO

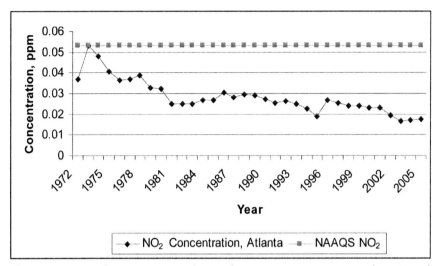

**Figure 5.7.** Annual $NO_2$ Concentrations, Atlanta, GA, 1972–2005 Based on Annual Averages

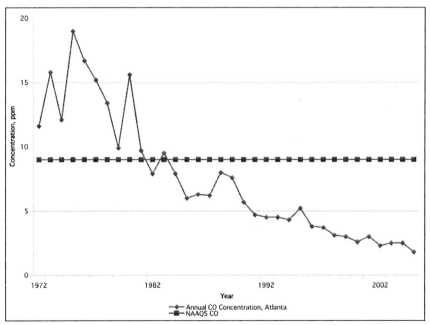

**Figure 5.8.** Annual CO Concentrations, Atlanta, GA, 1972–2005 Based on 8-Hour Second Maximum Annual Averages

emissions. CO emissions also occur from indoor sources, such as furnaces, wood stoves, and fireplaces. CO can have serious health impacts, including cardiovascular effects, central nervous system effects, and respiratory problems (EPA 2006b; 2006d). In Atlanta, CO concentrations have gradually decreased since 1972, falling below the NAAQS level in the early 1980s. Figure 5.8 depicts this trend in concentrations (EPA 2007).

Overall, Atlanta has experienced a downward trend in most air pollutants. Lead decreased significantly between 1971 and 1987 and then remained relatively stable through 2005. $PM_{10}$ decreased overall since 1986, and $PM_{2.5}$ only decreased slightly since 1999. Ozone fell before 1987 and then fluctuated between 1987 and 2005. While there was an overall decrease (17%) in ozone, the concentrations were above the NAAQS for most years. Sulfur dioxide dropped significantly in 1973 and then steadily decreased through 2005. Nitrogen dioxide and carbon monoxide steadily decreased between 1972 and 2005. While air pollution concerns still dominate much of Atlanta's urban environmental policy, specifically with respect to ozone and particulate matter, the recent trends clearly depict improving air quality. Whether these trends hold for Atlanta's future is a topic addressed following a discussion of the relationship between air quality measures and contributing factors (e.g., population, transportation, industry).

## DETERMINANTS OF AIR QUALITY TRENDS

Air quality trends for Atlanta can be assessed by examining trends in potential indicators of air pollution. Air pollution indicators are based on many different factors, such as population, industrial activity, technology developments, vehicle miles traveled, and fuel consumption (EPA 2003). By observing the relationship between these indicators and measured air quality in Atlanta, trends in Atlanta's air quality prior to formal measuring ("backcasting" before 1970) and in air quality after today (forecasting after 2005) can be estimated.

### Population

Atlanta's roots and growth link closely to transportation. The city of Atlanta was founded in 1837 when the railroad was extended into Georgia. Atlanta thrived from the railroad. After Sherman burned Atlanta to the ground in 1864, it was quickly rebuilt. Five years later, its population had doubled its pre-war levels (State of Georgia Secretary of State 2006). Atlanta's population peaked in 1970 (496,973), at which point the population began to drop until 1990 (394,017). There has been a resurgence of its population in the

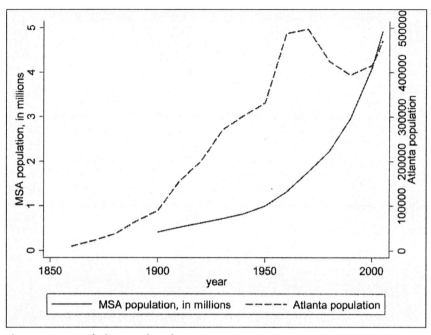

**Figure 5.9.   Population Trends, Atlanta, GA, 1860–2005**

late 1990s and early twenty-first century, reaching about 471,000 in 2005 (U.S. Census Bureau 1998; 2006). Figure 5.9 shows some of the population trends from U.S. Census data. The Metro Atlanta region experienced similar growth, without the decline after the 1970s. After World War II, urban sprawl began to take effect as suburbs began springing up around the city. Today, Metro Atlanta includes 8,376 square miles, has a population of nearly 5 million, and is expected to grow to nearly 6 million by 2015 (Metro Atlanta Chamber of Commerce 2006a). Clearly, better air quality is not correlated with Atlanta's exponential growth in population as we might have expected over the last several decades.

## Industry

Industrial activity is another indicator for identifying air quality trends over time. Metro Atlanta's industrial activity has generally increased along with its population. Some of the world's largest firms began moving their headquarters to Atlanta in the 1970s and 1980s. Today, Metro Atlanta is home to more than 137,000 businesses and serves as the primary hub for transportation and manufacturing in the southeastern United States (Georgia Department of Labor 2005).

Trade, transportation, and utilities (TTU) occupy the largest percentage (22.9%) of the industry sector and currently employ about 23 percent of the workforce (Metro Atlanta Chamber of Commerce 2006b). The transportation industry's large presence in Atlanta dates back to its inception, when the railroad was extended into Georgia and the city of Atlanta was established. Atlanta was dependent on the railroad for economic stability (Preston 1979) and growth (State of Georgia, Secretary of State 2006). The high railway activity in Atlanta indicates that Atlanta was probably exposed to high levels of air pollution from coal emissions as early as the nineteenth century. Railroads were considered a large source of smoke pollution, and communities with railroads had special regulations for emissions (Stern 1982). Today, Atlanta continues to be the largest rail center hub in the South although transportation concerns have shifted away from rail.

In addition to the railroad, Atlanta has significant road and air infrastructure. Atlanta is home to four major interstates for truck and car transport. As early as 1946, Atlanta recognized the importance of highways in maintaining Atlanta's leadership as a commercial transportation center and developed a regional highway transportation plan. The leaders of Atlanta also placed importance on the promotion of the airport (Brookings Institution 2006). Atlanta's airport eventually became the busiest in the world. Today more than 1,200 flights depart per day and more than 85 million passengers travel through the Atlanta airport per year (Metro Atlanta Chamber of Commerce 2006b).

**Figure 5.10.   Manufacturing Employment and Sector Size, Metro Atlanta, 1969–2005**

Manufacturing is another important industrial activity often linked to air quality. Manufacturing is the fifth largest industry sector in Metro Atlanta (Metro Atlanta Chamber of Commerce 2006a). The manufacturing industry grew from 3,513 establishments in 1990 to 4,997 in 2006 (Georgia Department of Labor 2005). Interestingly, employment in the manufacturing industry had the opposite effect—overall, it slightly decreased over the last several decades from about 190,000 employees in 1969 to approximately 185,000 in 2004 (Bureau of Economic Analysis 2006a) [see figure 5.10]. More, smaller establishments are producing increasingly valuable manufacturing output. Although the manufacturing sector in Metro Atlanta is hardly shrinking in raw size (measured in terms of real earnings), its share of total earnings has declined from 22 percent in 1969 to under 8 percent today (BEA 2006b). While industry in general has increased substantially and does not correlate with the air quality trend in Atlanta, employment in manufacturing appears to be somewhat correlated with the downward shift in air quality, which may indicate an increase in technological capabilities.

**Technology**

Technological shifts in energy and transportation can also affect air pollution. Electricity generation is a major source of air pollution (EPA 2004). Coal has traditionally been the primary source of electricity generation, and coal-fired power plants release pollutants into the air. Georgia's first electric company was established in 1883. By 2004, Georgia was home to twelve coal-fired power plants and 63 percent of the electricity was generated by coal (Energy Information Administration 2006). Numerous pollution control technologies have been implemented over the past few decades in the electricity generation industry.

Technological advances in the automobile may also have played a significant role in the air quality of Atlanta. The automobile was one of the primary forces that boosted Atlanta's economy in the early 1900s. The automobile was viewed as the means to bringing prosperity to the South. Between 1909 and 1930, automobile businesses grew from none to twenty-seven. The number of vehicles registered in Fulton County increased 435 percent from 1916 to 1923. During the 1920s, the city began to outgrow the streetcar, and by 1930 the primary source of transportation was the automobile instead of the streetcar. In 1930, 38 percent of Atlanta's commuters used private automobiles for transportation (Preston 1979). With the extensive suburban growth in Atlanta, this rate has continued to grow, and today Metro Atlanta residents utilize the private automobile more than ever. Against this trend in rising automobile use are the changes in automobile technologies, most notably the introduction of the catalytic converters in 1973 and new fuel mixes (e.g., unleaded and reformulated gasolines). These changes in technologies used in transportation appear to have had the most profound impacts on emissions since 1970. As automobile technology has improved over the last several decades, so has the air quality in Atlanta.

### Vehicle Miles Traveled and Congestion

The perception that auto transportation is linked to and even causes air quality problems appears firmly held by the media, interest groups, and the population at large. "Whether they live in urban communities or in the farthest suburban settings, most people in the Atlanta Region agree on the cause-and-effect relationship of these three points: Our air quality is poor, traffic congestion is a critical issue and public transportation is inadequate" (ARC 2004). Air quality and transportation problems are commonly portrayed side-by-side with causality implicit or explicit. Understanding Atlanta's air quality requires an analysis of its traffic.

Atlanta's increase in population, land expansion, and industry led to an increase in the number of miles driven. One popular metric is annual vehicle miles traveled (VMT) [see figure 5.11]. VMT increased by 55 percent between 1990 and 2004 in Fulton County alone.[4] The 3.2 percent annual growth rate for VMT lags somewhat behind Metro Atlanta's 3.4 percent population growth rate over the same time span (Georgia Department of Transportation 2006). Over the past fifty years, the nation experienced a dramatic increase in the number of vehicles per household. For example, only 2.5 percent of U.S. households owned three or more vehicles in 1960 compared with 18 percent in 2000 (U.S. Dept. of Energy, Transportation Energy Data Book). The EPA claims that VMT will continue to rise, and that the VMT growth rate for Atlanta is expected to be 103 percent between 1996 and 2030 (EPA 2006c). This amounts to a 2.1 percent annual growth rate, a substantial drop-off from recent trends.

In addition to VMT, commute times in Atlanta also increased. According to the Census, average commute times in Metro Atlanta grew by 20 percent from 1990 to 2000, compared to a 14 percent growth nationwide. Atlanta now has the highest traffic congestion growth rate (76% between 1993 and 2003) in the country (Metro Atlanta Chamber of Commerce 2006b). It has surpassed large cities such as Denver, Houston, and Dallas. The roads in Atlanta are more congested, and the average number of hours commuters are delayed due to congestion increased by 43 percent between 1993 and 2003 (Metro Atlanta Chamber of Commerce 2006b). Today, Atlanta has more vehicles on the road, more traffic congestion, and longer commutes than ever before, which are frequently touted as indicators of air pollution. Interestingly, however, these rising statistics

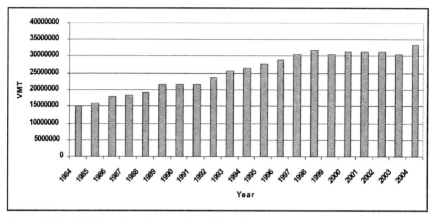

Figure 5.11. VMT Trends, Atlanta, GA, 1984–2004

are vastly different than the downward trends seen in air quality. As discussed in the section on technology, these dramatic differences are likely due to the improvements in automobile technology.

## Climate

The final indicator of air quality is climate. Weather patterns are important determinants of air quality, directly as in the case of ozone (which requires favorable weather conditions for its formation) and indirectly insofar as weather affects emissions (e.g., more air conditioning and driving in the hot summer). Weather plays a crucial role in determining Atlanta's compliance with the Clean Air Act. The temperatures in Atlanta fluctuated from year to year, but have experienced a slight overall increase since 1940 (see figure 5.12). Atlanta experienced its highest recorded average annual temperatures in the 1990s. Warm temperatures are a necessary condition for some air pollutants and, therefore, warming trends could lead to greater amounts of air pollution (Georgia State Climatology Office 2006). The average temperature increased by approximately 5 percent between 1940 and 2003 in Atlanta. However, ozone concentrations, which tend to increase with higher temperatures, slightly decreased since the 1980s.

## Summary of Key Indicators

Population, industrial and manufacturing activity, VMT and congestion, climate, and technology are contributing factors which routinely receive the bulk of regulatory and planning attention. Understanding the determinants of air quality can help one predict or forecast air quality trends.

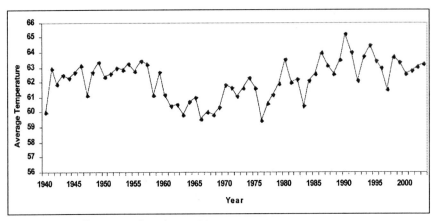

**Figure 5.12.   Climate Trends, Atlanta, GA, 1940–2003**

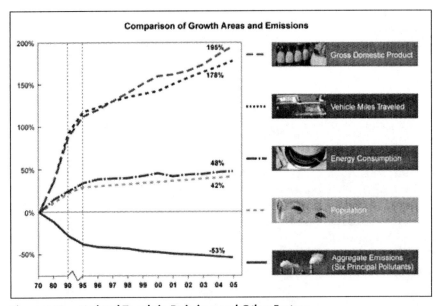

**Figure 5.13.   National Trends in Emissions and Other Factors**

At a national level, the EPA regularly produces reports to tout the efficacy of their efforts. Figure 5.13 reprints a graph from one of the EPA's recent reports (EPA 2006a). While reductions in emissions are not the same as reductions in ambient concentrations, the steady declines over the past twenty-five years suggest some success. This accomplishment occurs alongside fairly steady increases in population, VMT, energy use, and economic activity. Comparable measures for the Atlanta area suggest a similar story by overlaying figures 5.1 to 5.8 on top of figures 5.9 to 5.11.

Clearly, either the simple model used in policy discussions (more cars and people and industry means worsened air quality) does not adequately represent air quality trends. Most likely, the story of Atlanta's air quality history has been dominated by technological shifts. These changes have made the other factors second-order at best. Whether the technologies have been "forced" via regulation (e.g., unleaded gasoline, catalytic converters, smokestack scrubbers) or arisen with macroeconomic shifts (e.g., growth of service- and information-based industries) or something else is unclear from the available data. Moreover, simply examining trends cannot identify the counterfactual or "what would have happened" in the absence of one factor or another. At this point, even after thirty or more years of intensive federal air quality regulation, there are a great many unanswered questions about urban air quality. Yet, estimating future air quality trends is critical to public policy decision makers. In the following section, we discuss these implications and estimate possible future trends using a vector autoregression (VAR) model.

## THE FUTURE OF ATLANTA'S AIR QUALITY

Determining the future of Atlanta's air quality is paramount to public policy makers as they make decisions about the appropriate resource allocations for air quality improvements. The limited direct historical evidence of Atlanta's air quality poses a serious challenge to understanding Atlanta's air pollution problems in a longer context. Furthermore, the inadequacies of conventional measures and models pose enormous problems for identifying the determinants of air quality changes. In particular, the role of the 1970 and 1990 extensions to the Clean Air Act is difficult to determine. While some analysts such as Goklany (1999) go so far as to suggest that air quality was already dramatically improving before the advent of CAA regulations, the case of Atlanta might not permit any bold conclusions. With the exception of lead and TSP, no systematic, direct measures of concentrations of other criteria pollutants are publicly available. Lead levels appear to fall dramatically during the 1970s, consistent with a major influence of the federal regulatory regime. Measures of TSP in Atlanta also exist pre-1970, but visual inspection of the downward trend does not suggest a regime change following the CAA or its 1990 amendments (see endnote 2).

We attempt to estimate the time trends of concentrations of major air pollutants in Atlanta using a vector autoregression (VAR) model.[5] The forecasts from the VAR model take little account of other important trends that might affect pollution levels. They only rely on the time paths of each of the concentration measures. These patterns only implicitly reflect changes in other determinants of air pollution levels. The conventional wisdom and mental models of discussants (as well as many formal air quality models) posit very close relationships between pollution and these measures of economic activity.[6] The relationship is often thought to be quite direct, even if a bit noisy. Holding all else equal, it is commonly expected that ambient concentrations of pollution will rise when population, industrial activity, transportation, and temperatures rise. Yet even casual inspection of the graphs displayed thus far suggests that rising populations, VMT, and industrial activity are not positively related to ambient concentration levels. If anything, they are negatively related to them.[7] As Atlanta has experienced a population and transportation boom since 1970, its air quality has noticeably improved (or, perhaps in the case of ozone, stagnated).

Overall, it does not appear that there is a strong interaction across air pollutants in the VAR model for Atlanta. The VAR model predicts lead, $SO_2$, CO, and NOx levels in the atmosphere to continue to decrease toward zero over the next fifty years. The data range from 1958 to 2005. An example of a resulting forecast of one of the more volatile air quality measures, the fourth highest recorded value of the eight-hour ozone average, is presented in figure 5.14A. For the projected values in years after 2005, a 95 percent confidence interval is also displayed.[8] The forecasted ozone levels stabilize by 2015 to approximately 0.12 ppm, roughly the level experienced in the 1990s.[9] Figure 5.14B depicts similar forecasts for the other pollutants in the VAR model. In these graphs, notice that the projected concentrations are expected to stay below current levels and continue gradual declines.

The casual visual scans of graphs and correlations are inadequate to form predictions of what might be a much more complex system. It is possible that there is no relation between the economic indicators and the air quality measures. But it is also possible that the relationship appears in more subtle ways. For instance, a steady decline in ambient pollutant levels associated with the passage of time (perhaps because of technological innovation or regulation) might well fade over time and be overcome by the effects of population, VMT, or some other determinant experiencing rapid growth.

Measuring air quality is not a simple matter in the best circumstances. Air quality may vary substantially over space. The airshed in Atlanta is quite large, and a single "air quality index" value might not do well to describe the air quality in the area. Air quality can also vary widely over time, whether time is measured in hours or in months. The graphs above depict variation at an annual level, but they obscure important and dra-

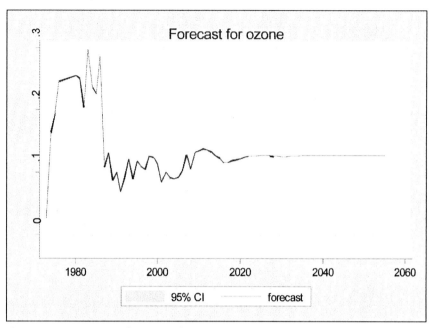

**Figure 5.14A.  Forecast for Ozone from VAR**

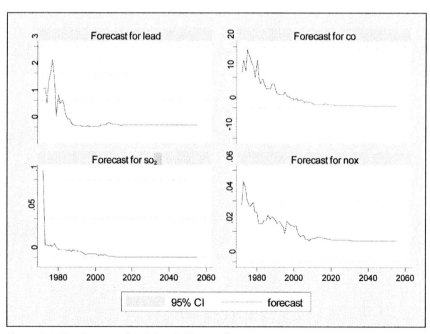

**Figure 5.14B.  Forecast for Other Pollutants from VAR**

matic variations at smaller time scales. Ozone levels, for instance, fluctuate dramatically over the course of a day, can vary widely from day to day, and certainly have important seasonal fluctuations as well. Air quality is also multidimensional with respect to the many chemicals that constitute the ground-level atmosphere. Atlanta may be relatively clean with respect to some pollutants, like lead, but remains polluted with respect to others, like $PM_{2.5}$, ozone, or even airborne carcinogens.[10] Measuring air quality, across the many dimensions of time, space, and chemicals, poses an enormous practical challenge to any agency tasked with monitoring it. It may be little wonder that the data that do exist suffer from coding errors and other possible outliers (e.g., the average and maximum $SO_2$ levels fell six-fold from 1972 to 1973).

The lack of data has not slowed the debate over the Clean Air Act, its implementation, and its subsequent reforms. Some might argue that this uncertainty fuels the debate. Much of the policy debate has featured advocates on all sides reaching conclusions about empirical questions (e.g., Is the air cleaner today? Is it cleaner than it would have otherwise been?) even when evidence does not exist. Most importantly, perhaps, the impressions of many Atlantans may not be well grounded in evidence such as that portrayed above. For whatever reasons, Atlantans tend to perceive major air quality concerns in the city, appear to possess mental models that link more transportation to worsening air quality, and feel confident that population and VMTs are rising in the area. Many interest groups and media outlets reinforce these relationships. Little effort is spent exploring these relationships, however. Those who admit Atlanta's air quality has improved often immediately follow the acknowledgement with a plea to do more.

## WHERE DO WE GO FROM HERE?

Overall, the story of Atlanta's air quality is dynamic and, thus far, promising. Despite powerful growth trends in most of the major urban air pollution indicators, Atlanta has experienced little deterioration and, in most instances, great advances in quality. Recent history has seen major improvements in many air pollution levels. This has occurred against a backdrop of growing population, rising VMT, and growing manufacturing and construction sectors.

Considering the weak relationships between prominent determinants of air quality and ambient concentrations in Atlanta, forecasting air quality for more than a few years is a difficult task. Without the benefit of hindsight, someone standing in downtown Atlanta in 1950 would have been hard-pressed to imagine what the next fifty years would bring to the metropolitan area in terms of population, traffic, and air pollution. The trends in ambient air quality do share common features across pollutants. As the time series stretches on, the ambient concentrations do tend to consistently fall to a low, background level. This much has been seen in lead, $SO_2$, CO, and possibly even $NO_2$. In the cases of ozone and perhaps $NO_2$, further declines may be both feasible and likely. Other criteria pollutants, like particulate matter, may experience similar trends, although data are severely lacking at this point. This is not to say that such trends are inevitable or "natural" in the sense that they will arise without costly, concerted effort. Accomplishing similar improvements in other pollutants, and maintaining the trends to date, may require a great deal. All that our analysis shows is a common historical trend. This may give reasons for environmental optimism or continued regulation of growth. Most of all, it should suggest that broadly speaking air quality has improved for certain pollutants and similar achievements may be possible for others. Unfortunately, however, the decrease toward a background level of a pollutant also suggests that additional future gains may be hard or impossible to come by. Crudely put, future air quality may easily worsen if for no other reason than it cannot get any better.

These results point to technology and policy as playing a dominant role in the air quality system. To date, far too little effort has gone into understanding how (technology and policy) innovation responds to environmental and economic dynamics, and vice versa. The shortcomings of the conventional predictions (more traffic, population, construction leads to worsening air quality) reflect this "partial" modeling of the situation. Understanding the innovation and diffusion of new technologies that impact air quality is no small feat, and predicting it is still tougher. Regulations can favor certain technologies, with both positive and negative impacts on air quality. A holistic approach to the air quality system appreciates the complex interactions between technology, policy, economics, and the environment. Just as one affects the other, those changes are likely to feedback and influence the other aspects of the system.

The rest of the system remains a mystery—one for political debate and opportunism. Lacking the ability to forecast air quality with much confidence, we might be content in knowing that the sky is neither falling nor pristine. Our air quality fate is likely to be determined by the winds of change that blow elsewhere. This may take the form of larger technological innovations (perhaps induced by policy, perhaps by continuing deindustrialization) that are difficult to foresee by just looking at air quality monitoring stations and regional planning documents. While we have made tremendous progress in improving air quality over the last several decades, important gaps remain in our understanding of the system that generates that air quality. It seems we understand least the most salient determinants of air quality. In the coming decades, Atlanta faces a formidable task in filling in those knowledge gaps and achieving additional improvements. If the past three decades are any guide, there is cause for guarded optimism.

## NOTES

1. Perhaps the earliest evidence of air pollution was written in poems and letters by classical writers living in overcrowded ancient cities. In ancient Rome, Seneca, Emperor Nero's tutor, wrote in a letter to Lucilius that he left Rome due to the "oppressive fumes and culinary odours" (Brimblecombe, 1987).

2. The lead values between the years 1959–1962 were unavailable. The average of 1958 and 1963 were used for these years.

3. "Good" ozone rests 10–30 miles above ground in the stratosphere, and "bad" ozone is at ground level (EPA, 2006).

4. Fulton County encompasses the majority of the city of Atlanta.

5. The basic VAR model describes the path of a variable, like lead concentration measures in Atlanta, over time as a linear combination of its historical values. The estimation here employs three lags of each endogenous variable. We estimate the VAR model for a system of air pollution measures, where each of the five ambient measures (ozone, lead, CO, $SO_2$, NOx) depends on the first three lagged values of the other four ambient concentration measures. With the system parameters estimated, forecasts can be made based on the historical time path and interactions across air pollutants. The VAR estimation makes adjustments for the small sample nature of the data, which is of use in estimating confidence intervals around forecasts.

6. Even the simple heuristic common to environmental studies of I=PAT (where I=impact, P=population, A=affluence, and T=technology) supports the intuition that as Atlanta's population, affluence, and use of emitting technologies increases, its air will become more polluted. Obviously, a key variable in this relationship is technology, which has changed dramatically over time.

7. Glancing at the pairwise correlations between ambient concentrations of the six criteria pollutants and economic measures (population, real per capita earnings, real manufacturing earnings, real transportation earnings, and average temperatures) confirms this. Each of the pollution levels has a negative and statistically significant correlation (at a 5% level) with each of the economic variables; the only exception being $PM_{10}$, which lacks sufficient observations. Many of these correlations are quite strong, and all are negative. The same set of pairwise correlations, when examined in first-differences, exhibits no significant correlations. Annual changes in ambient concentrations, up or down, appear uncorrelated with annual changes in the economic indicators. This suggests that the air quality and economic variables may be structurally unrelated, but both enjoy their own independent (and opposite) trends. Interestingly, this pattern also holds for the pairwise correlations between the changes in concentrations and the changes in economic indicators in the preceding year. One exception to this arises for NOx,

where NOx levels tend to rise in the year following increases in income and manufacturing and decreases in temperatures.

8. These 95% confidence intervals (CI) represent the range of values that the future concentrations of ozone (or other pollutant) are 95% likely to fall within. A small confidence interval indicates greater reliability in the results than a large confidence interval. Even when the models for air pollutants in Atlanta exhibit large confidence intervals, indicating low forecast precision, only in the case of ozone does the 95% confidence interval include the NAAQS.

9. Including $PM_{10}$ measures into the VAR system does little to change the results presented here. The forecasted levels of $PM_{10}$ resemble the predicted pattern for ozone, stabilizing at a level near 2001 levels.

10. This analysis has focused on the criteria air pollutants. These chemicals fall under a separate regulatory category from air toxics, or cancer-causing chemicals. These air toxics might pose some of the greatest threats to public health, although they are only more recently receiving much attention. For the purposes of this paper, however, it should suffice to note that trends in air toxics in Atlanta have roughly followed similar patterns to criteria pollutants like $SO_2$.

## REFERENCES

ARC (Atlanta Regional Commission). *RDP Technical Report– 2004 Update*. 2004. www.atlantaregional.com/cps/rde/xbcr/arc/rdp_Ch3_Natural_Resources.pdf.

Bureau of Economic Analysis. CA25 - Total full-time and part-time employment by SIC industry. 2006a. www.bea.gov/regional/reis/action.cfm.

———. CA05 - Personal income by major source and earnings by SIC industry. 2006b. www.bea.gov/regional/reis/action.cfm.

Bowler, C. and P. Brimblecombe (1992). Archives and air pollution history. *Journal of the Society of Archivists* 13, no. 2 (1992): 136.

Brimblecombe, P. Attitudes and responses towards air pollution in Medieval England. *Journal of Air Pollution Control Association* 26, no. 10 (1976): 941–5.

———. *The Big Smoke: A History of Air Pollution in London since Medieval Times.* Methuen: London, 1987.

Brookings Institution. Moving Beyond Sprawl: The Challenge for Metropolitan Atlanta. 2006. www.brookings.edu/es/urban/atlanta/lessons.htm.

Census, B. O. T. No. HS-28. National Air Pollutant Emissions: 1900 to 2000. www.census.gov/statab/hist/HS-28.pdf.

CVIOG (Carl Vinson Institute of Government). "Report on the Public Opinion Research for the Atlanta Regional Commission's 'Platforms for Progress' Project." (December, 2002).

Energy Information Administration. Georgia Electricity Profile. 2006. www.eia.doe.gov/cneaf/electricity/st_profiles/georgia.html.

Georgia Department of Labor. Georgia Labor Market Explorer: Historical Data. 2005. explorer.dol.state.ga.us/mis/historical.htm.

Georgia Department of Transportation. *Office of Transportation Data: Georgia's Roadway Mileage and Characteristics Reports (400 Series Reports)*. 2006. www.dot.state.ga.us/DOT/.

Georgia State Climatology Office. *Historical Climate Data and Summaries*. 2006. climate.engr.uga.edu/historic.html.

Goklany, I. M. *Clearing the Air: The Real Story of the War on Air Pollution*. Washington, D.C.: Cato Institute, 1999.

Metro Atlanta Chamber of Commerce. A Look at Atlanta: An Executive Profile. 2006a. www.metroatlantachamber.com/macoc/business/img/alookatatlanta.pdf.

———. Metro Atlanta Chamber of Commerce: Transportation Briefing. 2006b. www.metroatlantachamber.com/macoc/initiatives/img/transbrief.ppt.

Preston, H. L. *Automobile Age Atlanta: The Making of a Southern Metropolis, 1900–1935*. Athens: University of Georgia Press, 1979.

Sabatier, P. An Advocacy Coalition Framework of Policy Change and the Role of Policy-Oriented Learning Therein. *Policy Sciences* 21 (1988): 129–68.

State of Georgia, Secretary of State. *History of Atlanta*. www.sos.state.ga.us/tours/html/atlanta_history.html.

Stern, A. C. History of Air Pollution Legislation in the United States. *Journal of the Air Pollution Control Association* 32, no. 1 (1982): 44.

U.S. Congress. *Bureau of Economic Analysis: Regional Economic Accounts*. 2006. bea.gov/bea/regional/reis/.

U.S. Department of Energy. *Energy Information Administration: Official Energy Statistics from the U. S. Government*. 2006. www.eia.doc.gov/.

U.S. Census Bureau. *Population of the 100 Largest Cities and Other Urban Places in the United States: 1790 to 1990*. 1998. www.census.gov/population/www/documentation/twps0027.html.

———. *U.S. Census Bureau Fact Finder*. 2006. factfinder.census.gov/.

U.S. EPA. *Air Info Now. What is Particulate Matter?* U.S. Environmental Protection Agency. 2008. www.airinfonow.com/html/ed_particulate.html.

———. *Air Quality System*. U.S. Environmental Protection Agency. 2007. www.epa.gov/ttn/airs/airsaqs/.

———. *National Ambient Air Quality Standards*. U.S. Environmental Protection Agency. 2006a. www.epa.gov/air/criteria.html.

———. *What are the Six Common Air Pollutant?* U.S. Environmental Protection Agency. 2006b. www.epa.gov/air/urbanair/6poll.html.

———. *VMT Growth Factors (%) by County*. U.S. Environmental Protection Agency. 2006c. www.epa.gov/ttn/naaqs/ozone/areas/sitemap/vmtgagf.htm.

———. *The Inside Story: A Guide to Indoor Air Quality*. U.S. Environmental Protection Agency. 2006d. www.epa.gov/iaq/pubs/insidest.html

———. *Air Emissions Trends— Continued Progress through 2005*. U.S. Environmental Protection Agency. 2006e. www.epa.gov/airtrends/econ-emissions.html.

———. *Approval and Promulgation of Implementation Plans Georgia: Vehicle Miles Traveled State Implementation Plan for the Atlanta 1-Hour Ozone Nonattainment Area*. U.S. Environmental Protection Agency. 2005. www.epa.gov/fedrgstr/EPA-AIR/2005/April/Day-12/a7333.htm.

———. *Air Emissions Trends— Continued Progress Through 2004*. U.S. Environmental Protection Agency. 2005. www.epa.gov/air/airtrends/2005/econ-emissions.html.

———. *The Particle Pollution Report: Current Understanding of Air Quality and Emissions through 2003*. U.S. Environmental Protection Agency. 2004. www.epa.gov/

air/airtrends/aqtrnd04/pmreport03/pmlooktrends_2405.pdf#page=1.

———. *National Air Quality and Emissions Trends Report, 2003 Special Studies Edition*. U.S. Environmental Protection Agency. 2003.

———. *1994 Air Quality Trends Summary Report*. U.S. Environmental Protection Agency. 1994.

———. *EPA Sets National Air Quality Standards*. EPA Press Release. 1971. www.epa.gov/history.

# Chapter 6

# Transportation Issues and Opportunities Facing the City of Atlanta

## *Truman A. Hartshorn*

Transportation has always been Atlanta's lifeline, and Achilles heel. Indeed, transportation is the reason for its very existence and contemporary media reports remind us that mobility (and congestion) constitutes the number one public policy issue in the region. The city painfully experienced a gridlock event illustrating this problem one morning in late January 2007 when several major events attracted over 50,000 out-of-town delegates (mainly by automobile) during the busy morning rush hour, creating a chaotic commute both for them and for downtown workers.

In this chapter we discuss the transportation roots underlying the growth of Atlanta and examine issues and future prospects for the city. Transportation facilities drove both the magnitude of growth in Atlanta and the shape and density of development. Notwithstanding the early imprint of the rail and trolley lines on the landscape, the automobile primarily shaped both the city of Atlanta and the region over the years. Historically, the city remained small and compact in pre-automobile days, only reaching a population of 100,000 as recently as 1900. A small physical imprint continued to characterize the city even as the region exploded its population and areal extent. The city now accounts for less than 10 percent of the region's population. The last annexation of land to the city of Atlanta occurred in 1952 just as the post-World War II growth spurt overtook the region. Today, over 4.5 million of the 5 million residents of the region live outside the city.

The transportation system that evolved as a result of the evolving planning process in the post World War II era will be discussed here in three phases following a discussion of the early transportation imprint. Each of the phases will be discussed in the context of the issues and opportunities they presented to the city of Atlanta. A discussion of the transportation options and priorities facing the city of Atlanta today in terms of both planning and policy will also provide a lens with which to assess future prospects.

## TRANSPORTATION CONNECTION ORIGINS: PRE-1945

Beginning in 1837 when engineer Charles Long drove the stake establishing the southern terminus of the Western and Atlantic railroad built by the state of Georgia to connect with Chattanooga, the seed for a future city sprouted. Soon a transportation hub emerged as several rail lines converged on the fledgling frontier town, unleashing a massive growth spurt. The imprint of the original rail lines remains to this day as an important land use feature and perhaps a renewed force if the yet to be realized but oft-promised commuter rail network unfolds along this historical radial alignment.

The trolley network that evolved in the late nineteenth century and early twentieth century democratized transportation with its cheap 5-cent ride and generated burgeoning first-ring suburbs ringing the city in the early 1900s. First, the Victorian communities, such as West End and Inman Park and later, the bungalow neighborhoods, including North Boulevard Park and Grant Park fleshed out an ever-broader residential footprint for the city. Indeed, off-street parking for the automobile in these areas, now considered in-town communities, emerged as a major issue as these areas later adapted to the automobile culture.

The pioneering rail and trolley transportation lines that focused on downtown remained the major forces in shaping the spatial structure of Atlanta through the post-World War II years. Indeed, the automobile came into wide use by the 1920s but not in the way we now use it. In the early twentieth century the car primarily served as a toy of the rich, and, mainly for recreational purposes. The first automobile dealers in the city clustered downtown on West Peachtree Street to cater to the wealthy families living on large estates in the area now called Midtown. The last of these dealerships remained active through the 1970s and the final vestiges of car sales facilities only disappeared in the last decade. The former site of Hix Green Buick dealership at North Avenue became part of the Allen Plaza redevelopment in the mid-2000s and the Beaudry Ford location on Piedmont Avenue, a mid-rise housing complex for Georgia State University in 2007.

Indeed, Atlantans' became early adopters of the automobile. The first automobile show held outside New York City came here as early as 1913. But the car at that time was not generally used for the journey to work and did not become a major city shaper until after World War II. At first the automobile functioned as a "feeder" mode in the sense that it served as a "station wagon" used to shuttle workers to train stops and trolley lines. The automobile allowed urban development to fill in areas between the radial rail lines and encouraged the growth of a wealthy estate community in Buckhead and middle and upper middle class communities in Druid Hills and Ansley Park in the first one-third of the twentieth century. The first structured parking deck for automobiles did not rise downtown until the 1930s.

An elaborate system of elevated street viaducts bridged over the rails in the downtown area in the 1920s and 1930s to accommodate automobile and trolley traffic. These viaducts remain a mixed blessing, on the one hand facilitating vehicular movement and creating the space for parking and entertainment venues such as the Underground Atlanta festival center beneath elevated streets, but they are now old and in constant need of maintenance. The disruption of traffic on Peachtree Street at Five Points in 2006 and 2007 as one viaduct was replaced reminds us of this dilemma. A few viaducts received needed repairs or replacement over a decade ago in connection with the infrastructure improvements associated with the 1996 Summer Olympic Games, but much more work remains.

## ALL ROADS LEAD DOWNTOWN: 1945–1975

Early transportation planning documents such as the 1929 Atlanta Traffic Survey, Mayors Traffic Commission (1929), the Beeler Report (1924), and the Lochner Report (1946) all grappled with accommodating growth and the automobile. The rail and trolley system received attention as well. For example, the Lochner Report, fresh on the heals of the tremendous flows of rail passengers in and out of the city during World War II, called for a massive new rail passenger depot as well as offering a blueprint for the future freeway network for the city and region (figure 6.1).

The one thing all early transportation planning documents in Atlanta had in common was that they focused on the downtown area, a trend that continued well into the 1970s. The old adage that "all roads lead downtown" served as the dominant principle well into the 1950s and 1960s, guiding the philosophy of creating more highway gateway capacity on arterial streets and the alignment of the legs of the emerging interstate highway network to promote downtown access.

The expanding radial network of the Interstate highway system in the 1960s and 1970s closely paralleled the pattern the railroads developed a century earlier. The interstate routes greatly enhanced the capacity of the highway system and primarily focused on bringing workers into the city at a time when residences began to rapidly decentralize. The downtown

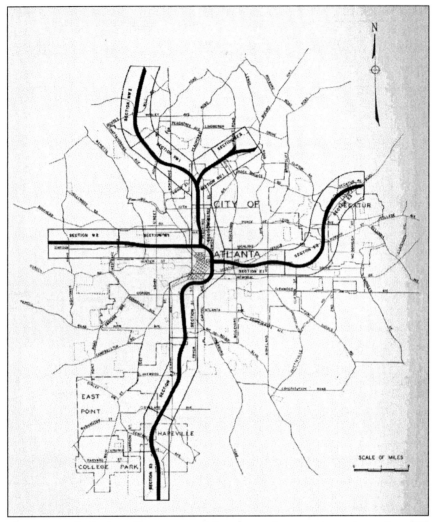

Figure 6.1. The Lochner Report map of the proposed expressway system released in 1946 became the model for the construction of the interstate highway network in Atlanta in the 1950s. Note the two north side legs that became I–75 and I–85 and single spine through the downtown area, becoming I–75/I–85 downtown connector.

in the 1960s remained the dominant work center in the region and planners envisioned a future doubling of employment in the greater downtown, referred to as the central area. The rail cordon boundary of that area is referred to as the Beltline today and will be discussed in a later section. Projections in the 1970s indicated that the massive growth of central area employment would in turn require even more freeway capacity than that offered by the original six legs of the Interstate highway system, as well as new arterial highway access.

A closer examination of the transportation planning process in Atlanta in the 1960s, and the future projections for subarea population and employment growth developed at the time, revealed that the decentralization of activity already underway undermined the growth projections. In a short time, powerful decentralization forces literally turned the region inside out. In addition to residential decentralization which the interstate system promoted, an unparalleled and unanticipated employment decentralization also occurred. Indeed, the interstates became two way streets, not just avenues to bring employees into the city but also conduits for employers to move out as well. To be sure, a large share of suburban growth in employment represented new jobs created in the region made possible by the growing role of Atlanta in the regional economy, but downtown breakaways became an important trend as well.

In the latter half of the 1960s and in the 1970s, the population and employment levels in the central area and in the city of Atlanta began to plateau even as suburban expansion accelerated. As it turns out, the earlier global projections concerning the overall growth of the Atlanta region were very accurate, while the small area forecasts as to where this growth would occur were seriously flawed (Hamer and Hartshorn 1974). To better understand the thinking of planners in the 1950s when downtown employment dramatically expanded, let us look more closely at the planning documents and guiding planning philosophy at the dawn of the freeway era.

The original interstate network consisted of twenty-eight lanes and a six-lane downtown connector (figure 6.2). The clamor for even more freeway capacity began almost immediately with a series of reports released by the regional planning agency created in 1947. The first report, "Access to Central Atlanta," Expressway Policy Study Report Number One, sounded the alarm in April 1959 (Atlanta Region Metropolitan Planning Commission April 1959). The report recommended an intermediate loop expressway around the downtown area (figure 6.3), a one-way downtown street plan, and the widening of several major streets to create an arterial network.

A second report, issued in June 1959, "Crosstown and By-Pass Expressways," expanded the scope of concern by citing the potential for a total breakdown of the downtown connector during peak hour use based on expected traffic increases (Atlanta Region Metropolitan Planning Commission June 1959). The problem arose due to the expected rapid growth of downtown employment which would generate unmanageable increases of trips into central Atlanta.

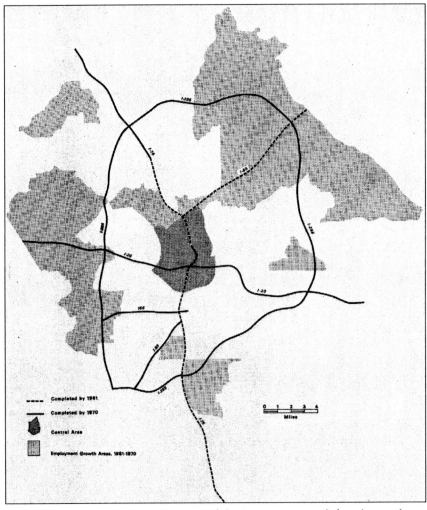

Figure 6.2. The north/south radial arms of the Interstate network focusing on downtown, I–75 and I–85, were the first sections of the Interstate highway network in Atlanta, built by 1961. The perimeter highway, I-285, was completed by 1969. Note the locations of the major employment growth areas in the 1960s in the suburbs, outside I–285.

According to ARMPC, even a close-in by-pass loop expressway, which was never built, would have decreased only slightly the astronomical number of expressway lanes "needed" to preserve stable flow conditions in and out of central Atlanta in 1970. Thus the downtown connector, with an alleged "deficit" of ten lanes in 1958, was to "need" roughly thirty

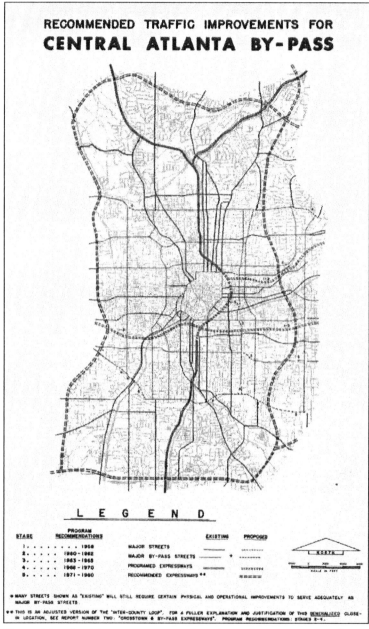

Figure 6.3. A 1959 report proposed an inner loop expressway bypass around downtown that was never constructed. The one-way downtown street pattern and the widening of several "by-pass" streets to create an arterial network also proposed in the study did materialize.

lanes (with a close-in bypass loop) or more than forty lanes (without the loop) in 1970. In fact, the estimates were accompanied by a warning that 128 expressway lanes radiating to and from central Atlanta, along with as many as forty-six lanes in the connector, would be the minimum required to service peak hour travel in 1970 (Hamer and Hartshorn 1971, 291–292).

An important document that became a cornerstone for transportation planning purposes in Atlanta for the next two decades, *"Facts and Forecasts 61/83,"* deserves special consideration (Atlanta Region Metropolitan Planning Commission 1969). The population and employment projections in the report were completed by consultants in the mid-1960s as inputs to the *Atlanta Area Transportation Study,* the long range planning program at ARMPC, and for the use of the Metropolitan Atlanta Rapid Transit Authority (MARTA) (State Highway Department of Georgia 1967). Planners chose the 1961 base year to coincide with the timing of the origin and destination surveys conducted by the State Highway Department tabulated for 700 small area units. The horizon year of 1983 represented the projected year that the region would reach a population of two million persons. In retrospect, the global forecasts of future growth were quite accurate but the small area forecasts were not. Virtually all new white collar office employment in Atlanta between 1961 and 1983 was forecast to occur Downtown, with some job increases in outlying municipalities such as Decatur, East Point, Buckhead, and Marietta.

A coalition of Downtown business interests led by Central Atlanta Progress with the backing of city officials produced the *Central Atlanta: Opportunities and Responses* document in 1971 (Central Atlanta Progress 1971). The central area also roughly corresponds to the pre-1952 Atlanta city limits (figure 6.2). While never adopted as an official report this study became an important planning document in justifying massive new freeway capacity for the city, a rail system, greater gateway capacity into the downtown area on major arterials, the development of parking reservoirs to intercept downtown-bound traffic on its margins, and the decking of Peachtree Street to create a pedestrian promenade above a transit corridor (figure 6.4). This report continued to endorse the earlier *Facts and Forecasts 61/83* figures that anticipated a near doubling of central area employment from 1960–1983 and a continuation of the rapid growth trajectory through 1995.

By 1970, actual employment figures released by ARMPC noted a dramatic tapering off of growth in the Downtown and central area, due to ongoing suburbanization of office and retail employment. The downtown in fact added only 7,000 jobs in the decade (Hamer and Hartshorn 1971, 296). Nevertheless, transportation consultants used the projections in the report to justify the addition of nearly twice the existing highway capacity to handle future growth.

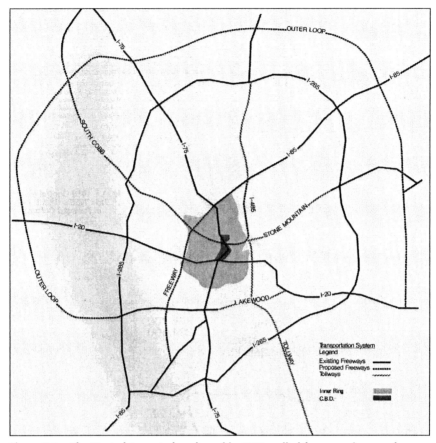

Figure 6.4. The Central Area study, released in 1971, called for a massive new freeway and tollway construction program. Citizen opposition led to the cancellation of several of the proposed routes through the city including the I-485 tollway through the Morningside neighborhood, the Stone Mountain tollway, and the Lakewood tollway to the east. On the Westside, the I-85 freeway extension and the South Cobb freeway were also canceled. The proposed outer loop expressway was defeated in the 1990s.

Planners for the MARTA rail system also used the 61/83 projections to justify the need for the rail network by extending the forecasts forward to 1995. The earlier projections also assumed that a rail system would be in place by 1983 to assist in the movement of employees in the Downtown area using the proposed 62-mile system proposed in 1962 as a framework. MARTA-enabling legislation passed the state legislature in 1965, creating a five-county transit district.

The MARTA Board submitted to voters a referendum for approval to construct of a pared-down 40-mile rail system in the fall of 1968. The public did not see the rail plan until two months before the election and had no say in its development. Cobb County residents did not vote on the proposal as they had already determined that they did not want to be a part of the rail system. Not surprisingly, a cross section of community interests questioned the plan. The proposed rail network did not include a tie-in with the privately held Atlanta Transit System that provided city bus service. The board chose an unpopular property tax levy to finance construction. As a result of this poor planning, a coalition of middle class, African-American, and largely redneck white conservative opposition led by racist leader Lester Maddox, coalesced to defeat the proposition.

As the MARTA Board regrouped from the stinging rejection of its plan, additional studies led to the development of other options. The Voorhees transportation consulting firm released a draft plan for a transit system for Atlanta in 1969 (A. Voorhees and Associates 1969). That study placed emphasis on busways for the region due to the extent of low density residential areas that would not likely generate needed ridership levels to justify rail transit. A 10-mile north/south rail spine in the Peachtree Street corridor in the highest density corridor of the region was to have rail service and a 54-mile busway network would serve other corridors. The Voorhees draft study was not well received by local officials and the final report, issued in 1971, reversed itself, noting the high costs of busways in separate rights-of-ways and the comparable service levels offered by buses and rail such that a predominantly rail-based system would be preferable.

The recommended transit system unveiled in the final Voorhees report included 14 miles of feeder busways in addition to fifty-seven miles of rail transit (figure 6.5). The MARTA Board returned to the taxpayers to seek approval of this system in the fall of 1971. This time the proposal called for a one cent sales tax to finance the local share of construction costs. MARTA would also purchase the private bus system and integrate it into the network, and fares would be reduced to fifteen cents. The referendum passed in the city of Atlanta, Fulton County, and DeKalb County. It was defeated in Clayton and Gwinnett counties.

A buzz of enthusiasm and optimism engulfed the community in the early 1970s in anticipation that the new MARTA bus and rail system might be able to solve many of Atlanta's traffic woes as the new busses hit the streets and rail construction began. But the forces of decentralization were already deeply entrenched, driven by the automobile. Moreover, it would be nearly a decade later before the rails would open, and then only on a phased basis. Given these trends it is not surprising that MARTA never did establish a leadership role in shaping growth nor help deliver on the promise of establishing large gains in downtown employment.

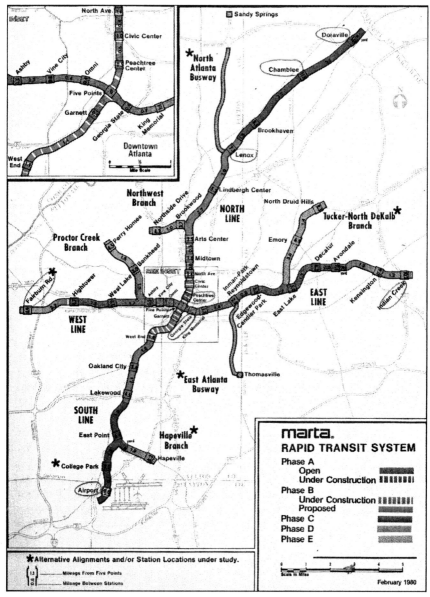

Figure 6.5.   The MARTA rail and bus network approved by voters in Fulton and DeKalb Counties in 1971 included a fifty-seven-mile network of heavy rail on north/south and east/west routes crisscrossing in the downtown.  In addition, fourteen miles of busways were proposed in three feeder corridors.  None of the busways were constructed, but the North Atlanta busway route later morphed into the north rail line aligned in the median of the Georgia 400 tollroad that opened in this corridor.

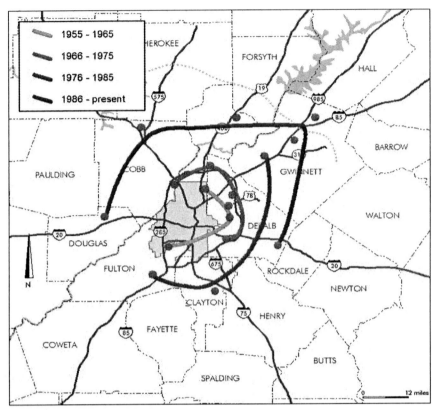

Figure 6.6. The four-stage interceptor ring model of regional mall development in Atlanta portrays the sequential development of shopping centers from the city outward. The inner ring, 1955–1965, reflects the expansion of malls into DeKalb County. The next ring, 1966–1975, roughly approximates the route of the I–285 perimeter highway. The third (1976–1985) and fourth (1986–present) rings show the expansion of malls into the outer suburbs.

## FREEWAYS (AND TRANSIT) AS TWO-WAY STREETS: 1976–1989

The suburbanization of all activities—residential, retail, office, and industrial—accelerated in the 1970s. By 1972, regional malls had sprouted at key northside intersections of the I–285 beltway at Ashford Dunwoody Rd. (Perimeter Mall), and Northside Dr./Cobb Parkway (Cumberland Mall) (figure 6.6). Office parks also gravitated to radial expressway legs and the I–285 circumferential highway (figure 6.7). In the mid-1970s the suburbs reached parity with the city of Atlanta in employment shares and became increasingly independent as centers of growth. In short, the truck/auto/freeway trilogy associated with the interstate and arterial

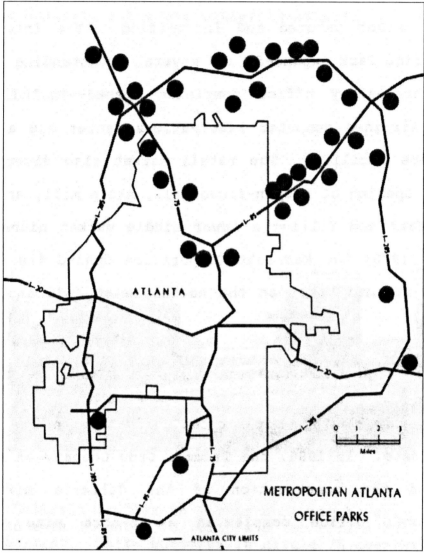

Figure 6.7. The pattern of office parks in Atlanta revealed in this 1970 map shows the close correspondence of their locations along the radial freeways and the I–285 perimeter highway. Note the paucity of office parks on the Southside.

highway network turned the city inside out. No longer did highways only carry workers to the city of Atlanta to work, as they became two way streets in the sense that they allowed employers to expand operations outside the city in the burgeoning suburbs. Reflecting these decentralization trends, crosstown suburb-to-suburb commuting and reverse commuting from the city outward increased.

The city began losing population during this time and the downtown struggled to maintain its employment level at 100,000. Still the leading work center in the region, the downtown had to find new functions to replace lost jobs and maintain its supremacy. Long gone were the days when the central area would double in growth, but projects on the books continued to add capacity to radial corridors serving downtown. The "Freeing the Freeways" program initiated by the State Department of Transportation involved adding lanes to the existing expressway network in the late 1980s. MARTA radial rail service to downtown began on the east line in 1979.

To be sure, the downtown found new roles to replace many jobs lost in this era, showing its adaptability and resilience. The hotel and convention industry provided most of the magic in generating new downtown employment to partially offset lost office and retail employment. The Peachtree Center area at the northern end of downtown benefited the most from the expansion of the hospitality industry even as the Five Points area, the original city hub, languished. For a time Underground Atlanta offered a promising downtown entertainment venue but it closed in 1979. The New Underground Atlanta opened again a decade later but never lived up to its potential.

Transportation planning by necessity adopted a more pluralistic regional approach in the 1980s, more realistically reflecting emerging trends. The Atlanta Region Metropolitan Planning Commission (ARMPC), predecessor planning agency to the Atlanta Regional Commission (ARC), acknowledged the emergence of a major activity center unfolding in Perimeter Center and Buckhead as early as 1968, but did not adopt its first Regional Development Plan until 1975.

The 1985 comprehensive update of the regional plan accurately portrayed regional growth. At that time office buildings and hotels began to ring suburban malls and the foundation for suburban downtowns began to unfold (Hartshorn and Muller 1989). Soon these centers, also known as edge cities, developed their own skylines and offered the same range of functions as the original downtown, if in a more dispersed setting oriented to the automobile rather than to the pedestrian. These edge cities at first only included Buckhead, Perimeter Center, and Cumberland, but by the 1990s were joined by a burgeoning urban center in the Roswell/Alpharetta area in north Fulton County (figure 6.8).

Reflecting the prevailing pattern of employment growth on the north side of the region, these new downtowns all developed within a wedge-shaped area between the I–75 and I–85 highway corridors. Often referred to as the "favored quarter," this area includes Buckhead and the three suburban northside edge cities (Leinberger 1995). While edge city employment grew steadily until 2000, it dropped after 9/11 and by 2005 had not regained the 2000 level, but growth soon returned only to be thwarted again at the end of the decade as the grip of the global recession intensified (table 6.1).

The emergence of these edge cities transformed the Atlanta region from a monocentric city focused on the downtown into a polycentric

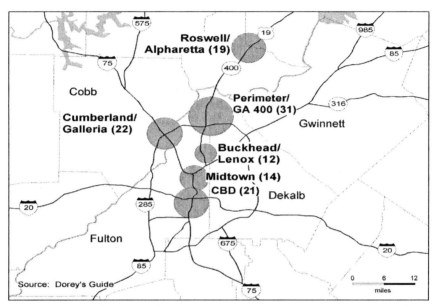

Figure 6.8. The relative size of the suburban downtowns or edge cities are shown here based on millions of square feet of office space, shown in parentheses, in relation to the three urban cores in the city of Atlanta: the central business district (CBD), Midtown, and Buckhead. The perimeter edge city is by far the leading commercial office center and leading headquarters area of the Atlanta region. The Cumberland edge city and the emerging Roswell/Alpharetta edge city are also located on the northside. No major edge cities occur on the Southside.

Table 6.1   Edge City Employment in Atlanta (in thousands)

| Super District | 1990 | 2000 | 2005 |
|---|---|---|---|
| Perimeter Center | 183 | 231 | 196 |
| Cumberland | 83 | 122 | 109 |
| Buckhead | 75 | 100 | 96 |
| Roswell/Alpharetta | 34 | 108 | 138 |
| Total | 375 | 561 | 539 |

Source: Atlanta Regional Commission

region with many centers. While long range transportation and land use planning did not anticipate nor plan for such high density centers, the accessibility advantage created by the freeway network, particularly at intersections of radial routes with the I–285 circumferential beltway, did bid up land values at those locations, which in turn generated high density development. For transportation planning purposes, the positive outcome of such concentrated development offered more options for transit alternatives to the automobile and the potential to shorten the length of work trips. Moreover, mixed-use development would enhance the prospect for the emergence of self-sufficient communities. In retrospect, that scenario might have unfolded, but it did not.

Unfortunately, a strong transit focus never developed in Atlanta's edge cities. With the exception of Buckhead (located in the city), no edge city gained a strong high density residential sector. Nevertheless, the employment levels of the edge cities continued to grow in the 1990s. Work trips also lengthened as the outward movement of residential areas continued. The suburb-to-suburb commuting flow mushroomed with the expansion of the polycentric development pattern, soon accounting for the largest share of regional work trips (table 6.2).

The dominant suburb-to-city flow that characterized the monocentric city focused on the pre-1975 downtown area, accounted for less than one-fifth of all trips in Atlanta's polycentric metropolis of the 1990s. That is not to say that radial traffic on the downtown connector (the combined I–75 and I–85 corridor through downtown) decreased, because it did not due to the massive north/south suburb-to-suburb flows through the city. The spatial mismatch in employment levels between the northern and southern suburbs continued to play a major part in growing traffic congestion as the jobs-poor southside exported workers to the jobs-rich northside. This situation will be addressed again in a later section.

Only an estimated 10 percent of the work trips began and ended in the city in the 1990s. The reverse trip from the city to the suburbs accounted for about 14 percent of all trips. The reverse trip form was the least well served by the transportation system as it typically involved a lower skilled transit-dependent commuter that had to transfer modes one or

**Table 6.2   Metropolitan Atlanta Regional Work Trip Flows (est.)**

| Trip Type | Percent of Total |
|---|---|
| City to City | 10 |
| City to Suburbs (Reverse) | 14 |
| Suburb to City | 18 |
| Suburb to Suburb | 58 |

Source: Author

more times in order to access suburban work places. The rail network, as was the case with the interstate system, was designed to bring persons into the city, not take them out, as most routes did not terminate at major employment hubs.

## DECENTRALIZATION AND RECENTRALIZATION: BARBELL GROWTH—1990–PRESENT

Two diverging growth trends have added more complexity to Atlanta's urban form in the past fifteen years. A barbell pattern of growth emerged reflecting the continued outward growth of the region on the one hand and a growing back to the city movement on the other. These dual patterns of growth both represent responses to the continued dominance of the automobile in shaping growth. By substituting longer work trips for access to cheaper land and a bigger home, many young families continued to prefer exurban locations. At the other end of the spectrum, the increased traffic congestion associated with longer commutes, and associated issues including higher gasoline prices and increased air pollution, induced many residents to leave the suburbs in favor of central city locations, including the downtown and midtown areas where a significant residential transformation unfolded, particularly after the 1996 Summer Olympic Games.

Rather than driven by a particular transportation planning paradigm, this most recent phase of growth and change in the Atlanta region resulted from consumer responses to the pro-growth market-driven real estate development process that the automobile-based lifestyle facilitated in the region. Largely fueled by the liberal funding of infrastructure improvements at the county level, this growth boom led to the expansion of the metropolitan area to twenty-eight counties in 2003. Not surprisingly, this unprecedented expansion process led to a counterveiling redevelopment process as a result of increasingly difficult commutes due to traffic congestion and long travel times.

We will discuss both ends of this barbell growth pattern here by first discussing the outward expansion in the context of the edgeless city concept often associated with unbridled sprawl. This will be followed by an examination of the back to the city movement occurring in the city of Atlanta.

### Edgeless City: Sprawl

The Atlanta metropolitan area added about one million persons and 500,000 jobs in the 1990s, placing it among the top three fastest growing large urban regions in the country. This growth plunged the exurban fringe farther into the countryside and work trips expanded in number and length. A recent report by the Transportation Research Board indicated that commute times in Atlanta increased on average from twenty-six to thirty-one minutes, the fastest rate of increase in any area in the nation between 1990 and 2000 (Hart 2006). Jobs/housing mismatches also increased in this period as the dominance of employment on the north-side increased to 60 percent in 2005, while the shares in the city of Atlanta and in the Southside stabilized at 20 percent each. In these suburban settings employment scatteration also increased. High technology-related firms, back offices, and distribution centers were among the leading types of businesses to locate in dispersed suburban locations. This lower cost work environment provides an effective alternative for highly entrepreneurial and competitive firms associated with the information age. Local government officials continued to endorse zoning practices that favored dispersed live, work, and play environments.

Ongoing decentralization of activity revealed yet another transformation of the region. This time the suburbs turned inside out as the edgeless city form became more prominent. The edgeless city, a term coined by Robert Lang, refers to market-driven growth process involving the sprawling expansion of development he labeled a "huge countrified city across a vast space" (Lang 2002). Single family residential subdivisions on relatively large lots often not connected to a public sewer system lead the outward expansion process and employment activities follow. The prevailing car culture, informal lifestyles, and access to quality schools typically drive the process. Even lower cost new school sites gravitate to fringe locations generating more sprawl as roads and subdivisions evolve to serve them.

A recent report brought home the enormity of the problem associated with this sprawl-like growth process. "The Atlanta region is the least dense of any of the top fifteen metros (2.3 persons per acre), has the largest median single family lot size (at three-fourths of an acre). As of 2000, the Atlanta region had half the density it had in 1970. . . . The average newcomer to the region today consumes twice the land as the average newcomer in 1970, with every two newcomers to the region consuming over an acre of land" (Metro Atlanta Quality Growth Task Force 2004). Nowhere is the lack of linkage between land use and transportation more apparent than in the outer suburbs where low density, segregative zoning practices still dominate.

By examining the employment shares between edge cities and edgeless cities one can gain further insight into the dilemma facing the region with respect to transportation planning. The edge city share of total employment in the region now stands at 40 percent while the edgeless share a much larger 60 percent of the total. The dispersed nature of employment in these locations makes effective transit services exceptionally difficult to implement. Shuttle buses, van pools, car pools, and rush hour bus service offer the most potential as alternatives to the single occupancy automobile in edgeless locations.

In 1998 a transportation crisis unfolded as the Regional Transportation Plan expired at a time when the Atlanta region failed to meet clean air standards. As a result federal transportation funds were frozen until the region could show progress in meeting compliance standards. Air quality deficiencies affected thirteen counties. Both short and long-term reforms would be needed to bring the region into compliance. Stricter automobile emission testing standards were adopted and in 1999 the state legislature created a new agency, the Georgia Regional Transportation Authority (GRTA) to have more oversight and enforcement responsibilities concerning land use, transportation, and air quality issues. Shortly thereafter the region adopted a new regional transportation plan, and modeling indicated that air quality would improve, and federal funding was restored.

### Back to the City: Maturing Downtown and Midtown Residential Markets

An alternative lifestyle to the suburban pattern has gained stature in the Atlanta region in the past fifteen years. While a slow and thin back to the city movement had been under way since the 1970s, it did not lead to a population turnaround in the city at that time as the gentrification process associated with the trend in older close-in Victorian and other architecturally desirable neighborhoods usually involved the displacement of previous residents. Eventually, infill housing in the former Buttermilk Bottom community (Bedford Pine) brought new units to the market in the 1980s, and together with a loft housing movement that began in Castleberry Hill to the west of downtown Atlanta sparked interest in converting old warehouses to residential use.

By the time that the buildup for the 1996 Summer Olympic Games emerged, the residential loft movement had spread to the city center in the Marietta Street Corridor, the lower downtown area near City Hall, and to the Five Points area (Hartshorn 1998). Many units came on line after the Olympics, financed by revenues generated by using the spaces as hospitality venues during the games. In the meantime, new high rise housing construction gained momentum in Midtown, a process that spread to downtown, especially around Centennial Park in the early 2000s. The bottom line of this trend is that a significant population turnaround has occurred in the city as this process accelerated and more housing came to Buckhead. The population figures for the city show that while there was only a slight population increase in the 1990s, the city is now growing at an impressive rate of about 9,000 persons per year, a trend that is expected to continue (table 6.3). Of course, these numbers pale in comparison to the robust growth of the metropolitan region, which now approaches 5 million persons.

## TRANSPORTATION IMPLICATIONS FOR THE CITY OF ATLANTA

Of particular relevance to the city of Atlanta is the long term impact of both the outward growth of the region and the back to the city movement. The current pattern of barbell growth in the region presents a picture of a very different set of transportation needs for the higher density and more mature infrastructure environment found in the city and close-in suburbs in comparison with the skeletal transportation network associated with the emerging exurbs. Scarce resources also exist for new transportation investments as funds must be allocated among an ever-larger array of competitors. The attitude of many suburban players is that the city of Atlanta has MARTA bus and rail service and does not need the additional funds for streets and roads as much as they need them. Unfortunately this is not the case. Moreover, real estate prices are generally higher in the city, requiring even more dollars for any given project. In the city, streets and traffic signals need rebuilding as well as more intensive traffic management approaches, whereas in outlying areas, new arterials and connectors are needed.

The city of Atlanta transportation needs run the gamut, including transit improvements, traffic management, signalization, pedestrian enhancements, parking management, and others. Different parts of the city have different needs as well. The needs of Buckhead, Midtown, and Downtown are much different than those of residential neighborhoods. Transit needs differ in the city and region as well. Whereas, rail service already exists in the city it must be supplemented by improved feeder services such as those provided by bus loops and a trolley network. In the suburbs, local and express bus service improvements are needed along with shuttle services. We will discuss several of these needs here.

**Table 6.3   City of Atlanta Population Trends**

| Year | Population |
|------|-----------|
| 1970 | 495,000 |
| 1980 | 424,922 |
| 1990 | 415,200 |
| 2000 | 415,474 |
| 2006 | 451,600 |

Source: Atlanta Regional Commission

The most important task facing the city of Atlanta in order to remain competitive in growth and transportation investment will be to reassert the historic hub role of the downtown and to showcase its inherent competitive advantage as the center of the region. In this regard, it is of utmost importance to have direct high capacity transit linkages between downtown Atlanta and all outlying edge cities. Buckhead and Perimeter Center, and to some extent the Roswell/Alpharetta cores already possess such connections, but a conspicuous missing link occurs with Cumberland and the Cobb county market. This northwest transit corridor link played an important role in the transit planning process in the 1960s and 1970s. The development plans for the Atlantic Station complex also incorporated a light rail link along this corridor but did not materialize, and no timetable or funding currently exists for this critical link.

Even more troubling is the lack of sensitivity of the current MARTA bus route network to the mobility needs of the city of Atlanta labor force. Essentially, this network remains frozen in the 1950s format wherein most employment occurred downtown and radial service to the core provided an effective service footprint. Once the MARTA rail network came on line in the late 1970s and 1980s many routes were diverted to "feed" the radial rail network. For many residents, service deteriorated at that time, even those seeking radial service into downtown due to the need to transfer between modes.

Overall, the growing crosstown and city-to-suburb (reverse) commute flow has not received effective service upgrades as the MARTA system evolved and employment decentralized. Reverse commuting has dramatically increased and this trip type remains poorly served. Expanded express bus HOV service on the expressways offering direct connections with edge cities should also be implemented to address this need. The reverse commuting needs for city residents can be anticipated to explode in the future given the growth of city population which far outpaces employment expansion. The continuing disparity in the jobs/housing balance between the city, the northside suburbs, and the southside suburbs will also lead to more reverse commuting (table 6.4).

Recent population growth in the city has not been matched by an employment turnaround. Employment totals in fact declined in the city (and

**Table 6.4   Regional Employment Shares—Ten-County ARC Region (percent)**

| Region | 2000 | 2005 |
|---|---|---|
| Northside | 58 | 60 |
| Southside | 20 | 20 |
| City of Atlanta | 22 | 20 |

Source: Atlanta Regional Commission

much of the region), between 2000 and 2005, and ARC projections indicate that it may take until 2015 for city employment totals to again reach 2005 levels. This lack of robust employment growth in the city means that more reverse commuting will be necessary in the future for those new middle class central city residents in the labor force.

While it is possible to use MARTA rail and bus service for the reverse commute, the fact that only the north rail line and south line directly connect with major employment centers, creates a dilemma for the passenger. The northeast line and the east and west lines do not terminate at major employment nodes, but the northeast line does provide Buckhead service.

The jobs/housing mismatch between the north and south sides of the region also creates another traffic dilemma for the city of Atlanta due to the huge flow of traffic through the city from south to north in the morning rush hour and the reverse in the evening. That traffic will largely remain automobile-based in the future due to the dispersed nature of employment. In order to reduce the congestion on the downtown connector a serious look at the proposal by the Reason Foundation to develop a tunnel through the center city to carry the heavy through-traffic loads should be carefully studied (Poole 2006). The proposal calls for such a connection between the southern terminus of GA 400 on the north and I–675 on the southside. More extensive carpool and vanpool programs could also alleviate some of the congestion. By converting HOV lanes to HOT lanes and implementing more southside/northside express bus routes, additional congestion relief would occur.

As currently constituted, the Xpress commuter bus routes offered by Georgia Regional Transportation Authority (GRTA)[1] provide radial service from suburban neighborhoods to the downtown on a dozen or more routes during the rush hour but no through reverse flow service for southside workers to access northside jobs exists. By just focusing on downtown service, the commuter bus network artificially limits its potential. Since the downtown only accounts for 10 percent of regional employment totals, the upside potential of attracting more radial transit trips into the area remains limited.

At the intercity scale, the proposed commuter rail network linking outer suburbs to the city by rail would also help reassert the ascendancy of downtown centrality, especially the proposed eastside "brain train" route linking Athens and Atlanta, due to the proximity of these two sizable markets and the high levels of interaction that already occurs between them. Other routes would likely generate lower ridership levels, including the proposed southside Lovejoy route, but until state-level and local funding emerge for these lines, commuter rail service to the city will remain a long shot. The proposed downtown multimodal rail station to consolidate several modes of service under one roof would also reinforce the hub function and assist with the revitalization of the railroad gulch area on the west side of Downtown, once the home of the downtown rail passenger stations.

Automobile parking issues also present a dilemma for the city. The city of Atlanta does not operate parking garage services, which are exclusively provided by the private sector, which aggressively added to the parking capacity of the downtown area over the years on surface lots as commercial building demolitions accelerated, and in large-scale parking deck structures. In the downtown alone there have been more than 50,000 parking spaces for many years. Nearly all new buildings provide additional capacity in parking decks. This relatively liberal provision of parking capacity detracts from making the downtown (and the city) more transit oriented.

The city appears to follow a laissez-faire approach in approving downtown parking capacity expansion. Two recent developments reflect this dilemma in making the city more transit oriented. First, the Georgia Bar Association greatly expanded the parking deck at the former Federal Reserve Bank on Marietta Street within three blocks of two MARTA rail stations. This parking expansion involved the destruction of a pocket park. The second case involved the controversial "green" parking deck in Piedmont Park at the Atlanta Botanical Garden that opened in 2009.

Indeed, even at transit-oriented development sites, liberal parking capacity is deemed necessary in Atlanta to attract patrons. At the Lindbergh Center, a MARTA-sponsored Transit Oriented Development (TOD), huge parking structures occupy a considerable footprint. Across Piedmont Avenue from this development, the new Lindbergh mixed-use complex heavily relies on automobile access.

As Atlantic Station Vice President Brian Leary has noted, in Atlanta "we drive where we want to walk." The massive 40-acre 7,000 parking deck platform on which the retail district of Atlantic Station lies provides a case in point. Marketed as Atlanta's premier mixed-use development, Atlantic Station depends almost exclusively on the automobile for access. Free shuttle bus service to the Arts Center MARTA Station provides supplementary access, but scheduled transit service is not yet available as originally envisioned. The new $38 million 17th Street bridge across the downtown connector is designed to carry a light rail line but no funds or approvals for a direct transit link appear to be on the horizon.

The Peachtree Street Corridor between downtown and Buckhead offers the greatest potential in Atlanta for genuine mixed-use development. The many new proposed high rise projects and those under construction in Midtown offer tremendous potential to create such a continuous mixed-use urban corridor between downtown and Buckhead. The proposed Atlanta Streetcar may revolutionize mobility in the corridor and should receive funding priority.

In the new projects department, the Beltline also promises to become the catalyst for the redevelopment of the 22-mile railway cordon encircling downtown and midtown (see www.beltlinepartnership.org). Once an important rail freight axis supporting manufacturing and warehouse activity, this area fell into neglect over the years as the city grew and industrial activity decentralized. In 1999 Ryan Gravel, a Georgia Tech graduate student, proposed the placement of a new transit line in the area to link in-town neighborhoods. While it is not clear when the transit piece of this redevelopment might unfold, plans are now underway to develop a continuous 1200-acre linear park and trail complex in the corridor and it is now envisioned as a major live-work-play community that could sprout up to 30,000 jobs. Financing setbacks and recessionary times suggest that the full realization of these promises may be a generation or more away.

In other centers and corridors in Atlanta, expanded shuttle bus service should be encouraged to supplement automobile access and to assist pedestrian access. The BucRide program in Buckhead provides an example of such a service. Shuttles are also gaining in popularity in other areas such as the Emory University campuses and medical complex and Perimeter Center. The Livable Centers Initiative (LCI) of the Atlanta Regional Commission must be applauded in this regard for showcasing the potential of redeveloping and increasing the density of corridors and centers, making them more attractive for the transit and walking alternative to the automobile.

The city of Atlanta should also consider placing higher priority on transportation and traffic management alternatives such as prohibiting rush hour deliveries that essentially block one or more lanes of traffic on busy downtown streets. The same strategy could be used during rush hours at construction sites, much as the State of Georgia Department of Transportation (GDOT) prohibits lane closings for maintenance and repair work on Interstate highways during rush hours. More effective management of traffic and coordination with the police department at peak times at major tourist venues as is practiced at sporting events should be implemented. Educating the public about the scheduling of special events and potential traffic tie-ups should also receive more priority. A proposal to eliminate one-way traffic on several arterial highways serving downtown in favor of a return to two-way traffic corridors would assist with traffic calming and encourage pedestrian movement as well as disciplining the automobile, which in turn would improve the prospects for transit ridership.

## CONCLUSION

The city of Atlanta comprises a small part of the metropolitan area but functionally represents the most important part. Throughout most of its history, needed transportation investments served the city well. In the past twenty-five to thirty years as the region has grown into a metropolitan area of 5 million in population, the city increasingly finds itself competing with many more interests for scarce transportation dollars. The needs of the city today are not appreciated or effectively served by the region as a whole or the state of Georgia. Moreover, the region finds itself in a quandary as to its priorities and finds itself in a difficult position of not being able to secure funding to fulfill its transportation needs.

This uncertainty facing transportation infrastructure improvements, and a lack of leadership allows many competing voices to seek recognition and validation, adding to the confusion. Columnist Maria Saporta from the *Atlanta Journal-Constitution* noted in a column in 2005 that the many overlapping and duplicative transportation voices remind one of a process of "rearranging deck chairs on the Titanic." The plethora of agencies having a responsibility for various aspects of transportation planning and implementation in the Atlanta region lend credibility to the "Titanic" theme. ARC, GRTA, GDOT, SRTA (State Roads and Tollway Authority), and MARTA each has its own constituency and responsibility in this regard and as a group these agencies create an ineffective and inefficient bureaucratic system. Several other groups and organizations have also been formed over the years to crack the transportation juggernaut in the Atlanta region, such as the Congestion Mitigation Taskforce, the Transit Planning Board, and the Regional Executive Steering Committee of Transit Operators.

Fragmented planning detracts from the effectiveness of transportation management in the Atlanta region. Websites are literally littered with dozens of references to studies focusing on various technologies, alternatives, and strategies to solve transportation problems. Compared with other metropolitan areas the Atlanta region has too many actors responsible for implementing transportation solutions, too many fragmented/polarized interests—city/suburban/environmental/rich/poor. Racism plays too important a role and no regional consensus or vision as to priorities exists. There are too many subarea studies that detract from big issue questions such as the appropriate role of transit in the future of the region. But there is no shortage of money for consultants for ever more studies even though there is a shortage of financing for project implementation. Perhaps the biggest problem lies with the state Constitution which specifically prohibits the use of state gasoline sales tax dollar proceeds for any other transportation use than roads and highways, including bridges. As a result there is no state money available in Georgia for transit funding. MARTA is the only major transit system in the country with no state-level funding.

The newly created City of Atlanta Transportation Department in the Bureau of Planning and Community Development may be able to raise the profile of the needs of the city vis à vis the rest of the region at the technical level, but the real test for the city will be to develop a political coalition at the mayoral and county commission level among the five urban core counties (DeKalb, Cobb, Fulton, Gwinnett, and Clayton) that have the most similar transportation needs to that of the city. It is incumbent on these areas to develop a unified voice and strategy to lobby for solutions to common transportation issues facing the most mature and most densely settled areas of the region that claim the largest share of population and employment. Support by private sector voices such as those represented by Central Atlanta Progress, the Chamber of Commerce, and the media will also be needed to educate the public and lobby public officials to support the needs of the urban core counties and the city of Atlanta.

Resistance to new urban transportation initiatives on the part of rural legislators and lobbyists remains a critical stumbling block and must be overcome. A recent editorial in the *Atlanta Journal-Constitution* (Jan. 11, 2009) suggests that "After years of denial, much of Georgia's leadership now acknowledges that the state's transportation system is in crisis and that the situation in metro Atlanta is particularly dire." Atlanta's future, city and suburb, clearly will be jeopardized unless critical transportation issues receive proper attention.

## NOTES

1. The Georgia Regional Transportation Authority (GRTA) is an agency created by the state of Georgia legislature in 1999 to assist the thirteen counties in the metropolitan Atlanta area deemed in noncompliance with federal clean air standards to regain satisfactory air quality levels.

## REFERENCES

Atlanta Region Metropolitan Planning Commission. "Access to Central Atlanta." Expressway Policy Study, Report No. 1. Atlanta, April, 1959.

Atlanta Region Metropolitan Planning Commission. "Crosstown and By-Pass Expressways," Atlanta, June 1959.

Atlanta Region Metropolitan Planning Commission. *Facts and Forecasts*, 61–83, March 1969.

A. Voorhees and Associates. "Summary of Highlights: Recommended Transportation Program." McLean, Va., 1969.

Beeler, John. *Report to the City of Atlanta on a Plan for Local Transportation*. New York: Beeler Organization, 1924.

"Beltline: Atlanta Connected" Atlanta Beltline, Inc. 2008. www.beltline.org (8 April 2008).

Central Atlanta Progress. *Central Atlanta: Opportunities and Responses*. Atlanta: Central Area Study Policy Committee, 1971.

Hamer, Andrew and Truman Hartshorn. "Planning Massive Accessibility For Central Atlanta: A Study of Misleading Projections." *High Speed Ground Transportation Journal*, 8 (1974): 290–302.

Hart, Ariel. "Atlantans Crank Up Commute Times." *Atlanta Journal-Constitution* (October 16, 2006): B1.

Hartshorn, Truman. *Raising the Roof on Downtown Housing*. Atlanta: Research Atlanta, Andrew Young School of Policy Studies, Georgia State University, 1998.

Hartshorn, Truman A. and Peter O. Muller. "Suburban Downtowns and the Transformation of Metropolitan Atlanta's Business Landscape." *Urban Geography* 10, (1989): 375–395.

H. W. Lochner and Co. and DeLeuw, Cather and Co. *Highway and Transportation Plan for Atlanta, Georgia*. Prepared for the State Highway Department of Georgia. Chicago, 1946.

Lang, Robert. "Open Spaces, Bounded Places: Does the American West's Arid Landscape Yield Dense Metropolitan Growth?" *Housing Policy Debate* 13, no. 4 (2002): 755–778.

Leinberger, Christopher. "The Changing Location of Investment and Development Opportunities." *Urban Land* (May 1995): 31–36.

Mayor's Traffic Commission. *Atlanta Traffic Survey Report*, Atlanta: City of Atlanta, 1929.

Metro Atlanta Quality Growth Task Force. "Consolidated Final Recommendations." Atlanta: Atlanta Chamber of Commerce, May 2004.

Poole, Robert W., Jr. "Reducing Congestion in Atlanta: A Bold Approach to Increasing Mobility." Los Angeles: Reason Foundation and Atlanta: The Georgia Public Policy Foundation, The Galvin Mobility Project, November 2006.

State Highway Department of Georgia. *Atlanta Area Transportation Study, Existing Conditions Report*. Atlanta, 1967.

*Part IV*

# WORKERS

*Chapter 7*

# The Creative Class and Economic Growth in Atlanta

## Michael Rushton

Amongst urban planners, the first decade of the twenty-first century will be remembered as the time when significant attention was directed toward the "creative class," those young, educated, and mobile individuals who work in occupations involving some degree of creativity and judgment, and who are seen as the most important source of growth in contemporary urban economies. The creative class naturally includes artists, but also involves architects, software engineers, and industrial designers, among others. But artists are seen by some as particularly important as an anchor for the other parts of the creative class, in terms of providing innovation in ideas ("knowledge spillovers," to use the term from the literature on economic growth), and also as providing an urban environment with the cultural amenities favored by young and mobile knowledge workers.

This chapter has two goals. It will provide an accounting of the state of the arts in Atlanta in terms of how it compares with other American cities and its future prospects. And it will evaluate the claims made for the arts in terms of attracting highly educated workers and, in turn, generating economic growth. Is the "creative class" another fad in popular economics, soon to move from airport bookstores to the remainder bins? Or is there good evidence that there really is a link between fostering the arts and economic growth?

### HOW DO THE ARTS IN ATLANTA COMPARE TO OTHER CITIES?

In terms of the presence of the arts, how does Atlanta compare with other U.S. cities? This is not a straightforward question.

First, we need some quantitative measure of "the arts." This could be accomplished by looking at the number of people employed as "artists," but even that is not so simple: do we include everyone working in *any* sort of entertainment establishment, or do we restrict ourselves to only considering the high arts? Alternatively, we could count the number of arts organizations in the city. But this leads to similar problems: The Atlanta Symphony and the Center for Puppetry Arts are certainly "arts organizations," but should we also include nightclubs that feature live music, or cinemas?

Second, there is the problem of choosing the appropriate geographical unit for analysis. The principal theme of this book is to examine the trends affecting the city of Atlanta, but when we turn to the literature on evaluating the level of arts activities across U.S. cities we find that most studies use metropolitan statistical areas (MSA's) as their primary geographic unit. When we consider the purpose of quantifying the arts, the use of MSA's is not always appropriate. Research on the impact of the arts on economic development, particularly in knowledge-based sectors, generally looks for two sorts of linkages. First, a strong arts presence might generate a milieu that is particularly conducive to experimentation and looking at old problems from new, untried perspectives, and this could be attractive to the creative class and the firms that employ them. Second, a vibrant cultural scene might be a valuable quality-of-life amenity independent of its impact of creativity in the workplace; the educated and well-paid members of the creative class might highly value the arts as something to engage in after work. But will we observe either of these linkages at the MSA level? It is hard to see how the activities of artists and arts organizations in Midtown Atlanta could have much impact on the creativity of firms located in the outer reaches of Gwinnett or Cobb counties. And few residents of the outer exurbs are going to see centrally-located arts organizations as relevant cultural amenities (a study of voting patterns in a referendum on a property tax increase earmarked for the arts in metropolitan Detroit found that, other things equal, the more distant from the city center, where most of the significant arts institutions were located, the less support for the proposal (Rushton 2005)).

Furthermore, the use of MSA's to measure the arts in a city can give quite misleading results. For example, Markusen and Schrock (2006) attempt to measure the concentration of artists in metropolitan areas, based on the number of individuals who self-identify as artists in the census (whether working independently or as employees, including employees for firms not categorized as arts organizations). Using year 2000 data for the largest U.S. MSA's, metropolitan Atlanta has an "artistic concentration" (i.e., the proportion of the workforce that is classified as artists) measured at 1.08, where the U.S. average is normalized to 1.00. However, they go on to note that from 1980 to 1990 the *number* of artists in the Atlanta MSA grew by 64 percent, and from 1990 to 2000 the number grew by a further 53 percent, more than in any other MSA. The "artistic concentration" in Atlanta is low—in fact lower in 2000 than in 1980—because the total workforce of the Atlanta MSA grew even faster than the number of artists over those two decades. But it is certainly possible, and one could make the case that it is probable, that the increase in the number of artists in metropolitan Atlanta was disproportionately in the city (indeed, below we see that if we focus on the city of Atlanta, the artistic concentration ranking is in fact *much* higher than what is found in the MSA data).

That being said, if research that attempts to quantify and rank artistic activity in the U.S. tends to use MSA's, it is worth considering here at least for the reason that, if nothing else, it affects perceptions of the city of Atlanta.

Without a doubt the most influential and popular work on measuring creativity in cities is by Richard Florida (2002a; 2002b). Analysis of Florida's hypotheses on artists and economic growth is given in the next section of the chapter; for now consider his rankings of metro Atlanta as a center of creativity. Florida (2002a) attempts to link the concentration of artists in a metro area with high levels of human capital and population growth. He uses a fairly narrow definition of artists, whom he labels "bohemians": authors, designers, musicians and composers, actors and directors, craft-artists, painters, sculptors and artist printmakers, photographers, dancers, and the catch-all census category of "artists, performers, and related workers" (in my empirical analysis, below, I use the same definitions). Florida reports that metro Atlanta has a concentration of 1.34, where the U.S. average is normalized to 1.00; in other words, the proportion of metro Atlanta's workforce that was employed as artists was 34 percent higher than the national average. This placed metro Atlanta fourteenth among large MSA's.

In his book *The Rise of the Creative Class*, Florida (2002b, 328) widens his attention to a "super-creative core," which includes, in addition to those working in the arts, design and entertainment, "computer and mathematical occupations; architecture and engineering occupations; life, physical and social science occupations; education, training, and library occupations; . . . [and] sports and media occupations," which for the Atlanta MSA is 12.3 percent of the workforce (in 1999), ranked fifteen among the forty-nine largest MSA's [in the South, Atlanta ranks behind Raleigh-Durham (first, nationally), Washington, D.C. (fourth), Austin (tied for fifth), and Houston (tied for eleventh)]. Opinions will differ on whether Florida's "super-creative core" is a relevant statistic for predicting economic growth, or whether it is well-defined in the first place. For example, a violinist with the Atlanta Symphony who performs, and perhaps teaches, but does not compose music, is certainly an "artist," but it is hard to see what makes this person "super-creative." Furthermore, we might ask whether what really matters for a creative economy is the absolute number of workers in the creative core, rather than the proportion of the total workforce. In Florida's analysis, metropolitan Buffalo has a higher proportion of its workforce in the "super-creative core" than does New York City, but it is not obvious that this makes Buffalo a more creative economy.

That being said, Florida's rankings in terms of arts, and more generally creative, employment are close to the findings of a recent study conducted by the Urban Institute, which, using 2001 data, ranks the Atlanta MSA at sixteenth place in terms of artists' employment (Jackson, Kabwasa-Green and Herranz 2006). However, they find that metro Atlanta ranks even lower in other arts indicators: twentieth in arts establishments per capita, fifty-first in arts nonprofits per capita, and forty-eighth in nonprofit arts contributions per capita. These low numbers for nonprofit arts activity echo the findings of Brooks and Kushner (2000; 2002) who conclude that Atlanta has low levels of nonprofits arts activity per capita, lags in private philanthropic support, and that even confining our attention to the South, Atlanta is not really the regional arts leader.

Should we evaluate the state of the arts in a city by focusing on nonprofits? In the U.S., nonprofits are the dominant organizational form for the high arts: live performances of classical music, opera, theatre, and dance, as well as the museum sector (DiMaggio 2006). One reason is the presence of high fixed costs in these art forms, necessitating private donations if costs are to be covered. The fine arts also benefit from the nonprofit form where artists place high value on the quality of their performances and on their artistic autonomy (Hansmann 1981).

Prior to the contemporary focus on the links between a city's arts environment, the attraction of an educated workforce, and economic growth, arts policy was directed towards the high arts, on the grounds that production and consumption of the fine arts generated more benefits to the community than was represented by market demand for the arts (Frey 2003; Peacock 2006), and that fine art has an intrinsic value that warrants efforts by the state to encourage the development of finer tastes amongst the public (Scitovsky 1972). A consequence of these assumptions was that public funding for the arts in the U.S. was devoted almost exclusively to nonprofit arts organizations, which came to be seen as synonymous with fine art (and in more recent decades, ethnic and folk art that also warranted subsidy). This is perhaps an explanation for the focus on the nonprofit arts as the measure of the cultural vitality of cities.

But it is now the case more than ever that consumers of the arts are "cultural omnivores" (Peterson and Kern 1996), where it is entirely possible that a regular visitor to the High Museum or the Atlanta Symphony is also an avid fan of *The Sopranos* and the (for-profit) local, live rock music scene. "Cool cities," to use the Richard Florida jargon, are not wholly defined by their nonprofit arts organizations, but also by nightclubs, coffee-houses, and galleries of contemporary art. Of course, "coolness" will be impossible to measure, except perhaps by surveys. But it is worth remembering that statistics on arts nonprofits in cities are not capturing the whole story; it is telling that a recent *New York Times* profile on cities' efforts to attract the creative class, describing Atlanta as a success story in this regard, shows a picture of young, hip, new Atlantans enjoying themselves at the Midtown "Verve Lounge," not at the High Museum (Dewan 2006).

## THE ARTS, THE CREATIVE CLASS, AND URBAN ECONOMIC DEVELOPMENT

Can cities spur economic growth with the development of policies and amenities that will attract the "creative class": highly-skilled and mobile individuals whose work is all about the creation of new ideas in technology, art, and design, and who combine a strong work ethic with a preference for active and exciting uses of their leisure time? Some legislators have certainly come to believe so. The governor of Michigan has developed a 'cool cities' initiative, where the homepage tells us that:

> Michigan cities of all sizes and the regions surrounding them are our future. To survive and thrive in the future, Michigan's cities must retain and attract more people including urban pioneers and young knowledge workers to its cities. We want them to choose Michigan as the place they want to live, work and play by creating attractive, vibrant and diverse cities that anchor vital and prosperous regions throughout the Great Lakes State [www.coolcities.com].

Michigan cities are eligible for awards for developing cool downtowns and "neighborhoods of choice." The creative class of Memphis, Tennessee produced a "Manifesto for Building a Community of Ideas," which in its preamble proclaims:

> Creativity is fundamental to being human and is a critical resource to individual, community and economic life. Creative communities are vibrant, humanizing places, nurturing personal growth, sparking cultural and technological breakthroughs, providing jobs and wealth, and accepting a variety of lifestyles and culture [www.creativeclass.org/acrobat/manifesto.pdf].

Among the policies called for in Memphis include investing in the "creative ecosystem," which is "arts and culture, nightlife, the music scene, restaurants, artists and designers, innovators, entrepreneurs, affordable spaces, lively neighborhoods, spirituality, education, density, public spaces and third places."

The summit that produced the Memphis Manifesto was hosted by Richard Florida, whose book *The Rise of the Creative Class* (2002b) has provided so much inspiration for urban planners and for arts advocates, who see Florida's ideas as a fresh case for state support for artists and arts organizations. In this section we try to shed further light on Florida's claims that a city that attracts artists will also attract the highly skilled creative class, and so bring economic growth.

Why would a concentration of artists in a city attract the creative class, and more generally be a spur to economic growth? As we noted above, arguments can be made from the perspectives of consumption and production.

On the consumption side, a concentration of artists (of all art forms) leads to better leisure options for individuals, especially those more educated knowledge workers open to hearing new music, visiting galleries, attending the theatre, and so on. With an increased proportion of the workforce involved in services, which unlike manufacturing need not locate close to natural resources or primary shipping routes, there is more flexibility regarding where employers and employees can be located. Urban amenities and quality of life issues, both natural and developed, become relatively more important in location choice. Glaeser, Kolko, and Saiz (2001) find high amenity cities have been enjoying faster growth than low amenity cities. Further, even the choices in amenities have changed:

> The important local amenities are no longer schools, churches, and neighborhood associations. . . . A residential population of young professionals with more education and fewer children creates a social profile geared toward recreation and consumption concerns (Clark, et. al. 2002, 500).

Glaeser and Gottlieb (2006) show that the decline in crime rates in U.S. cities has also facilitated the ability of people to enjoy social interaction outside of work and cultural amenities, furthering the demand for living in cities with good consumption options. The goal for the members of the creative class interviewed by Florida is "to 'live the life'—a creative life packed full of intense, high-quality, multidimensional experiences. And the *kinds* of experiences they crave reflect and reinforce their identities as creative people" (Florida 2002b, 166). Furthermore, there is evidence that as educated and creative individuals are attracted to a location, the quality of life can further improve "because more educated individuals spur the growth of consumption amenities in cities in which they reside, or because their influence on the political process leads to desirable outcomes such as reductions in crime and pollution" (Shapiro 2005, 2–3; but also see Glaeser and Saiz [2003] who claim that over the long term it has been productivity alone, and not quality of life, that has caused the higher growth rates in skilled cities).

A concentration of artists is also predicted to have a positive impact on the productivity of knowledge workers. First, there may be "positive externalities" from artists to other creative workers; the presence of artists serves to increase productivity in other creative sectors, as they provide a stimulus for new ideas. "Technological and economic creativity are nurtured by and interact with artistic and cultural creativity" (Florida 2002b, 5). While there are obvious opportunities for some high-technology industries to benefit from close proximity to artistic creation—the technology associated with digital animation, for example—the mechanisms by which knowledge and creativity actually spillover from one sector to another remain somewhat hazy. That is not to say the positive externalities do not exist, but only to remind ourselves that much remains to be learned about the process of the transmission of ideas and "cultural creativity" across firms.

If it is in fact the case that artists attract the creative class of knowledge workers, then a virtuous circle arises, since there are also knowledge spillovers between workers in creative industries, who thus find it productive and profitable to cluster in particular locations. A software engineer may be attracted to Seattle by its arts and music scene, but she or he will also be attracted to Seattle because of all the other software engineers who are already there, and will serve to make her or him more productive through the sharing of ideas, often in very informal ways. The idea that there are increasing returns to scale in a city's accumulation of human capital (Lucas 1988; Romer 1990) is borne out by evidence that in recent decades cities with the higher initial levels of human capital have not only had higher levels of income, which is not very surprising, but have also tended to have better records of economic growth, which is evidence in favor of some sort of knowledge spillovers and positive externalities (Glaeser and Shapiro 2001; Furdell, Wolman, and Hill 2005).

As Glaeser (2005) points out in a review of *The Rise of the Creative Class*, Florida's innovation is to combine the economic observation that cities with high human capital enjoy not only higher levels of income but also faster rates of growth, an idea that does not originate with Florida, with the idea that high human capital is attracted by opportunities for cultural consumption and other amenities. With that it is hard to argue. However, Florida goes further, claiming that the quality of life aspects desired by the creative class are specifically the "bohemian" lifestyle, which is a combination of varied cultural and recreational offerings with liberal social policies and cosmopolitan neighborhoods: "the increasing importance of creativity, innovation, and knowledge to the economy

opens up the social space where more eccentric, alternative, or bohemian people can be integrated into core economic and social institutions" (Florida 2002a, 57).

Florida could be criticized for glossing over the chicken-and-egg problem of whether artists and bohemia attract other creative workers or the
other way around (Lang 2005), but there are additional areas where Florida leaves himself open to criticism. While there might be some evidence
for the correlations between quality of life, artists, and a highly skilled
workforce, it is less evident that Florida's particular conception of what
makes a desirable quality of life is in fact what the creative class wants.
As Glaeser (2005, 594) tells it:

> I know a lot of creative people. I've studied a lot of creative people. Most
> of them like what most well-off people like—big suburban lots with easy
> commutes by automobile and safe streets and good schools and low taxes.
> After all, there is plenty of evidence linking low taxes, sprawl and safety
> with growth. Plano, Texas was the most successful skilled city in the country
> in the 1990s (measured by population growth)—it is not exactly a Bohemian
> paradise [also see Postrel (2006)].

This is a crucial question for growth in the city of Atlanta: are talented
members of the "super-creative core" going to want to live in Midtown
Atlanta or in Alpharetta? Are software designers looking to live "a creative
life packed full of intense, high-quality, multidimensional experiences" as
Florida would have it, or are they Patio Men (or Women) (Brooks 2002)
looking for a home in the sprawl of exurbia?

Malanga (2004) takes the criticism of Florida a step further:

> A far more serious—indeed fatal—objection to Florida's theories is that the
> economics behind them don't work. Although Florida's book bristles with
> charts and statistics showing how he constructed his various indexes and
> where cities rank on them, the professor, incredibly, doesn't provide any data
> demonstrating that his creative cities actually have vibrant economies that
> perform well over time.

## SOME NEW EVIDENCE ON ARTISTS
## AND URBAN ECONOMIC GROWTH

In this section I provide some updated evidence on whether artists tend
to attract human capital and in turn stimulate economic growth, or if
Florida's new economy of the creative class was ephemeral. In order to focus the analysis, instead of addressing directly the various arguments put
forth in *The Rise of the Creative Class*, I will look at a more tightly focused

article by Florida (2002a), in which he develops his "Bohemian index" and uses it for evidence of his creative class hypothesis.

Florida's Bohemian index uses the 1990 U.S. Census to find the degree of concentration of certain occupations in the arts, narrowly defined, on a per capita basis. He finds it is strongly correlated with various indices of the degree to which the local economy is based on high technology, on whether there is significant ethnic diversity, the proportion of the local population that is gay (as measured by the proportion of households where the householder and an unmarried partner are both male), and a "coolness" score developed by *POV* magazine in 1999 that considers the proportion of the population in their twenties, and various indices for nightlife and culture.

Florida (2002a) works with Metropolitan Statistical Areas, which in the United States can represent very large geographical areas. However, thinking about why it is that artists are likely to lure the creative class to cities, it seems to be more interesting to focus on the city core.

The first step is to define who exactly counts as an "artist." In this I follow Florida (2002a) and look for a narrow definition, meant to exclude those working in supporting roles in what could generally be called the hospitality industry. Using data from the US Census for the year 2000 [www.census.gov/eeo2000/index.html], I include seven job codes (the code number is given in parentheses) in the definition of artist:

- Artists and related workers (201)
- Designers (263)
- Actors (270)
- Producers and directors (271)
- Dancers and choreographers (274)
- Musicians, singers and related workers (275)
- Entertainers, performers, sports and related workers, all others (276)

The next step is to create, for each city, an "artists' index," which is defined as the number of artists per capita in the city relative to the number of artists per capita in the whole of the United States. I include the fifty-nine largest U.S. cities in the dataset. In the United States as a whole, there are just under 1.4 million artists as defined by the above list, or 4.95 individuals per 1,000. Not surprisingly, most cities have an artists' index greater than one, since artists tend to congregate in cities [artists, like other knowledge workers, have many incentives to locate where the other artists are, both for ideas about art, but also because buyers will tend to look for product where there are many producers; see Caves (2000)]. San Francisco had the highest level of the artists' index (4.28), followed by Atlanta (3.76), Orlando (3.47), Salt Lake City (3.44), Minneapolis (3.28), and Seattle (3.32).

Contrary to the results for MSA's described above, the *city* of Atlanta actually has a high concentration of artists. Data on the concentration of artists in the wider Metro area can thus be quite misleading.

For a measure of human capital, I consider the proportion of the city's population over the age of twenty-five having at least a bachelor's degree. For the cities in this sample the figure ranges from 9 percent in Newark, New Jersey, to 47.2 percent in Seattle, with Atlanta at 34.6 percent. A simple regression line fitted through the data indicates a strongly significant and positive correlation between the artists' index (A) and the proportion with a college degree (C), lending some support to Florida's hypothesis about artists and the creative class:

$$C = 16.6 \ (1.8) + 6.0 \ (1.0) \ A$$

where standard errors are in parentheses and the adjusted R-squared is 0.39. In terms of magnitude, a city with a concentration of artists equal to the U.S. national average, and so having an artists' index of one, could expect to have 22.6 percent of its population over the age of twenty-five with at least a bachelor's degree. But if the artists' index rises to two, double the national average, then we expect 28.6 percent to be college educated. The national average for the year 2000 was that 25.6 percent of those over twenty-five had at least a bachelor's degree.

Note that in showing this correlation (and those that follow) there is no pretense of there being a formal model that generates the relationship, or even that a direction of causality has been established; all that is being shown is that there is a correlation in cities between those who make a living as artists and the college educated.

As a next step I consider the correlation between the artists' index, which we now know to be correlated with levels of higher education, and population growth. The next regression compares the artists' index (A) for the year 2000 with the total growth in city population (P) from 1990 through 2004. I find no significant correlation between the two variables:

$$P = 9.1 \ (6.1) + 0.9 \ (3.3) \ A$$

where standard errors are in parentheses and the adjusted R-squared is -0.02.

Whether this result indicates a refutation of Florida depends on how one thinks about economic growth. Employment in regions closely tracks population; people are mobile and relocate because of job opportunities. But population growth is not necessarily a measure of success, because it tells us nothing of what is happening to the standard of living for the individuals who live there. Especially in cities that lack land on which to expand (San Francisco or New York, for example), economic success will be indicated by higher earnings, not rising population. Malanga (2004) takes Florida to task for failing to see that some very non-Bohemian cities, such as Las Vegas, Oklahoma City, and Memphis experienced strong population growth during the 1990s, while San Francisco had a virtually constant level of employment and population. But while it is common for politicians, especially in the United States, to make promises on how many jobs they will create if elected, it is the quality of employment that matters to our welfare, not the quantity of employment.

With that in mind, the final regression shows the correlation between the artists' index (A) and the total increase in per capita income (I) from 1990 through 2004. Income figures are not adjusted for inflation. I find a significant correlation between the artists' index and income growth:

$$I = 53.7 \ (5.8) + 6.7 \ (3.1) \ A$$

where standard errors are in parentheses, the coefficient on A has a p-value of .034, and the adjusted R-squared is 0.06.

To summarize what we have found to this point: using year 2000 data on the concentration of artists and the college educated in U.S. cities, we find a significant link between artists, high education levels, and income growth over the period 1990 through 2004. This confirms what has been found elsewhere in the literature on human capital levels and rates of economic growth, and lends further support to the basic hypotheses on the creative economy proposed by Florida.

The policy goal of attracting the new creative class has replaced, for the most part, economic development policies aimed at luring large firms through tax breaks and land deals. Local development now targets occupations rather than firms (Feser 2003; Markusen 2004). For arts advocates, there is a shift away from the economically dubious "economic impact studies," which measured the economic contribution of the arts to local economies by the amount that was spent on the arts plus various concocted "multiplier effects" (Bille and Schulze 2006), to arguments in support of the arts that rely on the special qualities of the arts: experiment, creativity, engagement (McCarthy, et. al. 2004; Gertler 2004).

But there is much to be done. In particular, we know little about how the process begins for a city that will become a center for artists and the creative class. For the past few decades, success has bred success in urban growth. But what was the primary cause? How do Bohemian enclaves begin, and what works in attaining the necessary critical mass? We await research on whether there can be deliberate urban policies that set what becomes a virtuous circle in motion.

## THE ARTS OUTLOOK IN ATLANTA

In April of 2006 Mayor Franklin announced the creation of the Arts and Culture Funding Task Force (ACFTF), whose mandate was to consider the funding levels for the arts necessary to have a culturally vibrant city, and to consider mechanisms used in other cities for funding the arts in order to help determine what might work well in Atlanta. The ACFTF issued its recommendations (which I discuss below) in March 2007, but it is worth stepping back in time to see the steps that led to the creation of the task force.

Cremin and deNobriga (2002) direct us to December 1996, when a small group of arts leaders in Atlanta began to gather for informal "think tank" discussions about the state of the arts in Atlanta, especially in light of the disappointment that the Olympic Games had not generated any sense of cultural renaissance. The discussion sessions eventually led to discussion forums, but there was a realization that for all the talk about the state of the arts in Atlanta, there was little data or means to methodically compare Atlanta to similar sized U.S. cities. This led to funds being raised for the first Research Atlanta study on the arts in Atlanta (Brooks and Kushner 2000), which looked at the state of nonprofit arts organizations in Metro Atlanta, describing a situation that was middling at best. The report received significant attention in local media, and at this point the baton was passed to the Metro Atlanta Chamber of Commerce (MACC).

The MACC, as might be expected, was interested in the arts in terms of the potential impact on economic activity in the region, and especially wanted to generate for the city an image as a cultural center. North Highland (2001) produced a somewhat anecdotal report for MACC on the links between arts and growth in business, and a Regional Arts Task Force was created, with the mission "to make the Atlanta region a premier center for the arts, and for it to be recognized as such," holding its first meeting in June 2002.

There were two major outcomes from the MACC Regional Arts Task Force. First, the Metro Atlanta Arts and Culture Coalition (MAACC) was formed, a lobby group aimed at increasing participation in the arts, and working to secure increased funding for the arts. The MAACC also works to bring together the many government, nonprofit, and commercial stakeholders in the arts in the region, seeking avenues for collaboration and coordinated actions. Second, a study was commissioned, again through Research Atlanta (Rushton 2003), to consider options for "sustainable" public funding for the arts, which in practice tends to mean an earmarked source of government revenues. This study did not call for an earmarked tax source, but focused on the key issues surrounding such a policy.

For nonprofit arts organizations, an earmarked source of funding is certainly an attractive policy innovation. San Francisco's dedicated funding for the arts through the hotel occupancy tax has been in place since the 1960s and is now a very significant source of funding. St. Louis funds its major cultural institutions through additional mills on the property tax, and Denver and Salt Lake City use one-tenth of one percent of the retail sales tax to devote to the arts and culture (see Martell (2004) for a detailed analysis of Denver's Scientific and Cultural Facilities District, and Rushton (2004) for general considerations on earmarked taxes for the arts).

Finally, in 2006, the mayor explicitly formed the task force designed to look into possibilities for sustainable funding for the arts. In its deliberations, the task force needed to grapple with some difficult questions of principles: What is public funding of the arts for? What does the city of Atlanta want to achieve in the arts? (Author disclosure: I provided some services to the task force, working through The Schapiro Group, which was contracted to assist the task force in its work.)

These questions are far from straightforward. A typical prior assumption is that the goal of a source of public funding for the arts is to provide income to the city's nonprofit arts organizations. It is certainly true that nonprofits in the arts face challenges. Live performing arts, which in the "high" arts are predominantly nonprofit, in particular are subject to "cost disease." Over the long-term, live performing arts organizations do not have much ability to increase the productivity of their artistic workers—an orchestra needs a certain number of players and a certain amount of time to mount a performance, and these numbers cannot be reduced through technological innovation in the same way that an auto manufacturer can improve its assembly line and so produce more cars per worker per hour. Yet performers' wages must rise in concert with wages for other skilled workers through the economy. Therefore, the live performing arts will always exhibit increasing real costs (Baumol and Bowen 1965). While a city's most prestigious arts organizations might be able to weather cost disease through philanthropy, second-tier arts organizations tend to struggle (Wyszomirski 2002). A recent example of the slow pressures of cost disease taking their toll might be in the switch to recorded music by the Atlanta Ballet (Elliott 2006).

Recent figures show that Atlanta has five nonprofit arts and culture organizations with annual revenues over $10 million: the Atlanta Symphony Orchestra; the Atlanta History Center; the High Museum of Art; the Alliance Theater Company; and, the Fox Theater. Nine other arts and cultural nonprofit organizations have annual revenues over $1 million. Of these fourteen organizations, only the National Black Arts Festival receives over 10 percent of its revenues from public funding.

If a new fund were to be devoted to increased support for arts and culture organizations, it would need to be determined what sort of organizations would qualify for funding. If history museums are included, then ought science museums to be eligible? And if science museums, should the zoo be eligible? In fact many cities that have adopted earmarked funding for the arts have included science museums, zoos, and botanical gardens; achieving a broad base of public support suggests including as many organizations as possible that individuals and their families like to attend.

But that only serves to highlight the fact that in order to gain public support, there needs to be consideration of what is in the public interest. Is the goal to help preserve important cultural institutions for future generations? To allow organizations to reduce admission fees and thereby increase access, perhaps including outreach programs? To provide small amounts of support to the widest possible range of arts organizations, down to the neighborhood level, and so increase participation and youth programs in the arts? The provision of new public funding to existing Atlanta arts nonprofits cannot be an end in itself.

A further question is raised by the "coolness" issue discussed above: Should cultural policy in Atlanta focus on what would attract the highly-educated and mobile "creative class" to move to the city and to remain? If so, how would this inform the allocation of public funds for the arts and culture? Specifically, how would cultural life be enhanced for the two-thirds of the workforce that Richard Florida estimates is *not* a part of the creative class? This is hardly a trivial question for the city of Atlanta, which, as is being discussed by other authors in this book, is a city with significant inequality in wealth, income, and opportunity.

In its report released in March 2007, the ACFTF stressed the intrinsic benefits of the arts. The opening statement of the report holds that "A city is defined by its arts and cultural vibrancy. Arts and culture preserve and communicate our values, lift up voice throughout our city, challenge our conventions, and transform our city's space into meaningful *place*" (Arts and Culture Funding Task Force 2007, 4). The task force recommended a dedicated funding source for the arts that would have the goals of "increasing access to arts and culture" and "enhancing the presence of arts and culture." The funds would be raised through an earmarked tax with a target of about $10 million per year, to be managed by a new not-for-profit organization, and distributed broadly to cultural organizations, including museums in the humanities and sciences. While the final recommendations of the ACFTF recommended some general principles for the selection of the appropriate tax base, it was beyond the scope to make a specific recommendation.

## SOME FINAL CAVEATS

If the ACFTF's recommendations were to be adopted, what impact might it have? We should note the underlying assumption of advocacy for increased public funding of nonprofit arts organizations, that if only there were increased funds for the production of the arts, there would be increased audiences and cultural consumption. But to what degree does increased "unearned" revenue, whether from government or philanthropy, actually change the cultural consumption habits of the local population? The Metro Atlanta Chamber of Commerce expressed hope that Atlanta could come to be perceived as a vibrant city for the arts, but that induces us to ask why it is not perceived as such presently. Are Atlanta residents constrained in their consumption of the arts because of insufficient supply, or is it simply the case that tastes are not those that favor the live, performing high arts, or serious visual art? Thirty-seven years ago, economist Tibor Scitovsky (1972) proclaimed "what's wrong with the arts is what's wrong with society": the high arts, particularly in the United States, struggle because the consumer demand is not there. Classical music, opera, ballet, serious theater, visual art, can only be enjoyed by those who have been educated in the art form and who have typically had some immersion in the arts in their home environment. Lack of an audience without these qualities is not something that can be changed in the short term; developing audiences for the high arts requires a deep cultural change, involving significant changes in attitudes towards leisure time and what constitutes the good life. There are public policies that can attempt to make progress in these directions, starting with schools and after-school programs, especially those that favor participation in the fine arts. But it is not as simple as just granting more money to existing nonprofit arts organizations. And it would require recognition that in fact the cultural tastes of Atlanta residents are perhaps not as sophisticated as some might prefer to assume.

Finally, looking at the future of the arts in Atlanta there needs to be a link to other urban amenities that impact the ability to enjoy what culture the city has to offer. Jane Jacobs (1961) begins her pathbreaking work on *The Death and Life of Great American Cities* (a work that is strongly influential on Richard Florida) by talking about the uses of *sidewalks*; a city that is culturally alive must present an environment where residents can be out and about, on foot, enjoying the diversity of the arts, restaurants, shops, and green space. Atlanta is not (yet) that city: residents drive to cultural events and drive home, and if that is the case it is not wholly surprising that high culture will relocate to where people live, and that Atlanta has become the first (but probably not the last) major U.S. city to have its opera relocate to the suburbs (Ruhe 2006).

And so the arts in Atlanta are something of a paradox. Atlanta has a very high concentration of its workforce in the arts, and this is accompanied by a highly educated population and economic growth. But arts organizations are not well-supported, and the city is far from being seen as an important cultural center. How culture, defined narrowly, affects economic growth is a question that has not yet been decided; Florida's ideas are provocative but there is not yet a large set of significant empirical work on the complex development of culture and economies, much less on what the arts policy response ought to be.

## REFERENCES

Arts and Culture Funding Task Force. *Atlanta's Cultural Investment Fund: Recommendations*. Atlanta, 2007.

Baumol, William J. and William G. Bowen. "On the Performing Arts: The Anatomy of Their Economic Problems." *American Economic Review: Papers and Proceedings* 55, no.1/2 (1965): 495–502.

Bille, Trine and Günther G. Schulze. "Culture in Urban and Regional Development." Pp. 1051–99 in *Handbook of the Economics of Art and Culture*, edited by Victor A. Ginsburgh and David Throsby. Amsterdam: Elsevier, 2006.

Brooks, Arthur C. and Roland J. Kushner. *The Arts Economy in 20 Cities: Where Does Atlanta Stand?* Atlanta: Research Atlanta, 2000.

———. "What Makes an Arts Capital? Quantifying a City's Cultural Environment." *International Journal of Arts Management* 5, no. 1 (2002): 12–23.

Brooks, David. "Patio Man and the Sprawl People." *Weekly Standard*, 12 August 2002.

Caves, Richard E. *Creative Industries: Contracts between Art and Commerce*. Cambridge, Mass.: Harvard University Press, 2000.

Clark, Terry Nichols, Richard Lloyd, Kenneth K. Wong, and Pushpam Jain. "Amenities Drive Urban Growth." *Journal of Urban Affairs* 24, no. 5 (2002): 493–515.

Cremin, Lisa and Kathie deNobriga. "Where do the Arts in Atlanta Stand?" *Grantmakers in the Arts Reader* 13, no. 1 (2002).

Dewan, Shaila. "Cities Compete in Hipness Battle to Attract Young." *New York Times*, 25 November 2006, A1.

DiMaggio, Paul. "Nonprofit Organizations and the Intersectoral Division of Labor in the Arts." Pp. 432–61 in *The Nonprofit Sector: A Research Handbook*. 2d ed., edited by Walter W. Powell and Richard Steinberg. New Haven: Yale University Press, 2006.

Elliott, Susan. "Taking a Musical Leap: Can Atlanta Ballet Hope to Soar without a Live Orchestra?" *Atlanta Journal-Constitution*, 22 October 2006.

Feser, Edward J. "What Regions Do Rather than Make: A Proposed Set of Knowledge-Based Occupation Clusters." *Urban Studies* 40, no. 10 (2003): 1937–1958.

Florida, Richard. "Bohemia and Economic Geography." *Journal of Economic Geography* 2, no. 1 (2002a): 55–71.

————. *The Rise of the Creative Class*. New York: Basic Books, 2002b.

Frey, Bruno. "Public Support." Pp. 389–98 in *A Handbook of Cultural Economics*, edited by Ruth Towse. Cheltenham, UK: Edward Elgar, 2003.

Furdell, Kimberly, Harold Wolman, and Edward W. Hill. "Did Central Cities Come Back? Which Ones, How Far, and Why?" *Journal of Urban Affairs* 27, no. 3 (2005): 283–305.

Gertler, Meric S. "Creative Cities: What are they For, How do they Work, and How do we Build Them?" Canadian Policy Research Network, Background Paper F/48, 2004.

Glaeser, Edward L. "Review of Richard Florida's 'The Rise of the Creative Class.'" *Regional Science and Urban Economics* 35, no. 5 (2005): 593–596.

Glaeser, Edward L. and Joshua D. Gottlieb. "Urban Resurgence and the Consumer City." Harvard Institute of Economic Research, Working Paper #2109, 2006.

Glaeser, Edward L., Jed Kolko, and Albert Saiz. "Consumer City." *Journal of Economic Geography* 1, no. 1, (2001): 27–50.

Glaeser, Edward and Albert Saiz. "The Rise of the Skilled City." Harvard Institute of Economic Research, Working Paper #2025, 2003.

Glaeser, Edward L. and Jesse Shapiro. "Is There a New Urbanism? The Growth of U.S. Cities in the 1990s." NBER Working Paper #8357, 2001.

Hansmann, Henry. "Nonprofit Enterprise in the Performing Arts." *Bell Journal of Economics* 12, no. 2 (1981): 341–361.

Jackson, Maria Rosario, Florence Kabwasa-Green, and Joaquin Herranz. *Cultural Vitality in Communities: Interpretation and Indicators*. Washington, D.C.: The Urban Institute, 2006.

Jacobs, Jane. *The Death and Life of Great American Cities*. New York: Vintage, 1961.

Lang, Robert E. "Review Roundtable: Cities and the Creative Class." *Journal of the American Planning Association* 71, no. 2 (2005): 203–220.

Lucas, Robert E., Jr. "On the Mechanics of Economic Development." *Journal of Monetary Economics* 22, no.1 (1988): 3–42.

Malanga, Steven. "The Curse of the Creative Class." *City Journal* 14, no.1 (2004): 36–45.

Markusen, Ann. "Targeting Occupations in Regional and Community Economic Development." *Journal of the American Planning Association* 70, no. 3 (2004): 253–268.

Markusen, Ann and Greg Schrock. "The Artistic Dividend: Urban Artistic Specialisation and Economic Development Implications." *Urban Studies* 43, no. 10 (2006): 1661–1686.

Martell, Christine R. "Dedicated Funding for Arts, Culture, and Science." *Public Finance and Management* 4, no. 1 (2004): 50–74.

McCarthy, Kevin F., Elizabeth Ondaatje, Laura Zakaras, and Arthur Brooks. *Gifts of the Muse: Reframing the Debate about the Benefits of the Arts*. Santa Monica, CA: RAND, 2004.

North Highland Company. *Evaluating the Link Between Arts & Business*. Atlanta: Metro Atlanta Chamber of Commerce, 2001.

Peacock, Alan. "The Arts and Economic Policy." Pp. 1123–43 in *Handbook of the Economics of Art and Culture*, edited by Victor A. Ginsburgh and David Throsby. Amsterdam: Elsevier, 2006.

Peterson, Richard A. and Roger M. Kern. "Changing Highbrow Taste: From Snob to Omnivore." *American Sociological Review* 61, no. 5 (1996): 900–907.

Postrel, Virginia. "Greetings from Plano, Texas." *Texas Monthly* (December 2006): 114–124.

Romer, Paul M. "Endogenous Technical Change." *Journal of Political Economy* 98, no. 5, part 2 (1990): S71–S102.

Ruhe, Pierre. "Will the Atlanta Opera Solve its Problems by Moving to Cobb?" *Atlanta Journal-Constitution*, 16 July 2006.

Rushton, Michael. *Sustainable Funding for the Arts: Earmarked Taxes and Options for Metropolitan Atlanta*. Atlanta: Research Atlanta, 2003.

———. "Earmarked Taxes for the Arts: U.S. Experience and Policy Implications." *International Journal of Arts Management* 6, no. 3 (2004): 38–49.

———. "Support for Earmarked Public Spending on Culture: Evidence from a Referendum in Metropolitan Detroit." *Public Budgeting and Finance* 25, no. 4 (2005): 72–85.

Scitovsky, Tibor. "What's Wrong with the Arts is What's Wrong with Society." *American Economic Review, Papers and Proceedings* 62, no. 2 (1972): 62–69.

Shapiro, Jesse M. "Smart Cities: Quality of Life, Productivity, and the Growth Effects of Human Capital." NBER Working Paper #11615, 2005.

Wyszomirski, Margaret J. "Arts and Culture." Pp. 187–218 in *The State of Nonprofit America*, edited by Lester M. Salamon. Washington, D.C.: The Brookings Institution, 2002.

*Chapter 8*

# Recent Trends and Future Prospects for Low Income Working Families in Atlanta

*Fred Brooks*

Widely perceived as a classic Sunbelt economic juggernaut, metro Atlanta has experienced explosive growth over the last fifty years (see chapter 3). With an economy based more on services than manufacturing, Atlanta has grown steadily, with few economic setbacks compared to many other cities in the United States. A positive aspect of metro Atlanta's growth has been low unemployment rates and steady job growth. An often overlooked aspect of a service-based economy, like Atlanta's, is that many service sector jobs do not pay very much. The five jobs projected to have the most annual openings in Atlanta from 2001 to 2012 (see table 8.1) pay an average median wage of $8.54/hour (Georgia Department of Labor 2007). This hourly wage translates to $17,763 annually or $2,000 below the federal poverty guideline of $19,874 for a family of four (U.S. Census Bureau 2007).

The first part of this chapter describes three Atlanta families with demographic profiles typical of low income working families. The next part operationally defines low income family and working poor, presents statistical data on low income families in Atlanta, and describes national political and economic forces contributing to large numbers of low income families. The final section describes national and local efforts to raise wages and incomes, highlighting a recent grassroots campaign in Atlanta to win a living wage ordinance. Although Mayor Franklin and Atlanta's City Council in 2004 were poised to pass a living wage ordinance that would have significantly raised wages for several thousand employees of city contractors, the state legislature ignored the home rule precedent and passed legislation preempting cities in Georgia from passing any type of living wage ordinances. The conclusion speculates on what this means for Atlanta's low income families.

Table 8.1   **Median hourly wages of the top five jobs projected to have the most annual openings in Atlanta from 2002–2012**

| Rank | Occupation | Median Hourly Wage |
|------|-----------|--------------------|
| 1 | Cashiers | $8.38 |
| 2 | Retail Salespersons | $10.51 |
| 3 | Laborers & Freight, Stock & Material Movers | $10.10 |
| 4 | Waiters & Waitresses | $6.51 |
| 5 | Food Preparation, including fast food | $7.20 |
|   | Average Median | $8.54 |

Source: Georgia Department of Labor

## THREE FAMILY PROFILES[1]

Yolanda [not her real name] is a twenty-eight year old, single, high school educated, mother of two children (ages two and six) who earns $325–$375/week (~ $16,000/year) working forty-five hours a week at a popular nationally franchised family restaurant. Yolanda's base pay is $2.13 an hour, unchanged since the day she started the job six years ago. Since Yolanda does not own a car, and there is no bus route to her job, she pays $20 a day for cab fare to get to and from work. Her two bedroom apartment costs $800 a month. She signed the lease on the apartment when she was trying to make things work out with the father of her children, but things didn't work out and he moved back to Pennsylvania. Because of the lease she is stuck with rent she cannot afford. Yolanda had employer-sponsored health insurance, but had to cancel it when it did not cover $700 of co-payments for a medical procedure. She now has over $4,000 of medical bills she cannot pay. Although she does not have health insurance, her two children are on the state-sponsored PeachCare for Kids.[2] Yolanda applied for Food Stamps, but her caseworker cut her off after one month. She thought Yolanda was lying, since her monthly bills exceeded her income by such an extent, she was convinced Yolanda must have an alternative source of income she was not telling the caseworker about. Yolanda's mother provides child care while she works the evening shift six days a week. Yolanda applied for child care support five-six years ago, and based on her income was going to pay one half the weekly rate. She applied for public housing but was told there was a two year back-up, the waiting list was closed, and there were no Section 8 housing vouchers available. She wants to stay in her current neighborhood because the school is good and her daughter is doing well in school. She feels she has already moved around too much and would like to create some stability for her children. Since Yolanda's yearly income of ~$16,000 exceeds the poverty threshold of $15,720 (for her family size) the federal government does not consider Yolanda's family as poor.

Ellen is a fifty-one year old African American woman who makes $5.50 an hour cleaning offices twenty hours per week for a janitorial service. Ellen's take home pay is $202 every two weeks. She has worked for the same company for eight years. She has a Section 8 housing voucher which allows her to pay $67 a month for a $650 apartment. Ellen also receives $155 a month in Food Stamps. Ellen states she has a back injury from an accident that occurred in 2001 when some books fell off a shelf she was dusting and landed on her back. She has applied for disability through Social Security but has not yet been awarded disability. Although her claim has been denied before, she is more hopeful now because she has an attorney helping her with her claim. Ellen says she hasn't had health insurance since 1997 when she did janitorial work for a contractor with the city of Atlanta. She says she switched to part-time work because her back was hurting her, and she also had to spend more time taking care of her sick boyfriend who died earlier this year. Although Ellen says she does not have health insurance, she has a "Grady Card," which allows her to receive health care at Grady Hospital, but she insists this is not Medicaid. Ellen says that ever since her boyfriend died earlier this year she has struggled every month to pay her bills. Her boyfriend received $603/month from SSI and he paid all the utility bills. She says when he was still alive they got by okay month to month on their combined incomes. Ellen occasionally gets a little bit of financial help from her thirty-three year old son, who works as a bartender, but has two kids and a child support payment to keep up with, so he usually has little money to spare. When asked what she liked about her job, Ellen stated she enjoyed many of the people whose offices she cleaned. She likes talking with them and joking around. Some of them help Ellen make ends meet by giving her clothes, helping her pay her light bill once, and they even paid the entire bill for her boyfriend's funeral last spring. Ellen says without her housing voucher she would be homeless.

Madelyn is a thirty-eight year old mixed race, single woman with a nineteen year old son (at the time of the interview, August 2006, living with his grandparents out-of-state), a twelve year old daughter, and a six month old son. Madelyn earns $8/hour, working forty hours a week at a high-end car wash. She has only been working there a couple of months since she was off for several months after the birth of her son in January 2006. She has not been on the job long enough to qualify for health insurance, so she is currently uninsured. She tried to make things work out with her ex-boyfriend (the father of her infant son), but he was very physically abusive, so Madelyn ended the relationship. He provides no financial or any other help in raising the infant child. Madelyn and her children have been homeless for most of the past year. She was in a serious auto accident, where she was hospitalized for a week. She lost two jobs she had, her auto insurance had expired, and she has yet to get a settlement from the person who rear-ended her on I-75. When she applied for TANF she was six months pregnant, with a high-risk pregnancy, and with Department of Family and Children Services' "work first" policy was unable to find anyone who would hire her considering she was going to give birth in three months. The only way Madelyn is currently making it is that she is living in a transitional housing program that helps families transitioning from homelessness to independence. She is scheduled to be in the program for another two months and is expected to find her own housing. She is worried about finding market rate housing since she has bad credit because she broke a lease and was evicted from her last market rate apartment. Madelyn does not own a car, and pays $55 per week co-pay for her child care.

## DEFINITIONS OF WORKING POVERTY AND LOW INCOME

Yolanda, Ellen, and Madelyn have incomes near or below the official federal poverty line. Although the Census Bureau glossary says the government does not use the term working poor since it is defined differently depending on who is using it, the Bureau of Labor Statistics (2005) defines working poverty as "those individuals who spend twenty-seven weeks in the workforce (working or looking for work) but whose income falls below the official poverty threshold."

An extensive body of research challenges the validity of measuring poverty with the U.S. Federal Poverty Thresholds (for overviews see Bernstein and Sherman 2006; Pearce and Brooks 2002). The federal government established poverty guidelines in 1964, and based them on the assumption that food constituted 33 percent of the average family budget. The federal guidelines have never taken into consideration the costs of housing, utility bills, child care, transportation, taxes, or geographical differences in cost of living (Pearce and Brooks 2002). Further evidence that the poverty guidelines are considered too low is that state and local governments routinely offer many welfare programs targeted to families with family incomes that are well above the poverty level. For example, in Georgia a family may qualify for Medicaid or PeachCare with incomes up to 235 percent of the federal poverty level. In some states families earn up to 350 percent of the federal poverty threshold and still qualify for the Child Health Insurance Program (Pear and Hernandez 2007).

Since the federal poverty guidelines underestimate working poverty other measures have been developed for empirical research. One measure is the self-sufficiency standard developed by Pearce and Brooks (2002). Another is the Family Basic Needs Budget developed by the Economic Policy Institute. The self-sufficiency standard takes the local cost of living

Table 8.2   **Federal poverty thresholds compared to the self-sufficiency index for different family structures in Fulton County, Georgia**

| Measure | One Adult | One Adult & One Child[a] | One Adult & Two Children[b] |
|---|---|---|---|
| Federal Poverty 2005 | $9,973 | $13,461 | $15,720 |
| 200% of Federal Poverty | $19,946 | $26,922 | $31,440 |
| Self-Sufficiency Standard | $19,256 | $32,437 | $37,982 |

Source: US Bureau of the Census Federal Poverty Thresholds for 2005; Self-Sufficiency Standards from Pearce & Brooks, 2002.
[a]Assumes the child is a preschooler
[b]Assumes one child is a preschooler and the other is school age

into account for housing, utility rates, child care, transportation, and taxes. In the state of Georgia a self-sufficiency standard is calculated separately for each county. Table 8.2 compares the federal poverty thresholds for different family sizes to the self-sufficiency standard for Fulton County. The gap between the federal poverty rate and the self-sufficiency standard is quite enormous for all family sizes. While the federal poverty level for a family of three (one adult and two children) is $15,735, the self-sufficiency standard is almost two and a half times as much at $37,982 (U.S. Census Bureau 2007; Pearce and Brooks 2002).

In this chapter I will use the term "working poor" to refer to families, like the three women profiled above, where the head of household is working full time and her income is at or below the official federal poverty level. I will use the broader term "low income" to refer to all people living in families earning less than 200 percent of the federal poverty level. Since the ratio of the self-sufficiency standard to the official poverty level ranges from 200 percent to 240 percent this is probably a conservative measure of the number of low income people in Atlanta.

## RECENT STATISTICAL TRENDS FOR
## LOW INCOME FAMILIES IN ATLANTA

For the past quarter century Atlanta has had a relatively stable, high concentration of urban poverty combined with rising income inequality. Since the 1970s the percentage of people in Atlanta living in low income families has increased from 39 percent to 43 percent. Table 8.3 reports the ratio of income to poverty rate for residents of Atlanta from 1970 to 2005.

In 1970 39 percent of families in Atlanta were low income (< 200% of poverty rate). This rose to 51 percent in 1980 and then declined 4 percent over each of the next two decades to 43 percent in 2000, and remained at 43 percent in 2005. Examining the raw numbers for each income category since 1990 reveals differences between income strata. Since 1990 24,000 more

**Table 8.3   Ratio of income to Federal Poverty Level for individuals in City of Atlanta**

| Ratio of income to poverty level | 1970[a] | 1980[b] | 1990 | 2000 | 2005 |
|---|---|---|---|---|---|
| Under 1.00 | 19,023 | | 102,364 | 95,743 | 105,928 |
| | 16% | | 27% | 24% | 27% |
| 1.00 to 1.99 | 27,082 | | 73,876 | 76,630 | 65,077 |
| | 23% | | 20% | 19% | 16% |
| 2.00 and over | 73,221 | 199,403 | 198,579 | 220,033 | 223,219 |
| | 61% | 49% | 53% | 57% | 57% |
| Total | 119,326 | 409,424 | 374,579 | 392,406 | 394,224 |
| | 100% | 100% | 100% | 100% | 100% |

Source: U.S. Bureau of the Census
[a]Data from 1970 is households; data for all other years is for individuals
[b]Ratios for 1980 were reported differently from other years, 210,021 individuals (51%) lived in families with incomes from 0-1.99 of the poverty threshold; ratios the Census Bureau reported for 1980 are shown below

**Ratio of Income to Poverty Level for 1980**

| Ratio of income to poverty level | 1980 |
|---|---|
| Under .75 | 84,539 |
| | 21% |
| .75 to 1.24 | 55,982 |
| | 13% |
| 1.25 to 1.99 | 69,500 |
| | 17% |
| 2.00 and over | 199,403 |
| | 49% |
| Total | 409,424 |
| | 100% |

Atlantans are living in families with incomes above 200 percent of poverty. For people earning between 100 percent and 200 percent of poverty the numbers rose during the 90s then declined by 11,000 between 2000 and 2005. The number of people living below 100 percent of poverty declined by 6,000 from 1990 to 2000 but rose by 10,000 from 2000 to 2005. In 2005 27 percent of the population of Atlanta was living below 100 percent of the poverty rate. This is 11 percentage points higher compared to 16 percent of the population living in poverty in 1970.

The data do not tell us how many of the families living between 100 percent and 200 percent poverty from 2000 to 2005 either went up or down to other income categories or moved out of the city. The data clearly show that from 1990 to 2005 the percentage of Atlanta residents living below 100 percent of poverty remained constant at 27 percent while their raw numbers increased by 4,000. This suggests that while near poor families might be leaving Atlanta, the poorest of the poor have remained in the city.

These statistics suggest a continuing trend of rising income inequality in Atlanta that Keating (2001) documented has been happening since the 1950s. According to Keating (2001) and Smith (1987) inequality between blacks and whites in Atlanta increased between 1950 and 1990. In 1950 the ratio of median family incomes between predominately white and predominately black census tracts was 2.02 (whites earning twice the amount of blacks). By 1990 the ratio had grown to 5.28 ($88,029 to $16,667 respectively). Keating (2001) cites a multiplicity of factors contributing to rising inequality in Atlanta. These factors include affluent whites and blacks leaving the city, the (primarily northern) suburban growth of major office complexes and business development, and the distribution of jobs by race and gender.

Data from 2005 suggest poverty in Atlanta is still related to race, gender, and family type. Table 8.4 shows the percentage of Atlanta residents living above or below the poverty level by race and gender. For people living above the poverty line the distribution by race and gender is fairly equal compared to an extremely skewed distribution of race and sex for people living below the poverty line. Fifty-two percent of the poor in Atlanta are black females while only 5 percent of the poor are white females. Only 11 percent of the poor are white males compared to 31 percent being black males.

Table 8.4  **Poverty status in Atlanta by race and gender in 2005**

| Poverty Status | White | | Black | | Totals |
|---|---|---|---|---|---|
| | Male | Female | Male | Female | |
| < 100% of Poverty | 12,100 | 5,927 | 33,751 | 56,721 | 108,721 |
| | 11% | 5% | 31% | 52% | 100% |
| > 100% of Poverty | 71,661 | 59,225 | 66,095 | 74,463 | 271,444 |
| | 26% | 22% | 24% | 27% | 100% |

Source: US Bureau of the Census, American Community Survey 2005

Table 8.5  **Ratio of income to poverty level by family type**

| Ratio of income to poverty level | Family Type | | | |
| | Married Couple | Male Head of Household | Female Head of Household | Totals |
|---|---|---|---|---|
| < 1.3 | 2,298 | 2,416 | 19,594 | 24,308 |
| | 9% | 10% | 81% | 100% |
| 1.3-1.84 | 1,959 | 983 | 3,637 | 6,579 |
| | 30% | 15% | 55% | 100% |
| > 1.84 | 33,629 | 4,450 | 10,683 | 48,762 |
| | 69% | 9% | 22% | 100% |

Source: US Bureau of the Census, American Community Survey 2005

Family structure is also related to poverty levels in Atlanta. Table 8.5 shows poverty levels in Atlanta by family type. In 2005 81 percent of families in Atlanta with incomes less than 1.3 of the poverty level were female-headed households.

In summation, since 1990 the number of affluent people living in Atlanta has increased while concentrated poverty remains relatively constant, and the number of near poor people has decreased slightly. Poverty in Atlanta is still strongly correlated with race, gender, and family structure. Many of the macro-economic trends affecting Atlanta are related to the national and even global economy.

## NATIONAL AND LOCAL FACTORS CONTRIBUTING TO LOW INCOMES AND WORKING POVERTY

Although working poverty has only recently attracted the attention of scholars, journalists, and the popular press, many of the economic, institutional, and political trends that contribute to low incomes have been operating for the past quarter to half century. Many of these trends are national, or even global in scope, such that Atlanta cannot be blamed for being the perpetrator of these trends. At the same time, powerful political and economic interests in Georgia have done little to help low income families. In the case of the recent campaign in Atlanta for a Living Wage Ordinance, the legislature and governor decided living wage ordinances, passed by democratically elected local officials, were not in the best interest of Georgians. (These trends will be analyzed later in the chapter.) This section will briefly describe the following trends and how they contribute to working poverty in the United States and Atlanta: decline of organized labor, the global economy and rise of neo-liberal economic policies, the hegemony of Wal-Mart's business model, and several policy positions of the federal government. These are not necessarily discrete variables; many of these factors are mutually reinforcing and often work in combination with each other.

### The Decline of Organized Labor

Many scholars credit the rise of organized labor during the first half of the twentieth century as a major factor in moving millions of families in the United States from working poverty to middle class (Conlin and Bernstein 2004; Murolo and Chitty 2001). Organized labor played a role in creating the forty hour work week, overtime pay, benefits such as paid sick leave and paid vacation, in addition to raising wages so that people with high school educations could earn enough to buy homes, automobiles, and live middle-class lifestyles.

Union density in the U.S. private sector labor market peaked in 1954, with 39 percent of the workforce belonging to unions (Clawson and Clawson 1999). In 2006 only 7.4 percent of private sector workers belonged to unions (Bureau of Labor Statistics [BLS] 2007). Forces both inside and outside the labor movement contributed to labor's decline. Unions can only blame themselves for being racist and sexist during the mid-twentieth century and failing to see the organizing opportunities brought about by the civil rights movement and the dramatic influx of women into the labor force over the last half of the twentieth century (Clawson and Clawson 1999). Unions can also be faulted for complacency about their size and influence in mid-century. Most unions adopted a business unionism model that placed an emphasis on maintenance rather than growth, which is emphasized in an organizing model. The schism between organizing and maintenance was never completely reconciled, and the most recent manifestation of the tension was the secession from the AFL-CIO of several large and fast-growing unions (e.g., SEIU, Teamsters, and UFCW) claiming the old coalition of labor unions was not placing enough emphasis on organizing new members (Greenhouse 2005a).

Another factor contributing to union decline in the U.S. is the transition from a manufacturing/industrial-based economy to a service-oriented economy. Much of that transition has also been geographic, from old industrial northern cities (e.g., Detroit, Cleveland) to fast-growing Sunbelt cities (e.g., Atlanta, Phoenix, Las Vegas, Orlando). Simply put, the most unionized sectors of the economy and country have been declining, while the least unionized sectors have been growing so fast unions have been unable to keep up (Clawson and Clawson 1999).

The decline of union density has had enormous impact on wages in blue-collar industries. Although traditionally union jobs paid approximately one third more than the same non-union jobs, this gap has increased recently. According to a report from the Economic Policy Institute (Conlin and Bernstein 2004) blue-collar workers in labor unions earn 54 percent more than non-unionized workers doing the same exact jobs.

Organized labor has never established a strong mass-base in Georgia or Atlanta. The only unions that have attained reasonable density are those strongly associated with heavily unionized national industries such as autoworkers. The Ford plant in Hapeville, which closed in October 2006, was unionized, as is the General Motors plant in Doraville (scheduled to shutter in 2008). Georgia has been a so-called "right-to-work" state since 1947 (U.S. Department of Labor 2007). Currently, Georgia has the third lowest rate of unionization in the U.S.; only 4.4 percent of private sector workers in Georgia are union members. The only states with lower unionization rates are North Carolina and South Carolina (BLS 2007).

## Neo-Liberal Economic Policy and the Global Economy

One reason union density has declined in the United States is the rise of the global economy, where corporations seek to build manufacturing plants anywhere in the world they find the lowest labor costs. Many American companies claim they are unable to compete with foreign industries that pay wages that are pennies on the dollar compared to wages in the United States. American industries that appear to be unable to compete in the global economy include textiles, shoemaking, steel, and some electronics.

Job growth trends in metro Atlanta reflect the nationwide shift from a manufacturing to a service-based economy. In the decade from 1995 to 2005, while metro Atlanta lost 23,000 (-11.3%) manufacturing jobs, service sector jobs grew at a steady rate. For example financial sector jobs increased by 45,000 (+40%), education and health jobs increased by 81,000 (+54%) (BLS 2006; Georgia Department of Labor 2006 in Chamber of Commerce 2006).

## The Hegemony of Wal-Mart's Business Model

The primary features of Wal-Mart's business model include low wages, minimal benefit packages, squeezing suppliers, and doing whatever it takes to prevent unions from organizing their employees (Rathke 2005). The growth of this business model is called the Wal-Martization of the economy (Conlon and Bernstein 2004). Rathke (2005) argues that Wal-Mart is the GM, Ford, and US Steel of the current age, that is, their business model sets the standard for similar stores (e.g., Home Depot, Lowe's, Target, etc.) and much of the service economy. When unions organized auto and steelworkers in the early twentieth century it helped raise wages and improve working conditions for millions of workers across the U.S. If Rathke is correct, the fate of the working poor will be determined largely by the wage and benefit standards that Wal-Mart sets. The clash between Wal-Mart and a more employee friendly business model was recently portrayed in stark relief in Southern California. Wal-Mart announced a plan to build forty supercenters in southern California. The unionized chains that currently dominate the southern California market (Albertson's, Kroger, and Safeway) pay an average of 30 percent more to employees compared to Wal-Mart (Conlon and Bernstein 2004). The unionized chains also pay a greater percentage of employee health insurance compared to Wal-Mart. Fearing being unable to compete with Wal-Mart, these stores attempted to cut wages and benefits, resulting in a five-month-long strike. Although current jobs were protected, all new hires in the union chains will make lower wages and pay a much higher percentage of their health insurance compared to current union members. Many new employees are expected to be unable to afford the higher health insurance premiums (Conlon and Bernstein 2004).

Trends on the uptake of employee-paid health insurance suggest more companies are adopting Wal-Mart's business model. According to Reynolds and Kern (2003) the percentage of employees with health insurance wholly paid by their employer dropped from 71 percent in 1980 to 37 percent in 1993. In 2006, only one out of every three entry level jobs filled by those with high school diplomas offered health insurance. This was a 50 percent decrease since 1979 (Greenhouse 2006). In Georgia, 1.6 million people (18.1% of the population) do not have health insurance. Georgia was one of only eight states with a statistically significant decline in health insurance rates from 2004 to 2005 (Coffey 2006).

One consequence of companies like Wal-Mart offering benefits packages its own workers can't afford, is that many working people end up relying on government benefits such as PeachCare. In 2004 10,261 children of Wal-Mart employees in Georgia were enrolled in PeachCare for Kids. Wal-Mart employees led all companies in Georgia with the highest number of children enrolled in the PeachCare program (Miller 2004).

**Federal Government Policies**

The federal government has enormous power to positively or negatively affect the working poor by the policies it adopts or does not adopt. New Deal legislation from the 1930s helped close the gap between rich and poor, and created safety net programs such as unemployment insurance to help working families cope with the vicissitudes of capitalism. It also helped set the stage for the tremendous post-war economic expansion where Americans in all economic quintiles experienced significant financial gains (Krugman 2006).

Although the federal government has never been "pro-labor," [3] at times the government has been neutral rather than hostile in policy making that affected union organizing. The National Labor Relations Act (NLRA) enacted in 1935 helped even the playing field between labor and management and contributed to the growth of unions in the 1930s and 1940s.

Since 1980, when Reagan took office and put the power of the presidency squarely against organized labor by firing 11,500 striking air traffic controllers, the federal government has trended anti-union for two and a half decades. The president appoints the chair and members of the National Labor Relations Board (NLRB). The NLRB has tremendous power adjudicating labor elections and setting labor policy. Although Clinton appointed some pro-labor members to the NLRB, Reagan and George W. Bush appointed unabashedly anti-union members to the NLRB (Meister n.d.; Meister 2005). A recent board decision widely perceived as anti-union was the NLRB's decision designating lead shift nurses as managers rather than employees. This decision makes lead registered nurses ineligible for union membership. Some labor scholars believe this decision could eliminate eight million workers from potential union membership across the United States (Greenhouse 2006b).

## The Minimum Wage

Beyond the federal government's policy making influence on organized labor, the government's decisions on the minimum wage also affect the quality of life of the working poor. "The purchasing power of the minimum wage peaked in 1968. In 1996, even after the increase of the minimum wage to $5.15/hour, the purchasing power of the minimum wage was 30 percent below its peak in 1968" (Reynolds and Kern 2003). In 2006, the value of the minimum wage was at its lowest level since 1955 (Bernstein and Shapiro 2006 in Brooks 2007, 438). In December 2006 the federal government broke the record (10 years) for the longest time elapsed without increasing the minimum wage (Bernstein and Shapiro 2006).

"An astonishing feature of the stagnation in wages and the decline of the minimum wage over the past thirty years is the fact that the U.S. economy and worker productivity have both increased significantly over the same time period" (Reynolds and Kern 2003 in Brooks 2007, 438). For much of the last century, wages and the minimum wage experienced gains somewhat commensurate with increases in gross domestic product and worker productivity. "In 2001, worker productivity was roughly 80 percent higher than when the minimum wage peaked in 1968. If the minimum wage had kept pace with worker productivity it would have risen to $14.65" by 2005 (Pollin 2005 in Brooks 2007, 438). In January 2007 within its first one hundred hours of business, the newly elected (majority Democratic) Congress passed the first increase of the minimum wage in over ten years. President Bush signed the legislation in the summer of 2007. The credit for making the minimum wage increase a congressional priority can probably be attributed to the dozens of local and statewide grassroots campaigns conducted over the past ten to fifteen years.

## NATIONAL AND LOCAL FORCES
## COMBATING WORKING POVERTY

### Minimum and Living Wage Campaigns

Although low-income working families traditionally have had little political power, they have not sat idly by watching their wages stagnate, health insurance erode, and jobs ship overseas. Although the federal government since the 1980s has largely abandoned issues of working poverty, numerous labor and grassroots organizations have been organizing and affecting policy on two of the levels of government where average citizens are still able to influence public policy: state and local levels. Although the federal government refused to raise the minimum wage from 1996 to 2006, twenty-two states raised their minimum wages above the federal level (Caplan 2006).

Over 140 cities, towns, and counties have passed living wage ordinances. Most living wage ordinances set a minimum wage that is significantly higher than the federal minimum wage for employees of companies with city contracts. The wage rates mandated by living wage ordinances in 2006 ranged from $6.25 in Milwaukee County to $14.00 in Santa Barbara, California (ACORN Living-wage Resource Center 2006). Since most ordinances only apply to companies with sizable contracts with the city (but some apply to companies receiving tax breaks, or operating on city owned property) they only directly affect a limited number of jobs.

Living wage campaigns and the resulting ordinances are based on two simple ideas. First, anyone who works full-time should not have to raise their family in poverty. Second, public dollars should not be subsidizing poverty wage jobs. These ideas have wide public support, and when combined with well organized, strategic, energetic, coalition campaigns (see Reynolds and Kern 2003 for numerous case studies of campaigns) have won more often than lost, resulting in 140 new ordinances and raising the wages of an estimated 250,000 low-wage workers.

A few cities have passed bolder ordinances that raised the minimum wage significantly for all businesses operating in the city. For example, the minimum wage in Santa Fe, NM is $9.50 an hour for all businesses operating in the city limits (Gertner 2006). In 2006, another seventy-five coalitions were waging living wage campaigns in cities across the United States. This level of local organizing has been justifiably called a "living wage movement" (see Gertner 2006; Pollin and Luce 1998; Reynolds and Kern 2003). Economist Robert Kuttner (1997) described the living wage movement as "the most interesting and (underreported) grassroots enterprise to emerge since the civil rights movements . . . signaling a resurgence of local activism around pocketbook issues."

### Innovative Union Organizing

Besides the living wage movement, many unions have reinvented themselves by experimenting with new organizing strategies and techniques. Some of these strategies have succeeded, resulting in hundreds of thousands of new members, primarily in the service sector (see Brooks 2005a; 2005b; Delp and Quan 2002). While globalization and economic restructuring continue to take a toll on the old industrial unions in the auto and textile industries, the Service Employees International Union (SEIU) has been the fastest growing union in the United States. Between 1995 and 2005 SEIU grew from 1.1 to 1.8 million members (Greenhouse 2005b). In some cases the wins were large and dramatic. In California in 1999 a majority of 74,000 home health workers voted to unionize (Delp and Quan 2002). This was the largest successful union election since the 1941 United Auto Workers victory at the River Rouge plant in Dearborn, Michigan (Stone 2000). In 2005, Local 880 SEIU in Illinois won an election representing 49,000 home child care providers. This was the largest successful union election of child care providers ever, and one of the largest union victories ever in the state of Illinois (Brooks 2005a). Major drives of child care workers are currently taking place in New York and New Jersey (ACORN 2007).

Since the 1980s, in what is widely perceived as the most successful union drive in the United States, the Hotel Employees and Restaurant Employees Union Local 226 (also referred to as "the Culinary," an affiliate of UNITE/HERE) has organized 60,000 housekeepers, waitresses, busboys, and hotel workers on the strip in Las Vegas, Nevada. Unionized waitresses earn $10.14 an hour before tips, the highest rate in the entire United States (Greenhouse 2004).

Although the Atlanta affiliates of SEIU and UNITE/HERE have not organized up to the same scale as their sister locals in California, Illinois, or Las Vegas, they have made steady, methodical progress in several areas. SEIU Local 1985 headquartered in Atlanta represents over 5,000 state employees ranging from parking lot attendants, to Head Start teachers, to caseworkers at the Department of Family and Children's Services (Local 1985 n.d.). UNITE/HERE has organized a unit of concessionaire workers at Hartsfield-Jackson International Airport. In addition to these union efforts, in 2001 a coalition of community, labor, and faith-based organizations came together and launched a citywide campaign to win a living wage ordinance in Atlanta. The following section tells the story of the Atlanta living wage campaign.

## THE ATLANTA LIVING WAGE CAMPAIGN

By 2001, fifty local governments in the United States had passed living wage ordinances (ACORN Living Wage Resource Center 2006). Leaders of community and labor organizations in Atlanta decided the time was right to fight for a living wage ordinance. Four organizations played significant leadership roles in the campaign: Atlanta 9to5 Working Women, Georgia Citizens Coalition on Hunger and Homelessness,

The Central Labor Council of North Georgia, and Project South. Several of these organizations had just collaborated on a successful statewide campaign raising the Georgia minimum wage to the same level as the federal minimum wage. With all fifteen city council seats and the mayor's position up for election in November 2001, the coalition felt the campaign was auspiciously timed. The coalition quickly grew to more than fifty organizations (later over one hundred groups joined the coalition), and members began attending candidate forums asking the various candidates where they stood on a proposed living wage ordinance. The campaign also began researching city contracts, tax breaks, and engaged the Brennan Center for Financial Justice at New York University to help write a draft ordinance for Atlanta. According to a coalition member, mayoral candidate Shirley Franklin stated that not only did she support a living wage ordinance, but that "she could make things happen." Based on a combination of factors including strong support from the potential mayor, the quick growth of the coalition, and the widespread success of living wage campaigns across the country the draft ordinance proposed by the coalition was considered quite strong. Not only would the ordinance require all contractors (with contracts over $50,000 annually) to pay their employees $10.50 an hour, the ordinance would apply to employers receiving city grants, loans, leases, subcontracts, and subtenants. Since the city owns Hartsfield-Jackson Airport, it would have applied to an estimated 10,000 low-wage workers at the airport. Compared to other living wage ordinances across the nation the proposed Atlanta ordinance would be one of the stronger ones, covering the maximum number of jobs with companies receiving public subsidies. The coalition held a kickoff rally in October 2001 at the old city council chambers, attended by over 200 supporters in addition to a dozen candidates for city council.

In the winter of 2002, shortly after Mayor Franklin and new city council members took office, the coalition began office visits and determined that ten out of fifteen council members supported the living wage ordinance. Although neither the mayor nor city council seemed in a hurry to pass the ordinance, Mayor Franklin ordered a review of all employees on city payroll. The audit found 800 city employees earning less than $10.50 an hour, which was the hourly wage the living wage coalition was trying to win for any jobs directly subsidized by city monies. Mayor Franklin immediately raised the wages of all city employees to a minimum of $10.50 an hour. She stated that 800 employees received increases ranging from $400 to $4,000 per year (Cindia Cameron, personal communication 2006). The Atlanta Living Wage Coalition had scored its first victory.

Since the coalition felt it had solid support from the mayor and the majority of city council it adopted a slow "under the radar" approach to the ordinance, hoping to get the bill passed before attracting opposition from the business community. Compared to living wage campaigns in other cities, like Chicago, where Mayor Daley opposed a living wage ordinance (Reynolds and Kern 2003), in Atlanta there was little confrontation between living wage activists and city officials. Since the key city officials had expressed support for the ordinance there was no need for confrontation. City council spent most of 2002 studying the issue, and in 2003 Councilman C.T. Martin and nine other city council members[4] introduced a very strong ordinance which was almost identical to the draft ordinance proposed by the coalition. The proposed ordinance would require contractors to pay $10.50 an hour and would apply to businesses operating at Hartsfield-Jackson airport.

The City Finance committee had a public hearing on May 28, 2003. The Atlanta Living Wage Coalition was well represented; over a dozen coalition members testified including several low-wage workers who stood to receive substantial pay raises if the bill became law. By this time the business community was well aware of the ordinance and they presented a number of witnesses testifying against the proposed ordinance. Delta Airlines and AirTran in particular were opposed to the living wage ordinance. One living wage coalition member recalls either the Delta or AirTran spokesperson saying if the city passed the living wage ordinance they would "stop it."

In the summer of 2003 it seemed clear that the business lobby had finally gotten the ear of the mayor. As politicians often do when they are on the hot-seat between powerful business interests and grassroots organizations, in August 2003 Mayor Franklin announced the formation of the "Independent Living Wage Commission" to study the issue and report back to her in ninety days with recommendations. In December over ninety days had passed with no announcement of the commission's formation. On January 8, 2004 the mayor's office announced that Walter Massey, the president of Morehouse College, would chair the Mayor's Independent Commission on the Living Wage.

The mayor's goal was to appoint an independent commission with no partisans on either side of the issue. The commission began work in January by reviewing over "1000 pages of economic analysis, opinion columns, and research reports on the subject of the living wage and its projected and actual impacts in other cities" (Massey 2004; 3). The commission also scheduled two hearings on the issue for January and February 2004.

Although the anti-living wage lobby[5] had witnesses testify at both hearings, it decided to take its case to the state legislature, which had just become majority Republican, and the governor, who was the first Republican governor in power since Reconstruction. The business lobby found an enthusiastic and powerful legislator in the person of Representative

Earl Ehrhart (R–Marietta), who had just become chairman of the Rules Committee. Representative Ehrhart introduced HB 1258, which would preempt all local government entities in Georgia from passing living wage ordinances. The House Industrial Relations Committee held hearings on HB 1258. One pro-living wage witness attended the hearing and described it thusly: "I remember I testified [against HB 1258] and it was like in this little conference room. And it was all these guys, I mean they didn't give a rat's ass about it. I mean, it was obvious that all of them were just going to let it . . . fly right through." She went on describe the committee chair's reaction to any testimony against HB 1258: "he shot it down, he completely shot it down!"

The Atlanta Living Wage Coalition had been implementing a citywide strategy for almost three years and was unprepared to mount a statewide campaign on such short notice. Coalition members lobbied as many legislators as they could from their base in Atlanta, but were unable to influence many legislators outside the city. What had been an offensive campaign quickly became defensive. On March 24, 2004, HB 1258 was passed by the legislature. One week later, on April 1 the mayor's Independent Living Wage Commission released their report recommending that Atlanta pass a "carefully tailored living wage ordinance." HB 1258 rendered all of the commission's work moot once Governor Perdue signed it and it became law on May 13, 2004.

Although the city of Atlanta could have protested this raw exercise of state power into city affairs by either passing a living wage ordinance anyway or filing a lawsuit against the state, Mayor Franklin and the city attorney decided against challenging the state's preemption law. The city studied the new state law and crafted a much milder ordinance which, rather than requiring contractors to pay employees $10.50/hour, stated that one criterion the city would examine when considering bids for contracts would be the wages and benefits companies offered their employees. They would award points to companies paying higher wages and offering benefits. In 2004, the city passed this ordinance believing it was a small concession to the living wage coalition and was also in compliance with HB 1258.

During the following legislative session in January 2005 the legislature decided the new Atlanta ordinance was too intrusive between businesses and the wages they paid their employees. Representative Ehrhart introduced an amendment to HB 1258 which would preempt the new Atlanta ordinance and anything similar. Like HB 1258 the amendment flew through the legislature and passed with 105 yeas to fifty-seven nays in the House and thirty-three yeas and seventeen nays in the Senate (Georgia General Assembly 2005). According to Jen Kern (personal communication July 7, 2006), the director of ACORN's Living Wage Resource Center, this new law was the most restrictive living wage preemption legislation in the entire country. No other states have preempted the power of cities to favorably consider contractors who paid their employees good wages and benefits.

## Implications of the Living Wage Campaign

Although living wage ordinances are criticized for being symbolic rather than substantive poverty reduction measures, the symbolic and instrumental messages in Georgia are clear: the legislature and governor in Georgia are against local government initiatives that would raise the wages of low-income working people. The state government's blunt force instrument approach to squashing local initiatives suggests at least for the immediate future working poor families in Georgia cannot look to local or state government for policies that might help them. An immediate implication for community and labor organizations is that to wield power at the local level they also need a statewide base and organizing strategy. Local organizations have responded by developing statewide strategies. The Atlanta Living Wage Coalition changed its name to the Georgia Living Wage Coalition and with over one hundred endorsing organizations is waging a multi-year campaign to raise the minimum wage in Georgia. In 2008 the coalition failed to get the minimum wage bill out of committee, but it plans on trying again in 2009. Since this is a modest proposal to raise wages for several categories of workers not covered by the federal minimum wage laws (e.g., home health care, fishermen, recreation workers) whether it passes or not will show where state lawmakers stand on initiatives to help low-income working people.

Another implication of the legislature's recent rejection of policies that would help the working poor is that community and labor organizations should get more directly involved in electoral politics. If low and moderate income people want influence over state legislators they have to remove those who do not represent them and elect politicians who will. Currently the most successful electoral strategies appear to be in states like New York, Oregon, and Connecticut, where community and labor organizations have established the Working Families Party. This third party strategy is most effective where election laws allow fusion or open ballot voting. Open ballot voting historically was legal and widely practiced in every state in the United States. It allows more than one party to endorse a candidate on the ballot (see Working Families Party n.d.). Open ballot voting is currently not allowed in Georgia, so election laws would probably have to change first. The New York chapter of the Working Families Party seems to be particularly effective. In 2004 it pushed the New York legislature to override Governor Pataki's veto of a minimum wage increase.

## SHORT AND LONG-TERM PROSPECTS
## FOR LOW INCOME ATLANTANS

The statistics since 1990 suggest increasing inequality in Atlanta with the number of poor people recently increasing (from 2000 to 2005), while more affluent people are also moving into the city. At the time of this writing (February 2008) economists are predicting either no economic growth or a recession for the remainder of 2008. Local and state policy initiatives don't appear poised to reduce inequality or poverty rates in the city of Atlanta. At least for the immediate future I predict that poverty and inequality in Atlanta will remain unchanged or will get worse.

Long-term prospects for the working poor will probably be determined by the success of national movements to revitalize the labor movement and reform education. Historically the road from the working poor to the middle class was paved by either organized labor (for people with a high school education or less) or higher education. One reason hourly wages have been stagnant for the past thity-five years is the decline of organized labor. There are millions of service sector jobs that will never require college degrees to perform (janitorial, retail, food service, etc.). It is difficult to imagine employees in these sectors significantly improving their wages without organizing into some type of labor union.

With the decline of the U.S. industrial base and the effects of a globalized economy, earning a middle class income today depends more than ever on obtaining a college degree. Economists and pundits of all political persuasions argue that for the U.S. economy to successfully compete globally and for inequality and poverty to be reduced education reform is essential (see Brooks 2008; Reich 2008). Inequality and working poverty are unlikely to be reduced in Atlanta until education reform and a revitalized labor movement have succeeded in other regions or at the federal level. If that occurs the politics of change are much more likely to affect the state of Georgia and Atlanta. At least for the near term, low-income uninsured Atlantans, like Yolanda, Ellen, and Madelyn, might see their wages increase and finally get health insurance because of federal legislation rather than anything initiated at the state or local level.

### NOTES

1. In order to give a human face to the issue of working poverty in Atlanta I interviewed 6 families where the single head of household was working, but the families were struggling to make ends meet. Four families were referred to me by a social worker who worked for a non-profit agency that provided homeless families with transitional housing. Two interviews were with women who were living in apartments with the assistance of Atlanta Housing Authority vouchers which paid

a major portion of their rent. I had interviewed these women on a previous research project, and I knew that both had jobs and were struggling to pay their bills. Based on this convenience sampling technique it is unknown if these profiles are representative of the population of working poor families in Atlanta. The demographic profiles of these families are strikingly similar to working poor families described by Shulman (2003) and Shipler (2004) in their books on the working poor in the U.S.

2. PeachCare for Kids is Georgia's version of the federally sponsored State Child Health Insurance Program (SCHIP), passed in 1997. The program is designed to insure the children of low income working families who have been most impacted with the declining rates of employer sponsored health insurance. The federal government currently pays 73% of the costs of PeachCare, with the state paying the remaining 27%. The program has been in effect for ten years and is up for reauthorization in 2007. Current indicators suggest the Bush administration is going to push for states to pick up more of the costs of SCHIP (Pear and Hernandez, 2007).

3. An argument might be made that the federal government was "pro-labor" from 1935 to 1947 between passage of the Wagner-Connery Act (which prohibited much anti-union behavior by companies) and the Taft-Hartley Act which was unquestionably anti-union legislation. Without question the federal government has trended anti-union since 1947.

4. Other sponsors included H.L. Willis, Natalyn Archibong, Jim Maddox, Ivory Lee Young, Jr., Derrick Boazman, Ceasar Mitchell, Carla Smith, Debi Starnes, and Mary Norwood. A City Council member I interviewed who supported the proposed ordinance stated in retrospect that he wondered if it might have been a strategic mistake having 10 cosponsors for the ordinance. It might have given the opponents of the ordinance the impression that it was a *fait accompli* in the city chambers and prompted them to go to the state level to stop it.

5. I attempted to interview members of the anti-living wage lobby for this paper. I contacted The Chamber of Commerce, Central Atlanta, Progress, and Georgia State University Professor Emeritus of Economics Dr. Donald Ratachek. Neither the Chamber of Commerce nor Donald Ratachek responded to my invitation for interviews. Central Atlanta Progress stated no one on staff in 2006 had been involved in the 2004 campaign.

## REFERENCES

ACORN. Best of ACORN organizing—2006. 2007. www.acorn.org/fileadmin/ ACORN_Reports/2007/2006AnnualReport.pdf (18 Feb. 2007).

ACORN Living Wage Resource Center. Living Wage Wins. 2006. livingwagecampaign. org/index.php?id=1959 (18 Feb. 2007).

Bernstein, Jared, and Isaac Shapiro. *Buying Power of Minimum Wage at 51 Year Low: Congress Could Break Record for Longest Period Without an Increase.* (20 June 2006). www.cbpp.org/6-20-06mw.htm (12 Sept. 2006).

Bernstein, Jared and Arloc Sherman. Poor Measurement: New Census Report on Measuring Poverty Raised Concerns. Center on Budget and Policy Priorities and Economic Policy Institute. (28 Mar. 2006). www.epinet.org/issuebriefs/222/ ib222.pdf (12 Feb. 2007).

Brooks, David. Fresh Start Conservatism. *New York Times*, p. A23, (15 Feb. 2008).

Brooks, Fred. "Historic Union Victory for Family Child Care Providers in Illinois." In *Critical Solidarity: Newsletter of the Labor and Labor Movements Section American Sociological Association* 5, no.1 (2005a): 7–8.

———. "The Living Wage Movement: Potential Implications for the Working Poor." *Families in Society* 88, no. 3 (July–September 2007): 437–42.

———. "New Turf for Organizing: Family Child Care Workers." *Labor Studies Journal* 29, no.1 (2005b): 45–64.

Bureau of Labor Statistics [BLS]. In S. Fogel (Guest Editor) "Working but Poor: New Directions for Social Workers." *Families in Society* 88, no.3 (2005): 1–2.

Bureau of Labor Statistics [BLS]. Union Member Summary. 2007. www.bls.gov/cps/ (9 Jan. 2007).

Caplan, Jeremy. Where to Get a Pay Raise. *Time*, p. 51, (21 Aug. 2006).

Chamber of Commerce. Metro Atlanta Nonagricultural Employment. Atlanta MSA Growth Statistics. www.metroatlantachamber.com/macoc/metro%20ATL%20stats/MSA%2003.17.08.pdf (25 Nov. 2008).

Clawson, Dan and Mary Ann Clawson. "What Has Happened to the US Labor Movement? Union Decline and Renewal." *American Sociological Review* 25, (1999): 95–119.

Coffey, Sarah Beth. The State of Working Georgia 2006. Atlanta: Georgia Budget and Policy Institute, 2006.

Conlin, Michelle and Aaron Bernstein. "Working . . . and Poor." *BusinessWeek* (31 May 2004).

Delp, Linda and Katie Quan. "Homecare Worker Organizing in California: An Analysis of a Successful Strategy." *Labor Studies Journal* 27, no.1 (2002): 1–23.

Georgia. Department of Labor. 2002 – 2012 Long-Term Occupational Projections, WIA #03 and #06, Most Annual Openings. 2007. explorer.dol.state.ga.us/mis/occupation/mopeno03.htm (12 Feb. 2007).

Georgia General Assembly. HB 59–Minimum Wage Mandates by Local Governments; Change Certain Provisions. 2005. www.legis.ga.gov/legis/2005_06/search/hb59.html (5 Oct. 2006).

Gertner, Jon. What is a Living-Wage? *New York Times Magazine* (15 Jan 2006): 38–68.

Greenhouse, Steven. Crossing the Border into the Middle Class. *The New York Times*, p. A 22, (3 June 2004).

———. AFL-CIO Leader Says Split Hurts Labor. *The New York Times*, p. A 14, (29 July 2005a).

———. Splintered but Unbowed. *The New York Times*, p. C 1, (30 July 2005b).

———. Many Entry-Level Workers Feel Pinch of Rough Market. *The New York Times*, p. A 10, (4 Sept. 2006a).

———. Labor Board Broadens Definition of Supervisors. *The New York Times*, p. A 16, (4 Oct. 2006b).

Keating, Larry. *Atlanta: Race, Class, and Urban Expansion*. Philadelphia: Temple University Press, 2001.

Krugman, Paul. Wages, Wealth and Politics. *New York Times*, p. A17, (18 Aug. 2006).

Kuttner, Robert. Boston's 'Living-wage' Law Highlights New Grassroots Efforts to Fight Poverty. *The American Prospect*: 1997.

Local 1985 (n.d.). About Local 1985. www.seiu1985.org/whoweare/ (21 Feb. 2007).

Massey, Walter. Report of the Living Wage Ordinance-Independent Review Commission. City of Atlanta (1 April 2004).

Meister, Dick. The President's Anti-Labor Relations Board. 2005. www.dickmeister. com/id160.html (15 Feb. 2007).

———. Ronald Reagan's War on Labor. www.dickmeister.com/id89.html (15 Feb. 2007).

Miller, Andy. Wal-Mart Stands Out on Rolls for PeachCare. *Atlanta Journal Constitution*, B1 (27 Feb. 2004).

Murolo, Priscilla and A. B. Chitty. *From the Folks who Brought you the Weekend: A Short, Illustrated History of Labor in the United States.* New York: New Press, 2001.

Pear, Robert, and Raymond Hernandez. States and U.S. at Odds on Aid for Uninsured. *New York Times*, A1, A14 (13 Feb. 2007).

Pearce, Diana and Jennifer Brooks. *The Self-Sufficiency Standard for Georgia.* 2002. www.sixstrategies.org/files/GA-FINAL-fullreport.pdf (30 Jan. 2007).

Pollin, Robert. "Evaluating Living-Wage Laws in the United States: Good Intentions and Economic Reality in Conflict?" *Economic Development Quarterly* 19, (2005): 1–2.

Pollin, Robert and Stephanie Luce. *The Living-Wage: Building a Fair Economy.* New York: New Press, 1998.

Rathke, Wade. "Leveraging Labor's Revival: A Proposal to Organize Wal-Mart." *New Labor Forum* 14, no. 2 (2005): 59–66.

Reich, Robert. Totally spent. *New York Times*, p. A23 (13 Feb. 2008).

Reynolds, David and Jen Kern. *Living-wage Campaigns: An Activist's Guide to Building the Movement for Economic Justice.* Detroit, MI: Labor Studies Center, Wayne State University and the Association of Community Organizations for Reform Now (ACORN), 2003.

Shipler, David. *The Working Poor: Invisible in America.* New York: Alfred A. Knopf, 2004.

Shulman, Beth. *The Betrayal of Work: How Low-Wage Jobs Fail 30 Million Americans and Their Families.* New York: The New Press, 2003.

Smith, David M. *Geography, Inequality and Society.* Cambridge: Cambridge University Press, 1987.

Stone, Deborah. Why We Need a Care Movement. *The Nation* (13 Mar. 2000).

U.S. Census Bureau. (2007). Poverty Thresholds 2005. www.census.Gov/hhes/ www/poverty/threshld/thresh05.html (17 Jan. 2007).

U.S. Department of Labor (2007). State Right-to-Work Laws and Constitutional Amendments in Effect as of January 1, 2007. www.dol.gov/esa/programs/ whd/state/righttowork.htm (15 Feb. 2007).

Working Families Party (n.d.). Open Ballot Voting – Our (not so) Secret Weapon. www.workingfamiliesparty.org/fusion.html (18 Feb. 2007).

*Part V*

# RACE AND ETHNICITY

## Chapter 9

# Black, White, and Browning: How Latino Migration is Transforming Atlanta

## *Charles A. Gallagher*

### ATLANTA: THE SOUTH'S ELLIS ISLAND

Like much of the United States at the turn of the twentieth century, Georgia and Atlanta have experienced a tremendous growth in their immigrant population, the overwhelming majority coming from Mexico, Central, and South America. The Latino population increased about 300 percent from 1990 to 2000, the third largest growth rate in the country. Georgia now comprises the eleventh largest Latino population in the United States (National Council of La Raza 2004). Latinos now make up 14 percent of the U.S. population, almost 43 million, making them larger than the black population and the largest minority in the United States. Half of all of Georgia's nearly 600,000 Latinos live in five counties: Gwinnett, Clayton, DeKalb, Fulton, and Cobb. This pattern of settlement is in and of itself unique. Typically immigrant groups have settled in inner city neighborhoods and then moved out to first and second ring suburbs over the course of a generation or two. In part because Atlanta is more decentralized than older cities like Chicago and Philadelphia, Latino migration in the Southeast has been characterized by settlement in counties that the census and demographers define as suburban. It is also the case that by skipping inner city residence Latinos in the South are less likely to share social space with the resident African American population.

What makes this particular wave of Latino immigration also different from the past is the destination is no longer restricted to the border states in the Southwest region of the country. North Carolina, Arkansas, Tennessee, South Carolina, and Alabama had Latino rates of population growth similar to that of Georgia. These six states had the highest rate of Latino growth in the country. Within these six states 57 percent of all Latinos were foreign born, and in counties that serve as rural destination points two-thirds of Latinos were foreign born (Kochhar, Suro, and Tafoya 2005). To put this in a broader historical context, 10.3 million immigrants entered the country from 2000 to 2007, the single largest number of new-comers in U.S. history. The majority of these new immigrants are from Mexico and Central America (Preston 2007).

The rapid growth of the Latino population to Georgia and the South-east region of the United States is a relatively new phenomenon. How-ever, the social and economic issues arising from the relatively sudden arrival of new immigrant populations to this region are not. Tensions over language acquisition, competition for jobs and housing, worries over miscegenation, and concerns that these new groups refuse to assimilate to the norms of American society now dominate the political discourse. This tension between new immigrants and the native population was made painfully evident in the "English First" initiative in January 2009 in Nashville, Tennessee. The ballot measure would have required that all city government business be conducted in English. Although the "English First" initiative (labeled "English Only" by its detractors) was defeated, 44 percent of the Nashville population voted for the ballot measure. The backlash against these new immigrant populations is thought to be at least in part a response to the economic downturn that has created a sharp decline in the need for the types of labor that immigrants are typically concentrated in, namely construction and service employment.

The current backlash directed at immigrants crossing our borders today has been a reality for almost every group arriving to our shores since the Pilgrims established themselves as the dominant ethnic and racial group in England's "new" colony. A clearly agitated Benjamin Franklin had this to say about the new German immigrants he saw as unwilling to assimi-late to the norms and folkways of the Anglo-dominated majority. Franklin lamented that he had "great misgivings about these immigrants because of their clannishness, their little knowledge of English, their press, and the increasing need of interpreters . . . I suppose in a few years [interpreters] will also be needed in the [Congress] to tell one-half of our legislators what the other half say" (Yzaguirre 2004, 18). Viewed today, the political and cultural takeover of the nascent Anglo-American colony by German immigrants seems a quaint and comical historic footnote. Unfortunately such anti-immigrant sentiments have always been a central political con-cern throughout the history of this country. It is in fact only during the distraction of crisis (civil war, world war, economic dislocations) or when our borders were almost completely closed that issues of immigration were not a major focus of the body politic. Ironically the lulls in anti-immigrant activities were typically due to acts of Congress that had been motivated by nativist social movements. Concerns about a west coast cultural and economic takeover by the Chinese immigrants brought in to connect the Pacific and Atlantic railroads resulted in the Chinese Exclusion Act of 1882. The relative calm around immigration after WWII was a result of the 1924 U.S Immigration Exclusion Act, which effectively closed our borders until 1965 (Myers 2007). Since its inception the norm in the United States has been one of pitched battles over who should be allowed to enter our country, how many immigrants should be let in, under what conditions or stipulations should immigrants be granted citizenship, and what set of stereotypical attributes (lazy, model, socialist leaning, diseased) are linked to these newcomers (Steinberg 1989).

What I wish to suggest in this chapter is that the current political hysteria concerning immigrants, much like the immigration panics of yesteryear, are part of an immigration ebb and flow that is both manageable and in the long run, beneficial to the United States. A large, comparatively undereducated immigrant population arriving in a relatively compressed amount of time does present a number of challenges. Without question the rapid increase in immigrant populations has taxed local social service agencies and strained many public school systems. Schools located in new destination locations have experienced a sudden increase in their student population and have scrambled to put in place bilingual educational programs.

However the historical record and research emerging on immigrant assimilation suggests that today's Latino immigrants (by far the largest group) are on the same trajectory of "becoming Americans" in a manner similar to past immigrant "newcomers" like southern Italians, Greeks, Russian Jews, and the Irish (Alba and Nee 2003). While a snapshot of what is taking place in many of the new destination communities where Latinos are locating may appear to be pluralistic communities in the making, the long view of this process is that these groups, like the German immigrants Benjamin Franklin disparaged, will assimilate. The reality is that this process of assimilation, that is becoming like the dominant group in language, culture, and aspirations, is well underway.

The first part of this chapter will explore the demographic changes that have taken place concerning Latino immigration to the United States in the last two decades with a particular focus on Atlanta. I will then examine how Latino immigration is challenging the existing black-white political and cultural binary that has defined Southern (and Atlanta) race relations since our nation's inception. What is taking place at unprecedented speed is the extent to which Latino migration to Atlanta and the Atlanta metropolitan area has shifted the politics of race from one focused almost myopically on black and white issues to one that now comprises a triangulation of black, brown, and white concerns, anxieties, aspirations, and resentments. These issues, race, identity, and belonging, play out within the context of resources like housing, education, employment, and how Latino immigration is reshaping the racial dynamics of Atlanta.

The influx of Latinos to the city of Atlanta is part of the flow of Latinos to the South, to Georgia, and to metro Atlanta. Outside the magnitude of the population change, the characteristics of the Latinos are very similar across the different geographies. I rely on data from all levels of geography in describing the Latino population and its behavior. To discuss the implications of the increase in this population, I rely on the literature that discusses these issues, not just Atlanta-specific research, since such research is not available. The more national or regional-based research findings are relevant to Atlanta.

## LATINO GROWTH IN THE SOUTH

Latino immigrants today mirror the historical experiences of previous waves of immigrants from Europe. Typically a majority of immigrants tend to be young men with educational levels that are below the national average (Durand and Massey 2004). Given that these new immigrants are in their prime child-bearing years, large scale immigration characteristically results in the expansion of public schools in new-destination areas. Latinos now constitute the single largest minority population in U.S. public schools. Nationally, Latinos comprise 19 percent of public elementary and secondary schools compared to blacks at 17 percent and whites at 58 percent (NCLR 2007). In Georgia, Latinos now comprise about one in twelve students in the public schools. However, half of Latinos (49.6%) in Georgia will not complete high school, a statistic somewhat lower than the nationwide Latino average of 53 percent. This high school graduation rate for Latinos in Georgia is lower than it is for blacks (56.8%), Asians (76.6%), or whites (71.8%) (NCLR 2005). The lower rates of high school graduation reflect the correlation between immigration status, length of time in the United States, and poverty. It is often the case that male immigrants quit high school because the perceived opportunity cost of being in school rather than earning income is too high, they are the sole bread winner for an extended family, and/or there are cultural expectations for remittances to kin who remain in the native land.

An overwhelming majority of Latino immigrants to the Southeast work in manufacturing, food production, agriculture, and construction. In rural counties in the new destination states Latinos comprise a majority of manufacturing workers and have been credited in some towns with the regeneration industries that had been experiencing labor scarcity (Kochhar, Suro, and Tafoya 2005). According to the U.S. Census, Latinos accounted for 8 percent of the construction workers in Atlanta in 1990. By 2000, Latino construction workers in Atlanta were estimated at close to 50 percent (Feagans 2006). Typically as length of time in the United States increases and levels of formal education rise, poverty rates go down. In Georgia 18.8 percent of Latinos are at or below the poverty threshold as defined by the U.S. Census, compared with 13.4 percent of non-Latino Georgia residents (U.S Census 2003). What is important to note is that Latinos are more likely to be in the labor force (78.1%) than the non-Hispanic population (67.3%). What these relatively high labor force participation rates suggest is not an aversion to work but the simple fact that Latinos are concentrated in low-wage employment that places them in the category of the working poor. The concentration of Latinos in low-wage work is reflected in median family income in the state of Georgia. In 2003 non-Hispanic median household income was $42,742 compared to $33,289 for Latino households (National Council of La Raza 2004).

Like immigrants of the past, many Latino males establish themselves in the labor market and then send for their wives, travel back home to find a bride, or, as is increasingly the case, meet a partner in the United States and marry (Steinberg 1989). Being a younger, overwhelmingly Catholic population with lower levels of formal education Latinos, like many immigrant groups of the past, have families that are on average larger than the general population. The median age for Latinos is twenty-seven years while the median age for non-Latinos is thirty-four. The average family size for Latinos is 3.8 compared to 2.4 for white non-Hispanics (Kochhar, Suro, and Tafoya 2005). Between 1990 and 2002 Latino births in Georgia grew by 643 percent, from 2,263 to 16, 819 (NCLR 2005).

## RETHINKING RACE CATEGORIES

Every large-scale immigration wave to the United States has reshaped the dynamic and contours of race and ethnic relations. From initial contact and the genocide of indigenous populations to enslaved Africans brought to our shores in the 1600s, to the selective immigration policies of the 1960s, contact with and each group's entrance to the United States alters the existing ethnic and racial hierarchy. In a similar way Latino immigration in the South is reframing the centuries old black-white racial dichotomy. The established "black and white" framework for race relations is being rendered anachronistic by the arrival of immigrants from Asia and Latin America. The immigration trends over the last two decades are blurring and redefining existing racial boundaries, forming new identities and allegiances, and perhaps most significantly changing the existing black-white race relations model.

Many race scholars are arguing that what is supplanting the black-white model is a racial hierarchy better characterized as "black and non-black" or the Latin Americanization thesis. Within the "black and non-black" race relations paradigms (Gans 1999; Gallagher 2003) the "non-black category" includes whites, middle class, mixed or light-skinned Asians and Latinos, and newly arrived white immigrants from Eastern Europe. The "black" category will include African Americans, poor multiracials, and dark-skinned Latinos, Asians, and Caribbeans. A middling or "residual group" are those groups on the socioeconomic and racial margins who are effectively waiting to be pushed or pulled into the "black" or "non-black" category. In many ways this model looks like the racial hierarchy that exists throughout Latin America, where light skin and European features are a form of social and cultural capital. Using this model as a framework U.S. race scholars (see Bonilla-Silva 2004) argue that immigration is transforming our biracial order to a triracial one that will in effect reconfigure the existing racial boundaries to include groups that historically have not been considered part of the dominant group.

What is taking place among Latinos today is the type of sorting based on phenotype and socioeconomic status these models would predict. Light-skinned, middle class Latinos, many who self-define as white already, are marrying non-Hispanic whites. It is likely the children of these unions will self-identify and be viewed as members of the white race. The "racial redistricting" (Gallagher 2004) or redrawing of the color line that is taking place in the United States points to an expansion of the white population over the next fifty years.

The question is, how is this transition playing out in Georgia and Atlanta and what does it mean for race relations? The question of whether Latinos can or are willing to assimilate has become a lighting rod in the national debate on immigration. Harvard University political scientist Samuel Huntington (2004) argues in his latest book, *Who We Are: The Challenges to America's National Identity*, that America's core Anglo-Protestant culture is doomed because Latino immigration differs "fundamentally from those of previous immigration, and the assimilation successes of the past are unlikely to be duplicated with the contemporary flood of immigrants from Latin America." Proximity to Mexico and the ease with which Latino immigrants can cycle back and forth to their home village and the United States is, according to Huntington, the key factor that will keep Latinos from ever being "truly" American citizens. The Pacific and Atlantic Oceans forced Asian and European immigrants to leave their immigrant cultures behind once and for all because they were unable to ever visit the motherland. It is Huntington's view that easy access to Mexico and Central America delays and diminishes American assimilation for Latinos.

As scholars like Huntington see it, Salsa surpassing ketchup as the number one condiment is more than a factoid—it is a dire cultural metaphor of things to come. Huntington is however wrong on almost all counts. Demographically, Latinos are in large part identical to immigrant populations of the past. Like the groups that came to the United States before them, Latinos tend to be younger than the general population, come with lower amounts of formal education, initially struggle learning English, have lower median incomes and slightly larger families than the national norm. These characteristics mirror almost every group that has ever come before them, and like immigrant groups of the past the inevitable march towards assimilation is very much underway for much of the Latino population. In Georgia nearly a third of this population speaks English "very well." Research has found that by the third generation 60 percent of Mexican Americans speak *only* English at home. Over 90 percent of Latinos believe that mastery of English is the means for upward mobility in the United States. Just over 40 percent of Latinos own their own homes compared to 68 percent of Georgia householders. Home ownership rates among Latinos who have been in the Unites States for thirty years are however identical to the national average of 68 percent.

## STICKY FLOOR, SEGMENTED ASSIMILATION, OR UPWARD MOBILITY?

An excellent body of longitudinal research on Latinos provides a withering critique of Huntington's nativist screed that Latinos do not wish to assimilate or throw themselves into the melting pot. The important question that Huntington does ask is whether Latinos will be able to reproduce the intergenerational upward mobility of white Europeans from Eastern and Southern Europe. The upward mobility *high wage* manufacturing jobs provided to first and second generation European immigrants are for the most part gone. What is also different today is that Latinos represent an ethnically diverse, class stratified, and culturally distinct population. What many race scholars suggest is taking place is a reordering of racial categories that will privilege some Latinos and consign many to social and economic margins. A process similar to the incorporation of Southern and Eastern Europeans into the white race is taking place among certain parts of the Asian and Latino populations in the United States and here in Georgia. Just as the Irish, Italians, Greeks, and Jews went from being on the margins of whiteness to being members of the dominant group, some light-skinned, middle class Latinos and multiracial Asians are being incorporated into the dominant group as they  proceed to define themselves, and become viewed by others as being white, or perhaps more importantly they come to be viewed as "non-black" (Gans 1999; Gallagher 2003; Bonilla-Silva 2004).

A kind of "racial redistricting" is taking place where the boundaries of whiteness are expanding to include groups who until quite recently would have been on the margins of whiteness. Within the context of contemporary race relations those groups who do not conform to cultural and physical expectations of white middle class norms, namely blacks and dark-skinned Latinos who are poor, will be stigmatized and cut off from the resources whites have been able to monopolize for decades, like good public schools, social networks, safe neighborhoods, and access to primary sector jobs. Research recently conducted at Vanderbilt University made this variation on "color-ism" painfully apparent. After controlling for all the relevant variables (English proficiency, education, work experience, nationality) the researchers found that "those with the lightest skin earned an average of 8 to 15 percent more than immigrants with much darker skin." On average being one shade lighter had the effect of one year of additional education (*New York Times* January 28, 2007, 19). Membership does indeed have its privileges.

These dynamics are playing out in a number of ways and have implications for race and ethnic relations beyond the Latino community. For instance, the link between interracial marriage rates and racial attitudes points to how Latino immigration to Georgia may alter the state's racial hierarchy from a black-white dichotomy to one much more fluid and complex. A national study of marriage preferences found that "nonblack racial groups are more likely to reject African Americans as potential partners than any other group (Yancey 2003, 71). Research on racial attitudes found an "unambiguously greater average level of hostility" towards blacks by all non-black groups (Bobo and Smith 1998). In another national survey on racial attitudes whites, Asians, and Hispanics had the greatest resistance to a member of their racial or ethnic group marrying someone who was black (Herring and Missah 1997). Simply put, what Asians, whites, and Latinos share is a common antipathy, suspicion, and stereotyping of blacks. The result of continued high levels of residential segregation, social distance, and racial stereotyping results in marriage among white, Asian, and Latino populations who may intermarry, and are able to blend into the dominant group. These new pairings typically enjoy the prerogatives of the dominant group while dark-skinned groups (African American, Afro-Caribbean, black or dark Latinos) experience continued socioeconomic stagnation and pariah status (Gans 1997).

In *Assimilation in American Life*, Milton Gordon observes that "once structural assimilation has occurred, either simultaneously with or subsequent to acculturation, all of the other types of assimilation will naturally follow" (Gordon 1964, 81). According to Gordon marital assimilation would signal a point in the assimilation process where a minority group "loses its ethnic identity in the larger host or core society, and assimilation takes place" (Gordon 1964, 80). Gordon explains that "Prejudice and discrimination are no longer a problem" as widespread interracial marriage occurs because "the descendants of the original minority group become indistinguishable" from the dominant group (Gordon 1964, 80). The idea is that multi-color and multi-ethnic unions will result in a reduction of social distance between groups, a decline in racial conflict will follow, at least in theory, resulting in a reduction in racial inequality. It is no wonder that interracial marriage is "generally regarded, with justification, as the litmus test of assimilation" (Alba and Nee 2003, 90).

Unfortunately current trends in interracial marriages reflect a reshuffling rather than a razing of existing racial hierarchies. Sociologist Herbert Gans points out that "About half of all Asian-Americans and light skinned Hispanics now marry whites, and at that rate, they may be defined as near white in a few decades" (Gans 2003, 44). Almost 70 percent of young Japanese born in the United States marry individuals who are white (Alba and Nee 2003). When racial minorities marry out of their group it is most always to someone who is white. U.S. Census Bureau research has found that when one parent is white, which is very likely among Asians and Latinos, there is a very strong possibility that the child will be identified as white.

Another obstacle that will be play out in immigration, race relations, and racial conflict in metro Atlanta is a fundamental change in how the majority now perceives race as it relates to America's opportunity structure. The perception among a majority of white Americans is that the socioeconomic playing field is now level. A stunning 71 percent of the white population now believes that African Americans have "more" or "about the same opportunities in life" as whites, although black and brown unemployment is almost three times that of whites. Gallup polls tells us that eight in ten whites believe that there is no difference in educational opportunities between blacks and whites even though blacks graduate from high school or finish college at rates significantly below whites. A majority of whites perceive the "race problem" as having been solved at a time when every quality of life indicator shows persistent and in some cases growing racial disparities.

As many now see it, we are a color-blind nation. But this version of color-blindness does not ignore race; it acknowledges race while disregarding racial hierarchy and inequality. By taking racially coded styles, products, and media experiences that whites and racial minorities can purchase and share, race becomes nothing more to members of the dominant group than an innocuous cultural signifier, a benign cultural marker that has been stripped of all forms of institutional, discriminatory, or coercive power. America's racial "presentation of self," at least on television, in the multiplex, and in magazines is overwhelmingly depicted as an integrated, multiracial environment where individuals consume products in a post-race, color-blind world. Mainstream magazines routinely present advertisements in which whites, blacks, Asians, and Latinos gather together to shop, eat, work, and interact in spaces where race is meaningless. In this carefully manufactured racial utopia, television commercials depict actors of different races inhabiting race-neutral environments like Wal-Mart, Taco Bell or the company water cooler. On TV middle class friends across the color line share living rooms and bond over football, beer, and Domino's Pizza.

White America has been utterly saturated with images of middle and upper middle class couples from across the racial spectrum living a life quite similar to their own. Watching television depictions of well off, successful black, brown, and Asian Americans has the effect of convincing white Americans that racial minorities share the same socioeconomic opportunities.

Two black head coaches lording over the Super Bowl in 2007, George Lopez, J-Lo, Oprah, Condoleezza, and perhaps most important symbolically the election of the nation's first African American president, Barack Obama, are part of a new story being constructed about U.S. race relations. These symbols of racial equality and color-blindness suggest to *all* Americans that racism is past tense. In the media-constructed fictionalized world of race relations, everyone shares social space with individuals across the color line even though most whites in metropolitan areas in the United States live in suburban neighborhoods where non-whites account for less than 5 percent of the population. The non-white success stories in situation comedies, reality programs, and television dramas, much like the day-to-day experiences of most whites, convey a message that society is now free of institutional racism or discrimination. The ease with which individuals dance, date, love, and marry across the color line in the media is further evidence that race has been defanged of its institutional powers.

## COLORISM IN A NEW CONTEXT

However, these media-constructed images only tell part of the story. In the U.S. Census Latinos are free to choose from any of the racial categories offered because "Latino" is officially defined as an ethnic group. In 2000 47.9 percent of Latinos chose white as their racial identity. An additional 42.2 percent chose the category "some other race," which is understood as meaning that members in this category did not see themselves as being a member in the racial designations offered by the federal government. In subsequent follow-up interviews on the some other race population, researchers found that the Latinos in this category were "less educated, less likely to be citizens, poorer, less likely to speak English exclusively and are less often intermarried with non-Hispanic whites" (Tafoya 2004, 5). What appears to be happening is a Latino population that will be cleaved by socioeconomic status and color. Income data suggests that wages for all immigrants, and immigrants with little formal education in particular, are declining. The Pew Economic Mobility Project found that "wages are decreasing substantially for both first and second generation immigrants, raising questions about the degree of future potential economic mobility" (Moscoso 2007). If history is any guide, racial and ethnic tensions tend to flare up when the economic pie is shrinking. The target of such animosities is often new immigrant groups who are thought to be the cause of economic recession.

Indeed recent research by Qian and Lichter (2007) finds that having lighter skin has a variety of class-specific implications in terms of life chances and rates of intermarriage. They found that "it is native born, less educated Asian Americans and Hispanics who tend to share the same pool of marriageable partners as new immigrants" (2007, 90). On one hand we see poor native Latinos marrying Latino immigrants, and on the other hand a high level of marriage rates among well-educated Latinos to whites; not surprisingly, these Latinos tend to define themselves as white in the U.S. Census. Those Latinos who find themselves occupying the status of a racialized minority rather than an immigrant on the path to assimilation are likely to sour on the idea that the United States is the land of opportunity. Lopez and Pantoja (2004) find that second generation immigrants tend to report "higher levels of personal and structural discrimination as well as reflect a more pessimistic outlook toward occupational opportunities available to them" (2004, 640). It is unlikely that this group includes light-skinned, non-Spanish speaking, educated individuals who have white partners and live in the suburbs. This particular slice of the Latino population will have glided seamlessly into the dominant group. The great challenge to racial justice will not be the impending race war from white nationalists as Samuel Huntington suggests. The larger problem is Americans who truly believe the war on racial inequality, institutional racism, and discrimination has been fought and won. If the starting point for a national discussion about racial equality is that there is no problem, racial justice in the era of color-blindness is highly unlikely.

## A RISING TIDE BUT FOR FEWER BOATS

The implications of these trends for race relations in Georgia are numerous. In 2000, nearly half of all Latinos defined themselves as white. The 42 percent of Latinos who did not check the white box but instead marked "some other race" on the 2000 Census are less educated, younger, have greater difficulty speaking English, and are more likely than Latinos who marked white to *not* marry outside of the ethnic group. This group is overrepresented among Latinos who do not finish high school (Tafoya 2004). No doubt some might place parts of this Latino population in the "residual" or "black" part of the new racial hierarchy that is emerging.

This "some other race" category is likely to experience "sticky floor" mobility, that is no or little mobility, as they find themselves stuck in low-wage, dead-end service sector employment that results in economic and social marginalization. This prediction is all the more likely given the collapse of the construction industry and a general contraction of the services (landscaping and restaurants for example) that employ a sizable share of the Latino workforce. While Latinos may assimilate in a generation or two, there is evidence that the path to upward socioeconomic mobility previously taken by Southern and Eastern Europeans will not be available for a sizable part of America's new immigrant groups. The "new second generation" may be synonymous with segmented assimilation. What is likely to happen is a majority of the children of immigrants will experience downward social mobility while only a small segment experience upward mobility. If Latinos follow patterns similar to those in South America, lighter-skinned, educated, middle class Latinos will assimilate into the suburbs, attend white public schools and attain primary sector employment with "other" whites.

What we are also likely to see is a socioeconomically bifurcated population, similar to what we see among African Americans. Part of the Latino population may be trapped in low-wage manual or service employment while another slice, well educated and light-skinned may experience rapid mobility. This will only add to tensions among blacks and whites who believe Latinos "take" jobs from natives and suppress wages. As we see the labor market contract Latino successes will continue to be viewed by the black community as yet another example of being leaped-frogged in the labor market by a new immigrant group because of systemic and institutional racism.

In 2008, it is estimated that there will be over 100,000 registered Latino voters in the state of Georgia (Gonzalez 2007). Latinos already play a pivotal swing vote in counties with a high density of Hispanic voters. As a voting block it may be that the interests of Latinos are in opposition with the goals or concerns of black voters. In conversations I have had with black students at universities around the country it is an open secret among some in the black community that tensions run high with Latinos because of the belief that prejudice towards blacks is a common feature among Latinos. Unfortunately, the Latino community shares similar sentiments of animosity and distrust directed towards African Americans. In her study of Latinos in North Carolina McClain found that Latinos generally "hold negative stereotypical views of blacks . . . and that Latino immigrants do indeed feel they have more in common with whites than with blacks" (McClain 2006, 24). These are real social concerns that will only deepen. The black-white dichotomy that has defined much of Georgia's history has given way to a much more colorful and complex hierarchy. The question remains however as to what the next page will be for race relations in Atlanta and Georgia.

## REFERENCES

Alba, Richard and Victor Nee. 2003. *Remaking the American Mainstream.* Cambridge: Harvard University Press.

Bobo, L., and R. Smith. 1998. "From Jim Crow Racism to Laissez-Faire Racism: The Transformation of Racial Attitudes." In *Beyond Pluralism: The Conception of Groups and Group Identities in America*, Wendy Katlin, Ned Landsman, and Andrea Tyree, editors. Chicago: University of Illinois Press.

Bonilla-Silva, Eduardo. 2004. "From Bi-racial to Tri-racial." *Ethnic and Racial Studies* 27(6): 931–50.

Durand, J., and D. S. Massey, eds. 2004. *Crossing the Border: Research from the Mexican Migration Project.* New York: Russell Sage.

Feagans, Brian. 2006. "One Man's Ruin and Recovery." *The Atlanta Journal-Constitution.* A1. March 12, 2006.

Gallagher, Charles A. 2003. "Color Blind Privilege: The Social and Political Functions of Erasing the Color Line in Post-Race America." *Race, Gender and Class* Vol. 10, 4: 22–37.

———. 2004. "Racial Redistricting: Expanding the Boundaries of Whiteness." Pp. 59–76 in *The Politics of MultiRacialism*, Heather M. Dalmage, editor. Buffalo: State University of New York Press.

———. 2004 "Playing the White Ethnic Card: Using Ethnic Identity to Deny Contemporary Racism." Pp. 148–58 in *White Out: The Continuing Significance of Racism*, Ashley W. Doane and Eduardo Bonilla-Silva, editors. New York: Routledge.

Gans, Herbert. 1999. *The Possibility of a New Racial Hierarchy in the Twenty-First Century United States.* Chicago: University of Chicago Press.

Gonzalez, Jerry. 2007. "Latino Voting Strength in Georgia: Building Towards Greater Voter Engagement and Participation in 2008." GALEO, November 14, 2007.

Gordon, Milton. 1964. *Assimilation in American Life: The Role of Race, Religion and National Origins.* New York: Oxford University Press.

Herring, C., and C. Amissah. 1997. "Advance and Retreat: Racially Based Attitudes and Public Policy." Pp. 121–43 in *Racial Attitudes in the 1990s: Continuity and Change*, J. K. Martin, ed. Westport, CT: Praeger.

Huntington, Samuel. 2004. *Who We Are: The Challenges to America's National Identity.* New York: Simon and Schuster.

Kochhar, R., R. Suro, and S. Tafoya. 2005. *The New Latino South: The Context and Con-sequences of Rapid Population Growth.* Washington, D.C.: Pew Hispanic Center.

Lopez, Linda and Adrain Pantoja. 2004. "Beyond Black and White: General Sup-port for Race-Conscious Policies Among African Americans, Latinos, Asian Americans and Whites." *Political Research Quarterly.* Dec. 57, 4, 633–42.

McClain, Paula. 2006. "Racial Distancing in a Southern City: Latino Immigrants' Views of Black Americans." *Journal of Politics* 34, August 2006, 571–84.

Moscoso, Eunice. "Study: Wages Dip for Immigrants." *Atlanta Journal-Constitu-tion,* July 26, 2007, C3.

Myers, John P. 2007. *Dominant-Minority Relations in America: Convergence in the New World.* New York: Allyn and Bacon.

National Council of La Raza. 2004. *Georgia: State Fact Sheet.*

Preston, Julia. 2007. "U.S. Immigrant Population is the Highest Since the 1920s." *New York Times,* November 29, 2007, A15.

Qian, Zhenchao and Daniel Lichter. 2007. "Social Boundaries and Marital As-similation: Interpreting Trends in Racial and Ethnic Intermarriage." *American Sociological Review* 72, 68–94.

Steinberg, Stephen. 1989. *The Ethnic Myth: Race, Ethnicity and Class in America.* Boston: Beacon Press.

Tafoya, Sonya. 2004. "Shades of Belonging." Pew Hispanic Center December 6, 2004, 1–23.

U.S. Census Bureau. 2003. American Community Survey.

Yancey, George. 2003. *Who is White?: Latinos, Asians, and the New Black/Nonblack Divide.* New York: Lynne Reiner.

Yzaguirre, Raul 2004. "Huntington and Hispanics" *Foreign Policy,* May/June 2004, 142: 4.

*Chapter 10*

# Atlanta and "the Dream": Race, Ethnicity, and Recent Demographic and Socioeconomic Trends

*Obie Clayton, Cynthia Hewitt, and Gregory Hall*

The Atlanta metro area is rapidly living up to its self-designation as the capital of the New South and as an international city. Over the past twenty years the population has become much more ethnically diverse, particularly because of the large immigrant Hispanic population. The Atlanta region seems to be following the classic growth model of American cities with its development of labor force queues and niches based on gender, race, and ethnic hierarchies, increasing residential density in the inner city, and rapid ethnic and racial transition occurring in declining inner suburbs. However, the racial and ethnic hierarchies, while present, have shifted considerably, and the settlement patterns of immigrants differ from those observed in northern cities, reflecting both constraints and opportunities unique to Atlanta. This uniqueness perhaps gives it its tremendous draw, illustrated, for example, by the fact that in 2005, the Atlanta region was the number one destination for migration within the United States, for all types of people.

This chapter explores the changing ethnic and racial face of Atlanta and the implications of this change for the political structure and schools. The chapter also explores the changing economic conditions of racial and ethnic groups as reflected in the types of occupations held.

Table 10.1   Atlanta and Atlanta Metropolitan Area (MSA) Population, 1990–2005

| Year | City of Atlanta | | Atlanta MSA | |
|------|-----------------|----------|-------------|----------|
|      | Population | % Change | Population | % Change |
| 1960 | 487,455 | - | | - |
| 1970 | 496,973 | 2.0 | 1,312,474 | |
| 1980 | 425,022 | -15.0 | 1,684,200 | 28.3 |
| 1990 | 394,017 | -8.5 | 2,138,136 | 27.0 |
| 2000 | 416,474 | 1.5 | 2,959,950 | 38.4 |
| 2005 | 424,831 | 2.0 | 4,112.198 | 38.9 |

U.S. Census Bureau Decennial Censuses 1960-2000 and 2005 *American Community Survey.*

## DEMOGRAPHIC CHANGE

### City of Atlanta Population Trends

The rapid population expansion in the Atlanta region has occurred primarily outside the city of Atlanta. The population of the city of Atlanta reached its apex in the late 1960s or early 1970s. Thereafter, a decline was recorded until the decade of the 1990s; during the 1990s Atlanta experienced a reversal, with population growing by 5.7 percent (see table 10.1). By 2000, growth in the urban area began to display a maturing, with increased multifamily, particularly condominium development, and infill housing. In the five years to 2005, the city recorded a 13.0 percent population increase, double the rate of the last decade in half the time.

Atlanta, like most of the Southeast, was historically characterized by a one-dimensional racial profile—the relationship between whites and African Americans. In 1970, the successes of the civil rights movement created a climate for the reversal of the great migratory pattern of African Americans to the North. The rise of the automobile culture and spread of suburban development, as well as the demise of segregation led to the development of "white flight." The African American population share in Atlanta went from 51.5 percent in 1970 to a peak of 68 percent in 1980. However, the former factors also led increasingly to rapid suburbanization of the African American population. Atlanta's African American population fell from 1970 to 1990, as did Atlanta's overall population. By 1990, suburbanization and the dynamics of the advent of civil rights for African Americans had pretty much run their course. These processes left some enduring patterns of black/white population relationships.

In the 1980s, Atlanta increasingly became a destination of choice, culminating in the hosting of the 1996 Olympic Games, which might be seen as the turning point when the historically bimodal pattern of race relations became significantly more diverse. For instance, Atlanta's Asian-heritage population was only 1,998 in 1980, less than 1 percent, but grew 71

**Table 10.2   Atlanta Population by Race and Ethnicity, 1970–2005**

| Race/Ethnicity | 1970 | 1980 | 1990 | 2000 | 2007 |
|---|---|---|---|---|---|
| Total Population | 496,973 | 425,022 | 394,017 | 416,474 | 421,065 |
| Population Percent | 100.0% | 100.0% | 100.0% | 100.0% | 100.0% |
| White, Non-Hispanic | 241,529 | 138,260 | 119,266 | 130,222 | 143,112 |
| | 48.6% | 32.5% | 30.3% | 31.3% | 35.8% |
| Black, Non-Hispanic | 255,941 | 283,150 | 263,107 | 254,062 | 231,609 |
| | 5.15% | 66.6% | 66.8% | 61.0% | 57.5% |
| Native American | n/a | 595 | 511 | 594 | 502 |
| | <0.01 | <0.01 | <.001 | <0.01 | |
| Asian or Pacific Islander | n/a | 1,998 | 3,425 | 8,080 | 10,323 |
| | 1% | 1% | 2% | 2.4% | |
| Other Race | n/a | 1,019 | 183 | 630 | 11,643[a] |
| | <1% | <1% | <1% | 4.0% | |
| Hispanic | 497 | 594 | 7,525 | 18,720 | 23,876 |
| | <1% | <1% | 1.9% | 4.5% | 6.0% |

Source: U.S. Census Bureau Decennial Censuses and *2005 American Community Survey.*
[a]The 2005 other category includes both some other race alone and two race alone categories which accounts for the large category increase.

percent between 1980 and 1990, and 136 percent between 1990 and 2000. By 2007, the 10,323 people of Asian heritage constituted 2.4 percent of the population, and people of "other" heritage increased from 1,019 in 1980 to 17,036 in 2007 (see table 10.2). But most astounding was the growth of the Hispanic population from the 594 recorded in 1980 (less than 1 percent of the city's population) to 7,525 in 1990, 18,720 in 2000, and 23,876 in 2007 (6 percent of the population). As property values escalated, partly in response to inner city redevelopment spurred by Olympic investment, more of the African American population diffused into the southern and eastern suburbs, and an increasing gentrification of the city got underway, with the beginnings of a return of white population to the city of Atlanta.

### The Atlanta Metropolitan Area: Population Growth and Shifts

In the period 1990 to 2000, Atlanta grew by a modest 6 percent, but the metropolitan area grew by a startling 39 percent, as shown in table 10.3. The Atlanta metropolitan area grew from 1.7 million in 1970 to 4.1 million in 2000, and an estimated 4.8 million in 2005. Very significant in this growth is the number of people of immigrant status living in Atlanta. By 2000, approximately 10 percent of the Atlanta area population was foreign-born (see table 10.4). Of the 423,105 person immigrant population, 206,567 are reported to be of Hispanic or Latino origin, including 120,328 from Mexico. The Asian immigrant population was approximately 115,000, while approximately 37,000 people were from Africa and 33,000 were from the Caribbean. Part of this growth was fueled by the choice of the Atlanta metropolitan area as a location to settle refugees. However, many immigrants select Atlanta for their own reasons, particularly related to its reputation as a place where middle-class lifestyles are supported. With African immigrants recording the highest education level of any group in American society—domestic or immigrant, this distinction may also figure into their choice of the Atlanta metropolitan area (*Journal of Blacks in Higher Education* 2003). Additionally, over 53,000 immigrants are from Europe. Overall, taking into consideration internal U.S. migration and immigration, just a little more than half of the area residents—approximately 55 percent—were actually born in Georgia.

**Table 10.3   Atlanta MSA Population by Race and Ethnicity, 1990 and 2000**

| Race/Ethnicity | 1990 Population | 1990 Pop. Percentage | 2000 Population | 2000 Pop. Percentage |
|---|---|---|---|---|
| Total | 2,833,511 | 100.0% | 4,112,198 | 100.0% |
| White, Non-Hispanic | 1,990,255 | 70.2% | 2,460,740 | 60.0% |
| Black | 732,389 | 25.9% | 1,178,872 | 28.7% |
| American Indian/Inuit | 5,911 | <0.01% | 7,739 | >0.01% |
| Asian or Pacific Islander | 49,313 | 1.7% | 134,973 | 3.3% |
| Other Races[a] | 1,325 | <0.01% | 61,023 | 1.5% |
| Hispanic | 54,318 | 1.9% | 268,851 | 6.5% |

Source: U.S. Census Bureau, Decennial Censuses.
[a]And persons identifying with two or more races.

**Table 10.4   Atlanta MSA Population by Nation and State Origin, 2005**

| Origin | 2000 Population | 2000 Population of Total | 2005 Estimate Population | 2005 Estimate Percentage of Total |
|---|---|---|---|---|
| Total U.S. and Foreign | 4,112,198 | 100.0% | 4,828,838 | 100.0% |
| U.S. Origin | 3,689,093 | 89.7% | 4,216,079 | 87.3% |
| Born in Georgia | 1,973,007 | 48.0% | 2,273,993 | 47.1% |
| Born in other State/ U.S. Territory | 1,716,086 | 41.7% | 1,942,086 | 40.2% |
| Foreign-born population | 423,105 | 10.3% | 612,759 | 12.7% |
| Latin America | 206,567 | 5.0% | 418,888 | 8.7% |
| Mexico | 120,328 | 2.9% | 270,330 | 5.6% |
| Caribbean | 32,944 | <1.0% | n/a | -- |
| Asia | 115,102 | 2.8% | n/a | -- |
| Africa | 36,645 | <1.0% | n/a | -- |
| Europe | 53,228 | 1.3% | n/a | -- |
| Other | 1,174 | <1.0% | n/a | -- |

Source: U.S. Census 2000 and U.S. Census *2005 American Community Survey*.

By 2005, according to the U.S. Census' American Community Survey, approximately 612,800 Atlanta metro residents, or 12.7 percent, were foreign-born. There are approximately 418,900 (roughly equal to the entire population of Atlanta) who report Hispanic or Latino origin, including 270,300 from Mexico. Further, it has been found that generally the documented immigrant population is underreported (Feagans 2005). As the Latino and Asian population in-migration resulted in increased population percentages, so has the high rate of African American in-migration resulted in greater population proportions; African Americans comprised 25.9 percent of the area's population in 1990 and an estimated 30.4 percent in 2005. The city of Atlanta, alone, in 2000 contained 30 percent of the region's nonwhite population while accounting for only 13 percent of the total regional share of the population.

Given the desirability of Atlanta as a place to live, it remains primarily an African American and white city. Latino presence in areas of metropolitan Atlanta other than the city of Chamblee, the city of Doraville, and sections of northeast Atlanta still remains scarce. As with blacks, the Latino population is highly segregated. However, what is interesting about the residential patterns of Latinos is that unlike other ethnic immigrant groups, Latinos headed to the suburbs as opposed to the central city. In this regard, the change in Gwinnett County, in the northeast Atlanta metropolitan area, is particularly notable. Its white population proportion was 90 percent in 1990; 67 percent in 2000, and as of 2004, is estimated to be only 57 percent (Feagans 2005).

## Residential Patterns

Atlanta was historically characterized by white racial segregation of neighborhoods. Before the spatial integration of larger urban areas brought about by the spread of the automobile culture, Atlanta neighborhoods were racially segregated but interspersed. However, expanding black neighborhoods were primarily allowed on the south side of the city. Post-World War II, African American population growth led to the politically negotiated transition of all-white neighborhoods in the newly developing southern and western portions of the city to neighborhoods for the rising African American middle class as they moved out from the Atlanta University Center, and West End neighborhoods. Thereafter, with respect to residential development, the same north-south pattern emerged regionally.

Expansion areas were particularly demarcated by the construction of the first major interstate highway, Interstate 20, through Atlanta: neighborhoods to the south became unrestricted while neighborhoods to the north of I–20 were primarily white-only. As desegregation occurred, African Americans flowed primarily southeastward into DeKalb County and southwestward into Fulton County. Whites moved northward, up interstates I–75 and I–85 into north Fulton, Cobb, and Gwinnett counties. Today, Atlanta is still a city that is highly racially concentrated in its housing sector. For example, the majority of middle-class blacks reside in two areas: southwest Atlanta and south central DeKalb County (see figure 10.1). Moreover, more than 70 percent of the area's African American population resides south of I–20.

As with African Americans, the area's Hispanic population is highly concentrated. The largest concentration of Latinos is northeast of the city, along I–85 (see Figure 10.2). The Asian population is also concentrated in the northeast sector (Chamblee and Doraville) (see figure 10.3). Large numbers of Atlanta's newer immigrants have settled in the Chamblee area, a suburb of approximately 10,000 people that is among the most overcrowded areas in the United States (Fannie Mae Foundation 2002). These trends reflect the gentrification that has taken root in the city of Atlanta proper, which has compelled the newer immigrant groups, especially Hispanics, to seek more affordable housing in the city's suburbs where the housing stock is older. The surge in the Latino population has caused some racial strains in the inner suburban, and increasingly, in the outer suburban areas, primarily because most residents have had no direct

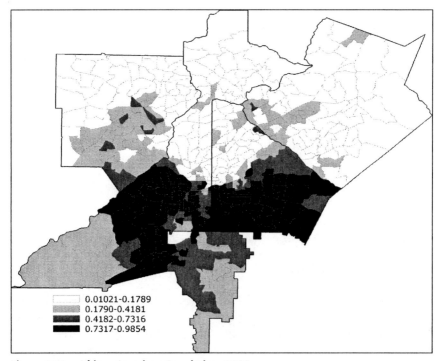

**Figure 10.1. African American Population, 2000**

experience with immigration or immigrants. Added to this is the little, if any pre-existing infrastructure of Spanish-language institutions, such as clinics, churches, social organizations, and so forth. Further, Latino immigrants must cope and exist in an area characterized historically by the uneasy racial divide between whites and blacks. African Americans continued to be concentrated in the city of Atlanta, which forms the basis for black political empowerment at the core of the metropolitan area.

## RACE, ETHNICITY, AND IMMIGRATION IN THE GEORGIA LABOR MARKET: OCCUPATIONAL AND EARNINGS SHIFTS 1985 TO 2005

One of the most frequently cited reasons for the rapid Atlanta metropolitan area growth is the strength of its economy. Just as with residential patterns, membership in particular racial and ethnic groups has a significant impact on an individual's outcomes in earnings, experience of poverty, and wealth. In addition, gender is a major determinant of labor market experience and outcomes. Many factors impact earnings outcomes, hence it is very difficult

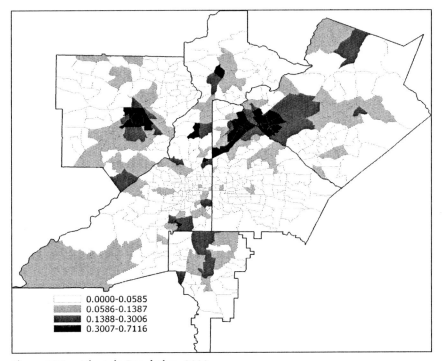

Figure 10.2. Hispanic Population, 2000

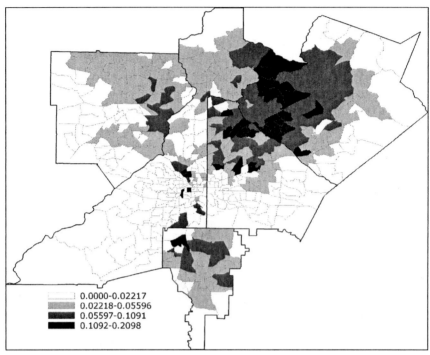

0.0000-0.02217
0.02218-0.05596
0.05597-0.1091
0.1092-0.2098

**Figure 10.3.   Asian Population, 2000**

to assess the impact of increased immigration into Georgia. Other important trends that affect group outcomes include changes in industrial composition, occupational growth and decline, occupational gender distribution shifts, educational outcomes, internal migration patterns, and so forth. We begin by looking at the earnings for particular occupations in Georgia,[1] and the overall distribution of occupations by gender, race, and ethnicity. We then assess which occupational groups account for the largest proportion of employed African Americans and Latinos and look for overlap and any displacement between African Americans and Latinos

The Atlanta metropolitan area labor force is comprised of approximately 2.1 million individuals, of whom about 64.3 percent are white, 26.0 percent are black, and 9.7 percent are Other (Census 2000 SF 4 data). According to the Census Bureau, approximately 6.2 percent are Hispanic; however, it is expected that the actual Hispanic workforce may be twice as large. Interesting gender patterns can be observed. Overall, there has been a reversal of the traditional predominance of men in the labor force. Both the white and African American labor force are characterized by a greater proportion of women, 50.2 percent and 54.8 percent respectively. The Hispanic workforce, shaped by distinctive gender dynamics stemming from immigration patterns (immigrants tend to be more male) and occupational niches (construction, laborers), exhibits the traditional pattern—only 38.9 percent are women while 61.1 percent are men. This is directly reflective of their population numbers, as they alone have a larger proportion of men in their overall population (U.S. Census 2000).

Unemployment and employment rates vary widely by race, ethnicity, and gender. Unemployment is lowest among white women and Hispanic men, 2.9 percent and 3.3 percent respectively, and highest among African American men and women, 10 percent and 8.1 percent, respectively. A look at the proportion of people age twenty-nine to sixty-nine who are not in the labor force reveals several factors, with gender implications. While women are more often intentionally out-of-the labor force as mothers and / or home-makers, men are generally expected to be in the labor force—employed or looking for work (unemployed). While disability conditions will remove a percentage of men from the labor force, not being in the labor force for the most part equates to a form of "hidden" unemployment, or working "off the books" in the informal economy. Approximately 16 percent of African American men are not in the labor force in comparison to 14.6 percent of white men and 10.5 percent of Hispanic men. (This does not include people who are incarcerated.) We can combine the unemployed and out of the labor force to get a full measure of the portions of the community not work-ing. Among men, 13.8 percent of Hispanic, 18.1 percent of whites, and 26.0 percent of African Americans are not working in the formal economy. This is a major difference by race, and requires a careful analysis of many factors to explain. These disparities correlate with disparities in outcome measures of well-being, such as poverty rates and per capita income.

According to the 2005 American Community Survey, the overall poverty rate for the Atlanta metropolitan area was 11.4 percent, while only 6 per-cent for whites. Among African Americans, almost 20 percent had family incomes below the poverty line as did almost 18 percent of Hispanics (see table 10.5). African American and Hispanic per capita income, approxi-mately $19,959 and $14,833 respectively, are considerably below white non-Hispanic per capita income, $34,527.[2] Although Black per capita income is higher than that of Hispanics, the greater rate of poverty may be accounted for by several factors. First, African Americans are most characterized by single-parent households, while Hispanics and Asians are the least affected by this form of social structure. A dual income family structure, and often even more streams of income in Hispanic households, may compensate for low earnings. Among blacks, comparatively, it is likely that there are relatively more very high income individuals whose incomes inflate aver-age overall income. Black earnings may also be more volatile with large proportions falling into poverty, perhaps due to periodic unemployment, while Hispanics' poverty may be due more to low wages.

## Theoretical Approach: Labor Force Queues

There are several critical approaches to labor market outcomes useful in understanding the Atlanta situation. One model of the labor market position of different population groups is the concept of the labor queue pioneered by Stanley Lieberman (1980). This approach asserts that workers with the status characteristics corresponding to groups who have greater privilege or prestige, such as males, whites, and Anglo-ethnicity, are likely to occupy the "better" jobs. Only when these workers are sorted into the cream of the jobs will workers of various other status combinations be hired. The job queue is a conceptualization of all the available jobs arrayed from best to worst. While prestige and other rewards, including different levels of benefits, are all factors of job ranking in the queue, the most determinant factor of ranking is earnings in an occupation. The highest status workers are allowed to match their skills to jobs, and have the resources to reproduce skills, and to fill the better positions. People of lower status characteristics on the other hand are more or less excluded from good jobs through various processes of disprivilege in the forms of pre-existing networks, racism, sexism, and anti-immigrant sentiment.

It can also be helpful to conceptualize that there exists both a "good" jobs queue and a "bad" or "reverse jobs queue." The concept of a reverse job queue suggests that a segment of the employers actually *prefer* to employ the lowest status and most vulnerable workers, because their main criteria for filling jobs is low pay. These are jobs necessary to processes and industries where there are low requirements for worker skill, training, self-motivation, and creativity, and thus where low cost is the overriding consideration when selecting workers. For these jobs, it is the most vulnerable and socially low-status workers who are preferred. Thus, the labor market job processes operate to select high privilege workers first for the good jobs queue and low privilege workers first for the reverse labor queue. We describe jobs as "good" or "bad," based on whether they provide a "living wage." The concept of a living wage is based on

**Table 10.5   Poverty Experienced within the Last Twelve Months and Per Capita Income, by Race and Ethnicity, Atlanta MSA**

| Category | Percent Experiencing Poverty | Per Capita Income | Per Capita Ratio with Whites |
|---|---|---|---|
| Total Population | 11.4% | $27,797 | 0.81 |
| African American | 19.8% | $19,959 | 0.59 |
| White | 6.0% | $34,527 | 1.00 |
| Hispanic | 17.8% | $14,883 | 0.43 |

Source: U.S. Census *2005 American Community Survey*.

analyzing what is needed to provide adequate housing, food, health care, transportation, and domestic goods for a family of three or four. Jobs that pay less create the "working poor"—people who work regularly but remain unable to meet their daily needs, leading to deficiencies in health care and educational expenditure, and lower overall social well-being in a community. A living wage is generally above the established minimum wage (see Brooks, this volume).[3]

Racial/ethnic-gender groups also come to fill job niches—where a group occupies a disproportionate proportion of the total available jobs in a particular occupational and/or industrial specialty, based on group solidarity, as exerted both in the economy, and sometimes via local, state, and national politics. For instance, white political power prevented African Americans from competing for most jobs at the middle to upper range of the job queues until the 1970s. And ever since then, with their control over resources through ownership, they have been positioned to continue to provide privileges for their group (Hewitt 2000; 2004). Further, the various ethnic groups, distinguished by cultural ties resulting in social solidarity, tend to specialize and concentrate in particular occupations. The group culture in ethnic occupational niches then provides a sort of training system to their co-ethnics, giving them a comparative advantage (Waldinger 1986; Sowell 1994). Thus, the area labor force comes to be characterized by relatively fixed, self-reproducing, or self-compounding divisions characterized by race and ethnicity. In-migration of members of the existing racial and ethnic groups may enhance or shift these queue and niche occupational structures, and an incursion in large numbers of a new racial or ethnic group can likely lead to a restructuring of these occupational divisions. We use a labor queue model to describe labor force structure and explain racial and ethnic distribution in jobs in the Atlanta metro area.

Our analysis here is focused on forty-two occupational categories, as defined by the U.S. Census Standard Occupational Code (SOC) listing. These forty-two occupations are those for which a racial or ethnic group occupied a disproportionate proportion of the jobs.[4] In particular, we define a racial or ethnic job niche as an occupation in which the group's share of positions exceeds its population proportion by 20 percent or more. For most of the occupational niches for the minority groups the concentration in the niche is 50 to 100 percent or more above their population percentage.

The analysis below (based on the data in tables 10.6 and 10.7) present a picture of the racial and ethnic distribution of jobs by gender because of the tendency for men to be employed in different occupations than women, and the gender composition of the labor force to be different among different racial and ethnic groups. A thorough gender analysis of women's job placement as opposed to men in terms of the job queue, however, would require close scrutiny not only of the distribution of jobs among women, but of the distribution of jobs between men and women, in order to reveal to what extent jobs in which women are concentrated, the "pink collar" jobs, are paying low to below living wages.

## RACIAL AND ETHNIC JOB NICHES AMONG MEN

An analysis of occupations of males in the Atlanta metropolitan area shows that they are characterized by hierarchal racial or ethnic concentration, or niches, with white males in occupations that pay higher salaries. Non-Hispanic whites constitute almost 66 percent of the male labor force, blacks constitute approximately 23 percent, and Hispanics, or Latinos, hold 8.2 percent of jobs. In 2000, whites constituted only 60 percent of the area population, but among men, they held 66 percent of the jobs, while blacks constituted almost 29 percent (28.7 percent) and held only 23 percent of the jobs. Hispanics, constituting 6.5 percent of the population, show rough parity in their share of jobs held (6.6 percent).

The advantaged position of white males is readily seen when we consider the distribution of jobs across occupations. White male job niches exist in fourteen occupations: twelve in the management and professional categories, one in the service category, and one in sales and office. White males are most overrepresented among lawyers (89.8%), top executives (87.4%), "advertising, marketing, promotions, public relations and sales managers," (85.8%), "judges, magistrates, and other judicial workers" (85.6%), and "sales representatives, services, wholesale and manufacturing" (86.1%). The average median hourly earnings available in these white male niche occupations are $36.78. These are occupations clearly at the top of the job queue.

Latinos are disproportionately represented in eleven occupations: three service occupations—cooks and food preparation workers (23.7%), waiters and waitresses (15.1%), and building and grounds cleaning and maintenance (25.4%), and among eight job categories toward the bottom of the queue, primarily as agricultural and related workers, construction, food processing, and textile related workers. Hispanics constitute 48.2 percent of all construction laborers, 41 percent of painters and paperhangers, and 40.5 percent of (documented) farm workers, including supervisors. The median hourly earnings available in these Hispanic male niche occupations are $11.55. These for the most part low-wage positions may be the top of the reverse labor queue.

African Americans occupy sixteen occupational niches distributed somewhat throughout the job spectrum, although more heavily at the bottom, and notably absent in construction categories. Blacks constitute 45.7 percent of male "counselors, social workers, and other community and social services specialists," almost 50 percent (49.9%) of protective service workers (excluding firefighting), 46.6 percent of "transportation, tourism and lodging attendants," 63.4 percent of bus drivers, 57.1 percent of motor vehicle operators (except truck drivers among whom they still constitute 40.6 percent), and 50 percent of "other material moving workers, except laborers." While these are the occupational categories which show the greatest concentration of African Americans among the male job holders, several others are clearly to be considered niches. These include special education teachers (33.9%), health-related, and financial and information sales and office occupations. These niches are characterized by moderate to substantial education, skill, and credentialing, and possibly by union protection. The average hourly median earnings available in the African American male niche occupations are $13.71.

## WOMEN AND THE RACIAL AND ETHNIC OCCUPATIONAL LABOR QUEUE

In general, in comparison to men, women are more concentrated in occupations where median earnings are below a living wage, particularly sales and office occupations and to a smaller degree, services, while male employment tends to cluster in construction (see table 10.6). Non-Hispanic whites constitute almost 63 percent of the female labor force, blacks constitute approximately 30 percent, and Latinas constitute approximately 4 percent. These proportions are more consistent with their population distribution than those for men, where the black share is particularly low. Niche occupational development for white women occurs primarily in the management, professional, and related categories; for African Americans in service, and sales and office occupations situated in the middle of the queue, and among Latinas, in the construction and production, transportation, and material moving occupations at the end of the list (see table 10.7). Outside of the occupations of "fire fighting and prevention" and "extraction workers," which have a negligible number of jobs, white women are concentrated only in "sales representatives, services, wholesale and manufacturing," which along with the professional and managerial occupations pays considerably above the metropolitan living wage of $13.10 an hour. Only one occupational niche for white women falls below the minimum wage—"religious workers"— which may often be part-time jobs and provide other intrinsic rewards.

**Table 10.6   Occupational Share and Hourly Earnings for Men by Race and Ethnicity, Atlanta MSA, 2000**

| Selected Occupation by Sex and Category[a] | Median Hourly Earnings | Latino Share of Jobs | White Share of Jobs | Black Share of Jobs | Other Share of Jobs | Number of Jobs |
|---|---|---|---|---|---|---|
| Male Employed Labor Force | | 8.2% | 65.7% | 22.5% | 3.7% | 1,127,536 |
| *Management, professional, and related occupations:* | | | | | | |
| Management, business, and financial operations occupations | $38.73 | 2.9% | 80.9% | 13.3% | 3.0% | 207,377 |
| Management Operations | $39.84 | | 82.1% | 11.9% | 3.0% | 152,361 |
| Top executives | $70.00+ | 1.6% | 87.4% | 7.6% | 3.3% | 34,987 |
| Advertising, marketing, promotions, public relations, and sales managers | $44.02 | 2.8% | 85.8% | 9.5% | 1.8% | 20,909 |
| Financial managers | $42.06 | 2.4% | 80.0% | 14.5% | 3.1% | 9,489 |
| Operations specialties managers, except financial managers | $38.89 | 3.3% | 81.0% | 12.9% | 2.9% | 23,110 |
| Professional and related occupations | | | | | | |
| Computer specialists | $31.22 | 2.9% | 70.6% | 16.4% | 10.1% | 55,689 |
| Architecture and engineering occupations | | | | | | |
| Architects, surveyors, and cartographers | $29.39 | 2.6% | 84.2% | 7.2% | 6.0% | 4,284 |
| Social scientists and related workers | $29.36 | 1.2% | 83.3% | 11.8% | 3.6% | 2,485 |
| Counselors, social workers, and other community and social service specialists | $17.55 | 1.6% | 52.1% | 45.7% | 0.6% | 4,063 |
| Lawyers | $53.15 | 1.8% | 89.8% | 6.8% | 1.5% | 11,067 |
| Judges, magistrates, and other judicial workers | $39.42 | 2.4% | 85.6% | 5.7% | 6.3% | 679 |
| Teachers, special education | $24.08 | 4.9% | 61.2% | 33.9% | 0.0% | 183 |
| Art and design workers | $21.42 | 2.5% | 81.3% | 12.0% | 4.2% | 7,958 |
| Other health diagnosing and treating practitioners and technical occupations | $23.35 | 2.5% | 82.4% | 11.3% | 3.7% | 5,601 |
| Health technologists and technicians | $17.74 | 2.1% | 53.4% | 39.9% | 4.6% | 4,144 |
| *Service occupations:* | | | | | | |
| Nursing, psychiatric, and home health aides | $10.18 | 5.1% | 31.2% | 63.3% | 0.4% | 1,338 |
| Fire fighting and prevention workers, including supervisors | $19.00 | 0.4% | 80.0% | 19.4% | 0.2% | 4,879 |
| Other protective service workers, including supervisors | $10.51 | 2.6% | 46.0% | 49.9% | 1.5% | 9,520 |
| Cooks and food preparation workers | $9.28 | 23.7% | 36.2% | 34.6% | 5.4% | 15,229 |
| Waiters and waitresses | $6.39 | 15.1% | 58.2% | 19.7% | 7.0% | 8,772 |
| Building and grounds cleaning and maintenance occupations | $10.05 | 25.4% | 40.6% | 31.0% | 3.1% | 35,949 |
| Personal appearance workers | | 2.8% | 38.2% | 39.6% | 19.4% | 3,530 |

Continued on next page.

**Table 10.6  Occupational Share and Hourly Earnings for Men by Race and Ethnicity, Atlanta MSA, 2000**

| Selected Occupation by Sex and Category[a] | Median Hourly Earnings | Latino Share of Jobs | White Share of Jobs | Black Share of Jobs | Other Share of Jobs | Number of Jobs |
|---|---|---|---|---|---|---|
| Transportation, tourism, and lodging attendants | $9.55 | 4.8% | 47.3% | 46.6% | 1.3% | 1,907 |
| Cashiers | | 4.9% | 46.7% | 35.8% | 12.6% | 10,530 |
| *Sales and office occupations:* | | | | | | |
| Sales representatives, services, wholesale, and manufacturing | $26.19 | 2.1% | 86.1% | 10.2% | 1.6% | 45,434 |
| *Office and administrative support occupations:* | | | | | | |
| Communications equipment operators | $12.98 | 7.6% | 52.0% | 40.4% | 0.0% | 369 |
| Financial clerks, except bookkeeping, | | | | | | |
| accounting and auditing clerks | $14.33 | 2.9% | 54.4% | 41.8% | 0.9% | 3,346 |
| Information and record clerks, except customer service representatives | $13.02 | 5.8% | 48.3% | 42.3% | 3.6% | 8,188 |
| Material recording, scheduling, dispatching, and distributing workers | $13.97 | 4.9% | 50.8% | 41.3% | 3.1% | 34,559 |
| *Farming, fishing, and forestry occupations:* | | | | | | |
| Agricultural workers including supervisors | $10.58 | 40.5% | 36.6% | 20.0% | 2.9% | 1,978 |
| *Construction, extraction, and maintenance occupations:* | | | | | | |
| Carpenters | $15.86 | 31.2% | 56.7% | 10.3% | 1.8% | 23,056 |
| Construction laborers | $11.21 | 48.2% | 33.7% | 17.0% | 1.1% | 22,872 |
| Painters and paperhangers | $14.31 | 41.7% | 44.5% | 12.0% | 1.7% | 11,539 |
| Pipelayers, plumbers, pipefitters, and steamfitters and construction laborers | $16.28 | 34.7% | 49.3% | 15.3% | 0.7% | 7,228 |
| Extraction workers | $11.93 | 16.6% | 76.0% | 7.5% | 0.0% | 362 |
| *Production, transportation, and material moving occupations:* | | | | | | |
| Food processing workers | $9.89 | 18.0% | 41.9% | 34.6% | 5.6% | 3,639 |
| Textile, apparel, and furnishings workers | $11.28 | 21.3% | 38.2% | 23.2% | 17.4% | 4,935 |
| Rail and water transportation workers | $18.04 | 2.1% | 53.8% | 42.2% | 1.8% | 1,314 |
| Bus drivers | $10.44 | 1.1% | 34.8% | 63.4% | 0.7% | 2,992 |
| Driver/sales workers and truck drivers | $15.44 | 14.4% | 25.7% | 40.6% | 1.5% | 40,871 |
| Motor vehicle operators, except truck drivers | $11.06 | 14.4% | 25.7% | 57.1% | 2.7% | 3,355 |
| Laborers and material movers, hand | $10.32 | 10.2% | 41.0% | 46.3% | 2.5% | 27,552 |
| Other material moving workers, except laborers | $10.19 | 8.9% | 39.1% | 50.2% | 1.7% | 12,148 |

[a] Figures highlighted where disproportionate racial/ethnic share defined as occupational niche.

As among men, African American women have niches in the "counselor, social workers, and other community and social service specialists" occupations among the top categories. Their occupational concentration is then heavily connected to the service sector occupations, including nursing aides (64.4 percent of jobs), protective services (59.6 percent and 60.2 percent), food preparation (36.8 percent) and building and grounds maintenance (42.9 percent). Outside of the protective services, these occupations have large numbers of jobs which do not pay a living wage. African American women also have occupational niches in the mid-range office and administrative support occupations, including cashiers (39.2 percent), financial clerks (39 percent), customer service (45.1 percent), "material recording, scheduling, dispatching, and distribution workers" (40.9 percent), and other office and administrative support (36 percent). Hourly earnings in the service occupations tend to be below the living wage, while sales, and office and administrative support occupations tend to be right around the living wage level, except among the large number of cashiers, whose median hourly wage is only $6.15. Finally, among women, African Americans tend to hold a disproportionate share of some production occupations in the production, transportation, and materials moving category, such as assemblers and fabricators (44.7 percent), metal workers and plastic workers (43.4 percent), and other production occupations, including supervisors (38.7 percent). The production occupations have median hourly earnings close to or above the living wage, while the transportation and moving niche occupations do not provide a living wage.

Unlike among men, considerable overlap occurs between African American women and Latinas in terms of occupations in which they are both disproportionately represented. As with Hispanic men, Hispanic women have no job niches within the top management, professional and related occupations, or among the mid-level office and administrative support occupations, and only one, cashiers, among the sales and office occupations. Cashier, an occupation with median hourly earnings below living wage, is consistent with the other low-wage occupations where Hispanic women have concentrations. In services, they have concentrations as cooks (17.3 percent), waitresses (6.9 percent), and building and grounds cleaning (18 percent). These pay below living wage. Hispanic women are also concentrated in occupations, which actually have negligible numbers of women employees, in the farming and construction categories. Otherwise, Hispanic women have niches in production, transportation, and material moving occupations, including assemblers and fabricators (6.4 percent), metal and plastic workers (7.8 percent), and other production occupations including supervisors (9.5 percent). These occupational niches are shared with African American women.

## EFFECTS OF WEALTH, CLOSURE,
## AND GOVERNMENT REGULATION

Explanations for the continued hierarchal placement of workers by race and ethnicity include the seemingly obvious issue of educational achievement; however, there exists debate among social scientists over the extent to which group educational achievement *reflects* a group's access to resources and ability to provide home support, that is, among the first outcomes of moving out of poverty (Bonacich 1981), or is the path the poor are able to take to achieve access to resources. The analysis of labor force queues and niches offers some other explanations. First, there are demand-side issues of levels of ownership, and in particular, the related dimension, authority. The privileged labor market position of white males clearly correlates to their greater wealth and asset holding, which is one proxy for ownership. It has been shown that differences in earnings are more strongly related to differences in level of authority, than education, or tenure (Wright 1978). Authority is a dimension characteristically associated with management of enterprises and service, positions that are critical to their functioning, and generally owners tend to feel comfortable turning decision-making over to people similar to themselves (Smith and Elliott 2002). And since authority is most effective if it is legitimated—when it is voluntarily acknowledged by the supervised—persons placed in authority positions are usually of equal or higher social status than those they supervise. Hence, the ownership structure of an industry is most telling on who acquires authority and the exercise of responsibility, with the attendant higher earnings.

The Atlanta area labor force queue also suggests various ways in which it is shaped by group closure and government sector regulation. Unionization is not a particularly salient factor in the racial and ethnic distribution of jobs in the South, in general, and in the Atlanta area in particular. Few jobs are likely to come under union protection, most noticeably in the absence of niches in the manufacturing sector of jobs. However, African Americans do occupy niches among the "production, transportation, and material moving occupations" where manufacturing jobs are found in the area of driving and material moving, which may come under union protection. Another form of closure—licensing and accrediting—also serves to limit the competition and raise wages for certain skilled jobs and in certain industries. The government sector also provides jobs with remuneration above the minimum level and that are less subject to racist and sexist discriminatory processes. Atlanta area African American occupational niches, in particular, reflect these factors, including health technologists and technicians and special education teachers. Some of the highest paying occupational niches held by male Hispanic workers are in

**Table 10.7  Occupational Shares and Hourly Earnings for Women by Race and Ethnicity, Atlanta MSA, 2000**

| Selected Occupation by Sex and Category[a] | Median Hourly Earnings | Latina Share of Jobs | White Share of Jobs | Black Share of Jobs | Other Share of Jobs | Number of Jobs |
|---|---|---|---|---|---|---|
| Female Employed Labor Force | | 3.9% | 62.7% | 30.2% | 3.3% | 965,458 |
| *Management, professional, and related occupations:* | | | | | | |
| Top executives | $70.00+ | 2.3% | 79.6% | 15.4% | 2.6% | 9,255 |
| Advertising, marketing, promotions, public relations, and sales managers | $44.02 | 3.0% | 80.8% | 14.2% | 1.9% | 14,139 |
| Farmers and farm managers | | 0.0% | 94.6% | 3.4% | 2.0% | 500 |
| Operations specialties managers, except financial managers | $38.89 | 3.3% | 81.0% | 12.9% | 2.9% | 13,102 |
| Professional and related occupations | | | | | | |
| Architects, surveyors, and cartographers | $29.39 | 5.6% | 80.9% | 9.2% | 4.1% | 934 |
| Social scientists and related workers | $29.36 | 3.2% | 82.6% | 12.1% | 2.1% | 3,101 |
| Counselors, social workers, and other community and social service specialists | $17.55 | 1.5% | 56.7% | 41.1% | 0.7% | 11,851 |
| Religious workers | $7.82 | 1.3% | 77.3% | 18.3% | 3.1% | 2,934 |
| Lawyers | $53.15 | 1.9% | 77.8% | 18.8% | 1.5% | 4,525 |
| Legal support workers | $21.31 | 2.4% | 75.3% | 21.3% | 1.0% | 7,199 |
| Teachers, special education | $24.08 | 1.0% | 80.2% | 17.9% | 0.9% | 2,095 |
| Art and design workers | $21.42 | 3.0% | 81.0% | 11.5% | 4.5% | 8,851 |
| Entertainers and performers, sports, etc. | n/a | 2.2% | 78.7% | 18.6% | 0.4% | 3,793 |
| (Health) Therapists | $25.77 | 0.5% | 77.8% | 20.7% | 1.0% | 4,815 |
| *Service occupations:* | | | | | | |
| Nursing, psychiatric, and home health aides | $10.18 | 2.1% | 31.9% | 64.4% | 1.6% | 10,905 |
| Fire fighting and prevention workers, including supervisors | $19.00 | 0.0% | 82.1% | 17.9% | 0.0% | 195 |
| Law enforcement workers, including supervisors | $17.67 | 2.0% | 37.3% | 59.6% | 1.1% | 3,320 |
| Other protective service workers, including supervisors | $10.51 | 1.3% | 37.5% | 60.2% | 1.0% | 4,651 |
| Cooks and food preparation workers | $9.28 | 17.3% | 40.4% | 36.8% | 5.4% | 13,320 |
| Waiters and waitresses | $6.39 | 6.9% | 70.7% | 17.5% | 4.9% | 17,193 |
| Other food prep and serving workers, including supervisors | $13.06 | 7.5% | 54.1% | 32.2% | 6.2% | 8,867 |
| Building and grounds cleaning and maintenance occupations | $10.05 | 18.0% | 35.1% | 42.9% | 4.0% | 22,222 |
| Child care workers | $7.94 | 5.5% | 63.3% | 29.5% | 1.6% | 16,217 |
| Transportation, tourism, and lodging attendants | $9.55 | 4.8% | 47.3% | 46.6% | 1.3% | 5,803 |
| *Sales and office occupations:* | | | | | | |
| Cashiers | $6.15 | 5.7% | 49.1% | 39.2% | 6.0% | 28,972 |
| Sales representatives, services, wholesale and manufacturing | $26.19 | 2.5% | 76.6% | 18.8% | 2.0% | 24,210 |
| *Office and administrative support occupations:* | | | | | | |
| Communications equipment operators | $12.98 | 2.3% | 57.3% | 49.2% | 1.3% | 2,153 |

Continued on next page.

Table 10.7  Occupational Shares and Hourly Earnings for Women by Race and Ethnicity, Atlanta MSA, 2000 (continued)

| Selected Occupation by Sex and Category[a] | Median Hourly Earnings | Latina Share of Jobs | White Share of Jobs | Black Share of Jobs | Other Share of Jobs | Number of Jobs |
|---|---|---|---|---|---|---|
| Financial clerks, except bookkeeping, accounting and auditing clerks | $14.33 | 2.1% | 56.2% | 39.0% | 2.7% | 16,981 |
| Customer service representatives | $15.14 | 3.4% | 50.4% | 45.1% | 1.1% | 33,136 |
| Material recording, scheduling, dispatching, and distributing workers | $13.97 | 3.6% | 52.7% | 40.9% | 2.8% | 21,930 |
| Other office and admin support workers, including supervisors | $11.36 | 2.1% | 60.1% | 36.0% | 1.8% | 64,876 |
| *Farming, fishing, and forestry occupations:* | | | | | | |
| Agricultural workers including supervisors | $10.58 | 30.6% | 47.4% | 15.7% | 6.2% | 859 |
| *Construction, extraction, and maintenance occupations:* | | | | | | |
| Supervisors, construction and extraction workers | $25.94 | 7.1% | 67.1% | 25.8% | 0.0% | 693 |
| Carpenters | $15.86 | 26.9% | 60.6% | 12.5% | 0.0% | 424 |
| Construction laborers | $11.21 | 30.8% | 49.2% | 16.4% | 3.5% | 736 |
| Painters and paperhangers | $14.31 | 15.2% | 73.3% | 7.3% | 4.2% | 896 |
| Pipelayers, plumbers, pipefitters, and steamfitters and construction laborers[b] | $16.28 | 19.3% | 58.2% | 15.5% | 7.0% | 114 |
| Other construction workers and helpers | $13.34 | 7.3% | 53.4% | 31.6% | 7.6% | 395 |
| Extraction workers | $11.93 | 0.0% | 100.0% | 0.0% | 0.0% | |
| Vehicle and mobile equipment mechanics, installers, and repairers | $18.15 | 5.2% | 38.4% | 49.0% | 7.4% | 539 |
| *Production, transportation, and material moving occupations:* | | | | | | |
| Assemblers and fabricators | $16.05 | 6.4% | 38.5% | 44.7% | 10.3% | 6,316 |
| Food processing workers | $9.89 | 21.2% | 43.8% | 27.8% | 7.1% | 2,387 |
| Metal workers and plastic workers | $14.51 | 7.8% | 39.3% | 43.4% | 9.5% | 2,735 |
| Textile, apparel, and furnishings workers | $11.28 | 13.4% | 35.9% | 35.9% | 14.8% | 9,068 |
| Woodworkers | $12.04 | 7.1% | 54.0% | 31.0% | 8.0% | 226 |
| Plant and systems operators | $18.90 | 0.0% | 47.1% | 52.9% | 0.0% | 104 |
| Other production occupations, including supervisors | $12.86 | 9.5% | 43.9% | 38.7% | 7.9% | 19,456 |
| Supervisors, transportation and material moving workers | $23.32 | 1.8% | 52.0% | 41.7% | 4.5% | 947 |
| Rail and water transportation | | | | | | |
| Workers | $18.04 | 0.0% | 15.2% | 84.8% | 0.0% | 66 |
| Bus drivers | $10.44 | 1.1% | 34.8% | 63.4% | 0.7% | 5,087 |
| Driver/sales workers and truck drivers | $15.44 | 2.3% | 49.6% | 46.5% | 1.7% | 2,482 |
| Motor vehicle operators, except truck drivers | $11.06 | 23.6% | 26.2% | 50.2% | 0.0% | 313 |
| Laborers and material movers, hand | $10.32 | 15.9% | 33.4% | 45.7% | 5.0% | 9,055 |
| Other material moving workers, except laborers | $10.19 | 2.8% | 34.9% | 60.5% | 1.8% | 958 |

[a] Figures highlighted where disproportionate racial/ethnic share defined as occupational niche.

[b] Some lack of clarity with definition of this category.

the construction industry, which can be characterized by both forms of closure and government regulation of wages. In the Atlanta context, the low level of unionization may have mixed effects, offering fewer apprenticeship barriers to entry into construction specialties for Latino workers and yet allowing lower pay scales than in other regions.

Another criterion regarding the queue ranking of occupations that is not well-represented in the SOC listing is the degree to which physical exertion and harsh or unpleasant work conditions or materials pertain in a job. In respect to this criterion, whites occupy a niche in no occupations likely to entail these factors, and in general, African American men also do not predominate in them, while Hispanic workers, who are often immigrants, and African American women predominate in several occupations characterized by these conditions. Relatedly, the lowest paying niche occupied by white men is one which is likely characterized by high workplace flexibility and satisfaction with materials—the category of art and design workers.

### Globalization and the Reverse Labor Queue

The reverse queue of jobs which pay less than what may be considered living wages has always existed in capitalism and has traditionally been filled by slave, migrant or immigrant, and female labor. Agriculture was the predominant sector built around low-cost labor until mechanization replaced much of the need for labor after World War I. The South, and Atlanta in particular, reemerged in the 1970s as economic contenders as part of the emerging service economy. As mentioned earlier, since the 1996 Olympic Games hosted by Atlanta, there has been an influx of workers who have occupied jobs primarily in the construction and service sectors, jobs that are mostly low-wage, often with no benefits. Today, most low-cost labor is in what Robert Reich (1992) described as "face-to-face services"—particularly services for domestic, health, and other reproductive needs that have to be delivered on the spot (such as child care, health care, food preparation, and cleaning)—and therefore which cannot be outsourced overseas.

In the globalized service economy, the outsourcing of risk and innovation to small start-up firms fostered a very competitive environment among the workforce, with big rewards for the successfully placed individuals, and little social protection for the vast majority of others. In fact, this competition unleashed among high end workers leads to their "outsourcing" functions necessary to their lives, such as cleaning, maintenance, cooking, and organizing recreation. They seek to maximize the gainful employment of their time and pay others whose labor is less expensive and specialized than their own, to do these chores, the "face-to-face" workers. As stressed by Sassen (1991), the labor market becomes characterized by a dualism where the existence of a relatively small sector of high-paid workers increasingly generates a sector, several times larger, of very low-paid service workers serving the high-paid workers. Since these low-wage positions cannot be outsourced, immigration is allowed to fill them here.

What is the impact of this immigrant labor on the existing labor force? Historically, in the United States, economic expansions have been consistent enough to open new opportunities to the existing labor force to improve their skills, experience, and credentials, and to move up in authority level—to experience social mobility. As particular ethnic groups were able to gain political power and organize unions, occupations providing important services were often protected—particularly in fields of education, protection services, and construction. This social mobility for the European immigrant group was also protected by racism, which excluded African, Native American, and Asian (to a lesser extent) heritage people from competing in upper end job markets. Thus the iniquitous situation whereby racial minorities were bypassed by each entering European immigrant group occurred. Today, a key question is whether the same racist social status system will pertain and certain minorities will be mired at the bottom of the labor queue.

There is evidence that the politically enforced low status of illegality attached to workers of Latin American and Mexican heritage in particular, language barriers along with ineffective education services, and racial and cultural prejudice, have situated this group today below African Americans in labor market status. However, Latin Americans' disadvantages make them the most desirable workforce for the reverse queue—the sector of the labor market whose labor selection is basically only on the basis of cost. By being at the head of the reverse queue, Latinos are serving a high demand market so unemployment is low. But poverty is high due to the generally less than living wage that is paid, and often below minimum wage. On the other hand, although African Americans experience high levels of unemployment, they are unlikely to accept the long hours and difficult conditions with low pay and low authority. State surveillance upon immigrant workers, particularly those who are undocumented, creates a compliance based on fear, shared to some extent by their documented family and friends by association as well. This makes acceptance of exploitative conditions characteristic of the reverse labor queue more likely.

Asian workers, on the other hand, have only been able to make the journey to the United States—in the absence of shared borders—by passing through documenting customs procedures. The intense U.S. military and investment intervention in some Asian countries, the rise of development, and consequent increase in education levels, has resulted in a significant flow of Asians engaged in high education endeavors in the United States, building skills, and obtaining skill-based visas—H1-B visas, for example. Further, a greater proportion of Asians arrive with investment capital resources to start businesses (Bates 1997). The only occupation category displaying a concentration of other people that includes the Asian American population, is computer specialties in the managerial and professional category. The education level of the Asian immigrant population reflects this,[5] and exempts them from much low-wage labor competition. A similar situation pertains to immigrants from Africa and Europe.

The South and East Asian populations in the Atlanta MSA are gradually developing an impressive commercial presence in Doraville, a city northeast of Atlanta that is home to many Korean, Vietnamese, and Mexican enterprises. There are plans for a new Asian shopping center, which has caused anxiety among non-Asian residents (Poole and Yoo 2007). The economic strength of Asians throughout the state may not only add to this group's political clout, but strengthen its standing in partisan politics statewide and nationally.

## POLITICAL AND SOCIAL IMPLICATIONS

Many factors have worked against the political participation of newer immigrant groups, Hispanics especially. As the Georgia Association of Latino Elected Officials (GALEO) reports, many Latinos have traditionally felt alienated from the political process, and do not understand it. While their political base is currently small (it is estimated that just over 2.0 percent of Georgia's registered voters are Hispanic, and Hispanic voters do not yet control a district), GALEO reports that Hispanics are registering to vote in growing numbers. They are pressing for greater access to various social services and are striving to combat the general anti-immigration tide that periodically sweeps the country (Smith 2006; Jones 2007; Center for Hispanic Studies 2005). These groups and initiatives generally seek to deny economic benefits and social services to illegal immigrants, as well as paths to citizenship. On the other hand, economic integration seems to be proceeding despite these barriers, as increasingly services are offered with bilingual choices, and some municipalities have welcomed the influx of a new labor force (Kirp 2000). We see these trends (of Asian/Hispanic population growth and residential concentration) nationally. How much more the Atlanta area immigrant population will grow will depend partly on the direction that immigration reform takes in this country, and partly on the vibrancy of the economic sectors that create demand for low-skilled labor, such as housing, manufacturing, and food processing.

Very interesting is the notion of a "black-brown" coalition in Atlanta. African Americans tend to overwhelmingly vote liberal and Democratic, while Hispanic immigrants, increasingly, as a group, tend to split their support between liberal and conservative political aspirants. Asian groups tend to be more conservative in orientation than Hispanics. There are large cultural gulfs between urban African Americans and rural immigrant Latinos and upwardly-mobile Asian immigrants. However, influential sectors of the African American community are making some efforts to reach out.[6] There is some public discourse about how blacks in this country have "lost ground" and concern about the economic costs of immigration, yet this has not resulted in political hostility between blacks and Latinos (Diamond 1998). Yet, in regards to the major national political questions, such as the war in Iraq, as shown in a 2004 poll just after its start, Hispanics were more similar to African Americans in their level of opposition to the war, particularly if significant numbers of civilian casualties were anticipated [85 percent of African Americans, and 75 percent of Hispanics were opposed in comparison to 48 percent of white Americans] (Basu 2003). Further, the majority of Hispanics have voted Democratic overall in every U.S. presidential election.

Effective analysis of the political orientation of the population with Hispanic ethnic background is complicated by the failure of most analysts to take both race and ethnicity (Hispanic culture) into consideration. While Spanish cultural background may be a master identity when the person arrives, its saliency is challenged by the dominant status division of race within U. S. society over time as they and their children become more likely to be able to vote. Based on the level of their African and/or Native American heritage, people of Hispanic culture assimilate very differently into United States society and political culture. To some extent, the same range of political stances is found among the population of Anglo culture, which varies highly by racial status, as is found among the population of Hispanic culture, which also varies highly by racial status. Without in-depth analysis, it appears that most of the Hispanic immigrant population to metropolitan Atlanta is by racial status Native American, not particularly European (Spaniard) heritage.

## State Level Implications

National, state, and county demographic trends in race and ethnicity provide a backdrop for understanding the Atlanta area. The U.S. Census Bureau projects that non-Hispanic whites will no longer be the majority nationally by 2050. In 2004, Texas joined the group of majority-minority states to bring the current total to five, with Georgia not far behind as seventh in terms of the greatest minority population proportions among states.

Georgia's white, non-Hispanic population proportion fell from 70 percent in 1990 to 63 percent in 2000, and to 60 percent in 2004. Quoting Doug Bachtel, a demographer at the University of Georgia, Feagans (2005) writes: "To a demographer, such change is lightening-fast. 'Usually demographic trends move at the speed of a retaining wall. But this rapid minority growth has just been coming like a freight train.'" The change in Gwinnett County, in the northeast Atlanta metropolitan area, is particularly notable. Its white population proportion was 90 percent in 1990; 67 percent in 2000; and as of 2004, is estimated to be only 57 percent (Feagins 2005).

**Implications for Schools**

There are many pieces of anecdotal information reflecting the social significance of the minority population influx over even the last five years. According to the Pew Hispanic Center, Georgia's increase by 390 percent over the last decade (1992–2003) of Hispanic students enrolled in public schools, was the fourth fastest in the nation, behind Arkansas and North and South Carolina (Moscoso 2006). The number of Hispanic students in Georgia schools increased from approximately 19,000 to 93,000. In Gwinnett County, the number of students with English as a second language grew from about 3,900 in 1994 to nearly 41,000 in 2003, approximately 20 percent of the student population. In Cobb County, in the northeast quadrant of the Atlanta MSA, Hispanic students went from about 2,215 to 14,000 in the same time period. In DeKalb County, Hispanic ethnicity students account for about 5 percent of high school students; 7 percent of middle-school students, and 11 percent of elementary school students. By 1998, there were seven area schools that were majority Hispanic, and fifty-seven metro-area schools experienced a change in the race/ethnicity of the majority of their students. In Clayton County, on the Southside of the Atlanta area, twenty schools changed from majority white to majority black, and of the fifteen schools that shifted proportions in DeKalb, three changed from majority black—non-Hispanic, to majority Hispanic. Concern about these shifts has been expressed because school racial and ethnic composition shifts are often more volatile than even neighborhood shifts, and a trend toward an outcome of racially and ethnically segregated schools is being observed (Orfield in Stafford 1999).

The relative youth of the Hispanic immigrant population accounts in large part for the impact on schools, and on hospitals as well. Age and cultural characteristics, among other factors, have combined to yield a Hispanic birthrate that is twice the rate of the general population in Georgia (Pascual 2004). For example, at Atlanta's sole major public hospital, Grady Memorial Hospital, 42 percent of the babies born in 2003 were to Hispanic parents, up from 30 percent in 2000, as were 37 percent of the babies born at the Atlanta Medical Center. At the Women's Pavilion at Gwinnett Medical Center, 24 percent of the women admitted were of Hispanic background. Among the positive factors influencing this level of fertility, beyond their age, is that the mothers of Hispanic heritage tend to be healthier and younger than other Georgian mothers, generally do not smoke or drink, and are at low risk for HIV. Rarely are their births the results of induced pregnancies for older mothers.

## CONCLUSION: ATLANTA AND THE POTENTIAL FOR RACIAL EQUALITY

There have been tremendous demographic shifts in population resulting in increased diversity yet continued separation and inequality with respect to occupations and earnings, residential patterns and socioeconomic outcomes. However, the groups and forces of moderation and acceptance of change have in the last twenty years maintained an overall peaceful coexistence as the predominant environment in Atlanta and its environs. There is not an absence of possibilities for conflict, but that type of outcome appears to be mitigated by several factors.

One hypothesis is that the African American status group with their high unemployment[7] has been "lapped," or more inciting, has been "displaced," by all other groups in terms of jobs obtained. However, we suggest an alternative perspective on the challenge faced by African American workers based on the existence of both a job queue and a "reverse job queue." When the squeeze comes in the labor market—in conditions of competition—it is felt most strongly among workers in the center of the queue, like African Americans, not those at the front of the good-job queue or the front of the bad-job reverse queue. Hence African Americans are likely to suffer from less secure job niches.

The fact that there is a weak union/organized labor presence in the Atlanta MSA means that worker interests are unlikely to be mediated through formal local political processes. This has several implications. In line with competition theory, it can then be predicted that less racial/ethnic identity politics will form if there is not a strategic move toward using it to influence political redistribution of economic benefits, such as jobs. Thus, it seems unlikely there will be more competitive interactions of an overtly racial/ethnic nature between groups as the area becomes more diverse. Blacks have "more to lose" as their job niches become less secure and as other immigrant groups grow in numbers, and possibly in political representation, however, without developing a "worker activism/union" form of social capital, a distinctly racial/ethnic clash over jobs is unlikely.

Among women, African Americans and Latinas share occupational niches in production, transportation, and material moving, particularly as assembler and fabricator factory workers. Some of these positions pay a living wage, can therefore be considered "good jobs," and could be a site for competition. It is an interesting question whether in these jobs competition will result or some form of solidarity, particularly given the tendency toward a downward trend or stagnation in the number of production jobs due to overseas outsourcing. However, the number of Hispanic women workers is still relatively small.

For Hispanic workers, much may depend on their ability to find opportunities such as previous generations of immigrants did where expanding economic sectors absorbed large numbers of new workers. In particular, one pattern facilitating group adaptation to the new society has been for migrants and immigrants to concentrate in the teaching profession as a route to middle-class status. The future of the Hispanic population, and indeed, of the entire metropolitan area is partially dependent on providing the new Hispanic youth generation with adequate tools to sustain "American" lifestyles. Given the current low level of academic achievement among Hispanic youth, and the research findings on the importance of cultural congruence between teachers and pupils, recruitment of Hispanics to the teaching profession is a clear social need. Despite the language barriers, and often low education among Hispanics, the effort to provide training and allow immigration of potential teachers would well serve the new Atlanta.

One area to the north of Atlanta, Dalton, Georgia, has committed to integrating its new population without prejudice. The city of Dalton is distinguished by recognizing that the influx of Hispanic workers to jobs in their manufacturing economic base (carpet manufacturing) is also an opportunity to reverse the depopulation trends and recessionary conditions in the town. They have committed to embracing bilingualism, not only among Hispanics, but for all the children in the city, and Hispanic cultural events are woven into the local social calendar (Kirp 2000). In Dalton, where ownership and control over society is firmly in corporate hands, there may also be little perceived political challenge posed by the immigrant influx because little power is held by any other working class population group to be contested.

Atlanta does present a somewhat different case where the white population's dominance is consciously challenged by African Americans, and because mutual integration does not take place, there is a lack of unity within the populace. This lack of unity seems to lead to a lack of self-confidence and ability to pursue long-term, coordinated policies. For instance, the energy crunch and environmental impact of a sprawling metropolitan area offer great challenges to finding alternative residential and transportation patterns, such as extension of the rapid transit system,

which has been stymied by racial controversy. Politically, the state legislature is dominated by more rural and suburban white representatives,
while the city government is more representative of the majority-black
population within its borders. This has led to a general internecine struggle where blacks lack control over adequate resources to project Atlanta
into the future, and whites seem to withhold resources rather than see
them enhance black resource control. The struggle over the rebuilding of
Atlanta's waste water system is reflective. This is currently typified by the
threatened bankruptcy of the Atlanta public hospital, Grady, despite its
importance as a regional trauma center for all.

In seeking to ameliorate this condition, the arrival of a third ethnic
group could be an opportunity to recast race relations and practice politics of collaboration. African Americans have the opportunity to co-opt
Hispanic leadership and voters into ruling coalitions, and thereby set the
stage for a more united majority that will be coming in the near future.[8]
There is some evidence of awareness of the possibilities of collaboration,
although still these community segments are almost completely separate
in lifestyles and social life. But there is cause for hope across racial lines.
Perhaps to be white and elect to live in the Atlanta metropolitan area is to
value diversity, because that is the base and direction this urban area is
moving. The large in-migrant population of whites and those who elect
to remain are staking their future on this diversity. A gradual diversifica-
tion of the economic base is necessary to support real diversity among
equals. Job equity is helpful toward wealth and asset equity, but it is the
"commanding heights" of the economy, ownership or control of industries and institutions that employ thousands, where social directions are
determined. How this equality will occur is problematic.

Latinos, from their base in construction and agriculture, may have a
real opportunity to consolidate home ownership through renovating
and building homes of their own, and to enter into wholesaling of construction materials related to the processing of lumber and agricultural
or forestry products, and other foodstuffs. From the construction base
there is always the possibility of moving into real estate, the backbone
of local economies. This is roughly the path taken by the Cuban-heritage
Hispanic population in the Miami area (Portes and Bach 1985);[9] however,
their success may have been partially a result of the capital resources that
the Miami Cuban upper-class refugees brought with them. Mexican immigrants, lacking those resources, were, and possibly are, unable to make
those inroads. However, it appears the Mexican immigrants to Atlanta
are a unique group in their own right, in comparison to those who had
settled in the Southwest and Miami in the past. The choice to branch into
Atlanta, where no legacy of settlement existed prior to 1980, may reflect
a spirit of opportunity seeking. The growing Hispanic population may

be self-selected self-starters, who will hopefully make the most of the opportunities which drew them to Atlanta.

Little has been said here of the East Asian, Indian, and Arab population, all of which is growing. Chinese Atlantans have begun formation of ethnic neighborhoods, particularly in DeKalb County. The Indian and Arab populations tend to be more dispersed. In general, while whites and blacks vie for political and cultural leadership, Atlanta's growth and emersion into global relationships offers alternative perspectives, and these may eventually highlight some commonalities. For the present, one thing seems largely agreed upon by all its residents, despite some resentments of the past and struggles for well-being in the present: they love Atlanta.

## NOTES

1. We use salary for Georgia because such data does not exist at lower levels of geography.

2. These figures represent a range defined as the figure, plus or minus a margin of 4 percent.

3. The living wage for Atlanta was $13.25 (Georgia Living Wage Coalition 2007).

4. The SOC has approximately 800 detailed categories which are combined and grouped according to skill, authority, and industry criteria.

5. There is, however, also a substantial Asian refugee-related population who are technically very low-skill.

6. For instance, New Birth Baptist Church, a DeKalb County megachurch, publicized its recent recruitment of a Puerto Rican minister to increase its outreach (Varela 2007).

7. Unemployment in the formal sector may possibly be offset by participation in the informal economy.

8. However, social-minority political majorities can be hamstrung without the participation of the "economic majority," the ownership class, which remains white and intact through inheritance. Since the economic elite is usually divided into local and international wings, something of a three-way coalition may develop with one of the wings.

9. This study highlighted the solidarity among Cubans in business/residential enclaves and their success in self-employment, in contrast to Mexican immigrants who assimilated as dispersed itinerant workers.

## REFERENCES

Basu, Moni. 2003. "Majority supports Iraq War, poll says." *Atlanta Journal-Constitution,* February 6, p. A1.
Bates, Timothy. 1997. *Race, Self-Employment & Upward Mobility.* Washington, DC:

The Woodrow Wilson Center Press.

Bonacich, Edna. 1981. *The Economic Basis of Ethnic Solidarity.* Berkeley: University of California Press.

Center for Hispanic Studies. 2005. "Anti-Immigration Groups in Georgia: The Current Context in 2005." Center for Hispanic Studies, Anti-Defamation League.

Diamond, Jeff. 1998. "African-American attitudes toward United States immigration policy." *International Migration Review* 32:2 (Summer), 0451–0470.

Fannie Mae Foundation. 2002. "Patterns and Trends in Overcrowded Housing: Early Results from Census 2000," Census Note 09, August 2002.

Feagans, Brian. 2005. "Census projects minority boom, Gwinnett tops influx in state." *Atlanta Journal-Constitution,* Aug. 11: D1.

Georgia Living Wage Coalition. 2007. www.atlantalivingwage.org.

Hewitt, Cynthia. 2000. "Job Segregation, Ethnic Hegemony and Earnings Inequality Among African Americans," in *The Atlanta Paradox, Labor Market Inequality in Atlanta,* edited by David Sjoquist. New York: Russell Sage.

———. 2004. "African American concentration in jobs: the political economy of job segregation and contestation in Atlanta." *Urban Affairs Review,* Vol. 39, No. 3.

Jones, Walter C. 2007. "Hispanics Claim Their Influence Rising at the Voting Booth." December 3, 2007, www.insideradvantagegeorgia.com.

*Journal of Blacks in Higher Education.* 2003. "In educational attainment, black immigrants to the United States outperform native-born white and black Americans." No. 40 (Summer), 51–52.

Kirp, David L. 2000. "The old south's new face." *The Nation,* June 26, pp. 27–30.

Lieberman, Stanley. 1980. *A Piece of the Pie.* Berkeley: University of California Press.

Moscoso, Eunice. 2006. "Hispanic kids bolster boom at U.S. schools." *Atlanta Journal-Constitution,* Oct. 6: A6.

Pascual, Aixa M. 2004. "Baby boom. High birth rate among women in Georgia's burgeoning Latino community leads to upsurge in business for many metro Atlanta hospitals and prenatal clinics." *Atlanta Journal-Constitution,* July 7: F1.

Poole, Sheila M. and Charles Yoo. 2007. "A clash of cultures in Doraville, some resent plans for Asian market," *Atlanta Journal-Constitution,* June 6, B1.

Portes, Alejandro and Robert L. Bach. 1985. *Latin Journey.* Berkeley: University of California.

Reich, Robert. 1992. *The Work of Nations.* New York: Vintage.

Sassen, Saskia. 1991. *The Global City.* Princeton: Princeton University Press.

Smith, Ben. 2006. "Number of Latino Voters, Candidates Don't Reflect Zeal of Recent Protests," *The Atlanta Journal-Constitution,* May 12.

Smith, Ryan A. and James R. Elliott. 2002. "Does ethnic concentration influence employees' access to authority? An examination of contemporary urban labor markets." *Social Forces* 81:1 (September), pp. 255–279.

Sowell, Thomas. 1994. *Race and Culture.* New York: Basic Books.

Stafford, Leon and Staff. 1999. "Ga. Schools becoming resegregated." *Atlanta Journal-Constitution,* June 17: A1.

U.S. Department of Commerce. 2000. *2000 Census.* Washington, DC

———. 2005. "The American Community Survey." U.S. Census. Washington, DC

Varela, Anna. 2007. "A bold move, a new birth, metro Atlanta mega church rolls out welcome mat for Latino community." *Atlanta Journal-Constitution* February 18, pp. A1.

Waldinger, Roger. 1986. "Changing ladders, musical chairs: ethnicity and opportunity in post-industrial New York." *Politics & Society* 15, 4:369–402.

Wright, Eric Olin. 1978. "Race, class, and income inequality." *American Journal of Sociology* 83, 6: 1368–1397.

*Part VI*

# GENTRIFICATION AND REVITALIZATION

*Chapter 11*

# The Development, Redevelopment, and Gentrification of Atlanta's Housing, 1980–2007

## *Larry Keating*

In the last three decades, housing in Atlanta evolved from a low density suburban pattern to a more eclectic agglomeration of high-rises, mid-rises, warehouse and school conversions, recycled office buildings, and a potpourri of shops, hotels, restaurants, and bars mixed with residences.

From predominantly single family and garden apartment stock with only one block of townhouses and three residential high rises in 1980, Atlanta has added over 25,000 new units, increased density by 6.7 percent overall and much more in urbane nodes, demolished over 20,000 homes, displaced thousands of uncompensated households, and restructured the physical form, tenure, and the racial composition of the city. The processes precipitating these changes are far from finished, and they present significant challenges and opportunities to both residents and policy.

This chapter summarizes these changes and examines some of their particular dynamics. Gentrification, both state-sponsored (urban renewal, publicly organized demolition, and public housing redevelopment) and market-stimulated is a subtext to several of these analyses. Local housing policy is intertwined with the evolution of the housing sector, so the analysis will periodically assess how policy changes affected outcomes. The chapter concludes with a characterization of likely futures and comments on how policy choices could construct different futures.

Table 11.1 describes the number of residential units' structure type and race as well as tenure by race for 1980 and 1990. Greater data accessibility in 2000 permits the analysis to combine tenure, units in structure, and race in a three way tabulation in table 11.2. One of the most striking phenomena revealed by these data is the static tenure for African Americans. The proportion of black households owning their homes rose only two-tenths of a percent in each of the two decades (from 37.3% in 1980 to 37.5% in 1990 and 37.7% in 2000). White ownership rates in the metropolitan area (not shown) rose from 57.2 percent in 1980 to 70.0 percent in 1990 and 75.5 percent in 2000. African American rates in the metro area initially declined from 41.8 percent in 1980 to 40.2 percent in 1990 but then rose to 48.6 percent in 2000. Seen in this context, black home ownership in the city began nearly four percentage points behind their metropolitan counterparts and fifteen points behind white households. Twenty years later white households had increased their lead over black households to twenty-seven percentage points and metropolitan area African Americans had an eleven point advantage over black households in the city. The substantial expansion of the Atlanta economy did not translate into comparable increases in home ownership rates for city of Atlanta African Americans.

There are multiple forces behind these changes: declining but continuing racial discrimination in both rental and sales housing markets; continuing racial discrimination in both employment and wages, particularly affecting black males; reduced asset accumulation due to historic discrimination; differential preferences between black and white households regarding city and/or suburban residential locations; and commercial underdevelopment in many African American neighborhoods. We will

**Table 11.1   City of Atlanta Occupied Housing, by Structure Type, by Race, by Tenure, 1980 and 1990**

| Units in | 1980[a] | | | | 1990[b] | | | |
|---|---|---|---|---|---|---|---|---|
| | White | | Black | | White | | Black | |
| Structure | Number | Percent | Number | Percent | Number | Percent | Number | Percent |
| 1 | 32,882 | 49.2 | 42,878 | 45.5 | 31,840 | 52.3 | 44,501 | 48.0 |
| 2 | 4,350 | 6.5 | 5,521 | 6.8 | 3,007 | 4.9 | 3,729 | 4.0 |
| 3 or 4 | 4,755 | 7.1 | 8,170 | 8.6 | 3,790 | 6.2 | 7,326 | 7.9 |
| 5–9 | 4,703 | 7.1 | 12,660 | 13.4 | 4,415 | 7.3 | 14,627 | 15.8 |
| 10–49 | 10,723 | 16.1 | 18,985 | 20.1 | 8,884 | 14.6 | 16,366 | 17.7 |
| 50 or More | 9,074 | 13.6 | 6,063 | 6.4 | 7,776 | 12.8 | 4,591 | 5.0 |
| Mobile Home[c] | 290 | 0.4 | 221 | 0.2 | 1,116 | 1.8 | 1,583 | 1.8 |
| Total | 66,777 | 100.0 | 94,498 | 100.0 | 60,828 | 100.0 | 92,723 | 100.0 |
| Own | 31,537 | 47.4 | 35,252 | 37.3 | 31,867 | 52.4 | 34,798 | 37.5 |
| Rent | 34,947 | 52.6 | 55,452 | 62.7 | 28,961 | 47.6 | 57,925 | 62.5 |
| Total | 66,484 | 100.0 | 94,570 | 100.0 | 60,820 | 100.0 | 92,723 | 100.0 |

Source: U. S. Census.
[a] 1980 data omits 897 households not classified as black or white; 688 of those households were Asian or Pacific Islanders
[b] 1990 data omits a small but indeterminate number of households not classified as black or white.
[c] 1980 Mobile Home; 1990 Mobile Home and other.

Table 11.2  City of Atlanta Occupied Housing, by Structure, by Race, by Tenure, 2000*

| Units in Structure | White Owner | | White Renter | | White Total | | Black Owner | | Black Renter | | Black Total | |
|---|---|---|---|---|---|---|---|---|---|---|---|---|
| | Number | Percent | Number | Percent | Number | Percent | Number | Percent | Number | Percent | Number | Percent |
| 1 | 29,686 | 79.6 | 4,295 | 13.3 | 33,981 | 48.9 | 32,827 | 95.0 | 13,182 | 23.1 | 46,009 | 50.1 |
| 2 | 637 | 1.7 | 2,127 | 6.6 | 2,764 | 4.0 | 333 | 1.0 | 3,307 | 5.8 | 3,640 | 4.0 |
| 3 or 4 | 830 | 2.2 | 3,265 | 10.1 | 4,095 | 5.9 | 284 | 0.8 | 7,206 | 12.6 | 7,490 | 8.2 |
| 5–9 | 849 | 2.3 | 3,820 | 11.9 | 4,669 | 6.7 | 290 | 0.8 | 11,363 | 19.9 | 11,653 | 12.7 |
| 10–49 | 2,328 | 6.2 | 8,431 | 26.2 | 10,759 | 15.5 | 314 | 0.9 | 11,539 | 20.2 | 11,853 | 12.9 |
| 50+ | 2,807 | 7.5 | 10,161 | 31.6 | 12,968 | 18.7 | 359 | 1.0 | 10,484 | 18.3 | 10,843 | 11.8 |
| Other | 136 | 0.4 | 78 | 0.2 | 214 | 0.3 | 163 | 0.5 | 107 | 0.2 | 270 | 0.3 |
| Total | 37,273 | 100.0 | 32,177 | 100.0 | 69,450 | 100.0 | 34,570 | 100.0 | 57,185 | 100.0 | 91,758 | 100.0 |
| Percent | 53.6 | – | 46.3 | – | – | 100.0 | 37.7 | – | 62.3 | – | – | 100.0 |

Source: U.S. Census.
*2000 Data for black alone and white alone; omits 1,632 owners (2.2%) and 5,402 renters (5.7%).

examine the interplay of many of these phenomena in the forthcoming analyses of residential development in Atlanta since 1980.

These data also reflect other significant changes in Atlanta's housing. The number of white occupied units declined by 8.5 percent between 1980 and 1990 (from 66,484 to 60,828) but then, as gentrification intensified, increased by 14.2 percent (to 69,450 in 2000). But, white home ownership increased in both decades in both absolute and relative terms even as overall white occupancy decreased and then increased (from 31,537 units in 1980 to 31,867 in 1990 and 32,273 in 2000; respective percentages were 47.4%, 52.4%, and 53.6%). Black occupied units decreased slightly in each of the two decades (from 94,570 to 92,723 to 91,758) as the African American proportion of the population peaked at 67.1 percent in 1990 and then dropped to 62.1 percent over the next ten years.

Table 11.2 shows that in 2000 almost all of black home ownership (95.0%) occupies single family units. While white home ownership is also concentrated in single family units (79.6%), the focus is not as exclusive, and future analyses will show that the establishment and subsequent expansion of the condominium submarket is responsible for increasing numbers and proportions of white occupied multifamily housing. Table 11.2 shows that this new sector is not exclusively white occupied, but it also shows that black participation is nominal.

After over 30,000 black occupied owned single family homes, the next largest number of black occupied units is the 13,182 rental single family homes. While some of these homes are only temporarily in the rental sector as their owners wait for better markets to sell them, most initially entered the rental sector because there was no market for them as sales housing. Forthcoming analyses will show that many of these homes are occupied by very low-income people, that their physical condition is deteriorating, and that they constitute a particularly difficult dimension of Atlanta's low-income housing problem because they are so costly to rehabilitate and manage.

There are a substantial number of white occupied single family units subject to similar fiscal and economic constraints, but their number is not so large (4,295).

There are some subtle distinctions in the data—many of the smaller-sized buildings in the ownership sector (3–4 units and 5–9 units) were formerly apartments that were converted to condominiums, many of the larger buildings (10–49 units and 50 or more units) are high-rise condominiums, and duplex structures have declined to 6,404 in 2000 from 9,871 twenty years earlier as gentrification consolidated units and demolished archaic structures.

These changes and others less revealingly captured by the data have had beneficent effects on many Atlantans. There are now at least two urban nodes in which car ownership is truly optional. Modest rental housing has been replaced by new high-rise condominiums opening onto wide sidewalks that lead to shops, bars, restaurants, theatres, and transit to other sections of the city in Buckhead and Midtown. Several other neighborhoods contain commercial districts in which shopping and entertainment are easily accessible, the street life is vibrant, the laundromats have become trattorias, and there are no vacancies.

Both of these types of residential and commercial changes fit Jason Hackworth's (2002) definition of gentrification; "the production of urban space for increasingly affluent users" (Hackworth 2002). From its modest beginnings in the 1960s and 1970s gentrification metamorphosed by the late 90s into a much more robust and extensive economic process. The consequences for many Atlantans have been wrenching and profound. Thousands of families have been involuntarily displaced without compensation or assistance. Former residents of private rental housing, privately owned subsidized rental housing, and publicly owned housing have been expelled into a shrinking rental housing market that frequently loses units to demolitions, succession to other land uses, and condominium conversions. Replacement of rental housing is severely constrained by new residents with distinctly classist preferences for neighbors. The new residents adroitly use the city's planning apparatus to block new rental construction.

Some of the upward class transitions are painless. Warehouses becoming artists' residences and hip shops damage almost no one. Development of vacant land is comparably benign unless the vacant state was produced by demolition of residences. But, most transitions involve displacement and redevelopment, and this sequence inevitably involves the forced relocation of people and the destruction of social networks that made peoples' lives more tolerable or enjoyable.

Often the processes require several years, and there are other differences between new and existing residents that exacerbate the transition. Differences in incomes, wealth, race, sexual preferences, and other values often add volatility. The following analyses will try to dissect how the major changes in the housing stock reflect both changes in the demand for housing and the sociology of the city.

## ATLANTA IN THE 1980s

The beginning of the current cycle of gentrification resulting in residential land use dates to the 1960s, but, because there were few early gentrifiers, measurement in the 1960s and 70s is difficult. A few neighborhoods north and east of the CBD (Ansley Park, Inman Park) were identified then as having gentrifying segments, but because both earlier awareness and analysis relied on limited anecdotal evidence, this investigation begins with the 1980s. Although the population of Atlanta declined from 425,022 to 415,200 between 1980 and 1990, the city's housing market added 4,010 net new homes, and there were substantial changes within the existing housing stock in multiple submarkets and neighborhoods during the 1980s.

Undeveloped peripheral areas within the city filled in with single family homes and garden apartments; gentrification increased from a few idiosyncratic pockets (Ansley Park, Inman Park, Midtown, and Virginia Highland) to approximately fifteen central, near eastside, and northside neighborhoods; land use succession and residential replacement intensified in upscale areas; and the poorest districts continued to lose previously standard homes, setting the stage for gentrification to follow. In addition, neighborhoods leveled twenty years earlier by federally and locally sponsored gentrification (urban renewal) began to slowly redevelop.

The most vigorous geographic submarkets surrounded Buckhead Village and the more than six million square feet of retail commercial anchored by Lenox Square and Phipps Plaza malls.[1] Development of over three thousand new units nearby followed two distinctly different patterns:

1. Residential land use succession (replacement of a residential use by another, usually higher density residential use) primarily but not exclusively along Lenox Road between I–85 and Lenox Square Mall;
2. Infill on underdeveloped sites passed over by the initial wave of suburban residential construction in both the northeast and northwest quadrants of the city.

Residential land use succession intensified residential uses along Lenox Road and at several points along Peachtree Street and Roswell Road. Over one thousand much higher density garden and mid-rise apartments and condominiums replaced single family homes on deep lots that had developed earlier along Lenox Road before the construction of Lenox Square Mall in 1956. On Peachtree Road south of the Buckhead Village, three high-rise apartments and multiple townhouses replaced lower density residences, adding several hundred housing units. More subtle but equally disruptive changes occurred along this section of Peachtree Road and further south along Peachtree Street to the Brookwood interchange (where I–85 and I–75 merge) as fifty-year-old rental apartments were converted to condominiums. These changes in tenure added no new units but displaced over one thousand households, many of them elderly. Because the economics of most conversions heavily favor converters and purchasers, original residents generally did not have the resources to purchase their units and were frequently required to move before their leases expired. They were usually not compensated for forced moves. Nationally, condominium conversions in the 1970s and 1980s led to some significant local legislation increasing protections for tenants on both the East and West coasts, but not in Atlanta.

Another form of housing development in the neighborhoods surrounding Buckhead Village filled in lots that had been passed over earlier by the first wave of suburban construction. Steep slopes and irregular shapes provided the rationale for initially bypassing these sites. This form of gentrification responded to two of the economic forces driving gentrification: the increasing demand for more central locations and the maturation of the surrounding neighborhoods, both of which increased land values to the point of development feasibility. Most of the new housing was single family, but in a few cases neighborhoods agreed to the rezoning of larger parcels for townhouses or, more commonly, large zero-lot line homes or large homes on relatively small plots. In the area south of the perimeter highway (I–285) just inside the city limits, nearly 700 primarily single family units were added. In response to these development pressures, the city of Atlanta revised their subdivision regulations at the end of the decade of the 1980s to incorporate requirements more germane to urban infill—such as sidewalks, shallower setbacks, smaller side and rear yards, and higher densities (Whitenhauer 1989).

Multifamily properties developed along major arterials on the northside (such as Roswell Road) accounting for over 700 additions to the housing stock. These units replaced smaller apartments and single family units that had earlier clustered along the transportation routes.

Development patterns in the southern half of the city were quite different. On the southwest periphery, the extensive suburban area developed by and for middle income African Americans after the passage of national open housing legislation in the 1960s expanded in the 1980s beyond the perimeter highway into the Ben Hill and Niskey Lake areas and added nearly six hundred units, one-quarter of which were single family houses. Prior land uses in these areas were agricultural and low density residential and commercial. Previous restrictions on development for middle class African Americans and the economic effects of racial discrimination, which retarded increases in black incomes, had constrained development in the southwest quadrant and contributed to the location of the I–285 interstate both closer to the Central Business District and within the city limits than is the case in other quadrants of the city.[2]

Adjacent to the core on the eastside where the Bedford Pine Urban Renewal Area had demolished over 1,800 housing units and the Buttermilk Bottoms neighborhood in the 1960s, long-awaited subsidized private development began in the 1980s under the auspices of Park Central, Inc., a subsidiary of Central Atlanta Progress.[3] In 1986 the Georgia legislature passed housing enterprise zone legislation providing for ten-year property tax abatements to subsidize new residential construction in the poorest neighborhoods and in areas where there were fewer than 1,000 persons. In a perversely ironic twist, the first area to qualify for the abatements was the Bedford Pine Urban Renewal Area where there had been concentrations of poor people whose displacement qualified the area on the absence of population criterion.

Substantial protests by (urban renewal) displacees of Bedford-Pine (just east of downtown) in the 1960s and 70s secured promises of a modest amount of replacement housing, but by the time redevelopment finally began, the resistance had dissipated and the modest number of temporary manufactured homes placed on the site to hold places for the original residents and preserve a remnant of the original community were themselves demolished by the Atlanta Housing Authority. Of the 1,145 units built during the 1980s, 218 were subsidized for low or moderate income households, at 19.0 percent, sixty-eight units short of the 25.0 percent required by the contractual agreement with representatives of the former neighborhood. Several hundred units were built in the 1990s, but while all the housing was subsidized by substantial federal write-downs and local tax abatements, no additional units were constructed for low and moderate income people, driving the proportion of units reserved for poorer people to below three-fifths of what had been agreed upon (Keating and Creighton 1989, 84).

In the poorest sections of the city east, south, and west of the core, eight primarily African American neighborhoods lost over 1,200 housing units as the lowest income residents could not marshal sufficient money to pay the carrying costs of an aging housing stock. Where urban renewal had earlier demolished thousands of units in Bedford Pine, Summerhill, Peoplestown, Mechanicsville, Vine City, and the other neighborhoods immediately surrounding the Central Business District during the 1960s and 70s, market failure in the 1980s in neighborhoods such as Butler Street, Grady-Antoine Graves, Summerhill, Peoplestown, Mechanicsville, Vine City, Pittsburgh, and the areas adjacent to the Atlanta University campuses caused many units to physically decline to the point of uninhabitability and demolition. Both government-financed, urban-renewal clearance and private, market-failure-induced demolition began gentrification processes that eventually led to higher income residential succession.

Farther south, in the southeastern section of the city, nearly 1,500 units were lost to market failure and land use succession to industrial and trucking uses in the Blair Villa, Poole Creek, Polar Rock, and Browns Mill areas.

Immediately north of the long-standing, east-side racial dividing line, Ponce de Leon Avenue, the more conventionally familiar form of gentrification produced differential effects in the Midtown and Virginia Highland neighborhoods. The 1960s/70s version of gentrification began circa 1968 in some of the older, architecturally significant homes in Ansley Park, Inman Park, Morningside/Lenox Park, and Midtown as well as in some sections of Virginia Highland. In this phase of gentrification, which was slower and initially less extensive than it became by the end of the century, developers and financial institutions waited until they could see confirming signals that gentrification would redevelop almost all of a neighborhood before they committed to produce new infill housing. Virginia Highland had reached that point by the 1980s and nearly 500 units of new construction were added on underutilized land on the west side of the neighborhood where proximity to a rail line (now the Beltline project) had previously retarded development. In Midtown existing residential uses covered almost all of the buildable parcels, and the housing market had not yet matured to the point where high rise condominiums could replace existing commercial or residential uses. Consequently, the consolidation of formerly two and three unit buildings into their original single family uses plus the demolition or consolidation of rooming houses removed over two hundred housing units from Midtown's inventory, but there was no new infill development.

Gentrification had occurred in a few neighborhoods in a few American cities in the first half of the twentieth century. Its reappearance in many cities in the 1970s elicited scholarly and policy-oriented inquiries. By the early 1980s an academic consensus concluded that the phenomena were real but relatively small (Berry 1985). In Atlanta there were approximately sixteen neighborhoods in various stages of gentrification, fewer than 8 percent of the total (Keating and Creighton 1989, 45–53). In the short run the prospects for extensive transformation of racial and class residential patterns were limited to the handful of areas then presently affected. The longer run prospects were frequently and incorrectly judged to be equally small.

Examination of the Atlanta data assembled by Ted Levangood of the Atlanta Bureau of Planning in 1986 both provides one of the first broad measures of gentrification in the city and retrospectively reveals some similarities with today's more vigorous and extensive gentrification.[4] Levangood analyzed turnover and sales price changes between 1975 and 1985, thereby isolating a northeast-east-southeast arc of ten neighborhoods one to three miles from the CBD that real estate commentators, consumers, and activists characterized as gentrifying (Morningside/Lenox Park, Midtown, Virginia Highland, Poncey-Highland, Inman Park, Candler Park, Lake Claire, Cabbagetown, Grant Park, and Ormewood Park), but

also revealing that there were six other higher income, gentrifying neighborhoods farther north (Underwood Hills, Martin Manor, Peachtree Hills,
Loring Heights, Collier Hills, and Wildwood-Spring Lake). Contemporary analysts had concluded that relatively lower income areas containing
historically significant, architecturally valuable housing were the focus
for gentrification. Indeed, areas with these characteristics constitute most
of the first list of ten neighborhoods. But the second group were neither
predominantly lower income nor generally recognized as architecturally
distinctive. Then, as now, the absence of this distinctiveness translated
into either replacement of the original structure or its transformation via
extensive remodeling/rehabilitation. In retrospect, the seeds of a much
more vigorous form of gentrification had established itself just north of
and beyond the more popularly recognized gentrifying neighborhoods.

An additional Atlanta study, prepared for the Anti-Displacement Coalition, found that in Grant Park 152 initial units (77 rental and 75 owned)
became seventy-five owned units as they gentrified (Keating, et al. 1982).
A fourth study found a fifty-six unit decrease in rental units and a twenty-
two unit increase of owner units between 1979 and 1986 in Cabbagetown
as it gentrified. At the time there was no new construction, and there were
no demolitions, so the increases/decreases occurred within the existing
stock (Creighton, Keating, and Elliott 1986, 35). The two case studies con-
firmed the conventional wisdom that gentrification frequently decreases
rental units and increases ownership units, though not necessarily on
a one-for-one basis. The Grant Park study also measured voluntary vs.
forced displacement and found that 45 percent of the decreases in rental
units triggered forced displacement. So, while the magnitude and extent
of early phases of gentrification were small relative to the overall stock,
the consequences for those original residents who were directly involved
and for the particular stock of lower income rental housing were substantial and negative.

In terms of compensatory or ameliorative policy, the Atlanta Anti-
Displacement Coalition never developed sufficient political traction to
affect local policy. Nationally, the Carter administration began to consider
policy alternatives in 1979, but the Reagan administration terminated
these inquiries early in 1980. In fact, under Reagan, the Department of
Housing and Urban Development explicitly forbade its funded gentrification researchers from attempting to measure gentrification-induced
displacement (DeGiovanni 1983). Since HUD was the primary funder of
this type of research, there was no science upon which to base policy.

In summary, the decline in Atlanta's population between 1980 and 1990
reflected demographic changes— smaller households and later and fewer
marriages— and the destruction or transformation of housing previously
occupied by lower income people. But the decline did not directly reflect

the multifaceted, vigorous housing market that expanded to the city's boundaries on the west side, that filled in or replaced earlier suburban development along northside arterials, and that developed parcels previously judged too difficult or expensive on which to build and subdivided some former estates. Land use succession from relatively modest owned housing to far denser condominium and rental uses along Lenox Road between Lenox Square mall and I–85 foreshadowed more intensive residential succession and development in the next fifteen years, as did the extensive upgrading and replacement of fairly modest units in the Loring Heights, Collier Hills, Underwood Hills, Wildwood-Spring Lake, and Peachtree Hills neighborhoods. Condominium conversions along Peachtree Street, Peachtree Road, and in a few of the more fully gentrified neighborhoods (Ansley Park, Virginia Highland, and Midtown) began to develop a condominium submarket. In the poorest areas of the city, disinvestment and the poverty of the residents led to extensive demolitions, thereby setting the stage for the gentrification of the 1990s and 2000s.

Gentrification became a firmly established but limited dynamic occurring in less than ten percent of the city's neighborhoods. Both local and national policies extended the status quo in choosing not to attempt to ameliorate the negative consequences for forced displacees and a shrinking lower income housing stock. State-supported gentrification expanded as additional local subsidies and contiguous gentrification combined with previous deep federal urban renewal subsidies to stimulate construction on the long dormant, long vacant Bedford Pine Urban Renewal site.

Finally, the 1980s marked the end of expansion for the primary provider of standard housing for Atlanta's poor. For forty-five years from 1936 the Atlanta Housing Authority consistently added to its supply of low rent public housing and elderly housing, so that by 1982 it owned and managed 14,852 homes, 9.0 percent of the city's total supply of housing units. The apex reached in 1982 held for thirteen years before abruptly declining, and no new additions to the Atlanta inventory were made during this period because federal policy shifted away from the expansion of publicly owned housing, and local housing authorities, Atlanta among them, began to struggle to maintain their existing stock.

## THE 1990s: GENTRIFICATION ACCELERATES

Elvin Wiley and Daniel Hammel introduced the term "resurgent" gentrification to the literature in their 1999 article documenting the 1990's acceleration of conventional mortgage capital investments in gentrified neighborhoods to more than twice the suburban growth rate. They attributed the expansion to contextual change occasioned by the cumulative effects

of over two decades of less vigorous but steady class turnover in central
city neighborhoods that had previously suffered disinvestment, outmi-
gration, and decline; to favorable macro-economic trends (especially low
inflation and low interest rates); to a substantial expansion of secondary
mortgage markets infusing more capital into housing, especially ownership housing; to the subsequently requisite standardization of underwrit-
ing; and finally and somewhat perversely to the transformation of initial
responses to discriminatory lending practices to mortgage products designed to profitably reach "untapped" or "underserved" submarkets. In
part, the latter phenomena substituted geography (gentrifying neighborhoods) for the racial and ethnic groups that had been the victims of prior
discrimination but who now were gentrification displacees.

Between 1990 and 2000 the city's twenty year decline in population
reversed, and Atlanta grew by 22,457 people from 394,017 to 416,474.
In spite of the increase in the population, the *net increase* in the number
of housing units was a modest 4,244, only slightly more than the 4,010
units added in the previous decade when the population declined by
over 30,000 people. However, the population increase was reflected in
the addition of over 11,000 units, some of which were newly constructed,
others conversions of warehouses to lofts, and some the adaptive reuse
of office buildings as condominiums. The demolition of over 7,000 units
of public and private housing in preparation for the Olympics and the
gentrification-induced consolidation of two and three unit buildings into
single family homes held the *net increase* to just over 4,000 units.

Joe Martin, the president of Central Atlanta Progress said in May 1991
"It doesn't take a genius to figure out what the story's going to be in 1996:
The splendor of the Olympics amid the squalor of Southern poverty."[5]
Some of the 1,203 units of housing demolished in the seven "Olympic
Ring Neighborhoods" between 1991 and the end of 1995 were unrepair-
able and threats to public health and safety. But other demolitions were
cosmetic, along transportation routes from central area hotels to the stadi-
ums and venue sites that ringed the CBD, some were around the venues
themselves, and others were adjacent to the universities that housed and
entertained the athletes and support staff. In the early 1990s the seven
Olympic Ring neighborhoods[6] were each primarily occupied by poor African Americans. Today five are well on their way to being gentrified and
the other two have begun to gentrify. Their locations and poverty would
have eventually stimulated their gentrification, but publicly underwritten
demolition paid some of the front-end costs and fostered the redevelopment process.

Some of the housing demolished to eliminate the visual evidence
of poverty could have been rehabilitated. Of the structures destroyed
between 1993 and 1995, 28.8 percent were assessed as beyond repair in

a survey conducted for the Corporation for Olympic Development in Atlanta. The CODA survey was for general planning purposes and was separate from analyses and decisions to demolish housing. Another 30.6 percent were severely deteriorated—meaning that the initial analysis concluded that they were repairable, but further analysis might have reversed this assessment. But, 40.6 percent were clearly repairable— they were either standard quality or required only minor repairs. According to this survey, fewer than one-half of the units[7] that were demolished had to be destroyed for reasons of physical inadequacy— they were substandard housing that could have been rehabilitated or they were standard quality housing (Lowe 1996). Approximately 662 units of economically repairable housing were demolished. The most likely explanation is avoidance of the stigma that Martin alluded to—Southern poverty in the midst of Olympic splendor. Their removal from the supply of modest housing for low income people facilitated the resurgent gentrification that followed and tightened an already inhospitable housing submarket. In addition, the expansion of the City's *In Rem* demolition program bankrupted the program and led to its being shut down in the latter years of the decade.

### Housing Authority Demolitions

In 1991 the Atlanta Housing Authority launched what became the Olympic Legacy Program. It destroyed 574 units at Techwood Homes before the Olympics and 5,050 public housing units by the end of the decade. This program marked the beginning of a substantial transformation in the major programs delivering housing services to Atlanta's poor. By 1999 AHA had replaced 627 of the 5,624 former units, but it had also expanded the number of Section 8 certificates or vouchers entitling the holder to rent housing in the private market for 30 percent of their income. By 2001, AHA assisted a total of 20,876 households through all of its programs (Boston 2005, 396), an increase of 192 over the total in the late 1980s, so the number of vouchers increased beyond the number of demolitions and replacement units by at least 192 units. Between 1995 and 2008, almost all of the 10,954 family units were demolished and a substantial start on the destruction of the 3,764 elderly units began. AHA now plans to demolish all of the remaining public housing units, including the buildings for the elderly. However, the voucher program is being cut, so the excess of vouchers over former physical units will not hold.

The physical developments that replaced the earlier public housing communities were mixed income developments that included approximately one-third public housing units, some moderate income units (usually Low Income Housing Tax Credit units), and 30–40 percent market rate units. While the new units were larger, more modern with larger closets and better cabinetry, few of the original residents were able to return to the new developments. At Techwood and its sister development (Clark Howell Homes) seventy-eight of the original 1,119 families returned (Keating and Flores 2000, 302). Techwood was on the National Register of Historic Places and, like all of the other family public housing in Atlanta, was two or three story apartment buildings. There were no high-rises for families in Atlanta.

The families living in the public housing displaced by redevelopment usually lost valuable dimensions of their daily lives by being forced to move. The social communities they composed and participated in were demolished, the proximity to health and transportation services was reduced, and they had to reestablish themselves in new communities.

Expert opinion differs on the extent and value of the former social communities to the residents in public housing. Having worked in a number of public housing developments, I can confirm the presence of social groups that watched out for, valued, and supported their members. The camaraderie was evident. Also present was social criticism for behavior outside accepted norms. Each development had tangible social capital. The extent of social capital is disputed. Critics contend that there was insufficient social capital in many communities and that, consequently, the problems associated with poverty infected large segments of the communities.

Federal regulations required extensive resident participation in planning for redevelopment, but they also stipulated that residents did not have veto power. The ambiguity deriving from the tension between these two requirements led to highly charged planning processes at the first few sites. At Techwood and Clark Howell, three consecutive planning processes each came to different conclusions, required five years, exhausted the residents who remained, and partially masked the reduction of the population from 530 families to twenty-six by the Housing Authority by the time the final plan was adopted three months before demolition began.

Part of the difficulty in managing large-scale redevelopment projects is sequencing the provision of relocation housing relative to demolition of the original units. In a world that sought to preserve the positive attributes of social communities, relocation housing would be available prior to the moves required by demolition.[8] The choice AHA made in the 1990s and 2000s redevelopment initially sought to construct off-site replacement housing simultaneously with redevelopment, but they subsequently decided that this approach was both legally too complex and too expensive. AHA also subsequently decided to emphasize Section 8 or vouchers as both relocation housing and replacement housing.[9] This strategy meant there was no possibility of preserving either parts of or most of the original sociological community.

This strategy is also contentious regarding its impact on the locality's capacity to provide low income housing in the future. There are two issues here: One is whether the stream of future housing services from socially owned or controlled physical units is more secure over time than the stream based on demand-side subsidies/vouchers. Second, will the volume of future housing services provided be more or less with physical units or vouchers? While the issues are different, they turn on the same set of arguments. Housing is, in economic terms, a durable good. Properly constructed, a unit should last for forty or more years. Some systems (roofs, furnaces, etc.) require replacement during this length of time, but the basic unit should last and provide services to low income people for at least forty years. In contrast, vouchers are currently issued for one year time periods.[10]

In addition, during the last three years the national administration has proposed changes that would have reduced or transformed the level and strength of the federal voucher commitment. First, the Bush administration proposed replacing payments for local housing support with a block grant to local governments.[11] One of the concerns housing authorities and local governments had with this proposal was that future federal governments might find it easier to reduce the size of the block grants (or, as has happened with the Community Development Block Grant program, hold the dollar amount of the appropriation constant and let inflation reduce the actual value of the grant). The worry is that future administrations might find it easier to cut (or eliminate) support for housing because they would not be the front line provider of subsidies—that is, local governments would have to implement the reductions/eliminations and thus would be the initial focus of the resulting political complaints.

This proposal was successfully resisted. The following year the administration policymakers again proposed block grants but to local housing authorities. These were also resisted. Subsequently, the administration reorganized payments to local authorities to accomplish much the same effect—that is, paying a particular (and reduced) dollar amount instead of paying for a unit of housing services. A central point here is that support for housing for low income people is not an agreed obligation of the federal government. Republican administrations have frequently been hostile to the commitment and sought ways to reduce, severely curtail, or eliminate the level of support. Democratic administrations have been more favorably disposed, but not always.

At the end of the day the issue of whether physical units will provide a longer stream of services in the future than vouchers turns on future political alignments and the political vigor that both opponents and proponents devote to threatened cuts. There are no guarantees that a future national government might not sharply reduce subsidy support for physical units and force their destruction or sale. But, many housing professionals and political supporters of housing subsidies for low income people think a future government would have a far more difficult political task disposing of housing units than reducing payments for a one year voucher program, and these differences could be translated into preserving more support for more families.

The tie between the housing authority's demolition program and gentrification extends beyond relying on an already inadequate and diminished private market to house relocated poor people, for the redeveloped former public housing sites are gentrified islands in seas of renewal. As private market gentrification has spread throughout the city, the housing authority's urban renewal program has produced attractive new urbanist, mixed income communities that neighbors, Central Atlanta Progress, other business leaders, and the *Atlanta Journal-Constitution* praise. With restrictive admissions policies and substantially higher income limits for public housing residents in the new mixed-income communities, the authority has populated the redeveloped communities (termed Signature Communities by AHA) with what the chair of the House Banking and Financial Services Committee, Barney Frank, accurately describes as "a better class of poor people." The truly disadvantaged poor people who occupied the previous public housing communities have been supplanted by state-sponsored gentrification that pleases all but the former residents and the thousands of families on public housing waiting lists.

## New Tensions

Between 1998 and 2000, resurgent gentrification in the Kirkwood neighborhood in eastern Atlanta generated significant tensions between in-movers and indigenous communities. Differences in race, class, sexual preferences, and values triggered confrontations and created antagonisms. The existing neighborhood was almost entirely African American while the gentrifiers were predominately white. Class differences centered on tensions between the majority poorer renters in the indigenous community and the purchase of homes by almost all the relatively wealthier gentrifiers. The in-moving community contained a significant proportion of gay and lesbian members. Some traditional members of the indigenous community had difficulty accepting neighbors with different sexual preferences. The steady progression of resurgent gentrification and the sense that gentrifiers would eventually replace the original community increased the original residents' anxiety, as did their seeming inability to affect either the direction or the pace of change.

In the context of tensions elevated by the differences between the two social groups, the increasing number of gentrifiers and the correspondingly smaller African American community, issues that affected both communities added flash points to the conflict. In particular, crime and street level drug sales triggered accusations and counteraccusations between the two groups. Neither group sought or approved of criminal activity in the neighborhood, but the level of antagonism surrounding their social and economic differences made mutual recognition of common problems difficult and often unattainable. Concerted community action under these circumstances was not feasible.

In other gentrifying areas of eastside Atlanta less provocative but very real tensions emerged in political struggles for control of city-recognized community organizations—neighborhood associations and the Neighborhood Planning Units, which are composed of multiple neighborhood associations. These institutions have substantial influence over some aspects of development policy in the city, particularly within their own areas, so their control is viewed as politically important by both those who would gentrify an area and those who are threatened by gentrification-induced displacement. In an atmosphere of class, racial, economic, and political conflict, the struggles for control become heated and consuming.

## 2000s: GENTRIFICATION POLICY EVOLVES

In March 2000 the city council created a gentrification task force. The initial proposal was sponsored by Sherry Dorsey, Councilperson from the eastside neighborhoods where these conflicts surfaced, and she was joined by a westside Councilperson, "Able" Mable Thomas as a cosponsor of the final bill. The council's central charge stated, "the task force will create a comprehensive plan addressing gentrification that will preserve affordable housing in the city of Atlanta while encouraging the economic growth of city of Atlanta neighborhoods."

Thirteen of the fifteen councilpersons appointed members of the task force, Ms. Valena Henderson served as vice-chair, and Ms. Peggy Harper served as secretary. I served as chair. Staff of the Atlanta Bureau of Planning and students at Emory University Law School and the Georgia Institute of Technology Graduate Program in City and Regional Planning[12] supplied research and analytical support.

The task force met for over a year, held twenty public meetings, and reviewed recommendations in five public hearings/forums in the four quadrants of the city and at City Hall. Emory Law Professor Frank Alexander summarized the task force's central factual conclusions: Middle-income and upper-income individuals and families fuel the market-driven demand for new housing. Individuals and families of low income are simply not able to compete in this market for housing, and they see their opportunities for life in the city continuing to dwindle. The blessings of this residential renewal are mixed blessings for large numbers of the city's residents.

Rising property values accompany both new construction and speculation of further development. The supply of residential facilities for low-income families decreases even more dramatically. Apartments and homes for middle and upper-income families replace properties for low-income families. Owners of facilities for low-income residents elect to cease maintenance in anticipation of converting the units to middle-income units. The Atlanta Housing Authority demolishes public housing facilities and replaces them with mixed-income units, only a small portion of which are available to extremely low and very low-income families (Alexander and Keating 2001, 2).

The task force further concluded that there were three specific damaging consequences of gentrification:

1. There is a loss of affordable housing.
2. Poor indigenous residents are forcibly displaced.
3. Indigenous sociological communities are destroyed.

The task force was only partially successful in constructing policy recommendations to address these impacts largely because the bulk of displacement and its ancillary effects occur in private housing markets that are especially difficult (and expensive) to affect or modify through public action. Therefore, the central thrust of the forty recommendations sought to preserve and expand affordable housing and argued that the inability to construct policies to directly mitigate or ameliorate forced displacement and destruction of sociological communities made more vigorous pursuit of affordable housing retention and expansion essential.[13]

The task force presented its recommendations to the city council in September 2001 and, working with the city's law department, developed legislation implementing five of the first seven recommendations. The legislation, which passed in December, included definitions of affordable housing and mixed income housing and set goals for housing subsidies and affordable housing. Affordable housing was defined as accessible to households with less than 50 percent of Area Median Income (AMI).[14] Mixed income housing was defined as containing a minimum of 33 percent affordable housing.

The goals in the legislation targeted two-thirds of the public subsidies for housing at households with 30 percent or less AMI, and all housing subsidies within the definition of affordability (thereby targeting public subsidies to households with no greater than 50 percent AMI and allocating one-third of public subsidies for housing to households with 31 percent to 50 percent of AMI. Finally the legislation set goals for tax increment financing (referred to as tax allocation districts in Georgia legislation) and housing enterprise zone tax abatements of 33 percemy of affordable housing.[15] The bill passed in the closing moments of the Campbell administration. During the final negotiations prescriptive requirements were transformed into goals, thereby sharply reducing their legal capacity to direct aid to those damaged by gentrification.

But in the early days of the Franklin administration that followed, the city bureaucracy pursued the spirit of the law. The commissioner of Planning Neighborhood Conservation and Development redirected Housing Enterprise Zone subsidies according to the formula contained in the law: two-thirds of public subsidies directed to households with less than 30 percent of AMI and one-third of public subsidies focused on households with 31 to 50 percent of AMI formula contained in the law. The Bureau of Housing followed suit in their administration of the two federal programs under their jurisdiction (Community Development Block Grants and HOME). But, the Atlanta Development Authority, responsible for the administration of tax allocation district subsidies, ignored the legislation.

The development community began to lobby against the targeting of Atlanta's most housing-deprived citizens by city administered programs. In spite of the fact that gentrification brought thousands of middle and upper class households to the city each year, advocates for the development community invoked the (by then obsolete) arguments that the *subsidized* expansion of middle class residents was essential to the city's functioning.

In addition, once the Franklin administration transcended inherited budgetary and infrastructure crises they began to chart a more developer-friendly housing policy. The first step was the appointment of the Mayor's Housing Task Force in 2001. It was composed entirely of developers and financiers of housing. Their recommendations sought to redirect housing subsidies to the middle and higher income households their products could profitably serve (Mayor's Housing Task Force 2002).

Because the city does not adequately monitor compliance with local housing policy and program regulations, it is not possible to say how many units were produced or how long the focused targeting remained in force. A partial analysis conducted for the Housing Element of the Atlanta Comprehensive Plan showed that in 2002 and 2003 most respondents to a Department of Housing inquiry were compliant. But the department did not compel response, and some companies/organizations did not respond, making the results incomplete and the conclusions less certain (Keating et al. 2005, 66).

Some recipients of HOME funds who were also receiving Low Income Housing Tax Credits were evidently permitted to use higher income targets (60% of AMI) in their developments, and by early 2003 private developers were publicly saying that while the city had ostensibly adopted regulations targeting subsidies at lower than 50 percent of AMI, persistence by developers could circumnavigate the requirements and obtain subsidies for households with higher incomes.[16]

In summary, for a brief period in 2001 and 2002, city of Atlanta housing policy shifted focus to both the lowest income households who have the greatest housing needs and those most damaged by gentrification. But, the sharpened focus on vulnerability could not withstand pressure from development interests, and policy eventually reverted to subsidizing development and fewer households with housing needs.

## CHANGES IN THE HOUSING MARKET 2000–2004

Residential sales in Atlanta expanded from 4,292 in 2000 to 7,570 in 2003 and dropped in 2004 to an annual rate of 6,078 as interest rates increased from record lows, and the boom in housing began to contract. In the 1980s and early 1990s new development had focused on wealthier areas of the city (along the Peachtree spine and in Buckhead) and on the still expanding African American periphery. But the 7,733 sales of new units between January 2, 2000 and October 31, 2004 were scattered throughout the city. Builders and developers gained confidence that after more than two decades gentrification was an established and enduring phenomena. This confidence led to a shift in the timing of new infill construction from the end of established neighborhood gentrification to early in the process. The first stirrings of increased consumer interest in previously stagnant neighborhood submarkets were now often accompanied by infill projects seeking to capture competitive advantage and lower land prices by being among the early gentrifiers.

The 19,459 sales of existing units during the same time period were also broadly distributed across the city. Every neighborhood planning unit save one had over 500 sales, eight NPUs had between 500 and 1,000 sales and fifteen had over 1,000 sales. Buckhead and NPU-B led the way with 2,501 sales, and the east side neighborhoods in NPU-W, which includes Grant Park, Ormewood Park, East Atlanta, and Boulevard Heights, also had over 2,000 sales (2,150).[17]

Average sale prices in the city increased from $206,934 in 2000 to $246,732 in 2004, a $39,798 (19.2%) increase. In 2004, Atlanta's average sales price was 28.3 percent higher than the average sales price of existing units in the metro area.[18] Because average sales prices reflect both changes in prices and the composition of each year's mix of different sizes of units sold, changes per square foot is a more accurate guide to price changes. In

2000, the sales price per square foot in the city of Atlanta was $125.33. The price increased each year until in 2004 it was $169.10, a $43.77 increase. In percentage terms, the increase was 34.9 percent.

Prices increased every year in twenty-three of twenty-four neighborhood planning units. The only NPU in which prices did not increase annually was at the upper end of the market in NPU-E (Midtown, Ansley Park, Sherwood Forest, Home Park, and Georgia Tech) where oversupply in Midtown caused prices to decline briefly in 2003. Nevertheless, square foot prices were $231.48 over the 4.8 year period, 155.4 percent of the city average and second only to the most expensive houses in the city in the Mt. Paran/Northside/West Paces Ferry neighborhoods.

Both the overall volume of new unit sales (7,733/28.4%) and the distribution throughout the city confirm the establishment of vigorous housing submarkets in every sector. Twenty-five of the twenty-six NPUs had over one hundred new unit sales between 2000 and 2004. The only NPU that did not have one hundred new unit sales was R (Southwest Atlanta) which had eighty new unit sales. In the central city, the leader in new unit sales was NPU-V Peoplestown, Mechanicsville, Summerhill, Pittsburgh, and Adair Park with 769 new unit sales. Sales of new units in NPU-V increased from eight-six in 2000 to 189 in the first ten months of 2004 (an annualized rate of 227 for 2004). The three neighborhoods of Peoplestown, Mechanicsville, and Summerhill averaged 9.5 sales each year at an average price of $30,169 between 1989 and 1991 (Keating and Creighton 1991, 53, 69, 117). From 2000 to 2004, the same figures are 139.0 sales per year at an average price of $165,584.

At one level these data reflect the substantial increase in the volume, prices, and extent of resurgent gentrification. But there are cautionary notes: While the data represent recorded sales, there is an indeterminate amount of contamination by less-than-arms-length transactions, flipping, speculative investments, predatory loans, and destructive subprime transactions. The preceding data are for 2000–late 2004 and do not include 2005–2007, when subprime, predatory, and "exotic" financing were most prevalent. The extent of these phenomena is not yet clear. For the period January 2000 to March 2005, 15.9 percent of mortgages in the city were listed for foreclosure auction at least once, an annual rate of 3 percent (Duda and Apgar 2005, 56).[19] EquaSystems, the source of the data, estimates that 30 percent of the listed foreclosures result in consummated foreclosures. Foreclosure listings were heavily concentrated in the southern sectors of the city in areas of high minority concentrations.

New housing development (sales and rental) within the city increased by at least 114% between the 1980s and the first four years of the 2000s. Average annual additions to the stock from 1980 through the early 1990s were 1,710 units. In the 2000–2004 period, an average of 3,683 new units were added each year.[20] The location and types of new development have changed as substantially as the volume. The 1980s witnessed

1) subdivision and infill in the northwest of the few difficult-to-develop lots that the initial wave of new construction passed over
2) land use succession on and around Lenox Road and the Peachtree spine
3) continued suburban development on the southwest side as the African American population built out the last remaining undeveloped properties within the city
4) sporadic and deeply subsidized completion of two-decades-old urban renewal properties east of the CBD
5) a modest number of small infill developments in established gentrified neighborhoods.

A much more diverse mix of geographic areas, economic classes, and building types characterize development recently. Earlier data documented the nearly complete geographic dispersion of new residential construction throughout the city. Sites vary from the last remaining undeveloped parcel in an area, to former commercial, industrial, or residential uses. Economic classes range from a few new units of public housing through a full range of rental and ownership levels to million dollar penthouses and mansions. Building types are equally diverse. Lofts have been developed in former warehouses, factories, office buildings, and built anew. As a suburban, sunbelt city, in 1980 Atlanta had fewer than fifteen townhouses. Now there are thousands. Similarly with high-rise (over twelve stories) condominiums: from three or four with peeling paint in the 1980s to more than fifty currently. Cluster homes, townhomes, hospital conversions, above-the-store, new-urbanist-on-the-street, accessory units, and on the golf course: there are multiple types of units in the reviving mix.

The condominium submarket has added over 22,000 new units since the beginning of the decade. Two-thirds of these (15,326/22,783=67.3%) were newly constructed and 7,457 were conversions. Conversions are most often existing rental properties but are less frequently industrial, warehouse, or former school uses. Thirty percent of the activity (30.8%/6,079 units) was in the Midtown/Brookwood submarket: residential infill around and along the Peachtree spine north of North Avenue. Buckhead accounted for another 30 percent (30.3%/6,001) as that luxury high-rise condominium submarket demonstrated substantial depth. The central area accounted for not quite one-eighth (2,338/11.8%)[21] of the new stock as sites became more difficult to find in the relatively circumscribed area.

Conversions are a particular form of gentrification that have differential effects depending on the type of units converted. Transformation of an empty school into condominiums can (often does) help revive an area by adding a residential presence where none or less existed. If there are damaging effects, they are indirect because no residents are immediately displaced. The indirect effects may consist of the redevelopment's contribution to the gentrification of that segment of the surrounding neighborhood. These are notoriously difficult to quantify or measure and damaging effects are usually minor in the short run.

Conversion of a renter-occupied structure (usually an apartment building but also lately some lofts), has the much more substantial immediate impact of requiring the uncompensated displacement of the existing residents. During the first wave of condominium conversions nationally in the 1970s, many local jurisdictions developed a range of protections or compensatory programs for residents in conversions: non-eviction conversions (wherein a unit is converted after the occupant decides to move out); preferential treatment of occupants in purchasing converted units (from relatively ineffective/inconsequential rights of first refusal to mandated post-conversion proportions of original residents); and specialized protections for elderly, disabled, low income, and/or female householder households. In addition, tenure extensions and payment of relocation costs were instituted along both U.S. coasts by municipalities to try to mitigate the effects of forced displacement.

In Georgia the pressure of an incipient Atlanta Anti-Displacement Coalition and the passage of local legislation around the country led the Atlanta Apartment Association (now the Apartment Association) to successfully lobby the Georgia Legislature to pass preemptive state legislation blocking local attempts to construct substantive mitigating measures to protect tenants.

## GENTRIFICATION AND RECENT CENSUS ESTIMATES

Due to the decennial conduct of the U.S. Census, the latter one-half of a decade is often a period lacking in recent empirical measurements of social changes. This is somewhat less true this decade with the American Community Survey for 2005 providing a mid-decade estimate of many characteristics. Given the complexity and limitations of interpreting changes in housing prices as indicators of gentrification, the analysis now turns to Charles Jaret, Robert M. Adelman, and Melissa M. Hayes's (2007) comparative analysis of 2000 and 2005 census data to try to discern what these data reveal about gentrification.[22]

Facts and estimates that point toward resurgent gentrification in Atlanta are the increase in population between 2000 and 2005 of 35,126 persons, (an 8.4% increase), the continuing decrease in the African American proportion of the population, the increasing proportion of the population that is white, the increasing proportion of the population that is rich, the high and increasing proportion of the population in managerial and professional occupations, the low and decreasing proportion of households composed of married couples with children, and the relatively lower proportion of family households.

Resurgent gentrification is characterized, among other dimensions, by increasing participation of African-Americans as gentrifiers and by the migration of white gentrifiers into black neighborhoods. There is no definitive measure of the relative strength of these two counterposed phenomena; however, the population of African Americans in Atlanta declined from 67.1 percent to 61.4% percent between 1990 and 2000. Conversely, the white population increased from 31.0 percent to 33.2 percent during the same period. Between 2000 and 2005, this trend continued, with the African-American population declining further to 58.6 percent (a drop of 2.8% points) while the white proportion increased from 33.2 percent to 36.2 percent.[23] The implication of these data is that gentrification continues apace and that there is greater net participation by whites. This, of course, could take multiple different forms: higher levels of in-migration by whites compared to blacks, lower levels of forced moves out of the city by whites, or combinations of these (and other) factors.

Occupational patterns, particularly the proportion of the workforce in managerial and professional occupations, have sometimes been used as surrogates for gentrification. The mean proportions for Jaret et al.'s (2007) cluster analysis cities, including Atlanta, on this dimension were 35.9 percent (2000) and 36.6 percent (2005). Atlanta measured 40.6 percent (2000) and increased to 45.7 percent (2005), substantially higher than the mean, but not as high as Seattle, San Francisco, and Washington, D.C.'s 2005 figure of 52.2 percent. Each of those three cities is characterized as intensively gentrifying, but Atlanta is not far behind on this measure.

The increasing proportion of rich households (incomes of $150,000 or more) is a relatively clear cut indicator of gentrification; Atlanta's proportion increased from 7.8 percent to 9.7 percent between 2000 and 2005 (an increase of 1.9 percentage points and of nearly one-quarter proportionately—24.3%). There are two types of new housing associated with this level of incomes: infill McMansions and luxury condominiums, both of which are features of resurgent gentrification.

The final dimension of change that implies a gentrifying city is the decrease in the proportion of married couples with children from 9.2 percent of households in 2000 to 7.1 percent in 2005. Compared to the mean in the larger sample (13.3% in 2005) Atlanta had slightly more than one-half the average proportion. This measure is subject to a number of qualifications (changes in social mores in the non-gentrifying population and a concentrated effort by some colonies of gentrifiers to be more child-centered among others) and is therefore less conclusively an indicator of gentrification.

Taken together, the substantial increase in total population, the increasing proportion of the population that is white, the decreasing African American proportion of the population, the high and increasing proportion of the workforce in managerial and professional occupations, the increasing proportion of the population that is rich, and the declining proportion of the population that are married couples with children all point to continuing resurgent gentrification, but, as with increases in housing prices and sales volumes, the evidence is not irrefutably conclusive. It is however, in my view, convincing.

Jaret and others note two measurements that are counter to resurgent gentrification. The first is the proportion of the population composed of children younger than fifteen, which increased from 19.0 percent to 19.6 percent over the 2000–2005 period. This proportion also increased in the highly gentrified cities of Seattle and San Francisco, but less and at considerably lower levels, from 12.7 percent to 12.9 percent.

The proportion of young adults aged twenty-five to thirty-four declined from 19.7 percent to 18.2 percent, but nevertheless exceeded most cities and trailed only Austin, Minneapolis, Raleigh-Durham, and Washington, D.C. Neither measurement is contradictory enough to overturn the conclusion.

## INCLUSIONARY ZONING

In late 1997, the commissioner of Planning, Neighborhood Conservation and Development, Michael Dobbins, initiated voluntary inclusionary zoning in selected redeveloping areas. The new policy recognized the increasing volume of residential and other development inside the city and sought to leverage the expanded attractiveness into some housing for low and moderate income people as a part of redevelopment.[24] In several instances new development supplanted existing modestly priced housing. In these cases the policy sought to recover some of the lost supply. The strategy was opportunistic in the sense that as particular areas petitioned the Bureau of Planning for revisions in zoning and land use regulations to accommodate and/or manage proposed redevelopment, the bureau proposed and lobbied for voluntary inclusionary zoning provisions that traded increases in density for affordable housing. Over the next three years this approach produced ordinance changes in two redeveloping commercial and residential areas (Midtown and Lindbergh); two primarily residential neighborhoods (Inman Park and Mechanicsville), and two of the generic "quality of life" districts (Mixed Residential Commercial and Live Work) designed to apply to different types of redeveloping areas across the city.

Unfortunately, inexperience and a lack of staff housing expertise compromised the program in defining affordability. Where almost all inclusionary zoning ordinances define beneficiary income categories for both renters and owners through references to federal measures that are updated annually, the Atlanta ordinance tried to use the income categories to define prices for sales and housing and veered off into federal definitions of fair market rents for rental housing. These atypical approaches produced the anomalous result that prices and rents were specified but incomes were not. Focusing on supply characteristics (prices and rents) also meant that household size categories were not specified, a flaw that worked to the advantage of small households by enabling them to afford the same price unit as large households and consequently encouraging developers (or more likely, limiting development) to produce only small units in exchange for higher densities.

Additionally, a disadvantage of the neighborhood-by-neighborhood strategy is that neighborhood organizations frequently exhibit a classist aversion to any low or moderate income housing. Organizations in each of the four neighborhoods that "accepted" inclusionary zoning restricted any new affordable housing produced in response to the zoning to commercial or industrial districts within their neighborhoods, thereby effectively blocking new affordable housing from established residential districts. Each of the areas also restricted the quantity of affordable housing to a small proportion of the units added by density bonus, thereby reducing the number of affordable units to minuscule proportions. One area excluded low-income housing, agreeing only to accept moderate-income housing. The same area required that a development had to provide "maximum open space and street square footage" before the small affordable housing density bonus could be accessed, thereby making affordable housing extremely unlikely or impossible.[25]

But the most severe limitation on the ordinances' productivity is the fact that they are all voluntary and not mandatory, which means that only in the very special circumstances of high demand and a clearly profitable bonus will affordable housing be produced. To date there has been no compliance monitoring or detailed empirical analysis of affordable housing production through the ordinances, but there is a general perception that Midtown is the only place to have seen any induced affordable housing. The specifics of the Midtown case raise serious questions regarding efficacy as incomes for households as small as one person could be as high as $57,762 or higher. An informal analysis of seventy-three permits in "quality of life" districts showed no affordable housing[26] in exchange for increased densities.

A further disadvantage of the opportunistic strategy is that when the driving force behind the individual area negotiations leaves, the impetus to continue to raise the issue and press for more productive terms may vanish. This appears to have happened when Dobbins left government early in the Franklin administration. His successor as commissioner, Charles Graves, was so uninterested in the policy that at an Inclusionary Zoning Task Force meeting in February 2003 he did not discuss any of the above ordinances. This lack of interest meant there were no new negotiations, no attempts to rectify deficiencies, and no compliance monitoring or analysis of the efficacy of the policy in the few areas of the city where it might have been applied.

## Proposed Inclusionary Zoning Legislation

Most studies of the housing situation in Atlanta during the past decade have recommended the adoption of a citywide inclusionary zoning ordinance. In 2002, HUD financed the Atlanta chapter of the Urban Land Institute to conduct a series of broadly based workshops designed to crystallize a specific inclusionary zoning approach that could be supported by different development interests and some housing advocates. Some progress was made, but the workshops failed to reach resolution on the most contentious issue of permissible beneficiary incomes. Most development interests sought higher ceilings (80% to 100% of AMI or $56,200 to $70,250 in 2007) while housing advocates lobbied for most of the production to be accessible to households with lower incomes (30% or $21,075) with none directed at over 50 percent AMI ($35,121).

This work did clarify some of the issues and set the stage for the consideration of inclusionary zoning by Mayor Franklin's newly appointed Affordable Workforce Housing Implementation Task Force in late 2005. Composed almost exclusively of developers, development organizations, and city officials, the task force produced legislation in late 2006 that two years later is still pending.

Because the legislation could change before adoption or not be adopted, only the central features will be considered here. The ordinance would be voluntary, that is, a developer would have the option of producing affordable housing in exchange for a density bonus or not. The city's law department argued that a mandatory ordinance raised constitutional problems and conflicts with other legislation, but they have refused to make their reasoning public. Voluntary ordinances have not produced much affordable housing in other cities. The task force opted for a voluntary ordinance and to subsequently seek state legislative approval for a mandatory law. Advocates have marshaled multiple highly regarded opposing legal opinions and unsuccessfully proposed a colloquy to air differing interpretations.

Multiple factors combined for over two years to retard progress on the legislation: a poorly drafted original ordinance, successive changes in the city's planning apparatus, tepid support from the mayor's office, the law department's recalcitrance, and later in the period, the mortgage finance/foreclosure crises, the degeneration of the housing market, and staff layoffs stemming from the city's declining revenues. Several planners and the Atlanta Housing Association of Neighborhood Developers worked assiduously to craft effective legislation, but a bill is now unlikely to be considered during the remainder of the Franklin administration. Beginning with the original legislation and continuing through present versions is the core concept that voluntary acceptance of a 20 percent density bonus would trigger a requirement for 10% of the total units to be affordable at the beneficiary incomes shown in table 11.3.

On the ownership side unit prices for a three bedroom unit would range from $122,235 for the one-fifth of the units reserved for those with less than $42,150 incomes to $232,725 for one-half the units at the $80,780 or less income level. Rents are more opaque because additional programs (Low Income Housing Tax Credits, etc.) would generally be used to finance these units.

Companion legislation proposed a $75 million bond-financed Housing Opportunity Fund, a revolving loan fund that would help finance below market rate units. One-third of the total was reserved for rental production where significant subsidies would be required to reduce rents to the inclusionary zoning targets. This legislation passed the council, was signed by the mayor, and bonds in the amount of one-half the total were sold.

Three-quarters of households with housing needs have incomes less than 50 percent of AMI. The proposed ordinance reserves 50 percent of the rental units for the two lowest income groups, both of which are within the less than 50 percent AMI ceiling. The ordinance proposes a ceiling of 60 percent of AMI for the other one-half of the units. These are commendable provisions that could, over time, make real inroads on At-

Table 11.3  **Proposed Allocations of Affordable Units Generated by Inclusionary Zoning Density Bonus by Tenure and Income, 2007**

| Owner | | Renter | |
|---|---|---|---|
| Proportion of Affordable Units | Income Level | Proportion of Affordable Units | Income Level |
| 20% | <60% AMI/$42,150 | 20% | 30% AMI/$21,075 |
| 30% | <80% AMI/$56,200 | 30% | 45% AMI/$31,612 |
| 50% | <115% AMI/$80,780 | 50% | 60% AMI/$42,150 |

lanta's housing problems. The proposed home ownership income limits will not have a similar effect but will subsidize development and middle and upper middle class purchasers. It is unfortunate that the homeowner provisions mirror many inclusionary zoning ordinances around the country. Political devolution of housing legislation to development interest groups, common practice in campaign finance-driven municipal politics, frequently results in the elevation of development industry interests over public purposes.

## TAX ALLOCATION DISTRICT HOUSING SUBSIDIES

Tax Increment Financing, or Tax Allocation Districts as they are known in Georgia, dedicates future increases in local property tax revenues for a particular area to the repayment of bonds used to subsidize multiple different forms of development, including housing in the area. The economic development perspective of the technique is usually that the TAD subsidy bridges the gap between development or redevelopment costs and limited capacity to pay those costs in depressed or underdeveloped areas. Their widespread usage in the U.S. and now in Atlanta has blurred the original rationale by making TADs mechanisms for competition to subsidize development between areas and other more particular local objectives.

Atlanta has defined ten TADs to date. The first six are actively being implemented, and they will exhaust almost all of the currently accessible revenue streams because there is a state mandated limit of ten percent of the tax digest pledged to TADs.

As gentrification intensified and as the city simultaneously became a more attractive focus for development and redevelopment, different roles for TAD financing have been proposed. The Gentrification Task Force legislation set a goal of one-third (33%) of the residential development in a TAD to meet the legislation's definition of affordability (less than 50% of AMI). Subsequent policy has generally sidestepped these goals, choosing instead to set income targeting policy at different levels of government, on an area-by-area basis, and at different, usually higher, income levels.

Of the first six TADs, only Perry Bolton/Northwest Atlanta Redevelopment Area specified income targets in the original authorizing legislation. Initially, on December 2, 2002 the council adopted legislation focusing 20 percent of housing units subsidized by that TAD funding on households with 50 percent of Area Median Income. That construct lasted only two days until the council revised the income target ceiling upward to 80 percent AMI, thereby reducing the potential beneficient impact on households with the greatest needs.

The city council set a proportional goal of 20 percent of residential de-velopment below market in the Eastside Redevelopment Area (the fifth TAD) but did not stipulate or reference a definition of affordability and further restricting the Housing Authority to 10 percent of the 20 percent.[27] The Atlanta Development Authority subsequently set the income target for sales housing at 80 percent of AMI.[28]

In the absence of more explicit direction from the council, ADA's board ignored the Gentrification Task Force recommended goals that were ad-opted by the council and has generally set income targeting of 80 percent of AMI for sales housing and 60 percent of AMI for rental developments. The Beltline TAD legislation dropped the proportion of affordable hous-ing to 15 percent from the 20 percent specified for the Eastside and Perry Bolton and established the Beltline Affordable Workforce Housing Board which will make recommendations that will very likely include specific income targets.

To date the first four TADs have produced over 3,400 units of variously defined "affordable" housing. Table 11.4 specifies the distribution of these units.

As the preceding discussion indicated, the definitions of affordability have not followed a uniform policy, making interpretation of these figures imprecise. The fact that both the Atlantic Station TAD and the Westside TAD set their approaches to affordability prior to the attempt to establish a uniform TAD affordability policy further complicates this issue.

Atlantic Station's sales housing was priced at between $139,000 and $172,290 which suggests affordability criteria in the range of 80–100 percent of AMI. Rental rates are listed at between $787 and $1,370 for a two bedroom unit, implying criteria in the 60-80 percent of AMI range. Sales units in the Westside TAD range from $160,000–$185,000 for a two bedroom unit, suggesting a 100 percent AMI ceiling. The 194 rental units appear to correspond to an 80 percent of AMI cap. Thus, the 1,386 owner-ship units were developed for households with incomes at 80 percent or

Table 11.4   Affordable Housing Produced by Atlanta Tax Allocation Districts, 2007

| Tax Allocation District | Sales | | Rental | |
|---|---|---|---|---|
| | Total | Affordable | Total | Affordable |
| Eastside | 847 | 213 | 857 | 514 |
| Westside | 922 | 45 | 261 | 194 |
| Atlantic Station | 2,849 | 401 | 645 | 547 |
| Princeton Lakes | 849 | 727 | 350 | TBD |
| Total | 5,467 | 1,386 | 2,113 | 1,255 |

Source: Atlanta Development Authority, Housing Production Database (accessed 10 March, 2007).

more of AMI (currently $51,250 for a family of three), and 59.0 percent of the 1,255 rental units were targeted at the same income group. Only the 514 rental units on the eastside reached below 60 percent of AMI (currently $38,450 for a family of three).

The Georgia Supreme Court ruled local school boards' diversion of future property tax revenues to TAD development subsidies unconstitutional in 2007. School boards had been contributing approximately one-half of the total TAD subsidies. Development interests and some municipalities convinced the state legislature to put a constitutional amendment establishing school boards' capacities to divert anticipated increases in educational property tax revenues to development subsidies in the fall 2008 election. The amendment passed.

In summary, the tax allocation district subsidies have produced substantial amounts of subsidized housing but mostly for households with high incomes relative to those with housing needs. After some initially relatively high income targets as the program began and in the absence of a clear policy direction, the council attempted to tie production quantity and income targeting to housing needs. This attempt to construct an overarching policy for TAD housing subsidies recognized the additional pressure gentrification places on lower income people and affordable housing. But the council has subsequently deferred targeting and production decisions to the Atlanta Development Authority or, in the case of the Beltline, a project-specific advisory board. The exceptions to this posture were to increase the allowable income ceiling on the Westside, to specify a lower production requirement on the Eastside, and to lower the production requirement on the Beltline. After its initial foray into setting a citywide policy for housing subsidized by the diversion of future property tax revenues, the council has abdicated its responsibility for exercising its stewardship of these funds.

## CONCLUSION

### Changes in Markets

Gentrification has accelerated from its modest beginnings in the mid-1960s when segments of the Northside and two or three central area neighborhoods were the focus of reinvestment. By the mid-1980s redevelopment affected over twenty neighborhoods, and by the mid-1990s economic transformation spread across much of the city.

The cumulative effect of over thirty years of gentrification demonstrated that class trumps poverty and race and in doing so changed the dynamics of reinvestment. By the 1990s white middle class gentrifiers moved into poor African American neighborhoods confident that their investments would appreciate. Idealists among them sought social integration. Some middle class African Americans invested in the new racially transitional neighborhoods while others gentrified existing black neighborhoods, but their numbers were small in comparison.

Condominium conversions trailed years behind the first gentrifiers in the 1960s and 70s, waiting to be certain of the establishment of economically viable submarkets. But, by the 1990s widespread confidence in the efficacy of resurgent gentrification led converters to focus on the earliest stages of gentrification, usually successfully. The condominium market matured from a few hundred conversions in the 1970s to over 30,000 units in 2005. Over 50 high-rise condominiums "urban-ized" Midtown and Buckhead, and office conversions to residential condominiums injected some new life into the old CBD and filled in some of the blank spaces in Midtown.

Predatory lenders preyed on poor households in the 1990s and state-enacted legal restrictions in 2001 provided only temporary relief as newly elected Republicans rescinded those protections in 2002. Atlanta escaped some of the speculative fervor that mauled many housing markets, but inept developers attempting to ride resurgent gentrification's new momentum, fraudulent turnover schemes, revived predatory lenders, purveyors of "exotic" and extortionate loans, and the subprime lenders wreaked havoc in many of the city's submarkets in the mid-2000s.

In the near term the subprime/predatory lending crisis will damage many submarkets, particularly in south Atlanta. The extent of the damage and the severity of residual effects will depend on the vigor and breadth of remedial efforts by governments. To date there has been no indication that the state will act. The national response is not clear at this writing.

## Policy and the Future

A central element defining the context for Atlanta's future housing is the needs of the lowest income citizens. Table 11.5 presents the measures of housing needs in Atlanta for 1980, 1990, and 2000. Needs consist of cost burdened households (defined as those paying over 30% of income for housing), overcrowded households (defined as housing over 1.01 persons per habitable room), and households lacking complete plumbing and/or kitchen facilities.[29] These measures disclose that in 2000, 54,252 city of Atlanta households had one or more of the three types of housing needs. Nearly one-third (32.5%) of the households in the city of Atlanta are either cost burdened, overcrowded, or live in units that lack basic plumbing and kitchen facilities. This figure represents only those households having less than 80 percent of the regional median income, which in 2000 was $50,400 for a family of four. The facts that over 50,000 households had housing needs in both 1990 and 2000 and that individual measures of needs changed very little between 1980 and 2000 means that extensive housing problems are beyond the reach of Atlanta's vibrant private markets and that the modest local and federal efforts during the same period predictably left problems undiminished.

**Table 11.5   City of Atlanta Housing Needs, 1980, 1990, and 2000**

| Year | 1980 | 1990 | 2000[a] |
|---|---|---|---|
| Gross Rent as a Percentage of Income >30% | | | |
| Renter | 33,530 | 38,947 | 36,707 |
| Selected Housing Expenses as a Percentage of Income >30% | | | |
| Owner | 12,320 | 15,587 | 12,053 |
| Overcrowding Persons per Room 1.01 or More | | | |
| Renter | | 7,728 | 8,221 |
| Owner | | 2,063 | 988 |
| Total | 10,236 | 9,791 | 9,209 |
| Lacking Complete Plumbing Facilities | | | |
| Renter | 1,940 | 890 | 1,048 |
| Owner | 266 | 192 | 306 |
| Total[b] | 2.206 | 1,083 | 1,354 |
| Lacking Complete Kitchen Facilities | | | |
| Renter | | | 1,371 |
| Owner | | | 336 |
| Total[c] | 4,695 | 1,613 | 1,707 |
| Lacking Facilities | | | |
| Renter | | | 1,932 |
| Owner | | | 504 |
| Total | | | 2,436 |
| One or More Housing Problems | | | |
| Renter | | 40,334 | 41,880 |
| Owner | | 14,417 | 12,372 |
| Total | | 54,751 | 54,252 |

Sources: 1980, 1990 Censuses; 2000 Public Use Micro. Sample estimate by author.
[a] Households with incomes 80% or less of regional median.
[b] Occupied units.
[c] All units (occupied and vacant).

In addition to the magnitude and intractability of housing needs, the poverty of households with needs further defines the setting around which the future will be built. Over one-half (53.4%) of households with needs had less than 30 percent AMI. One quarter (24.8%) of households with needs have incomes between 31 percent and 50 percent of AMI. In HUD's terms, 78.2 percent of households with needs have either extremely low incomes or very low incomes (Keating et al. 2005, 6).

A third dimension of the context for housing and housing policy is that most of the action will take place in previously developed areas. There are a few remaining Greenfield sites in underdeveloped neighborhoods, primarily on the south side, but most of the city has been developed, and many areas are in their second or third cycle of redevelopment.

A fourth contextual variable is the legally constrained room for local policy to maneuver regarding condominium conversions. The inability of the city government to construct equitable policies for condominium conversions because of state preemption will be a major impediment to social justice in Atlanta's future housing transformation.[30] The legal and institutional changes in ownership occasioned by conversions provide leverage points that can introduce some equitable protections for tenants without too adversely constraining profits. Unfortunately, the present alignment of state political forces make elimination of the state preemption unlikely in the short term.

In terms of gentrification policy, national and local politicians have been loath to interfere. The Carter administration began to ponder what an equitable gentrification policy might be in the late 1970s, but the Reagan administration dropped the issue. No subsequent national administration has broached the subject.

The racial and political conflict attending the acceleration of gentrification in the late 1990s pushed the issue of protecting existing residents into local political consideration. The city council grappled with a set of policies that focused public subsidies on the most vulnerable residents and sought to protect those most damaged by gentrification by expanding affordable housing for those with the greatest need. But, they stopped just short of prescribing the central policies as law, declaring that the focus on the poorest and least able to cope were *goals* and not *requirements* for spending city-administered resources. Under sympathetic administrators, the distinction did not diminish the thrust of policy, but administrations changed, developers complained, and, as the most recent task force dismissively observed, "the legislation was only an expression of intent" (Affordable Workforce Housing Implementation Task Force 2006, 5).

While the thrust of current Atlanta policy still pledges allegiance and devotes resources to the attraction of middle class residents as a premise for subsidies—an archaic and disingenuous argument in the face of resurgent gentrification's increasing middle and upper class migration into much of the city—some progress has been made in directing some subsidies to the most vulnerable.

Both the mayor's Implementation Task Force recommendations and Atlanta Development Authority practices cap subsidies to rental housing development at 60 percent of AMI. Because development will focus on income levels at and just below the stipulated cap, it is particularly important that the task force recommendations specified one-half of the rental units produced by its proposed inclusionary zoning program be accessible to two groups (30% of AMI and 45% of AMI) with far lower incomes. It is important that these recommendations remain part of the legislation. Unfortunately, the development authority does not subdivide its rental subsidy regulations below 60 pecent of AMI. The task force recommendations and the Housing Opportunity Bond Fund are the brightest spots on the recent policy front.

The current alignment of political forces does not argue well for more progressive local policies, but there are positive paths to more equitable governance within reach. As long as electoral politics is dependent on private and interest group finance, politicians will defer to real estate interests in crafting housing policies. These interests will continue to emphasize new construction and development because that is what they know and do. Without substantial subsidies new construction and development inevitably exclude the poorest households who should be the primary focus of housing policy.

The inclusionary zoning legislation's major flaw at this writing is its reliance on voluntary compliance. For technical reasons, density bonuses, the usual *quid pro quo* in inclusionary ordinances, under Atlanta's zoning ordinance are less attractive than in other places. Negotiations are ongoing with development trade associations to provide more and different forms of subsidies (impact fee waivers, reduced parking requirements, etc.), but experience in other cities indicates that it is unlikely that any plausible combination of density increases and modest exemptions will trigger many new units of affordable housing under a voluntary ordinance. There is also a substantial downside risk that the state legislature will ban inclusionary zoning legislation as they did with tenant protections in condominium conversions and living wages.

Unfortunately, too many of Atlanta's community development corporations, which were originally beacons of hope for progressive housing policies, have been trapped in the conundrum of classist constituents, development imperatives, self-preservation, and fading financial support. There is still promise in the network of institutions, and substantial external support could realize the original promises.

After these modest bright spots, the outlook for progressive low income housing policy in Atlanta is bleak. The housing authority has gambled, putting all its bets on the survival of a program that has been under sustained attack from the political right for decades. In a few years the authority will only own the few units in mixed income communities occupied by the highest income poor people. A national shift could rescue this strategy from the more extensive devastation that would accompany continued retraction of the voucher program. The coin of the realm for low-income housing is politics. Atlanta's private home ownership markets, subsidized by $127 million dollars annually by the federal and state tax systems, are poised to gentrify much more of the city. Rental markets face the twin pressures of demolition for redevelopment and condominium conversions with very weak security of tenure protections. In the absence of a forceful political shift, poor people's housing situations will worsen. There is some hope in the national Housing Trust Fund legislation that is under consideration in Congress. Passage could direct significant resources to those in need.

Although many American cities have constructed more humane housing policies than Atlanta has yet, only a few are truly progressive and equitable. In the future Atlanta's claim of national leadership in human and civil rights could include eminence in local housing policies, but that would require a major political shift.

## NOTES

1. Lenox Square Mall is six miles north of the CBD on Peachtree Street, the city's iconic artery and development spine connecting Buckhead and the CBD.

2. The only extensive segment of I–285 within the city is on the west and southwest sides and, at 6.1 miles from the CBD it is much closer than the 10.8 miles on the north side or the 8.9 miles on the east side. These distances reflect the extent of development at the time the land for the highway was targeted and acquired as the Department of Transportation sought to minimize acquisition costs by purchasing rights of way just beyond developed areas.

3. Central Atlanta Progress is the organization of central area businesses and corporations that plans, advocates, and promotes their mutual interests.

4. Ted Levangood, Lotus Spreedsheets 1 and 2, Atlanta Bureau of Planning, 1986. The criteria for determining gentrification were both a neighborhood turnover rate greater than 67.0% (1975–1985) and an increase in median sales price of 63.5% or more over the same period. Inman Park had the highest turnover rate at 110.5% and Cabbagetown had the highest increase in median sales price at 180.0%. Candler Park (117.4%), Inman Park (109.8%), and Midtown (109.6%) were the three neighborhoods in which prices doubled.

5. "Martin Eager to Help Dress Neighborhoods for Olympics," *Atlanta Journal-Constitution*, 30 May, 1991, E-3.

6. Atlanta University (the residential neighborhood around the schools), English Avenue, Mechanicsville, Old Fourth Ward, Peoplestown, Summerhill, and Vine City.

7. This estimate conservatively assumes that one-half of the severely deteriorated units could have been economically rehabilitated.

8. AHA followed this sequence in redeveloping portions of the McDaniel Glenn community in the 1980's. In another earlier approach, AHA constructed temporary housing adjacent to the redevelopment site in the Bedford Pine Urban Renewal area of Atlanta in the 1970's.

9. Relocation housing is the housing residents move to from the redevelopment site. Replacement housing is the housing that substitutes for the original housing in the inventory of lower income housing. They may or may not be the same.

10. In the past commitments to provide voucher subsidies extended to as much as 40 years and were therefore "bankable" in the sense that financial institutions recognized the long term obligation and were willing to loan money for the development of physical units. But, over the past 20 years, successive administrations have reduced the commitment to its present one year term.

11. The present Community Development Block Grant Program was initially a replacement for two categorical housing programs in 1974.

12. See Bruce et al. (2000).

13. For a more extended discussion of alternative policies, please see Keating 2003. Very briefly, low income members of the Task Force opposed expanded roles for community development corporations because they saw them as gentrifiers, and Atlanta's primary public provider of low-income housing, the Atlanta Housing Authority, is both shrinking its inventory and is an avowed gentrifier. These conditions precluded a neighborhood by neighborhood attempt to preserve or expand low-income housing supply. Strengthening security of tenure laws and payment of displacement compensation were judged politically infeasible.

14. Area Median Incomes are a set of figures defined annually by U.S. HUD. One advantage of using these figures in legislation is that they are annually updated. A second advantage is that they are the basis for almost all federal housing subsidy programs. In 2007 30% of AMI for a family of three = $19,200 and for a family of four = $21,350. Fifty percent of AMI for a family of three = $32,050 and for a family of four = $35,600.

15. Sec. 54-I.1(a) a Code of Ordinances of the City of Atlanta.

16. Michael McGuire at a Urban Land Institute Inclusionary Zoning Task Force meeting, Loudermilk Center, Atlanta, 28 February, 2003.

17. Sales data supplied by the Tax Assessors of Fulton and DeKalb Counties.

18. Georgia Multiple Listing Service. The average sale price of existing homes was $192,262 in 2004.

19. City is defined as inside I–285 in this report.

20. Atlanta Regional Commission; Some estimates range as high as 5,000 new units per year since 2000. See David Pendered, "Housing Hot," *Atlanta Journal-Constitution*, 27 December, 2004, E1(3).

21. Data are courtesy of Haddow & Company and have been compiled for an area extending from Decatur to downtown and from there north to Buckhead.

22. Caution is advised because the 2005 data from the American Community Survey has substantially wider confidence intervals than earlier census estimates. I have not followed this advice, however.

23. The 1990 and 2000 figures are from STF1 (100% data). The 2005 figures are from the American Community Survey and have 90% margin of errors of ±3.6% (total population), ±4.8% (black or African American alone population) and ±5.3% (white alone population). In addition the ACS data excludes people living in institutions, college dormitories, and other group quarters.

24. Interview with Michael Dobbins, former Commissioner of Planning, Neighborhood Conservation and Development, Atlanta, 2 April, 2007.

25. Sec 16-18O.029.8.b.iii Code of Ordinances of the city of Atlanta.

26. Benjamin W. Giles, Planning Intern, City of Atlanta, Personal Communication, 5 April, 2007.

27. Section 03-0-1840, 1 December, 2003.

28. Atlanta Development Authority, Eastside TAD Affordable Housing Purchase Program Fact Sheet, Undated, p. 2.

29. In January 2004, the Georgia Department of Community Affairs (DCA) adopted the above indices that U.S. HUD traditionally used to measure needs. In May 2005, the new Perdue administration reduced the Georgia definition of housing needs to cost-burdened households.

30. In other communities greater protection of existing residents is afforded by much stronger security of tenure laws than are likely in Atlanta or Georgia.

## REFERENCES

Affordable Workforce Housing Implementation Task Force. *Executive Summary of Recommendations*. Report for Mayor Shirley Franklin, Atlanta, November 2006.

Alexander, Frank and Larry Keating. *A City for All: Report of the Gentrification Task Force*. Report for the Atlanta City Council, 2001.

Berry, Brian J. L. "Islands of Renewal in Seas of Decay." Pp. 69–96 in *The New Urban Reality*, edited by Paul E. Peterson. Washington, D.C.: Brookings, 1985.

Boston, Thomas D. "The Effects of Revitalization on Public Housing Residents: A Case Study of the Atlanta Housing Authority." *Journal of the American Planning Association* 71, no. 4 (December 2005): 393–407.

Bruce, Bill, Brad Calvert, Dan Schultz, Brian White, and Dina Lewallen. *Policy Tools for Gentrification in Atlanta*. Report by the Graduate Program in City and Regional Planning, Georgia Institute of Technology, 2000.

Creighton, Max, Larry Keating, and Michael Elliott. *Community Improvement Priorities for the Cabbagetown and Reynoldstown Neighborhoods*. Report prepared for the Cabbagetown and Reynoldstown Neighborhoods and the Metropolitan Community Foundation, 1986.

DeGiovanni, Frank F. "Patterns of Change in Housing Market Activity in Revitalizing Neighborhoods." *Journal of the American Planning Association* 49, no. 1 (March 1983): 22–39.

Duda, Mark and William C. Apgar. *Mortgage Foreclosures in Atlanta: Patterns and Policy Issues*. Washington, D.C.: Neighbor Works America, December 2005.

Hackworth, Jason. "Postrecession Gentrification in New York City." *Urban Affairs Review* 37, no. 6 (2002): 815.

Jaret, Charles, Robert M. Adelman, and Melissa M. Hayes. "Atlanta's Future: Convergence or Divergence with its Suburbs and Other Cities?" Presentation at the "City of Atlanta: Recent Trends and Future Prospects" Conference, Atlanta, Ga., 2007.

Keating, Larry. "Gentrification in Atlanta: Policies and Politics." In *Housing and the African American Community*, edited by Robert E. Holmes. Atlanta: Southern Center for Policy Studies, 2003.

Keating, Larry, Nicki Belville, Judy Caira, John Harsha, and Jackie Sweatt. *Displacement Study*. Report prepared for the Anti-Displacement Coalition by the Graduate Program in City Planning, Georgia Institute of Technology, 1982.

Keating, Larry and Maxwell Creighton. *Nonprofit Housing Supply*. Report, Atlanta, Ga., 20 May, 1989.

Keating, Larry, and Max Creighton. *Olympic Impact Neighborhoods; Planning Assessments of Human Services, Housing and Transportation Issues*. Atlanta, 1991.

Keating, Larry, and Carol Flores. "Sixty and Out: Techwood Homes Transformed by Enemies and Friends." *Journal of Urban History* 26, no. 3 (March 2000): 275–311.

Keating, Larry, Melissa Mailloux, Maxwell Creighton, and Donald Wilborn. *Housing Element of the Comprehensive Development Plan*. Report, December 2005.

Lowe, Edward. "Demolition and the Spatial Distribution of Abandoned Structures: A Case Study of Seven Olympic Ring Communities." Thesis option paper, Graduate Program in City Planning, Georgia Institute of Technology, 1996.

Mayor's Housing Task Force. "Recommendations." In *A Vision for Housing in Atlanta: Great Housing in Great Neighborhoods*. Report for Mayor Shirley Franklin, Atlanta, 2002.

Whitenhauer, Thomas. "Atlanta Subdivision Regulations." Thesis option paper, Graduate Program in City Planning, Georgia Institute of Technology, 1989.

Wiley, Elvin K. and Daniel J. Hammel. "Islands of Decay in Seas of Renewal: Housing Policy and the Resurgence of Gentrification." *Housing Policy Debate* 10, no. 4 (1999): 711–771.

*Chapter 12*

# Exploring Mixed Income Neighborhoods in Atlanta, 1970–2010

*Douglas J. Krupka*

Mixed income neighborhoods have been hypothesized to be highly unstable in the urban economics literature. Yet, there are many plausible benefits of such neighborhoods that might lead us to place a positive social value on the existence of these places (Wilson 1987). These social benefits of mixed income neighborhoods may make it optimal for policy makers to attempt to induce their stability. In terms of equity, the widely reported negative externalities present in neighborhoods which host high concentrations of poverty fall squarely on the shoulders of those least able to deal with them: the poor. In the meantime, the positive externalities of living in areas of concentrated wealth are monopolized by those who need them less: the wealthy. From a cultural perspective, the exposure of the rich and poor to each other could help bridge cultural, political, and economic gaps between these groups, to uncertain betterment of society.

For these reasons, and possibly others, mixed income neighborhoods have become a priority for many levels of government. The U.S. Department of Housing and Urban Development gives grants and subsidies to developers who provide some "affordable housing" mixed into their market rate dwellings. Atlantic Station and the Cotton Mill Lofts in Cabbagetown are two examples in Atlanta. Furthermore, many lower levels of government, including Atlanta, also offer incentives for developers to produce mixed income housing opportunities.

Despite the policy interest and social import of mixed income neighborhoods, they are relatively poorly understood. Urban economic models predict that such neighborhoods should be unstable to the point of nonexistence, despite their persistence. While there is much anecdotal evidence that many of these neighborhoods are at or near tipping points, and veering towards a segregated outcome, we know almost nothing about how these neighborhoods develop over time, and what, if any, other factors determine the ability of a neighborhood to stay mixed.

This paper looks at mixed income neighborhoods (census tracts) in Atlanta. First, the paper explores the dynamics of mixed income neighborhoods. It examines the determinants and dynamics of the level of income mixing in a neighborhood, and how these relationships have changed towards the end of the twentieth century. An interesting pattern emerges. Income mixing has become more stable over the course of the late twentieth century. The large changes in the size and character of Atlanta's central counties appear to have also affected the dynamics of mixed income neighborhoods.

It is possible—though not necessarily advisable—to use the knowledge gained in the previous experiments to make predictions about the future of mixed income neighborhoods in Atlanta out to 2010. To make predictions about the future, we must make many assumptions. Most importantly, we must assume that the variables that predicted income mixing in the 1990s will predict income mixing over the 2000s *in the same way they predict today*. Given the instability of the dynamic relationships discussed above, these assumptions may not be too safe. Nonetheless, we present the results of some simple projections for the inner counties of the metropolitan area. These projections predict some reversion to the mean in levels of income mixing, with highly mixed neighborhoods becoming less diverse as more homogenous neighborhoods become more diverse.

The rest of the paper is organized as follows. The next section discusses some important literature and conceptual issues. A third section discusses the data used in the empirical sections, and describes in broad strokes the models to be used. The fourth section presents the results for the "historical" levels of income mixing. The fifth section examines the changes in the dynamics of mixing in Atlanta over the study period. The penultimate presents and discusses the projections, and a final section concludes.

## LITERATURE AND CONCEPTUAL ISSUES

The three most important papers about mixed income neighborhoods lay out models of residential choice. These models (Alonso 1965; Tiebout 1956; and Schelling 1969) arrive at the very stark conclusion that people of differing types should locate in separate neighborhoods. These models appear to overpredict income sorting, however. A broad array of evidence suggests that America's urban neighborhoods are fairly well mixed.[1] While this disagreement between theory and practice has stimulated the theoretical literature on mixed income neighborhoods,[2] we still do not know much about how and why mixed income neighborhoods persist.

Krupka (2008) stresses that the lack of supporting evidence for the three fundamental theories is due to the theories' focus on long-run equilibrium, while the cross sectional data used in the empirical literature is primarily static, and thus must assume (implicitly) that such a long-run equilibrium is reached. Given the sometimes fluid nature of American urban geographies, this distinction implies the importance of examining the dynamics of mixed income residence patterns with panel data. This paper follows on Krupka (2008) in the context of Atlanta over the time period 1970 to 2000, and then uses the insights to make predictions about residence patterns in 2010.

In any study about mixed income development two problems arise. The first is that the study forces the researcher to define practically what constitutes a "neighborhood." Neighborhoods are complex, geographically limited networks of relationships that are not easily observed. Coulton et al. (2004) examine just this question. Their evidence, which focused on disadvantaged populations in Denver, Colorado, has two almost contradictory implications. On the one hand, personal definitions of one's neighborhood vary tremendously among populations of the neighborhood, but tend to be fairly inclusive at the extensive margin. On the other hand, looking at internal consistency of neighborhood perceptions, the evidence suggests that the usual social-science definition of a neighborhood (the census tract) may be too large. In squaring this circle, this paper uses the census tract as the proxy for neighborhood, but this choice is driven by data availability more than any inherent advantage of that geography.

The second problem in the study of mixed income residential patterns is in the definition of mixed income itself. Intuitively, if people with very different incomes live in the same place, that constitutes a very mixed income neighborhood. In the racial context, there are a variety of measures available. Most of these measures are closely related to some measure of segregation because the measurement of segregation has a well-established literature.[3] These measures take advantage of the discrete distribution of race, which is not possible in the case of income.

For a measure of income mixing we can turn to the literature on the measurement of income segregation. Jargowski (1996) develops his neighborhood sorting index (NSI) as a measure of income segregation at some larger scale. The NSI is basically the proportion of the citywide standard deviation in income attributable to variance in neighborhood average incomes. Turning this measure on its head, one could also have a neighborhood *mixing* index, which would be the proportion of the citywide standard deviation in income attributable to variance of incomes *within* neighborhoods. This inverse measure of segregation suggests the neighborhood standard deviation of income as a candidate for use as a measure of income mixing. For reasons described below, the coefficient of variation in income is used instead.

## DATA

Until recently, the examination of the dynamic trends of neighborhood residence patterns was considerably complicated, if not made entirely impossible, by the lack of consistent neighborhood boundaries in the census data files. Each census, the boundaries of census tracts would change. While most changes involved the merging or splitting of existing tracts, these changes (and the difficulty in tracking them) made examination of more than a cross-section of census tracts very difficult.

With modern improvements in mapping software, however, these obstacles can be surmounted. The analysis in this paper was conducted using data from Geolytics™, which reprocesses data from the 1970, 1980, and 1990 censuses so that these data can be expressed in the 2000 census geographies. This allows researchers to take each census tract as an observation in a massive panel dataset. The word neighborhood suggests a complex web of relationships, travel patterns, and shared mental geographies. While I believe that this concept of neighborhood is valid, it can not be measured with any accuracy by social scientists. Here I take the census tract as a loose definition of a "neighborhood" and leave it at that. While there is some evidence (Coulton et al. 2004) that real neighborhoods may be smaller than census tracts, going down to the block group level would require us to drop the earliest year of our data, 1970.

From this data, I collect several neighborhood attributes from 1970 through 2000. These attributes include median and average income, the standard deviation of income, demographic characteristics of the population (population growth, race, age distribution, and education) and some housing characteristics (vacancy rates, ownership rates, and housing vintage).

The intermediate goal of the paper is to predict income mixing at the census tract level in the year 2000 using only 1990 and earlier level variables. To that end, I must first define income mixing. As discussed above, Jargowski (1996) measures income *segregation* using the standard deviation of income across neighborhoods relative to the area-wide standard deviation of income. This would imply that the standard deviation of income would supply a valid measure of neighborhood-level income mixing. However, because the income distribution is so skewed, the standard deviation of income is correlated with the average income very strongly ($\rho = 0.92$ in this sample). This strong correlation says more about how changes in income mean less as levels of income grow than about the tendency of richer neighborhoods to be more diverse.

Instead of standard deviation, I use the coefficient of variation as my measure of income mixing. The coefficient of variation is the standard deviation of income divided by the average income (each measured at the neighborhood level). It can be interpreted as the standard deviation expressed as a proportion of the neighborhood average family income. Thus, a coefficient of variation of one represents a standard deviation of family income that is exactly as large as the average income. This standardization also frees us from worries about the accuracy of price indices and dollar comparability across census years, a major concern since our time period in question includes both the high inflation period of the 1970s and the rapid technological changes of the 1990s.

The standard deviation of income is computed from the income bins for each census year, while the average family income is taken directly from the Geolytics™ data. The other variables are computed rather trivially from the same source. I cannot use data from the entire metropolitan area,

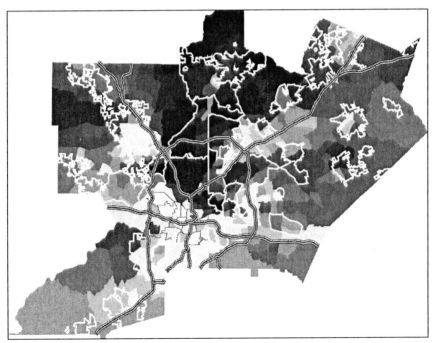

**Figure 12.1. Average Family Income, 2000. "Note: grey scale represents income deciles from lowest (lightest) to highest (darkest)."**

*Douglas J. Krupka*

however, because large portions of Atlanta were still underdeveloped in 1980 and 1970, several counties do not have data for those years, before the census had "tracted" the entire country. Thus, my analysis focuses on a subset of counties that have been tracted since 1970 and which I consider to be the "core" area of the region: Fulton, DeKalb, Cobb, and Gwinnett counties. None of the results are sensitive to this selection.

Table 12.1 presents the descriptive statistics for the variables used in the analysis. For the purposes of this paper, "pWhite" is the percent of the population that is white, "pOld" is the percent of the population above sixty-five, "pYoung" is the percent below fifteen, "pCollege" is the percent over age twenty-five and with a college degree, "Vacancy Rate" is the percent of housing units not occupied, "pOwner" is the percent of housing units that are owner occupied, "New Construction" is the percent of housing units built within the preceding five years, and "Pre-War Housing" is the percent of housing units built

**Table 12.1  Unweighted Descriptive Statistics**

| Variable | Year | | | |
|---|---|---|---|---|
| | 1970 | 1980 | 1990 | 2000 |
| Coefficient of Var. | 0.7203 | 0.6558 | 0.6399 | 0.7057 |
| | 0.1388 | 0.1560 | 0.1828 | 0.1828 |
| Population Growth | | 0.6909 | 0.5083 | 0.3431 |
| | | 1.1688 | 0.8017 | 0.5789 |
| pWhite | 0.8303 | 0.7298 | 0.6253 | 0.5132 |
| | 0.3051 | 0.3588 | 0.3640 | 0.3411 |
| pOld | 0.0656 | 0.0780 | 0.0825 | 0.0810 |
| | 0.0431 | 0.0555 | 0.0543 | 0.0487 |
| pYoung | 0.3017 | 0.2728 | 0.2098 | 0.2092 |
| | 0.0649 | 0.1908 | 0.0688 | 0.0692 |
| pCollege | 0.1325 | 0.2290 | 0.2972 | 0.3492 |
| | 0.1086 | 0.1491 | 0.1782 | 0.2095 |
| Vacancy Rate | 0.0477 | 0.0653 | 0.1069 | 0.0583 |
| | 0.0293 | 0.0434 | 0.0750 | 0.0512 |
| pOwner | 0.6532 | 0.6210 | 0.5802 | 0.5889 |
| | 0.2152 | 0.2708 | 0.2634 | 0.2715 |
| New Construction | 0.3025 | 0.1826 | 0.1948 | 0.1169 |
| | 0.2018 | 0.1853 | 0.1843 | 0.1266 |
| Pre-War Housing | 0.1773 | 0.1040 | 0.0794 | 0.0695 |
| | 0.1715 | 0.1471 | 0.1402 | 0.1207 |
| Med. Family Inc. | | | 42887.8 | 60433.0 |
| | | | 21265.3 | 31567.2 |
| Avg. Family Inc. | 12036.7 | 25064.0 | 51146.4 | 74528.5 |
| | 4125.5 | 10011.0 | 28261.1 | 42321.2 |

*Note*: These averages represent the 440 census tracts in the four "core" counties of the Atlanta Metropolitan Area. Standard deviations presented below the average in smaller font. Population growth represents the growth in population during the preceding decade, as a proportion of starting population.

before 1940. The census year is attached to the variable. These variables are included in some regressions to capture possible effects of the neighborhood housing and population mix on the income mixing of a neighborhood.

Figure 12.1 represents the geographic distribution of average family income across the metropolitan area in 2000. The map suppresses census tract boundaries for clarity's sake. The visual cues include the interstate highways and census designated places (in white lines). Within the city of Atlanta, neighborhood super districts defined by the Atlanta Regional Commission[4] are bounded by light black lines. Color gradations represent the deciles of tract average family income, with the lightest shade of grey representing the first (lowest) decile and the darkest grey representing the tenth decile. This figure shows the spread of wealthy families out into rural areas and down the eastern Atlanta gentrification zone (Midtown, Virginia Highland and toward Decatur).

Figure 12.2 shows the geographic distribution of the coefficient of variation in family income, with the same color scheme as figure 12.1. One shortcoming of this measure of income mixing is readily apparent from these maps: the strong negative correlation with average income. This

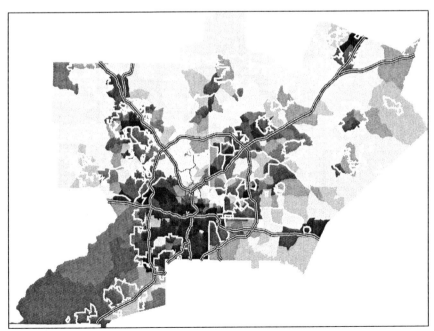

**Figure 12.2.** Coefficient of Variation of Family Income, 2000. "Note: grey scale represents CoVa deciles from lowest (lightest) to highest (darkest)."

correlation arises because of the standardization of the standard deviation of family income used to create the coefficient of variation: standard deviation was divided by the average. While this correctly adjusts for the heavy skew of the income distribution and the possibility that the same absolute difference in income probably means less in richer neighborhoods,[5] the strong negative correlation with average income admittedly reduces the use of the coefficient of variation as a policy objective. A better measure of income mixing might attempt to use a measure that is orthogonal to income levels, however the generation of such a measure is outside the scope of this paper.

## REGRESSIONS

This section presents the results from several sets of regressions of a neighborhood's coefficient of variation of family income (henceforth "*CoVa*") on previous levels of *CoVa* and (sometimes) other predetermined neighborhood characteristics:

$$1) \quad CoVa_t = \alpha_0 + \sum_{s=1}^{3} \alpha_s CoVa_{t-s} + \sum_{r=1}^{3} \alpha_{3+r} X_{t-r} + \varepsilon_t \, ,$$

where $t$ indexes census decades, $X$ is the vector of control variables listed in Table 3.1 and $\varepsilon_t$ is assumed to have all the desirable characteristics. The indices $s$ (the number of lags for *CoVa*) and $r$ (the number of lags for $X$) can vary independently. Table 12.2 presents results modeling only the dynamics by omitting all the control variables. Table 12.3 adds in the control variables.

Table 12.2 shows that *CoVa* is persistent: over 50 percent of the variation in neighborhood coefficient of variation is explained by previous levels of income mixing. Twice and thrice lagged levels of *CoVa* are statistically significant (at the 0.1 level), but add little explanatory power and have smaller coefficients. The negative and marginally significant coefficient

**Table 12.2  Dynamics of *CoVa***

|            | Coef.  | t     | Coef.  | t     | Coef.   | t     |
|------------|--------|-------|--------|-------|---------|-------|
| CoVa(90)   | 0.7883 | 21.07 | 0.5828 | 10.72 | 0.6164  | 11.77 |
| CoVa(80)   |        |       | 0.2900 | 5.09  | 0.3275  | 5.86  |
| CoVa(70)   |        |       |        |       | -0.0953 | -1.92 |
| constant   | 0.2013 | 8.08  | 0.1391 | 5.13  | 0.1593  | 4.36  |
| adj. r-sq  | 0.5021 |       | 0.5289 |       | 0.5675  |       |

on thrice lagged income mixing is interesting in suggesting that neighborhoods undergo cycles. Unfortunately, it is not possible to check for the stability of this relationship with these data. As we will see below, the temporal generalizability of these results is not something we should take for granted.

Adding explanatory variables improves explanatory power considerably, and allows the examination of some of the partial correlates of *CoVa* in table 12.3, which uses the full set of lagged dependent variables ($s = 3$)

**Table 12.3   Fuller Specifications**

|  | Coef. | t | Coef. | t | Coef. | t |
|---|---|---|---|---|---|---|
| CoVa(90) | 0.3104 | 5.33 | 0.2846 | 4.68 | 0.2035 | 3.25 |
| CoVa(80) | 0.1686 | 3.41 | 0.1634 | 3.06 | 0.1367 | 2.56 |
| CoVa(70) | -0.0193 | -0.41 | -0.0181 | -0.36 | 0.0466 | 0.83 |
| md.Fam.Inc(90) | $-6.80*10^{-8}$ | -0.05 | $9.27*10^{-8}$ | 0.06 | $5.72*10^{-7}$ | 0.39 |
| Pop.grwth89 |  |  | -0.0115 | -0.84 | -0.0223 | -1.46 |
| Pop.grwth78 |  |  |  |  | -0.0197 | -2.30 |
| Fam.avg.Inc9 | $-6.07*10^{-7}$ | -0.71 | $-4.58*10^{-7}$ | -0.48 | $-4.36*10^{-7}$ | -0.46 |
| Fam.avg.Inc8 |  |  | $-9.12*10^{-7}$ | -0.47 | $-1.13*10^{-6}$ | -0.48 |
| Fam.avg.Inc7 |  |  |  |  | $-1.79*10^{-6}$ | -0.37 |
| pWhite9 | -0.0022 | -0.09 | 0.0464 | 0.92 | 0.0096 | 0.18 |
| pWhite8 |  |  | -0.0595 | -1.19 | -0.0239 | -0.42 |
| pWhite7 |  |  |  |  | -0.0221 | -0.51 |
| pCollege9 | -0.0923 | -1.41 | -0.1167 | -1.03 | -0.1645 | -1.45 |
| pCollege8 |  |  | 0.0110 | 0.08 | -0.0113 | -0.07 |
| pCollege7 |  |  |  |  | 0.0547 | 0.35 |
| pOld9 | 0.3293 | 2.63 | 0.0736 | 0.32 | 0.0049 | 0.02 |
| pOld8 |  |  | 0.3054 | 1.25 | 0.2156 | 0.75 |
| pOld7 |  |  |  |  | 0.3609 | 1.09 |
| pYoung9 | 0.5405 | 4.34 | 0.4789 | 3.49 | 0.2967 | 1.84 |
| pYoung8 |  |  | -0.0074 | -0.22 | -0.0381 | -1.14 |
| pYoung7 |  |  |  |  | 0.3385 | 1.72 |
| VacRate9 | 0.7184 | 7.56 | 0.6931 | 7.01 | 0.6674 | 6.39 |
| VacRate8 |  |  | 0.0327 | 0.19 | -0.2144 | -1.13 |
| VacRate7 |  |  |  |  | 0.9151 | 3.65 |
| OwnRate9 | -0.0943 | -2.47 | -0.1558 | -2.84 | -0.1652 | -3.01 |
| OwnRate8 |  |  | 0.0620 | 1.18 | 0.0738 | 1.35 |
| OwnRate7 |  |  |  |  | -0.0089 | -0.18 |
| NewConst9 | -0.1106 | -2.59 | -0.1022 | -1.79 | -0.1346 | -2.36 |
| NewConst8 |  |  | 0.0262 | 0.40 | 0.0849 | 0.96 |
| NewConst7 |  |  |  |  | -0.0545 | -1.03 |
| PreWar9 | -0.0716 | -1.49 | 0.0644 | 0.69 | -0.1175 | -1.01 |
| PreWar8 |  |  | -0.2094 | -2.31 | -0.1529 | -0.95 |
| PreWar7 |  |  |  |  | 0.0442 | 0.43 |
| Constant | 0.3341 | 5.64 | 0.3995 | 5.15 | 0.3994 | 4.07 |
| adj. r-sq. | 0.7046 |  | 0.7038 |  | 0.7078 |  |

while adding the lags of the other control variables. In the full specification ($s = r = 3$), explanatory power is high, although not many variables are significant. The significant variables include the once- and twice-lagged dependent variable, the proportion under age fifteen in 1990 and 1970, and the vacancy rate in 1990 and 1970, which are associated with more mixed income neighborhoods, and the 1970–1980 population growth rate, 1990 ownership rate, and 1990 new construction rate, which are associated with lower levels of *CoVa* in 2000. All the measures of neighborhood income are insignificant, which should reassure us that our measure of mixed income neighborhoods is not simply picking up the effect of lower average incomes, which is in the denominator of the dependent variable.

As a final look at the results of the regressions, I also compared results of a regression run with only the significant variables from the full specification, and compared those results with results from a parallel model run using the standard deviation of family income (in 2000 dollars) as the dependant variable. The predictive power of the regression with real standard deviation as the dependent variable was higher, but this is partly due to the fact that *CoVa* has been standardized for average income, which is highly persistent. Also remarkable was the lack of agreement between the two models on which explanatory variables are significant: only 1990 and 1970 vacancy rates and the 1990 proportion of new housing units are significant in both models. The dynamic behavior of standard deviation of income is also simpler: 2000 mixing (as measured by standard deviation) depends only on 1990 mixing and not on 1980 or 1970 levels of mixing.

As these results will be used in projecting future levels of income mixing into 2010, any spatial patterns in the regression residuals would be of special interest. Figure 12.3 presents the deciles of the predicted coefficient of variation in family incomes for visual comparison with the actual levels in figure 12.2. The broad patterns are similar, and (importantly) there is little spatial pattern to the residuals, with large and small errors in prediction distributed more or less evenly around the core counties of the region.

## CHANGES IN THE DYNAMICS OF MIXING BEHAVIOR

Before I use the coefficient estimates presented in the last section to make projections about future levels of income mixing, I pause to examine the stability of these dynamic relationships over time. The stability of these relationships is interesting for two reasons. First, projections based on current dynamic behavior must be taken with at least some skepticism. Such projections into the future are only valid if the dynamic behavior is stable over time. In essence, using the relationships that existed over the broad

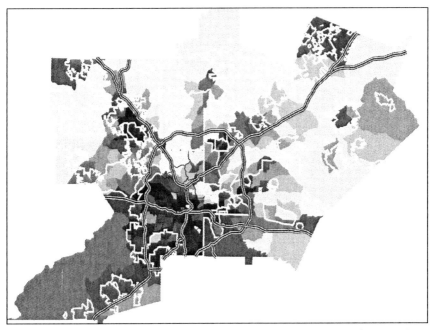

**Figure 12.3. Predicted *CoVa* (2000). "Note: grey scale represents deciles of predicted CoVa for 2000 from lowest (lightest) to highest (darkest), full specification."**

**Table 12.4 Stability of Relationship between *CoVa$_t$* and *CoVa$_{t-1}$*.**

Dependent Variable: *CoVa$_t$*

| | *t=* | | | | | |
|---|---|---|---|---|---|---|
| | 1980 | | 1990 | | 2000 | |
| | Coef. | t-stat | Coef. | t-stat | Coef. | t-stat |
| *CoVa$_{t-1}$* | 0.4623 | 8.38 | 0.7791 | 23.23 | 0.7883 | 21.07 |
| constant | 0.3359 | 8.30 | 0.1198 | 5.18 | 0.2013 | 8.08 |
| adj r-sq | 0.1364 | | 0.5509 | | 0.5021 | |

end of the twentieth century to project into the early twenty-first century is only valid if neighborhoods will continue to behave in a similar manner. If these empirical relationships are changing, we may not be able to put much faith in the projections.

A second reason to examine how neighborhood dynamics change is because it may interest some people in its own right. Over the past forty years, the Atlanta metropolitan area has undergone almost unimaginable change. The central city first began to empty out, and then filled up again. The population of the MSA as a whole and of the four core counties increased tremendously. The economy expanded and broadened. While it would be foolhardy to assume that these changes would not change the relationship between current and past income mixing at the neighborhood level, it is also interesting to see how these changes have affected those relationships. That is, the changes in the Atlanta economy may not have only changed neighborhoods, but also changed the way in which neighborhoods change. For these reasons, this section examines the stability of the dynamic relationship over time in this growing metropolis.

The four core counties of the Atlanta region had population of only 1.3 million in 1970. In 2000, this figure stood at 2.7 million, more than a 100 percent increase. In a city that has experienced as much change as Atlanta has, it would be surprising if the dynamics at work have remained unchanged through thirty years of development. Tables 12.4 and 12.5 show how the parameter estimates change as the time period $t$ in equations 1 and 2 changes. Because of data limitations, the full specification (with three lags in both the dependent and independent variables) is not possible except using the most recent, 2000 data. Table 12.4 shows how the relationship between *CoVa* and its realization in the previous period has changed. This coefficient has changed over the last thirty years, but in the last two decades it has remained fairly stable. Importantly, over the 1970s, mixed income neighborhoods appeared to be much less stable than they were over the 1980s and 1990s.[6]

Table 12.5 shows how the results change using three years of data, and when the additional control variables are included. For the regressions using only lagged dependent variables, the coefficients change substantially. When the control variables are added, the coefficient on the once-lagged dependent variable becomes very stable, but most of the other variables (including the twice-lagged dependant variable) had substantial changes in coefficients between 1990 and 2000. In fact, the simple correlation between the $t = 1990$ coefficients and the $t = 2000$ coefficients is -0.01! While the standard error for this correlation is no doubt incredibly complex, it seems safe to guess that this correlation is not statistically different from zero.[7] This instability in coefficients over time should give us pause when looking at projections made with any given set of regression results.

While the changes in the coefficients above may seem to be a narrowly technical point, it actually has some important practical implications. In the context of this chapter, it means that projections based on most recent information may be inaccurate if dynamic relationships continue to change. In a broader sense, it means that there is no reason to believe that casual observations even of very informed people can be trusted to yield useful predic-

**Table 12.5   Stability of Parameters with Three Years of Data**

Dependent Variable: $CoVa_t$

| | 1990 | | 2000 | | 1990 | | 2000 | |
|---|---|---|---|---|---|---|---|---|
| | Coef. | t-stat | Coef. | t-stat | Coef. | t-stat | Coef. | t-stat |
| $CoVa_{t-1}$ | 0.7474 | 20.52 | 0.5828 | 10.72 | 0.2473 | 5.53 | 0.2467 | 4.44 |
| $CoVa_{t-2}$ | 0.0774 | 1.71 | 0.2900 | 5.09 | 0.2292 | 4.89 | 0.1324 | 2.45 |
| $popgrw_{t-2}$ | | | | | 0.0096 | 1.46 | -0.0197 | -1.42 |
| $pWhite_{t-1}$ | | | | | -0.0951 | -3.19 | 0.0363 | 0.72 |
| $pWhite_{t-2}$ | | | | | -0.0172 | -0.51 | -0.0770 | -1.54 |
| $pOld_{t-1}$ | | | | | 0.2621 | 1.54 | -0.1931 | -0.85 |
| $pOld_{t-2}$ | | | | | -0.3322 | -1.25 | 0.5441 | 2.29 |
| $pYoung_{t-1}$ | | | | | 0.0080 | 0.27 | 0.3659 | 2.65 |
| $pYoung_{t-2}$ | | | | | 0.4723 | 3.32 | -0.0020 | -0.06 |
| $pCollege_{t-1}$ | | | | | 0.0114 | 0.14 | -0.1843 | -1.73 |
| $pCollege_{t-2}$ | | | | | -0.1633 | -1.45 | -0.0323 | -0.27 |
| $VacRat_{t-1}$ | | | | | -0.0499 | -0.31 | 0.6178 | 6.18 |
| $VacRat_{t-2}$ | | | | | 0.3407 | 1.54 | -0.0468 | -0.27 |
| $OwnRat_{t-1}$ | | | | | -0.1853 | -5.80 | -0.1856 | -3.75 |
| $OwnRat_{t-2}$ | | | | | -0.0387 | -1.01 | 0.0439 | 0.88 |
| $NewCons_{t-1}$ | | | | | -0.1692 | -3.02 | -0.1203 | -2.10 |
| $NewCons_{t-2}$ | | | | | 0.0043 | 0.09 | 0.0735 | 1.13 |
| $PreWar_{t-1}$ | | | | | 0.1959 | 1.78 | -0.0585 | -0.66 |
| $PreWar_{t-2}$ | | | | | -0.0694 | -0.80 | -0.0789 | -0.88 |
| Constant | 0.0857 | 2.59 | 0.1391 | 5.13 | 0.4125 | 5.49 | 0.5027 | 7.27 |
| adj. r-sq | 0.5431 | | 0.5289 | | 0.7027 | | 0.6848 | |

tions of future neighborhood outcomes. We all know that neighborhoods change. From past experience we may say that neighborhoods change in relatively predictable ways. The results in tables 12.4 and 12.5 suggest that the way in which neighborhoods change is changing. Experience with neighborhood change in the past will not necessarily give reliable foresight into a given neighborhood's prospects in the future, because the processes underlying neighborhood transition and evolution may themselves be evolving. This is an important point, as it draws our attention to the limits of our knowledge about neighborhoods and the complex dynamics playing out over a metropolitan area as it develops.

## PROJECTIONS

While the previous section highlights some limitations to our ability to foresee the future, we nonetheless can use the information from the most recent experiences to make predictions about the neighborhood level of income mixing in 2010. To do so, we use the estimated coefficients from the fourth section and multiply them by the independent variable for one less lag period than the coefficient was estimated with. In equations:

$$2) \quad \hat{\alpha}_0 + \sum_{s=1}^{3} \hat{\alpha}_s CoVa_{t-s+1} + \sum_{r=1}^{3} \hat{\alpha}_{3+r} X_{t-r+1} = E(CoVa_{t+1}).$$

In equation 2, the hat symbol represents an estimated coefficient, while the $E(.)$ operator represents the expected value of the variable in question. Thus, the coefficient for *CoVa*(1990) is multiplied by *CoVa*(2000), the coefficient for *Vacancy Rate* (1970) is multiplied by *Vacancy Rate* (1980), and so forth.

Figure 12.4 presents these projections. Figure 12.4 compares predicted levels of income mixing to the levels that pertained in 2000. In this figure, dark grey represents areas projected to become more income diverse, light grey areas are projected to become less income diverse, and middle grey areas are projected to have negligible changes (less than 10% in either direction). The presentation of the projections in figure 12.4 makes the spatial variation in projected trends easily visible. The projections suggest a major restructuring of neighborhood income mixing is underway. The concentration of highly mixed neighborhoods in the city's near southwest side is projected to become more homogenous, while the relatively stratified areas to the north and east are projected to become more diverse.

Some suggestive patterns come into focus. First, the homogenization of the near southwest side comes into focus as a solid block of light grey. Second, the inter-state highways seem to be associated with either positive or negative projected changes: the middle grey areas of the map generally do not straddle interstate highways.

Although the parameters are very unstable over time, the projections that arise from using these parameters are not as unstable. It is possible to take each of the sets of parameters in tables 12.4 and 12.5 and use them to create projections as in equation 2. Due to space limitations, I do not present these projections in detail, instead choosing to characterize the relationship between the sets of projections. These various sets of projections are correlated at between 0.85 and 0.99. However, the strong correlation does not imply that the projections are similar, only that they are generated from similar data.

Comparing the spatial pattern of predicted changes in income mixing across projections, one pattern emerges in most of them. In most projections, the impression emerges of a "border" area between the northeast and southwest sides of the city running approximately from the Bolton/Riverside area in the northwest of the city down through to the East Atlanta and Lakewood areas. This area is consistently projected to experience relative decreases in *CoVa* over the aughts. Roughly, this

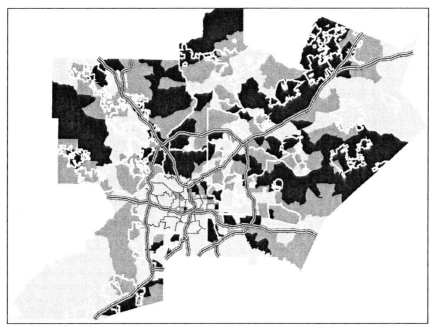

Figure 12.4. *CoVa2010/CoVa2000* Projected Changes. "Note: Projected CoVa for 2010 relative to actual CoVa for 2000. Dark grey: CoVa2010/CoVa2000>1.1; Light grey CoVa2010/CoVa2000<0.9; Middle grey: 0.9<CoVa2010/CoVa2000<1.1."

line across the city corresponds to the "gentrification border." The dire projections of declining income diversity there suggests that a process like that described in Krupka (2008) in which neighborhood transition leads to temporarily high income mixing may be taking place. The projected declines in mixing suggest that this process may be playing itself out. While there is some variation across the projections, most are consistent with this pattern, which is also apparent in the projections using the full set of predictors and most recent data.

While it would be foolhardy to trust too blindly in these projections, there are many reasons why one might favor the projections made using the most recent data. Intuitively, if parameters are changing, then the most recent ones would presumably be those most likely to be pertinent in the present period. One could also make a case that the instability of the parameters across the 1970s, 1980s, and 1990s is a result of the "filling up" of Atlanta over its development. If the core counties have stabilized over the 90s then the change in the parameters may be slowing in the aughts. Of course, only time will tell if the projections are accurate.

## CONCLUSION

This paper has examined the dynamics of income mixing in a major American city, Atlanta. Income mixing is persistent, but does not appear to be stable in the sense that the dynamics of income mixing will not preserve it in levels over time. These empirical results are similar to those presented for the national sample in Krupka (2008).

Whereas that paper uses contemporaneous data to predict income mixing, this paper focuses on the more speculative goal of predicting neighborhood level income mixing into the future. While the models appear to perform well, the projections that they produce are less stable. Depending on specification, the projections change. The projections made using the full specification provide sensible results, however they compete with several other sets of projections using fewer variables or different years.

Perhaps most interesting in these results is the change evident in the dynamic processes of mixed income neighborhoods. From decade to decade, the relationship between current income mixing and previous decade variables changes dramatically. This suggests that past experience may not always serve as a trustworthy guide of future changes in neighborhoods. Of course these results are only for one American city, and an exceptional one at that. Whether these results generalize to other metropolitan areas is an open and interesting question.

## NOTES

1. Duncan and Duncan (1955), Farley (1977), Massey and Eggers (1990), Miller and Quigley (1990), and Jargowski (1996) comprise a partial list of such direct evidence.

2. Miyao (1978), de Bartolome (1990), Frankel (1998), and de Bartolome and Ross (2003) are a few examples of this theoretical literature.

3. See Frankel and Volij (2007) and Massey and Denton (1988) for a longer discussion of the literature on the measurement of racial segregation.

4. Thanks to John Matthews of the Fiscal Research Center at Georgia State University and William J. Smith at West Georgia College for assistance with these neighborhood files.

5. It is also less strongly correlated with average income than the standard deviation is.

6. Specifications that also include the once-lagged control variables in all three years were also run to similar effect: the dynamic behavior of income mixing has stabilized since the 1970s.

7. The simple correlation between the t-statistics in the two columns is a much higher 0.57, suggesting that the same variables tended to be significant and have the same sign, however.

## REFERENCES

Alonso, William. *Location and Land Use.* Cambridge: Harvard University Press, 1965.

Coulton, Claudia, Thomas Cook, and Molly Irwin. "Aggregation issues in neighborhood research: A comparison of several levels of census geography and resident defined neighborhoods." CUPSC, Mandel School of Applied Social Sciences, Case Western Reserve University. 2004. digitalcase.case.edu:9000/fedora/get/ksl:2006052511/Cook-Agression-2004.pdf.

de Bartolome, Charles A.M. "Equilibrium and Inefficiency in a Community Model with Peer Group Effects." *Journal of Political Economy* 98, no. 1 (February 1990): 110–133.

de Bartolome, Charles A.M. and Stephen L. Ross. "Equilibria with Local Governments and Commuting: Income sorting vs. Income Mixing." *Journal of Urban Economics* 54, no. 1 (July 2003): 1–20.

Duncan, Otis D. and Beverly Duncan. "Residential Distribution and Occupational Stratification." *The American Journal of Sociology* 60, no. 5 (March 1955): 493–503.

Farley, Reynolds. "Residential Segregation in Urbanized Areas of the United States in 1970: An Analysis of Social Class and Racial Differences." *Demography* 14, no. 4 (November 1977): 497–518.

Frankel, David M. "A Pecuniary Reason for Income Mixing." *Journal of Urban Economics* 44, no. 1 (July 1998): 158–169.

Frankel, David M. and Oscar Volij. "Measuring Segregation." Working paper presented at the 2007 American Real Estate and Urban Economics Association Annual Meeting in Chicago, IL, January 2007. www.econ.upf.edu/docs/seminars/volij.pdf.

Jargowski, Paul A. "Take the Money and Run: Economic Segregation in the U.S. Metropolitan Areas." *American Sociological Review* 61, no. 6 (December 1996): 984–998.

Krupka, Douglas J. "The Stability of Mixed-Income Neighborhoods in America." Institute of the Study of Labor, Bonn, Discussion Paper No. 3370. 2008. ftp.iza.org/dp3370.pdf.

Massey, Douglas S. and Nancy A. Denton. "The Dimensions of Residential Segregation." *Social Forces* 67, no. 2 (December 1988): 281–315.

Massey, Douglas S. and Mitchell L. Eggers. "The Ecology of Inequality: Minorities and the Concentration of Poverty, 1970–1990." *The American Journal of Sociology* 95, no. 5 (March 1990): 1153–1188.

Miller, Vincent P. and John M. Quigley. "Segregation by Racial and Demographic Group: Evidence from the San Francisco Bay Area." *Urban Studies* 27, no. 1 (February 1990): 3–21.

Miyao, Takahiro. "Dynamic Instability of a Mixed City in the Presence of Neighborhood Externalities." *The American Economic Review* 68, no. 3 (June 1978): 454–463.

Schelling, Thomas C. "Models of Segregation." *The American Economic Review* 59, no. 2 (May 1969): 488–493.

Tiebout, Charles M. "A Pure Theory of Local Expenditures." *The Journal of Political Economy* 64, no. 5 (October 1956): 416–424.

Wilson, William Julius. *The Truly Disadvantaged: The Inner City, the Underclass and Public Policy*. Chicago: University of Chicago Press, 1987.

# Chapter 13

# Exploring Civil Rights Heritage Tourism and Historic Preservation as Revitalization Tools

## Glenn T. Eskew

Atlanta took the lead in civil rights heritage tourism by initiating the process of memorializing the movement in the months after the Reverend Dr. Martin Luther King Jr.'s tragic assassination in 1968. The vision of his widow Coretta Scott King to commemorate her husband's life and work for civil rights reform through the creation of a historic district that showcased sites in Atlanta related to movement history became a model for other cities. For the next twenty years, Atlanta boasted the only major shrine to the postwar racial struggle against segregation. A failure to capitalize on that advantage left Atlanta holding inadequate resources with which to compete against other cities such as Birmingham and Memphis when they developed their own products to market in the burgeoning civil rights industry. Despite having tapped corporate as well as local, state, and federal resources earlier in the process and with greater success, by the early 1990s, the King Shrine Area appeared lackluster, having failed to spark an urban renewal of historic Auburn Avenue as had happened in the restored civil rights districts surrounding the Lorraine Motel in Memphis and Kelly Ingram Park in Birmingham. When the National Park Service opened a new facility in time for the 1996 Summer Olympics, Atlanta finally had a functioning civil rights attraction with adequate interpretation, parking, and bathrooms for tourists, but the revitalization of the surrounding Old Fourth Ward neighborhood lagged behind. Not until Georgia State University expanded into the area did the long awaited redevelopment materialize. By reviewing the history of Atlanta's Martin Luther King, Jr. Civil Rights District, the use of historic preservation and heritage tourism can be evaluated as tools of economic revitalization in depressed areas while also shedding light on persistent problems that have plagued Atlanta's effort to memorialize the movement.

Tribute must go to Coretta Scott King who, as the martyred leader's widow, envisioned the memorial within a historic district as the appropriate way to honor the apostle of nonviolence and the movement he led. At first she confronted limited resources with which to commemorate the man, having inherited little money, few tangible personal items, and some private property owned by the family. Given the role of Ebenezer Baptist Church as the pastorate held by three generations of the family and that King's grandmother still owned King's birth home, the two block area along Auburn Avenue in which these properties were located provided the center for a historic district. Using the built environment that she had access to, Coretta Scott King linked together a King Shrine Area in the Old Fourth Ward that pilgrims could visit.

But a memorial based on historic sites proved incomplete given the man's philosophical teachings of nonviolence which promised to revolutionize the world, so Coretta Scott King proposed something grander: an "Institute for Non-Violent Social Change." Such a facility would allow an activist agenda to continue the work of Dr. King. In the institute she could place his many papers, speeches, and books, thereby providing a written repository of his life work for scholars and students to study. At first she thought the institute might be housed at Atlanta University on the city's West End. She asked the noted historian and civil rights veteran Dr. Vincent Harding if he might head the institute from his office at Spelman College, which he agreed to do in 1969.

Yet the very nature of Coretta Scott King's vision created a bifurcated mission for her civil rights memorial as it involved the management of a historic district as well as the promotion of King's teachings. Consequently what emerged as the Martin Luther King, Jr. Center for Non-violent Social Change, Incorporated set for itself two difficult objectives that competed over scarce resources. By the end of her direct involvement in the center, both objectives had met with limited success. On the one hand she had successfully built a monument to King and convinced the United States Congress to ratify the national King holiday celebrated every January. On the other hand, the King Center lacked an endowment to maintain its aging facilities and the King birthday observation did little to further the cause of civil rights. Nevertheless Coretta Scott King's bifurcated vision became a model for other cities such as Memphis and Birmingham that created monuments to the civil rights struggle that also promoted social justice.[1]

To achieve her objectives, Coretta Scott King set up and retained control of two entities that have played key roles in Atlanta's memorial effort. To settle King's personal affairs, she joined family attorneys in creating the

King estate as a trust that could hold intellectual and personal property including King's speeches, books, papers, and other memorabilia, handle issues of copyright, and determine licensing fees for the financial benefit of the heirs. To memorialize the man, she joined family attorneys in setting up the nonprofit Martin Luther King, Jr., Center for Nonviolent Social Change, Inc. that could institutionalize King's legacy in a memorial and accept gifts from well-wishers. On the board of directors managing the King Estate and the King Center, Coretta King placed King's sister, Christine King Farris, Jesse Hill, and other Atlanta black businessmen, and Ambassador Andrew Young and other trusted King advisors. With interlocking directorates linking the two boards, the lines between the King Estate and the King Center often blurred as when Coretta Scott King promoted a library for the nonprofit King Center that would house papers owned by the for profit King estate. Soon the King Center provided monetary compensation and other perks for King family members. Indeed through the King Center, Coretta Scott King created for herself a livelihood.[2]

Atlanta's leaders endorsed Coretta Scott King's idea of creating a King Shrine Area in a historic district carved out of Atlanta's Old Fourth Ward. White leaders eager to show their support for the King family, from Mayor Ivan Allen and Vice-Mayor Sam Massell to Coca-Cola's Robert W. Woodruff debated "how Atlanta can fittingly memorialize" its most famous native son through a "living, productive" memorial on Auburn Avenue. They saw the Old Fourth Ward as the perfect location for interpreting Atlanta's black history. Indeed they hoped that by developing some kind of memorial they might reverse the urban decline that seriously threatened the black residential and commercial area on the east side of the central business district.[3]

As the historic "black street" in Atlanta, Auburn Avenue, or "Sweet Auburn" as Atlanta's unofficial black mayor John Wesley Dobbs dubbed it, hummed with the bustle of black enterprise during the age of segregation. Originally called Wheat Street, the road stretched from the city's historic center of Five Points out into the leafy streetcar suburb of Inman Park. To dress up the neighborhood the city renamed the street Auburn Avenue. Prior to 1900, black and white people lived side-by-side in frame cottages and fine Queen Anne residences built by German immigrants and African Americans. With Atlanta's Race Riot of 1906 however, the city adopted segregation laws that divided the races and led to the relocation of many black businesses from the central business district to Auburn and parallel Edgewood Avenue. Black professionals followed, buying the houses once owned by whites who moved farther from the city center as this area of the Old Fourth Ward became predominantly African American. To house the black doctors, dentists, pharmacists, architects, builders, and lawyers, black investors such as Henry A. Rucker constructed offices such as the

Rucker Building, and fraternal groups such as the Odd Fellows and Prince Hall Masons built suites attached to auditoriums with other retail spaces available for rent. Black entrepreneurs such as former slave Alonzo F. Herndon founded such local institutions as Atlanta Life Insurance, a company located near the junction of Auburn Avenue and Atlanta's central business district. Nearby First Congregational Church anchored the corner of Courtland Street while further down Auburn Avenue stand Big Bethel African Methodist Episcopal, Wheat Street Baptist, and Ebenezer Baptist Churches, these four dominating the neighborhood although smaller churches existed on side streets.[4]

No sooner had "Sweet Auburn" emerged as Atlanta's principal black business address than a perceptible shift began to draw African Americans to the West End. The great fire of 1917 that skirted the sides of Auburn Avenue had left a scar between Fort and Young Streets and encouraged movement away from this congested low-lying area known as "Darktown." While spared the sweep of the blaze, the fire had threatened the nearby gabled Queen Anne and gothic cottages with their pine shake shingles farther up the avenue.[5] The black entrepreneur Heman E. Perry, who had arrived on Auburn in 1908 and over the next two decades built an empire that included an insurance company, several businesses, and a bank, began to speculate in real estate around the Atlanta University neighborhood. He founded the Service Realty Company to subdivide and develop a black housing district adjacent to the municipal Washington Park for Negroes. With the concentration of institutions of higher learning—Morehouse and Spelman Colleges as well as Atlanta University—all in the area, the West End became the new fashionable section of town for the black middle class. Soon black businesses and professionals followed the residents to the subdivisions being financed and constructed by Perry. Although he overextended himself and his enterprises collapsed in 1925 leaving only the bank—Citizens Trust Company—in operation, the area continued to draw new residents, especially given its easy accessibility to downtown made by public transit and the automobile. As a consequence, Auburn Avenue entered a period of decline after World War I that slowed with the Great Depression and World War II but picked up with increasing speed in the postwar era.[6]

Changes in Auburn Avenue's housing stock reflected the shift in the neighborhood. In the first half of the twentieth century, prominent black ministers and educators owned many of the finer two-story Victorian houses. Locals called the blocks on either side of Boulevard "Bishops Row" because here lived Colored Methodist Episcopal Church Bishop Lucius Henry Holsey, the Reverends A. D. Williams of Ebenezer Baptist, and Peter James Bryant of Wheat Street Baptist, and Principal Charles L. Harper of Booker T. Washington High School. Yet the large single-family houses that had been the norm in the neighborhood were replaced after 1900 by rental properties such as the rows of shotgun houses leased by black workers from the Empire State Investment Company. On nearby Houston Street at the turn of the century, stood the handsome homes of the Rucker, White, and other elite black families in Atlanta, but by the 1920s investors had constructed near these houses noisy factories, laundries, and other enterprises that employed African Americans.[7]

During the Great Depression and World War II, urban planners evaluated how best to grapple with Atlanta's many problems brought on by economic collapse, unchecked population growth, and increased traffic congestion. In 1946 the city's white elite endorsed the Lochner Report that called for three major expressways to cross in the city adjacent to the central business district with two of the roads combining into a downtown connector. A bond issue paid for the initial construction while in time the federal interstate program picked up the tab for much of the rest of Atlanta's highway construction that became Interstates 20, 75, and 85 as well as the 285 bypass that surrounds the city. Representatives from Atlanta's black and white community power structures negotiated the location of the roadways with a compromise worked out that had the downtown connector cut across Auburn with exit ramps accessing Edgewood in the low-lying area near where the 1917 fire had begun.[8] The construction split the Auburn Avenue neighborhood in half. While the more prosperous residents moved to the West End, many of those black Atlantans tied to the cultural institutions on "Sweet Auburn" remained behind in the East End.

For years the Williams and King families had lived at 501 Auburn Avenue. A white fireman stationed in Atlanta Fire Station #6 located on the corner of Auburn and Boulevard had built the house in 1895 but sold it to the Reverend A. D. Williams in 1909. As pastor of Ebenezer Baptist Church, the Reverend Williams used the house as the parsonage until his death in 1931. In 1926 his daughter Alberta had married a young Baptist preacher named Martin Luther King who joined his father-in-law on the ministerial staff of Ebenezer. The Kings moved into the home, and it was at 501 Auburn Avenue that Alberta gave birth to Martin Luther King, Jr. on January 15, 1929. The couple had two other children here, A. D. W. King and Christine King. With the death of A.D.'s widow Jennie C. Williams in 1941, the King family moved three blocks down the street to 193 Boulevard while retaining the ownership of 501 Auburn Avenue, which transferred to Alberta Williams King who kept the property and rented it out to tenants. While Martin Luther King, Jr., never again lived in the house, he returned to the neighborhood in 1960 when he joined his father, "Daddy King," on the staff of Ebenezer Baptist Church as an associate pastor. Also in 1960 the Southern Christian Leadership Conference, a civil rights group King had helped organize in Atlanta in 1957 and that had elected him president, opened an office in the Prince Hall Mason build-ing just a block down and across the street from Ebenezer Baptist Church. Although King purchased a home at 234 Sunset Avenue, Northwest in the Vine City area near the West End, for the rest of his working life in At-lanta—from the pulpit at Ebenezer or from his SCLC office in the Masonic lodge—King was on Auburn Avenue. This legacy provided the rationale for Coretta King's memorial district.[9]

Grand visions require funding, and private entities opened up to the King family. Friends and supporters donated money to the Martin Luther King, Jr., Center for Nonviolent Social Change which was incorporated as a nonprofit under the laws of the state of Georgia and which received 501 (c) 3 status from the Internal Revenue Service. With the money, Coretta King and the board purchased property for the site of the memorial on Auburn Avenue in the block of Ebenezer Baptist Church, just below Boulevard and the birth home. The center then hired the minority archi-tectural firm of Bond, Ryder, James, to design a cluster of buildings that could appropriately memorialize the civil rights martyr with a gravesite and a small chapel, house the center, and exhibit materials. The assort-ment of projects allowed for the memorial to be constructed in pieces. Private donors financed the buildings by making tax-deductible contribu-tions.[10]

Although the initial plan had been to place the archive of King speeches, books, and other materials at the Atlanta University Center, Coretta King decided to add a library and archive to her memorial thereby expanding the King Center's operations to include maintenance of these materi-als. In the short term, the papers remained in the West End where they were closed to scholars. In December 1969, the Ford Foundation gave the nonprofit King Center its first major grant, $100,000, to process King's papers, the first of many grants and awards to make these materials avail-able to the public. As the Ford Foundation explained, "the Institute is an experimental organization of intellectuals who seek, through research and reflection, to define, elaborate, and interpret the black experience," while the "Library-Documentation Project" which the grant funded, "is to collect and house the papers of Dr. King and other southern civil rights leaders."[11]

Organizers planned King's gravesite as the centerpiece of the memorial. The Bond, Ryder, James design featured the placement of King's tomb in the middle of the block equidistant from Ebenezer Baptist Church and the King Center's proposed Freedom Hall. With landscaping to Auburn Av-enue, pilgrims could drive up and pay their respects. Initially King's body had been interred in the family plot in South View Cemetery where now his father and mother are buried. A somber King Day ceremony in January 1970 relocated the martyr's remains from the cemetery to a marble sarcophagus placed on the memorial grounds.[12]

When black political empowerment achieved the election of an African American as mayor of Atlanta in the fall of 1973, city support for the King memorial project increased significantly. Within a year of Mayor Maynard Jackson's inauguration, the city had announced plans to construct a community center on the block of Auburn Avenue across from Ebenezer Baptist Church and King's crypt. In January 1975 Coretta King joined Mayor Jackson in unveiling plans for the $2.8 million dollar facility funded with federal grants and a $1 million dollar donation from Robert W. Woodruff. Once completed, the city-owned King Community Center housed offices for Atlanta Legal Aid, a branch of the Atlanta Public Library, a gymnasium and recreation room staffed by the city's parks department, and a child care program.[13]

By 1975 Coretta Scott King had raised $6 million dollars in private contributions, and so the King Center broke ground for its $10 million dollar administrative building and archives. That year the U. S. Department of the Interior listed the King birth home on the National Register of Historic Places. King's mother, Alberta Williams King, donated the house to the King Center that started to renovate the 1895 Queen Anne with the goal of restoring it to the appearance of King's childhood and then opening it up for tours.[14]

By 1977 construction at the King memorial site enabled the family to open the Interfaith Peace Chapel that filled in the property next to Ebenezer Baptist Church. A water feature of rectangular cascading pools stretched the length of the grounds, emptying into a large body of water in the center of which floated a circular island on which sat the relocated sarcophagus as the "permanent entombment of Dr. King." With its perpetual flame nearby, King's crypt became one of Atlanta's top tourist attractions.[15]

In 1977 industrialist Henry Ford II announced a campaign to raise the final $8 million needed to construct the Freedom Hall centerpiece with its auditorium, gift shop, and classrooms anchoring the corner of Boulevard and Auburn Avenues. The Ford Motor Company pledged $1 million while the United Auto Workers gave $600,000 from its strike fund. The King Center broke ground on this final phase of the Bond, Ryder, James design in October 1979. As Dexter Scott King later recalled, "We watched it all come up out of nothing—the reflecting pool and arched, covered walkway known as 'Freedom Walkway.' Next the administration building went up, then adjacent to it, Freedom Hall. . . . The construction of the center was rewarding to Mother, because it was her insurance that her husband's message and spirit would endure."[16] As the *Atlanta Constitution* recognized, Coretta Scott King had created "a thirteen million dollar complex of monuments and buildings in the heart of what the government officially calls a 'stricken area' surrounded by poor people."[17]

By 1979, the King Center listed other resources worth $1.8 million including rental property and other real estate. That year it received $218,000 in mailed donations and $50,000 from the Bee Gees. It sold $175,000 in souvenirs and made $5,000 on one-dollar tours of the King Birth Home. Yet expenses ate away at the King Center's revenues as it posted a $750,000 annual operating budget. Consequently the Atlanta *Constitution* noted, "a number of black Atlantans perceive a river of money flowing into the center and a trickle of services to the people."[18]

By the early 1980s the King Center had built out the Bond, Ryder, James design. It dedicated Freedom Hall in January 1982. It then retired its $10 million debt on the buildings in 1984 using donations from IBM, Coca-Cola, Disney, Southern Bell, Xerox, and the National Education Association. Also the U.S. government gave $4 million and money came from the kingdoms of Kuwait and Saudi Arabia. Coretta Scott King had successfully combined private and public monies to build her vision of a memorial to Dr. King. Yet once her initial wish that the federal government might get involved in the area came true, fears erupted over how the National Park Service would alter life in the Old Fourth Ward.[19]

During his last year in office, President Jimmy Carter pushed through Congress legislation designed to bring substantial federal support to the King Shrine Area. Already the U. S. Department of the Interior had listed the King Birth Home, Ebenezer Baptist Church, and the surrounding neighborhood on the National Register of Historic Places in 1974 and then designated this "Sweet Auburn Historic District" its highest status as a National Historic Landmark in 1976. What Carter and the Congress envisioned was the creation of a National Park at the historic site. On October 10, 1980, Congress passed legislation that created the Martin Luther King, Jr., National Historic Site and Preservation District, using the same "Sweet Auburn Historic District" area of nearly 24 acres enclosed on the north by Old Wheat Street, east by Howell Street, south by Edgewood Avenue, and west by Jackson Street. The legislation authorized the National Park Service (NPS) to get actively involved in the neighborhood.[20]

Having targeted the King Shrine Area, the NPS began its work cautiously. The legislation charged the NPS with the obligation "to protect and interpret for the benefit, inspiration, and education of present and future generations the places where Martin Luther King, Junior, was born, where he lived, worked, and worshipped, and where he is buried." Consequently the NPS initiated systematic studies of the area. Given the natural fear of federal encroachment on local authority, the NPS struggled to allay fears of area residents. It hired two noted African American historians from Atlanta, Dr. Alexa Henderson and Dr. Eugene Walker, to write a report which, once published by the U. S. Printing Office in 1984 became *Sweet Auburn: The Thriving Hub of Black Atlanta, 1900-1960*. Two years later the NPS Southeast Region under Regional Director Robert Baker published the *General Management Plan and Development Concept Plan for the Martin Luther King, Jr., National Historic Site & Preservation District*. Released in February 1986, this publication set forth the idea that federal involvement in the King Shrine Area would halt the decline of the neighborhood and lead to its redevelopment. As the report made clear "One purpose of the development program has been to identify ways to integrate the park with the surrounding area and to capitalize on the presence of the park as a focus of economic revitalization." Designed to direct NPS activities in the area over the next ten years, the plan charged the city of Atlanta with the need to adopt historic preservation guidelines for district buildings and to promote tourism in the area. Federal involvement proved crucial in stabilizing the properties around the King Birth Home, gravesite, and Ebenezer Baptist Church.[21]

With the hope of economic renewal along Auburn Avenue, the NPS also recognized the need to work with current residents and to protect their interests. The plan acknowledged "the low incomes of most residents make them extremely vulnerable to displacement caused by rising property values and rents. While the National Park Service will not force anyone out of the residences it acquires, it can do nothing to prevent displacement of residents from privately owned homes or apartments. If the area does revive economically, people could be involuntarily displaced from their homes and places of business." As late as 1983 there still lived in family homes descendents of the turn-of-the-century African Americans who had first moved to Auburn Avenue. Yet sixty-five percent of the area residents rented, many of them by the week. There developed in the neighborhood "a climate of distrust toward the Park Service and a general sense of anxiety among many residents of the Park who fear imminent eviction." Consequently the NPS developed plans to assist area residents to stay in their homes by stabilizing rents.[22]

During the 1970s, historic preservation strategies had developed that assisted neighborhoods in Atlanta fighting urban decline. Two such communities near Auburn Avenue had successfully turned around the decay that comes from cutting up houses into absentee-owned rental apartments with collapsing property values. In Inman Park, Atlanta's first streetcar suburb just down Edgewood Avenue from the King Shrine Area, preservationists in the 1970s had stopped commercial encroachment and the tearing down of houses by restoring these Victorian mansions to their former glory. A similar transition occurred during the 1980s in Cabbagetown, a mill village located just down Boulevard from the King Historic District. In support of efforts to use historic preservation in the Auburn Avenue area, the National

Park Service prepared a Catalog of Historic Structures that listed the properties in the area. Then the Atlanta Urban Design Commission prepared the Martin Luther King Jr. Landmark District Residential Design Guidelines. These were to be used by the commission to make sure that repairs to historic properties followed the requirements of the secretary of the U. S. Department of the Interior. The preservation strategies worked to maintain the historic look of the King district.[23]

Once on the site in the 1980s, the National Park Service began to reinterpret its mission in response to visitor needs. It assisted the King Center by stepping in to guide tourists through the King Birth Home, which became Georgia's number one tourist attraction, drawing a half million people in 1985. It established a kiosk for the distribution of information regarding historic properties in the King Shrine Area and it offered walking tours.[24] Yet the 1986 NPS plan recognized "the Martin Luther King, Jr., Center for Nonviolent Social Change (the King Center), which carries on the work of Dr. King, will continue to memorialize him and explain his philosophies and legacy to visitors. The National Park Service will not establish a major visitor center in the national historic site." While the NPS defined its responsibilities as "historic preservation," it also claimed the "interpretation of Dr. King's life" as one of its objectives. The 1986 management plan also noted "Visitors currently are limited in what they can see and learn about Dr. King and the Sweet Auburn community. Visitor services and facilities are lacking. And that current visitor use places a severe strain on the limited resources of the King Center."[25]

The announcement in September 1990 that Atlanta would host the 1996 Olympics offered an opportunity for the NPS to change all that. Park Service officials proposed a federal visitor center with rest facilities and interactive exhibits, the restoration of an 1896 fire station and other significant buildings, off-street parking for buses, and a new landscape for a total bill of $11 million. More than two million tourists visited the site in 1991 with an estimated five million projected for 1996. The proposal called for demolishing the city-owned Martin Luther King Community Center and building on that site an interpretative center and a new sanctuary for Ebenezer Baptist Church that would then turn its old National Historic Landmark sanctuary over to rangers for regular tours. The federal government won the support of Ebenezer's clergy, Atlanta's elected officials, and Georgia's Congressional delegation. Although the Bush administration had funded $2.2 million dollars for King-oriented restoration work in 1992, the Clinton administration secured the necessary $11 million dollars in November 1993.[26]

. As the federal government made its move, negative reports regarding the King Center appeared in the local media. Since the 1980s internal reports had decried "a serious cash flow problem" and "severe financial crisis" fueling speculation about mismanagement. With a bloated staff, the nonprofit began running deficits so staggering that when Coretta Scott King attempted to raise money for an endowment, she found few supporters. Disagreements within the family circle led to leadership changes at the King Center as Coretta Scott King stepped down as CEO, turning the operation over to her youngest son. In April 1989 a divided board of directors had appointed Dexter Scott King acting president of the King Center but he resigned after several months over conflicts with these elder advisors to Mrs. King. Five years later, a new board reelected him to the post in October 1994. He immediately took on the federal government.[27]

Trying to scuttle the National Park Service plans for an interpretative center in the King Shrine Area, Dexter Scott King proposed an alternative to be built by the private King Center. His proposal offered a Disney-like, "high-tech, virtual reality, interactive museum" called "The King Time Machine." Neither the King Center nor the King estate had funding in place for the estimated $40 to $60 million project, but both demanded that the city of Atlanta, Ebenezer Baptist Church, and the federal government reserve the land in question for the King Center and its envisioned high-tech "Dream." Nevertheless supporters of the NPS plan stood firm and in the end Dexter Scott King backed down.[28]

Barely making the Olympics, the National Park Service opened its King National Historic Site Visitor Center in June 1996. In addition to the bathrooms, bookstore, large lobby, and offices for staff, the center contains an interactive display. As in other civil rights museums, the exhibitory followed a Montgomery to Memphis trajectory using monochromatic lifecast mannequins to represent civil rights demonstrators fighting for racial justice. In support of the federal government's investment in the area, the city of Atlanta spent millions of dollars dressing up Auburn Avenue. It installed new granite and block sidewalks with interpretative stones that told the history of the neighborhood. It redeveloped the area under the downtown connector so that concessions might be offered there to the anticipated thousands of tourists headed to the King site during the Olympics. After completing its new building across Auburn Avenue from its old facility, Ebenezer Baptist Church turned over its historic sanctuary to the National Park Service. Indeed a perceptible shift had occurred in the look of the street, but surrounding properties remained plagued by low rents in a high crime area. The NPS stabilization of housing stock halted the decline and began a turnaround in housing prices that escalated with the return of middle class residents to in-town communities after 2000. The expansion of Georgia State University into the area convinced other local institutions such as Big Bethel African Methodist Episcopal Church to redevelop its properties. The university's purchase of major business offices, building of multimillion-dollar dorm complexes, and financing of condominiums at last secured the economic revitalization of the "Sweet Auburn" area around the King Memorial.[29]

In contrast to Atlanta, both Birmingham and Memphis at first shunned references to their civil rights legacies, perhaps an understandable outcome given their notorious reputations for violent race relations. In 1963, Birmingham's city commissioner for public safety pitted police dogs and fire hoses against nonviolent black children protesting for equal access to the system. In 1968 Memphis law enforcement was suspected of duplicity following the shooting death of King on the balcony of the Lorraine Motel. Nearly twenty years passed before municipal leaders in these two cities even considered memorializing the movement. About the time the National Park Service became a participant in the King Shrine Area, local activists in Birmingham and Memphis began calling for civil rights commemorations in their cities.

Historic preservation provided the impetus to memorialize the movement in Memphis. The vision for the National Civil Rights Museum belongs to D'Army Bailey, a black native of the city and Yale Law School graduate who early on recognized the importance of the Lorraine Motel as an appropriate site of conscience for civil rights heritage tourism. Once an anchor of black Memphis, the Lorraine and surrounding businesses had deteriorated into a drug and prostitute infested landscape. Foreclosure put the motel up for auction and Bailey helped organize the Martin Luther King Memphis Memorial Foundation in 1982 that raised money to buy the building for $144,000. Appeals to Coretta Scott King for an endorsement met with a threatened lawsuit because of the name of the group and a rebuke from the King estate because of its hostility towards the site of King's death. Al Davis, the spokesman for Coretta Scott King, explained she "opposes" the Memphis memorial because she "prefers that the focus on Dr. King be on his life and not his death." He added that "She's not in favor of making [the motel] a museum and she has told them that." Davis went on to say that the King Center in Atlanta "has a museum" but that "its primary focus is on working for causes King likely would be working for were he still alive." In early 1983, the Memphis group changed its name to the Lorraine Civil Rights Museum Foundation.[30]

D'Army Bailey struggled to raise seed money for the idea. He appealed to city and county leaders for support and received $45,000 from Center City Commission and Future Memphis to fund an exploration of the project. The money paid former Smithsonian curator Benjamin Lawless to conceptualize exhibits for the space. Using this museum proposal, the Lorraine Foundation worked Tennessee's halls of power. In a show of black political empowerment, the Tennessee General Assembly gave the effort $4.4 million dollars in April 1986. The city of Memphis and Shelby County governments contributed an additional $2.2 million dollars each for a total public outlay of \$8.8 million in tax dollars with which to fund the museum.[31]

Designers called for the renovation of the original Lorraine Motel into exhibitory space accessed from the back with new construction as additional square footage in the rear. The plans retained the historic façade with its motor court entrance and parking and restored the landmark sign, using its marquee for announcements. The Lorraine's exhibits, from Montgomery to Memphis message to monochromatic life-cast mannequins, set the tone of civil rights memorialization.[32]

In January 1989, the facility got its new name: The National Civil Rights Museum. As work neared completion, the Lorraine Foundation arranged a sneak preview for Rosa Parks and other dignitaries on July 4, 1991, including Coretta Scott King who, despite having opposed the museum every step of the way, agreed to attend in return for a \$15,000 payment. The grand opening of the facility took place on August 31, 1991. It met with mixed reviews, most damningly from *Time* magazine, which ridiculed what it called "a classic jumble of laudable intentions and bad taste." [33]

Despite a popular response, self-sufficiency proved illusive. Around 100,000 people toured the facility annually in the 1990s. Attempting to connect to other tourist attractions, the city created a "Civil Rights Plaza" linking the museum to the Main Street trolley as a "catalytic project" designed to revitalize the neighborhood by promoting art galleries and fancy restaurants that hinged on tourist traffic. The strategy worked as the number of tourist increased to 160,000 annually in 2007 with adults paying \$12 to tour the museum.[34]

In Birmingham, municipal leaders also used public money to build a civil rights memorial. The idea is attributed to Mayor David Vann, a veteran of the 1963 demonstrations who in 1979 toured a holocaust memorial and decided a similar museum would help heal the city's racial divide. Civic leaders picked up the idea for their 1980 *Master Plan for Downtown Birmingham* with the proposed museum anchoring a civil rights district that could revitalize the stricken area around Kelly Ingram Park. The election of Birmingham's first black mayor, Richard Arrington, signified black political empowerment, and Arrington appointed a biracial task force of dedicated civil servants, movement veterans, and historians that conceptualized what became the Birmingham Civil Rights Institute. Yet little happened until 1985 when the city government purchased for a half million dollars property across the street from Sixteenth Street Baptist Church and beside Kelly Ingram Park, the ground zero of the 1963 demonstrations. Six months later the Birmingham City Council allocated nearly a million dollars for the project and shifted another \$1.5 million dollars in federal revenue sharing funds to support the effort. Mayor Arrington explained the public's \$3 million dollar investment by saying "I believe that the Civil Rights Museum has great potential for our community in establishing Birmingham as a tourist attraction."[35]

Big plans require major funding. Twice Mayor Arrington appealed to the voters to pass a bond issue designed to pay for construction costs. Twice Birmingham's 65 percent majority black voters turned down the mayor's request, first in 1986, and then in 1988. Vowing to find the money Arrington sold city-owned surplus property and earmarked the $7 million dollars for construction costs. In July 1990 Arrington let the contracts that allowed the proposed Birmingham Civil Rights Institute to materialize in bricks and mortar. Following the 1980 *Master Plan*, city government promoted historic preservation and adaptive reuse strategies to renovate the neighborhood. The federal Street Improvements Warrant Program redesigned Kelly Ingram Park by adding brick walkways to a central water feature that declared "From Revolution to Reconciliation." Across the park the city positioned five art installations depicting scenes from the climatic civil rights struggle paid for through a National Endowment for the Arts-funded competition. The city financed the redevelopment of Fourth Avenue North, Birmingham's Auburn Avenue, by providing grants and loans to minority business owners. The once segregated Carver Theater found new life as the city funded the Birmingham Jazz Hall of Fame. The infusion of public monies halted the decline of this once thriving black middle class area.[36]

Just before it opened, the city government transformed the biracial task force into the Birmingham Civil Rights Institute Board of Directors, which incorporated as a nonprofit and filed for its 501(c)(3) status from the IRS. The board then leased from the city for $300 dollars a year the brand new museum that remained publicly owned. Independent from city management, the board hired its own employees and set up its own budget. It could solicit tax-deductible contributions from private corporations, citizens, and foundations as well as public support. In November 1992, Mayor Arrington and other dignitaries cut ribbons symbolizing the completion of the $12 million dollar project as crowds rushed to tour the Birmingham Civil Rights Institute. It had taken over thirteen years, but Birmingham's city government had planned and built what quickly became Alabama's number one tourist attraction, received rave reviews in national media outlets, and contributed greatly to the state's growing African American heritage tourism industry. Thirteen years later, the Birmingham Civil Rights Institute attracts a quarter of a million people annually and remains one of the state's top tourist draws with a $2.2 million dollar annual budget derived in part from $10 ticket sales. City government gives the institute substantial annual contributions such as $700,000 for FY 2007. And the Institute works to increase its endowment that had reached only $733,000 by 2007, much of which derived from corporate donations that followed the Institute's successful opening. Programming at the Institute promotes a greater understanding among the races in Birmingham.[37]

By comparing the institutional histories of the civil rights memorials in Atlanta, Memphis, and Birmingham, some general observations may be made. All three began by focusing on a historic landscape featuring buildings associated with the civil rights struggle. All three depended on public support to get the doors opened and continue to rely on tax dollars to keep them open. All three enjoy an expanding civil rights heritage tourism industry that attracts visitors to the area. And, with the contemporaneous building of the National Park Service's King facility, all three share a uniform look and design, from the Montgomery to Memphis interpretative refrain to the monochromatic life-cast mannequins on display. The difference between Birmingham, Memphis, and Atlanta is the legacy of the failed King Center.

Tax dollars paid for the Birmingham Civil Rights Institute and the National Civil Rights Museum in Memphis, with both of these properties becoming publicly owned although leased out to nonprofit corporations set up to manage them. Neither of these facilities had material relics or memorabilia for display when their projects began. Both created archives for manuscripts and other papers and hired curatorial staffs to manage these collections. Both retained as part of their missions the desire to be an agent for social change, although this has been interpreted largely through pedagogical strategies for teaching school children tolerance.

In contrast, only Atlanta had in hand historic materials and mementos from the movement that could comprise museum displays. Yet for whatever reason, the King estate failed to allow the King Center to develop extensive exhibits using loaned family materials. While the King Center received millions of dollars in taxpayer contributions and millions more from private foundations and worker-supported institutions, the facility remained privately owned and managed by Dr. King's friends and heirs. Public sympathy for the family inhibited demands for full accountability of the King Center's use of these financial resources. Pointed criticisms of the family's management of King's legacy have been ignored.

The intransigence of the King estate with its desire to profit but with its control over the King Center has left a quandary for Atlanta. What is to be done with the King Center complex if and when the King estate no longer cares to maintain the facility? The enabling legislation of 1980 which introduced the National Park Service into the King Shrine Area gives the federal government the first right of refusal to purchase the property. Will that occur? What will happen to King's home at 234 Sunset in Vine City?[38]

Ever one to feel inadequate with what it has and long known for ignoring its past, Atlanta turned its back on the millions of dollars invested along Auburn Avenue to embark on a new Civil and Human Rights Museum venture that just might top the experience of pilgrims to the Birmingham and Memphis shrines. When the King estate made good on its threat to sell King's papers, some of which had been previously housed in the King Center and all of which had been reviewed for publication in *The Papers of Martin Luther King, Jr.*, Atlanta, under the leadership of Mayor Shirley Franklin, pledged $32 million to buy them, arguing that the cache would become the centerpiece of a new $100 million Civil and Human Rights Museum that would appeal to tourists. The Coca-Cola Company provided a choice piece of real estate near its new museum, the Georgia Aquarium, and Centennial Olympic Park. Rather than locate the proposed human rights museum on the revitalized Auburn Avenue near the civil rights sites in the King Shrine Area where millions of dollars have already been invested over the previous four decades, the city has opted to build its memorial to the movement near the other high ticket attractions. To do so it will need more than one hundred million dollars to make this dream a reality.[39]

Thus forty years later, Atlanta found itself where Coretta Scott King stood in 1968, possessing an assortment of papers with the desire to house them in a library and museum. Unlike King's widow however, Atlanta does not own the copyright to the materials it bought from the King estate, so it may never profit from the publication of them, nor does it own the King Center with its gravesite, nor does it own the birth home, nor does it own all of Dr. King's belongings still housed at 234 Sunset including the Impala, all probably slated for the auction block one day. Indeed, Atlanta owns very little except a big vision and a lot of debt.

## NOTES

1. *Atlanta Constitution*, June 10, 1968, January 15, 1969; *Atlanta Journal*, June 4, 1968; *Atlanta Voice*, January 19, 1969.

2. King (2003, 70, 76, 164, 198–203).

3. King's birth home is at 501 Auburn Avenue in the Old Fourth Ward area of central Atlanta; *Atlanta Journal*, June 4, 1968, and June 10, 13A.

4. Durett and White (n.d. [1976]).

5. The fire began in a building used by Grady Hospital between Fort and Hilliard Streets in a black area of Atlanta that sat in the lowland between Edgewood Avenue and Houston Street where there were "many small dwellings packed close like rabbit hives, groceries, soda stands and the like. The fire burned through them faster than a man can walk," but it moved away from the Odd Fellows Building and other structures on Auburn and turned north along Jackson Street and Boulevard (Garrett 1969, 700–706).

6. Henderson and Walker (n.d., 1–18); Roth and Ambrose (1996, 132–33,150–51).

7. Henderson and Walker (n.d., 16–17); Blythe, Carroll, and Moffson (1994, 19, 71–72).

8. Hunter (1953, 214–15; 1980, 14); Stone (1989, 40); Martin (1987, 106, 144).

9. Blythe, Carroll, and Moffson (1994, 22–23); National Park Service (n.d., 70).

10. *Atlanta Journal-Constitution*, September 28, 1969, 2-A.

11. *Atlanta Constitution*, December 29, 1969; see also the *Reports* of the Ford Foundation.

12. *Atlanta Constitution*, December 29, 1969, 5-A.

13. Allen (1996, 180–182); *Atlanta Constitution*, January 16, 1975, 1-AF; September 17, 1975.

14. *Atlanta Constitution*, January 16, 1975.

15. *Atlanta Constitution*, April 4, 1977, 3-A.

16. *Atlanta Constitution*, October 4, 1978, 2B; January 14, 1979, 2B; December 9, 1977, 30-A; King (2003, 113).

17. *Atlanta Constitution*, October 17, 1979, 1-A.

*18. Atlanta Constitution*, October 17, 1979, 1-A.

19. *Atlanta Constitution*, January 7, 1985, November 17, 1985, January 17, 1986, January 11, 1995. The endowment drive attracted $500,000 from an Atlanta foundation and corporate support from the Stroh Brewery Company.

20. Public Law 96-428 adopted by the 96th Congress on October 10, 1980. The law also included the 234 Sunset Avenue, Northwest home of Dr. and Mrs. Martin Luther King, Jr.; Blythe, Carroll, Moffson (n.d., 7–11).

21. Henderson and Walker, *Sweet Auburn*.

22. National Park Service (1986, 3); Hamilton (1984, 15–19, quotation on 17).

23. Waldemer (2005); National Park (n.p., n.d.); McLean (1993). See also Atlanta Regional Commission (1979), and Winter (June 20, 1988; May 24, 1988).

24. *Atlanta Journal-Constitution*, January 9, 1983, January 8, 14, 1984.

25. National Park Service (1986, iii, 3).

26. National Park Service (1994 Update; 1996); *Atlanta Constitution*, August 11, 1994.

27. *Atlanta Constitution*, April 5, 1989, October 22, 1994, January 10, 1995.

28. Dexter King approached neighborhood leaders regarding the King Dream Center in June 1994; see *Atlanta Journal-Constitution*, August 11, 16, 1994; King (2003, 203–04, 207–09); *Atlanta Constitution*, April 5, 1989, October 22, 1994; January 1, 10, 14, 15, 21, 1995; and June 16, 1996.

29. King (2003, 207–09); National Park Service (1996); on Georgia State University see *Atlanta Journal Constitution*, July 25, 2007.

30. *Chicago Tribune*, December 12, 1982; *Memphis Commercial Appeal*, January 21, 1986; June 30, 1991; State of Tennessee historic marker at the Lorraine Motel; Davis quoted in the *Atlanta Journal Constitution*, November 30, 1986.

31. *Memphis Commercial Appeal*, January 21, April 2, 5, 8, 1986, June 30, 1991; Lawless (April 23, 1986); House Bill 1949 passed the Tennessee General Assembly on April 9, 1986.

32. *Memphis Commerical Appeal*, June 30, 1991.

33. *Memphis Commercial Appeal*, January 15, October 10, 1989, June 12, 15, 1990, "The Glory and the Glitz," *Time*, July 1991; unidentified clipping, perhaps *New York Times* or *Wall Street Journal*, October 7, 1991, 28, D'Army Bailey Papers

34. *Memphis Commercial Appeal*, June 12, 1995, September 26, 1996, April 3, 1998.

35. David Vann, interview with author, December 20, 1994, author's possession; City of Birmingham and Operation New Birmingham (1980); *Birmingham Post-Herald*, April 16, 1986, November 19, 1992.

36. *Birmingham News*, July 6, 1986; Task Force (July 11, 1986); *Birmingham News*, July 4, 1990, September 6, 15, 16, 1992.

37. Birmingham Civil Rights Institute, IRS Form 990, 2005; author's interview with Carol A. Wells, CPA for the BCRI, February 20, 2007, author's possession.

38. Public Law 96-428.

39. *Atlanta Journal Constitution*, December 21, 2006, June 10, 2007; *Atlanta Daily World*, March 22–28, 2007.

## REFERENCES

Allen, Frederick. *Atlanta Rising: The Invention of an International City, 1946–1996* (Marietta, GA.: Longstreet Press, Inc., 1996).

Atlanta Regional Commission. *Areawide Historic Preservation Planning: Potential Activities for the Atlanta Regional Commission, An ARC Staff Technical Memorandum*, October 1979.

Blythe, Robert W., Maureen A. Carroll, and Steven H. Moffson. *Martin Luther King, Jr., National Historic Site: Historic Resource Study* (National Park Service, 1994).

City of Birmingham and Operation New Birmingham, *Master Plan for Downtown Birmingham, Alabama*, December 1980.

Durett, Dan and Dana F. White. *An-Other Atlanta Tour: The Black Heritage* (Atlanta: The History Group, Inc., n.d. [1976]).

Garrett, Franklin M. *Atlanta and Environs: A Chronicle of Its People and Events, Volume II* (Athens: University of Georgia Press, 1969).

Hamilton, Susan. "The Sweet Auburn Community Confronts the National Park Service" (M.A. thesis, Georgia State University, 1984).

Henderson, Alexa and Eugene Walker. *Sweet Auburn: The Thriving Hub of Black Atlanta 1900–1960* (U.S. Department of the Interior, n.d.).

Hunter, Floyd. *Community Power Structure: A Study of Decision Makers* (Chapel Hill: University of North Carolina Press, 1953).

———. *Community Power Succession: Atlanta's Policy-Makers Revisited* (Chapel Hill: University of North Carolina Press, 1980).

King, Dexter Scott with Ralph Wiley. *Growing Up King: An Intimate Memoir* (New York: Warner Books, 2003).

Lawless, Benjamin. "A National Civil Rights Center: Technical Proposal," April 23, 1986, D'Army Bailey Papers, Mississippi Valley Collection, University of Memphis.

Martin, Harold H. *Atlanta and Environs: A Chronicle of Its People and Events, Volume III* (Athens: University of Georgia Press, 1987).

McLean, Angela. *Martin Luther King, Jr. Landmark District Residential Design Guidelines* (Atlanta: Atlanta Urban Design Commission, 1993).

National Park Service. *Martin Luther King, Jr., National Historic Site Land Protection Plan* (1994 Update).

———. *A Grand Endeavor For A Man With A Dream: The Story of Martin Luther King, Jr., National Historic Site and Preservation District* [1996].

———. *General Management Plan & Development Concept Plan*, February 21, 1986.

———. *Catalog of Historic Structures: Martin Luther King, Jr., National Historic Site and Preservation District* (n.p., n.d.).

Roth, Darlene R. and Andy Ambrose. *Metropolitan Frontiers: A Short History of Atlanta* (Marietta, GA.: Longstreet Press, 1996).

Stone, Clarence N. *Regime Politics: Governing Atlanta, 1946-1988* (Lawrence, Kan., University of Kansas Press, 1989).

Task Force. Minutes of the Task Force, July 11, 1986, Birmingham Civil Rights Institute Collection, Birmingham Public Library Department of Archives and Manuscripts, Birmingham, Alabama.

Waldemer, Sarah Virginia. "Historic Preservation As A Means of Urban Economic Revitalization: A Geographic Analysis of Atlanta's Cabbagetown Neighborhood (M.A. thesis, Georgia State University, 2005).

Winter, Nore V. *Design Guidelines for Historic Districts in the City of Atlanta*, June 20, 1988.

———. *The Atlanta System of Definitions and Criteria For Designating Historic Preservation Resources*, May 24, 1988.

**Katherine B. Hankins**
assistant professor of geography
Georgia State University

**Truman A. Hartshorn**
emeritus professor of geography
Georgia State University

**Melissa M. Hayes**
doctoral student in sociology
Georgia State University

**Cynthia Hewitt**
assistant professor of sociology
Morehouse College

**Charles Jaret**
professor of sociology
Georgia State University

**Larry Keating**
emeritus professor of city and regional planning
Georgia Institute of Technology

**Douglas J. Krupka**
senior research associate
IZA: Institute for the Study of Labor

**Douglas S. Noonan**
associate professor of public policy
Georgia Institute of Technology

**Glenwood Ross**
associate professor of economics
Morehouse College

**Michael Rushton**
associate professor of public and environmental affairs
Indiana University

**David L. Sjoquist**
professor of economics
Georgia State University

**Matthew Wooten**
graduate student
University of Texas

# Contributors

**Robert M. Adelman**
associate professor of sociology
State University of New York–Buffalo

**Fred Brooks**
associate professor of social work
Georgia State University

**Jennifer Chirico**
doctoral student in environmental policy
Georgia Institute of Technology

**Obie Clayton**
professor of sociology
Morehouse College

**Glenn T. Eskew**
assistant professor of history
Georgia State University

**Charles A. Gallagher**
professor of sociology, social work, and criminal justice
La Salle University

**Gregory Hall**
associate professor of political science
Morehouse College

# Index